Lecture Notes in Artificial Intelligence   12236

Subseries of Lecture Notes in Computer Science

More information about this series at http://www.springer.com/series/1244

Christoph Benzmüller · Bruce Miller (Eds.)

Intelligent Computer Mathematics

13th International Conference, CICM 2020
Bertinoro, Italy, July 26–31, 2020
Proceedings

 Springer

Editors
Christoph Benzmüller ⓘ
Department of Mathematics
and Computer Science
Freie Universität Berlin
Berlin, Germany

Bruce Miller ⓘ
National Institute of Standards
and Technology
Gaithersburg, MD, USA

ISSN 0302-9743   ISSN 1611-3349 (electronic)
Lecture Notes in Artificial Intelligence
ISBN 978-3-030-53517-9   ISBN 978-3-030-53518-6 (eBook)
https://doi.org/10.1007/978-3-030-53518-6

LNCS Sublibrary: SL7 – Artificial Intelligence

This Springer imprint is published by the registered company Springer Nature Switzerland AG
The registered company address is: Gewerbestrasse 11, 6330 Cham, Switzerland

Preface

With the continuing, rapid progress of digital methods in communications, knowledge representation, processing and discovery, the unique character and needs of mathematical information require unique approaches. Its specialized representations and capacity for creation and proof, both automatically and formally as well as manually set mathematical knowledge apart.

The Conference on Intelligent Computer Mathematics (CICM) was initially formed in 2008 as a joint meeting of communities involved in computer algebra systems, automated theorem provers, and mathematical knowledge management, as well as those involved in a variety of aspects of scientific document archives. It has offered a venue for discussing, developing, and integrating the diverse, sometimes eclectic, approaches and research. Since then, CICM has been held annually: Birmingham (UK, 2008), Grand Bend (Canada, 2009), Paris (France, 2010), Bertinoro (Italy, 2011), Bremen (Germany, 2012), Bath (UK, 2013), Coimbra (Portugal, 2014), Washington D. C. (USA, 2015), Bialystok (Poland, 2016), Edinburgh (UK, 2017), Linz (Austria, 2018), Prague (Czech Republic, 2019).

This 13th edition (CICM 2020) was originally scheduled to be held in Bertinoro, Italy. Due to the COVID-19 pandemic, the organizers decided to host the conference as an online event held during July 26–31, 2020. This year's meeting exposed advances in automated theorem provers and formalization, computer algebra systems and their libraries, and applications of machine learning, among other topics. This volume contains the contributions of this conference.

From 35 formal submissions, the Program Committee (PC) accepted 24 papers including 15 full research papers and 9 shorter papers describing software systems or datasets. With two exceptions, all papers were reviewed by at least three PC members or external reviewers. The reviews were single-blind and included a response period in which the authors could respond and clarify points raised by the reviewers.

In addition to the main sessions, the conference included a doctoral program, chaired by Katja Bercic, which provided a forum for PhD students to present their research and get advice from senior members of the community. Additionally, the following workshop was scheduled:

- Workshop on Natural Formal Mathematics, organized by Florian Rabe and Peter Koepke

Finally, the conference included three invited talks:

- Kevin Buzzard (Imperial College, UK): "Formalizing undergraduate mathematics"

- Catherine Dubois (ENSIIE, CNRS, France): "Formally Verified Constraints Solvers: a Guided Tour"
- Christian Szegedy (Google Research, USA): "A Promising Path Towards Auto-formalization and General Artificial Intelligence"

A successful conference is due to the efforts of many people. We thank Claudio Sacerdoti-Coen and his colleagues at the University of Bologna for the difficult task of first organizing what promised to be an enjoyable meeting in Bertinoro and then evolving it into an online event. We are grateful to Serge Autexier for his publicity work. We thank the authors of submitted papers, the PC for reviews, organizers of workshops, as well as invited speakers and participants to the conference.

June 2020   Christoph Benzmüller
                                                                          Bruce Miller

Organization

Program Committee

Akiko Aizawa	University of Tokyo, Japan
David Aspinall	University of Edinburgh, UK
Frédéric Blanqui	INRIA, France
Jacques Carette	McMaster University, Canada
James H. Davenport	University of Bath, UK
William Farmer	McMaster University, Canada
Jacques Fleuriot	University of Edinburgh, UK
Osman Hasan	NUST, Pakistan
Jan Jakubuv	Czech Technical University, Czech Republic
Mateja Jamnik	University of Cambridge, UK
Cezary Kaliszyk	University of Innsbruck, Austria
Fairouz Kamareddine	Heriot-Watt University, UK
Manfred Kerber	University of Birmingham, UK
Andrea Kohlhase	University of Applied Sciences Neu-Ulm, Germany
Michael Kohlhase	FAU Erlangen-Nürnberg, Germany
Laura Kovacs	TU Vienna, Austria
Temur Kutsia	JKU Linz, Austria
Adam Naumowicz	University of Bialystok, Poland
Karol Pak	University of Bialystok, Poland
Florian Rabe	FAU Erlangen-Nürnberg, Germany, and LRI Paris, France
Moritz Schubotz	FIZ Karlsruhe, Germany
Volker Sorge	University of Birmingham, UK
Geoff Sutcliffe	University of Miami, USA
Olaf Teschke	FIZ Karlsruhe, Germany
Josef Urban	Czech Technical University, Czech Republic
Makarius Wenzel	sketis.net, Germany
Abdou Youssef	George Washington University, USA

Additional Reviewers

Almomen, Randa
Betzendahl, Jonas
Brown, Chad
Butler, David
Cerna, David
Chevallier, Mark
Dundua, Besik
Greiner-Petter, André
Humenberger, Andreas

Korniłowicz, Artur
Marin, Mircea
Müller, Dennis
Palmer, Jake
Schaefer, Jan Frederik
Scharpf, Philipp
Seidl, Martina
Steen, Alexander
Tiemens, Lucca

Contents

System Descriptions and Datasets

Abstracts of Invited Talks

Invited Talks

A Promising Path Towards Autoformalization and General Artificial Intelligence

Christian Szegedy[✉]

Google Research, Mountain View, CA, USA
szegedy@google.com

Abstract. An autoformalization system is an AI that learns to read natural language content and to turn it into an abstract, machine verifiable formalization, ideally by bootstrapping from unlabeled training data with minimum human interaction. This is a difficult task in general, one that would require strong automated reasoning and automated natural language processing capabilities. In this paper, it is argued that autoformalization is a promising path for systems to learn sophisticated, general purpose reasoning in all domains of mathematics and computer science. This could have far reaching implications not just for mathematical research, but also for software synthesis. Here I provide the outline for a realistic path towards those goals and give a survey of recent results that support the feasibility of this direction.

1 Introduction

Today, AI systems are able to learn solving tasks that used to be thought of taking uniquely human capabilities until recently: computer vision [46], generating artistic images [13], music [21], mastering the game of go [43], discovering novel drugs [15] and performing symbolic integration [31], to name just a few. These and many other domains seemed to require uniquely human intuition and insight, but were transformed by deep learning in the past few years. While progress has been extremely impressive in those areas, each particular solution addresses a relatively narrow use case. On the other hand, general reasoning still seems a uniquely human feat and many [20] would argue that creating AI agents with general reasoning capabilities equaling to those of humans would take decades, maybe centuries, if possible at all.

This invited paper argues that in the coming years we will see automated systems to rival humans in general reasoning and the fastest path to achieve this is by creating automated mathematical reasoning systems via autoformalization.

Here, I give an overview of the hurdles involved, a realistic path ahead and indications on the feasibility of that path.

Mathematics is the discipline of pure reasoning. *Mathematical reasoning is not about mathematics per se, it is about reasoning in general.* Whether to verify

© Springer Nature Switzerland AG 2020
C. Benzmüller and B. Miller (Eds.): CICM 2020, LNAI 12236, pp. 3–20, 2020.
https://doi.org/10.1007/978-3-030-53518-6_1

the correctness or resource use of a computer program or to derive the consequences of a physical model, it is all mathematical reasoning, as long as it is based on fully formalized premises and transformation rules. Some tasks may require such a large number of logical steps that humans find it impossible to check them manually, but often they are easily solved by SAT-solvers [5] – programs whose sole goal is to decide if a Boolean expression can ever evaluate to true.

For certain classes of expressions, like those that occur frequently in chip design, SAT solvers work remarkably well [10]. An extreme demonstration of their power is their use in the computer generated proof of a previously unsolved famous conjecture in mathematics [25] – the Boolean Pythagorean triples problem. The final proof was 200 terabytes long.

However, SAT-solvers cannot verify statements about infinitely many cases. For example, they can't even verify that the addition of integer numbers is commutative. There are automated theorem provers (ATPs [11]) for finding moderately difficult proofs in first order logic that can deal with such problems. Proof automation via "hammers" [6,27] is also applied for higher order logic as well in the context of interactive theorem proving. Most existing proof automation is based on hand engineered heuristics, not on machine learning and is not capable of open-ended self-improvement.

Mathematical reasoning is just reasoning about anything specified formally. Reasoning about anything formal could be a powerful general tool. If we want to create an artificially intelligent system and demonstrate its general intelligence, it should be able to reason about any area of mathematics or at least it should be able to *learn to do so* given enough time. If it succeeds in practice, then we can be convinced that it is likely that it will be able to learn to cope with any scientific discipline as far as it can be formalized precisely.

Human mathematics consists of a large variety of loosely connected domains, each of them having its own flavor of proofs, arguments and intuition. Human mathematicians spend years studying just to become experts in a few of those domains. An artificial system engineered to produce strong results in a particular area is not a "general purpose" reasoning engine. However, if a system demonstrates that it can learn to reason in any area it is exposed to, then that would be a convincing demonstration of artificial general intelligence.

Therefore it is natural to ask: Will we ever arrive at the point where an AI agent can learn to do reasoning as well as the best humans in the world in most established domains of mathematics.

2   What is (Auto-)formalization?

The task of formalization is to turn informal descriptions into some formally correct and automatically checkable format. Examples of mathematical formalization include the formal proofs of the Kepler conjecture [22], the Four-Color theorem [16] and the Feit-Thompson theorem [17]. These formalization works required a lot of human effort. For example the formalization of the Kepler conjecture took over 20 man-years of work. The aim of autoformalization would be to automate such efforts and scale them up to process large chunks of existing mathematics in a fully automated manner.

More generally, "formalization" can refer to any process that takes an informal description for input and produces machine executable code. By this definition, formalization covers both programming and mathematical formalization. This generalized notion is also justified because computer verifiable proofs are in fact programs to feed some minimalistic verification kernel. For example, most proof assistants are complete programming languages that allow for running arbitrary programs while guaranteeing the correctness of the produced proofs.

Complex mathematics is especially time consuming to formalize by humans. Therefore, it is highly unlikely that a significant portion of mathematics will be formalized manually in the coming decades. Could formalization be ever automated completely? The ideal solution could process natural language text fully automatically, with minimal intervention from the user.

We call an automated system that is capable of automatically formalizing significant portions of mathematics from a natural language input and verifying it automatically an *autoformalization system*.

3   Why is Autoformalization Essential?

Is targeting autoformalization a prerequisite for training – and evaluating – AI systems for general purpose reasoning?

As was argued in the introduction, all formalizable reasoning can be viewed as mathematical in nature. Conversely, general purpose reasoning systems should be able to learn to reason about *any* domain of mathematics and should be able to discover new mathematical domains when needed or useful for another task.

Avoiding autoformalization (interpreting natural language text and communicating in natural language) would seem to simplify the engineering of formal reasoning systems. However, evaluating a highly sophisticated, general purpose, automated mathematical reasoning system without natural language communication capabilities would raise several problems:

1. Training and evaluation of a purely formal system would require a wide range of formalized statements. Creating a large corpus of diverse and correct formalized statements is a daunting task in and of itself.
2. Any human interaction with our system would be by formal inputs and outputs. If the system is trained by automated exploration and develops its own web of definitions (about which it does not need to communicate in natural language), it will resemble alien mathematics that is very hard to decipher and interpret by humans.
3. Every time the system needs to be applied to a new application domain, it would require full-blown manual formalization of that domain. This would limit its usefulness significantly.

Training a strong mathematical reasoning system without autoformalization might be still possible if one could develop a concise, well defined notion of "interestingness" that is used as the objective for open-ended exploration. However it would be very hard to communicate with such a system as it would not be able to communicate in terms of human mathematics. Furthermore, "interestingness" and "usefulness" of mathematical statements and theories are not easy to capture formally. It is hard to decide whether some mathematical area will ever have external applications or would provide insights for other domains down the line. Usefulness is highly contextual. There is no known way to guide a search process automatically towards useful theorems and notions in an open ended manner.

Since only a tiny portion of human mathematics is formalized currently, the only way for utilizing a significant fraction of accumulated human mathematical knowledge is by processing it from natural language. Therefore, the safest option is to use the entirety of human mathematics as a basis for training and benchmarking.

It could be easier to engineer and train an AI agent that can reason and formalize at the same time than designing one for just reasoning or just for formalization alone if one manages to initiate a positive feedback loop between reasoning abilities and formalization capabilities. Improving one aspect (translation or reasoning) of the system helps collecting new training data for the other:

- Improved reasoning allows for filling in larger holes in informal arguments, allows for translating and interpreting inputs specified more informally.
- Improved informal to formal translation expands the amount of data to guide mathematical exploration.

4   Potential Implications of Successful Autoformalization

Autoformalization is not just a challenge: successful autoformalization would represent a breakthrough for general AI with significant implications in various domains.

Autoformalization would demonstrate that sophisticated natural language understanding between humans and AI is feasible: machines could communicate in natural language over ambiguous content and use it to express or guide internal experiences. It would serve as a clear demonstration that natural language is a feasible communication medium for computers as well.

By nature, autoformalization would have immediate practical implications for mathematics. Initially, a strong autoformalization system could be used for verifying existing and new mathematical papers and would enable strong semantic search engines.

In the more general sense of formalization, a solution to autoformalization could give rise to programming agents that turn natural language descriptions into programs. Since programming languages can be formalized completely, reasoning systems trained on mathematical formalization could be fine-tuned for the task of creating algorithms in specific programming languages. By formalizing domain level knowledge, the system could learn to produce code from natural language input. Such reasoning systems should be able to create the formal specification of the task, the executable code and correctness proof of the newly designed algorithm, all at the same time.

Furthermore, this would give rise to strong and flexible general purpose reasoning engines that could be integrated into AI applications, combining reasoning with perception. This could be used to infuse strong reasoning capabilities into other AI systems and serve as a basis for a wide range of such applications (for example semantic search, software synthesis and verification, computer aided design, etc.).

5   Hurdles of Autoformalization

Designing and implementing a strong autoformalization system is a difficult undertaking and is subject to several current research efforts. Let us start with the outline of some straighforward attempt at its construction and analyze its most likely failure modes. We assume a system based on the following two components:

1. A reasoning engine (theorem prover),
2. a translation component for translating informal (natural language) statements into formal statements.

The translation component could generate multiple formal candidate statements in the context of the previously formalized statements and definitions. The system is successful if it creates formal translations for a substantial fraction of the informal statements after a reasonable number of attempts. (The automated verification of the correctness of translation remains a fuzzy, practical question that is subject to ongoing research, however.)

The first problem with mathematical formalization is that it requires at least some initial core formalization data-sets with a significant amount of parallel corpus in formalized and informal mathematical content. One limiting factor is the cost and effort of generating this seed corpus of translations.

Once we have a somewhat working "seed" translation model, one can try bootstrapping and training the system by generating several candidate translations of mathematical statements and trying to prove/refute each of them until we find a formalization that is correct, but not trivial. This means that we can see at least four major potential failure modes:

1. The seed formalization system is too weak to initiate a feedback loop that can open-endedly improve itself.
2. The system might start to generate mistranslations for further training of the translation model, entering a feedback loop of increasingly worse translations.
3. Translation gets stuck: it would generate a lot of incorrect statements that are never verified; and the system stops to improve.

4. The translation never crosses domain boundaries: it formalizes significant parts of some domain, but never succeeds in generalizing to new domains; and the training gets stuck after formalizing limited parts of the corpus.

Natural language is context dependent: it might contain hidden assumptions in far away parts of the text which are impossible to find without a thorough search. For example, papers tend to refer to text books for "basic terminology". The formalization system would need to look up the textbook and mine it for all the subtleties of its definitions and verify that those definitions are consistent with those in the repository of the formal system. If not, then the system would need to create new formal definitions that match those in the paper. Moreover, the paper itself might use inconsistent notations: "abuses of language". Additionally, it might just have plain errors obvious to the human reader. Therefore a straightforward translation attempt is not a robust solution and is unlikely to work in practice.

6   A Proposed Path to Autoformalization

It is hard to anticipate solutions of the potential problems from the previous section. Still, one can aim at designing a system that has a plausible chance of being bootstrapped without getting stuck or misguided.

Instead of direct translation, we propose to rely on a combination of exploration and approximate translation. By "approximate translation", we mean that the translation model does not produce concrete formal transcriptions but approximate embedding vectors thereof. These are then used as guides for an exploration algorithm as the following diagram shows:

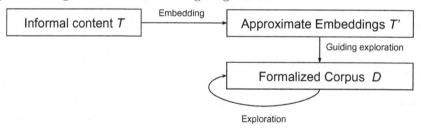

The first technical issue concerns the input format of informal mathematical content (i.e. mathematical papers and text books). A textual representation could work well for use cases that do not require the understanding of formulas, diagrams and graphs. However, mathematical content often uses a lot of formulas and diagrams. Geometric illustrations play a role in informing the reader as well. The safest path seems to rely on images instead of textual representation. While this puts more burden on the machine learning part of the system, it can reduce the engineering effort significantly.

Let S denote the set of syntactically correct formal mathematical statements in some formalization environment (e.g. HOL Light). By S', we denote those statements with a formal proof already present in our database. C is the set of possible forward reasoning rules called "conversions". C consists of partial functions with signature $c : S'^* \longrightarrow S$, that given a sequence s of true statements in S' it either generates a new true statement $c(s)$ or it just fails. Our system will rely on a few deep learning models:

- An embedding model $e_\theta : S \longrightarrow \mathbb{R}^n$ that embeds formal mathematical statements as low dimensional vectors.
- An approximate translation model $a_\xi : \mathbb{R}^{k \times l} \longrightarrow \mathbb{R}^n$, that outputs an approximate embedding of the formal translation of the informal input statement (given as a picture).
- An exploration guidance model $g_\eta : S \times \mathbb{R}^n \times \mathbb{R}^n \longrightarrow [0,1]^C \times [0,1]$. This model acts as a premise selection model, combined with a conversion type prediction, assuming a finite number of possible conversions. $f_\eta(s,t,p)$ which takes a formal statement s, a target embedding t and the embedding for additional conversion parameters and predicts probabilities for the best conversion steps $[0,1]^C$ and conversion parameter list p at the same time. The exact working of such models is described in [4].

For technical simplicity, we made the simplifying assumption that statements and input images are represented by fixed dimensional vectors, but this is not essential and could be easily changed. The parameters of the deep learning models e_θ, a_ξ and g_η are trained in lock step as described below.

The system is designed to learn to explore the set of true statements while this exploration is guided by a set of target embeddings. These target embedding vectors are produced by translation model a_ξ. During the process, we maintain the following data sets:

- A fixed set of informal target content $T \subseteq \mathbb{R}^{k \times l}$ in raw image format. (The pages containing the statements and definitions we are aiming to formalize.)
- The image of T'_ξ of T under the approximate translation model: $\{a_\xi(t)|t \in T\} \subseteq \mathbb{R}^n$. (The predicted embeddings of the informal statements on the formal side.)
- A set of already explored mathematical statements $D \subseteq S'$ of true and proven statements,
- The embeddings of the explored mathematical statements: $D'_\theta = \{e_\theta(s)|s \in D\} \subseteq \mathbb{R}^n$.

Our goal is to find a subset of $D' \subseteq D$, whose image under e_θ aligns well with T'. If our translation model is reasonably good, then true – but non-trivially true – translations are likely to correspond to their informal description. We train all the models simultaneously while we update the datasets T', D and D' as we go.

The goal of embedding model e_θ is to map semantically similar statements to vectors that are close. One can train such models in some supervised, end-to-end manner for one or multiple concrete semantic tasks. For example, the model could embed statements in order to predict whether the statement is useful for proving another specified statement, cf. [1] and [4]. Another related semantic task is that of reasoning in latent space [33], in which the model is trained to perform approximate rewrite operations in the embedding space.

For processing the natural language input, our computer vision model a_ξ predicts $a_\xi(p) = e_\theta(t(p))$, where $t(p)$ stands for the hypothesized formalization of page p. Since e_θ is assumed to be an embedding model that reflects semantic similarity, t can be multi-valued, reflecting that there are several correct formal translations of the same informal statement, the embedding vectors of which are expected to cluster in $\mathbb{R}^n$.

In order to create a feedback loop between training θ and ξ, we maintain a set of proved theorems, a large set of informal statements P and translations $T_\xi = \{a_\xi(p) | p \in P\}$ of approximate translations of informal statements. To generate the training data for training, we run guided exploration by sampling forward reasoning steps using another deep neural network g_η starting from our already proved theorems with the goal of getting close to as many of the approximate translated embeddings T_ξ as possible. For this purpose, η is trained via reinforcement learning in which the reward is based on the negative minimum distance to the closest target embedding vector. The guidance model g_η samples both conversions and conversion parameters ("premises" used for the conversion). Note that g_η can be trained while circumventing the sparse reward problem: even if we do not get close to any of our original targets, we can pretend that the embedding of the statement we arrived at was our original goal from the start. This idea is known as hindsight experience replay [2].

Once our guided search finds enough statements that match some of the prescribed embeddings in T_ξ, we would check that they are non-trivially true and use them as verified translations for retraining a_ξ. As we proceed, we can incrementally train e_θ and g_η as well. For example e_θ could be trained by analyzing the dependency structure of the explored statements (the tactic parameters that led to the new statement), while g_η is trained using reinforcement learning utilizing the rewards collected during exploration.

The main advantage is that this system is expected to be more robust to errors and incomplete inputs: if exploration is powerful enough, then it can work even if we fail to translate some of the statements properly. Also, if formalization gets stuck, the system can just relax the distance with which it accepts formalization attempts in the embedding space, still producing valid theories that might not exactly correspond to the informal corpus.

Also the system should be able to generalize to completely new domains more easily, as exploration is more likely to be efficient in the early stages. This can bootstrap the easy parts of the system and can prime the translation model and later exploration so that it can continue bootstrapping successfully.

7   Further Ideas and Considerations

The previous section has given a rough outline of a system that could bootstrap itself for mathematical reasoning via autoformalization. Here we consider additional details that are less critical but helpful for engineering a system described in Sect. 6.

7.1   Choice of Foundation and Framework

Traditionally, many people would argue that the choice of the right framework and foundation is crucial for the success of a formalization project. For human users of interactive proof assistants the right framework can affect the productivity of formalization, but generally these effects are hard to quantify and there had been several types of logical foundations and frameworks that have been applied successfully in large scale formalization efforts: Mizar [38], HOL Light [23], HOL4 [45], Isabelle [53], Coq [7], Metamath [37] and Lean [8]. We have only listed proof assistants that have demonstrated a significant amount of successful formalization efforts: tens of thousands of theorems, some of them of great complexity.

A few considerations apply when it comes to automatically formalizing from natural language. Theorem libraries based on purely constructive non-classical logic might have a significant mismatch with most mainstream mathematical text for non-constructive mathematical objects. Also it is useful if the proof assistant can be extended easily with new high level algorithms (new "tactics", for example). Engineering efforts required to interface with external libraries, especially machine learning systems is a point of consideration, too.

One last concern is the expressiveness of the logic. Although first order logic is generally capable of expressing the Zermelo-Fraenkel axiom system, it requires maintaining axiom schemes which is a handicap. Based on these considerations, higher order logic based systems with large theorem libraries (HOL, Isabelle, Coq, Lean) seem to be best suited to be the foundation of an autoformalization system.

7.2   Unsupervised Pretraining Tasks

Self-supervised pretraining might become an enabling factor for autoformalization system. BERT [9] style pretraining for both formal and informal corpora can pave the way, but formal content allows for much more creativity and possibility for pretraining models, these include training "skip-tree" models that generate missing trees from their context. This task subsumes a lot of other logical reasoning tasks

1. Skip-tree: removing some random or strategically selected subtree and predict the whole missing subtree.
2. Type inference model: Learn to do (partial) type inference of formulas.
3. Predicting the embedding or the text of possible useful lemmas that could help proving the statement.
4. Predicting the result (embeddings) of rewrites.
5. Predicting substitutions or inductive invariants.
6. Given a subtree, predict the containing tree.
7. Rewrite a formula with a sequence of rewrites, try to predict the sequence of rewrites that has lead to the result.

Prior work also includes predicting the symbolic integral of expressions [31] and predicting how general mathematical statements behave under rewrites in the latent space [33].

7.3   Additional Technical Considerations

For the neural representation of formal content, the network architecture has a significant effect on the performance of the reasoning system. Currently, deep graph embedding networks [40,52] with node-sharing do best, however transformer networks [51] have yielded breakthrough on formal integration [31], recently.

Our main approach is based on forward exploration. Aligning the result of forward exploration with the target statement might require reverse (goal oriented) proof search, however. As most research is done on reverse proof search e.g. [4,26,55], integrating with such methods is likely a useful idea and a fruitful engineering direction.

As described in the Sect. 6, we need to filter out translation candidates that are incorrect, trivial or uninteresting. The first criterion is clear: we do not expect wrong statements to be correct formalization candidates. It is harder to discard candidate translations that are trivially true (e.g. due to too general assumptions or other translation errors). This could be identified by observing the hardness of proving statements. Also, if a statement is overly long, or has a lot of redundant subtrees, then it is highly unlikely to come from formalizing human content. The usefulness of the produced statements should give another strong indication of good translations.

Curriculum learning is a promising way of learning to find longer proofs. A remarkable result demonstrating the power of strong curriculum is [61] in which they trained a reinforcement learning system to find proofs consisting of several thousand elementary proof-steps without any search, just by letting the policy network predict them in a single run.

Tactics in proof assistants are subroutines that perform complicated algorithms in order to produce long chains of arguments about the correctness of certain formulas. Examples of existing tactics include the application of SAT-solvers or first order automated provers to prove statements that require simple logical reasoning, but they can be as complex as using Gröbner bases of ILP solvers to reason about polynomial equations or linear systems of Diophantine inequalities. Given the complexity of such algorithms, it is unlikely that one could synthesize a general purpose computer algebra system from scratch initially. However, the vast majority of sophisticated human mathematics was discovered without the aid of computer programs, so we can hope that matching the performance of human mathematicians could be achieved without synthesizing complicated tactics.

For refutation and counterexample generation, it might be important to find substitutions into statements that provide a refutation of that statement. In general it is a promising research direction to use deep learning based models to embed not just the syntactic form of formulas, but also some experience stream associated with experimentation with the statements.

One difference between theorem proving and game playing engines is the much wider breadth of mathematics. For neural network based systems, this might mean that it could require very large neural networks to distill all the skills required to cope with all areas of mathematics at once. One could try to cope with that by utilizing mixture of expert models [58]. However, their fixed gating mechanism and rigid model architectures are relatively hard to extend. More flexible are multi-agent architectures using artificial market mechanisms that allow arbitrary agents to bet on the status of mathematical conjectures while the agents are rewarded for correct predictions, proving theorems formally and for introducing interesting new conjectures. The above direction opens a large box of interesting mechanism design [39] questions. [12] proposes that a betting market based multi-agent system under resource constraints is useful for assigning consistent probability values to mathematical statements. This could give some theoretical backing and guidance towards such solutions.

8 Short History of Autoformalization

The idea of autoformalization was first presented in 1961 by John McCarthy [36]. Another early attempt was the 1990 doctoral thesis of Donald Simons [44]. A first thorough study was performed in the 2004 doctoral thesis of Claus Zinn [60]. These works did not result in even partially practical solutions.

Josef Urban started to work on the topic in the early 2000s. He devised a first large scale benchmark for reasoning in large theories [48], motivated by the insight that reasoning in the presence of a large knowledge base of mathematical facts is a critical component in any autoformalization system. In 2007, he published the pioneering MaLARea [50] system for reasoning in large theories. From then on, with Cezary Kaliszyk they have been spearheading the research on reasoning in large theories and autoformalization [28,29].

9 Indications of Feasibility

Given the great complexity and breadth of the problem, it is justified to ask why is autoformalization even considered as a realistic goal in the short term – that is, within years. This section tries to give heuristic arguments for the feasibility of this task by methods that are either known or are on a clear improvement trajectory.

The success of autoformalization hinges on solving two difficult-looking tasks:

1. General purpose symbolic reasoning
2. Strong natural language understanding

The thesis of this paper is that deep learning will enable the advancement of both of those areas to the extent that is necessary for human level formalization and reasoning performance in the coming years. Let us review their recent progress in separation with the focus of exploring how they could enable autoformalization.

9.1   Search and Reasoning

Recently, it has been demonstrated by AlphaZero [42] that the same relatively simple algorithm based on Monte Carlo tree search (MCTS) [30] and residual convolutional networks [24] could achieve higher than human performance in several two-person games: go, chess and shogi, by self-play alone, utilizing the same algorithm for each of those games, **without** learning on any human expert games at all. Effectively, AlphaZero was able to rediscover all of the important chess, go and shogi knowledge in a few days that took human players centuries to discover.

However, mathematical reasoning differs from game playing in many respects:

1. The impossibility of self play: If open ended exploration is considered as an alternative, it is to decide what to explore. The lack of self play makes automated curriculum learning much harder for theorem proving.
2. Large, indefinitely growing knowledge base, resulting in a virtually infinite action space.
3. Very sparse reward: In the case of theorem proving, it is very hard to assign reward to failed proof attempts.
4. The diversity of mathematical knowledge: by nature, two-player games are very coherent, since each player has to be able to answer any move by any other player. Mathematics consists of wide range of loosely connected disciplines and it takes a lot of human experts to cover each of them.

DeepMath was the first attempt for applying deep learning at premise selection for the Mizar corpus [49] via convolutional networks and it yielded some initial improvements for this task. Also theorem prover E was improved by integrating neural network guidance [35]. In 2017, TacticToe [14], has demonstrated that tactic based higher order theorem proving via machine learning (even without the use of deep learning) is possible.

More recently the DeepHOL system [4] gave further demonstration of the power of deep learning in the more general case: for higher order logic and in the presence of a large knowledge base of premises to be used. However, formulas can be best described as graphs, suggesting the use of graph neural networks, which was suggested first in [52] and then yielded significant gains (40% relative increase in success rate) on the HOList benchmark in the end-to-end proving scenario [40]. DeepHOL-Zero [3] has demonstrated that relatively simple exploration heuristic allows for bootstrapping systems that can learn to prove without existing human proof logs to train on. While the proofs created by the above systems are very short, [61] demonstrates successfully, that with the right curriculum, in their limited setting, it is possible to train models that create proofs of several thousand steps without error.

9.2   Natural Language Processing and Understanding

Since 2017, natural language processing went through a revolution similar to that of computer vision, due to new neural model architectures, especially transformer networks [51] and large scale self-supervised training on vast corpora [9,41,56]. This has spurred fast advances in machine translation and language understanding. On some of the benchmark, this has resulted in human or close to human performance, for example on SQuAD 1.0 [57]. However this has lead to development of improved benchmarks to target the common weak points of those algorithms. Progress is still strong in this domain: improved model architectures and better tasks on larger corpora have yielded significant gains at a steady pace. On the analogy with computer vision, one can also foresee that natural architecture search will give rise to further advances in this field as well. Autoformalization systems can leverage all those advances for stronger translation models from natural language to the embedding space of formal statements.

9.3   Overview

Here is a short overview of the factors that support the potential success of autoformalization in the coming years:

1. The success of deep learning infused search in two person games, especially AlphaZero [42] style Monte Carlo tree search [30].
2. The demonstrations of the usefulness of deep learning in automated reasoning: premise selection [1] and proof guidance [4,35,40]
3. The demonstration that automated proof search can be learned without imitation [3].
4. The fast progress and success of neural architectures for formal and natural language content, especially graph neural networks [40,52,54] and transformers [51] for symbolic mathematics [31].
5. The success of imposing cyclic translation consistency [59] in image generation and unsupervised translation [32] give strong indications that autoformalization could be bootstrapped using very limited set of labeled pairs of formalized theorems.
6. The success of hindsight experience replay [2] to address the sparse reward problem for robotics applications.
7. The quick pace of progress in natural language processing via large, deep network models, and large scale self-supervised pretraining. Impressive results in several translation and natural language understanding benchmarks [34].
8. Generative neural models improve at a fast pace and yield impressive result in a wide range of domains from image generation to drug discovery.
9. Multi-agent system with agents specialized in different domains [12] could give a rise to open-ended self-improvement.
10. Automated optimization of neural architectures via neural architecture search [47,62] and other automated methods [19].
11. Computational resources available for deep learning purposes are still expanding quickly and are getting cheaper. For example, as of July 2019, Google' TPUv3 based pods can deliver over 100 petaFLOPS performance for deep learning purposes [18].

10 General Summary and Conclusions

We have argued in this paper that:

1. Autoformalization could enable the development of a human level mathematical reasoning engine in the next decade.
2. The implementation of autoformalization presents significant technical and engineering challenges.
3. Successful implementation of mathematical reasoning (theorem proving) and autoformalization has many implications that go far beyond just transforming mathematics itself and could result in the creation of a general purpose reasoning module to be used in other AI systems.
4. A reasoning system based purely on self-driven exploration for reasoning without informal communication capabilities would be hard to evaluate and use.
5. It is easier to engineer and bootstrap a system that learns to perform both formalization and reasoning than either task in separation.
6. It seems easier to create a formalization system from image than text data.
7. A naïve, direct translation approach for autoformalization would be brittle, hard to engineer and unlikely to work.
8. Combining approximate formalization (predicting embedding vectors instead of formulas) and guided exploration is a more promising direction to autoformalization than direct translation.
9. Deep Learning should be crucial for open ended improvement and reaching human level reasoning and formalization performance.
10. Recent progress in neural architectures, language modelling, self- and semi-supervised training, reinforcement learning, automated neural architecture search, and AI driven theorem proving paves the way for strong automated reasoning and formalization systems.

Acknowledgements. My warmest thanks go to my close collaborators and colleagues Sarah M. Loos, Markus N. Rabe, Kshitij Bansal, Francois Chollet, Alex Alemi, Stewart Wilcox, Niklas Een, Geoffrey Irving, Victor Toman and Aditya Paliwal for their contributions towards the goals sketched here. I am also indebted to Josef Urban and Cezary Kaliszyk for their pioneering work and selflessly sharing their vision and expertise and also for their collaboration on this area. I am also thankful to Ilya Sutskever, Henryk Michalewski, Daniel Huang, Quoc Le, Dániel Varga, Zsolt Zombori, Adrián Csiszárik for their feedback and valuable discussions on this topic. I would like to thank to Jay Yagnik, Rahul Sukthankar, Ashok Popat, Rif Saurous, Jeff Dean and Geoffrey Hinton for their support of deep learning based reasoning work at Google. I am grateful to Péter Szoldán, Christoph Benzmüller and Bruce Miller for proofreading the manuscript.

References

1. Alemi, A.A., Chollet, F., Eén, N., Irving, G., Szegedy, C., Urban, J.: Deepmath - deep sequence models for premise selection. In: Lee, D.D., Sugiyama, M., von Luxburg, U., Guyon, I., Garnett, R. (eds.) Advances in Neural Information Processing Systems 29: Annual Conference on Neural Information Processing Systems 2016, Barcelona, Spain, 5–10 December 2016, pp. 2235–2243 (2016)
2. Andrychowicz, M., et al.: Hindsight experience replay. In: Advances in Neural Information Processing Systems 30 (NIPS 2017), pp. 5048–5058 (2017)
3. Bansal, K., Loos, S.M., Rabe, M.N., Szegedy, C.: Learning to reason in large theories without imitation. arXiv preprint arXiv:1905.10501 (2019)
4. Bansal, K., Loos, S.M., Rabe, M.N., Szegedy, C., Wilcox, S.: HOList: an environment for machine learning of higher-order theorem proving. In: Chaudhuri, K., Salakhutdinov, R. (eds.) Proceedings of the 36th International Conference on Machine Learning, ICML 2019, Proceedings of Machine Learning Research, Long Beach, California, USA, 9–15 June 2019, vol. 97, pp. 454–463. PMLR (2019)
5. Biere, A., Cimatti, A., Clarke, E., Zhu, Y.: Symbolic model checking without BDDs. In: Cleaveland, W.R. (ed.) TACAS 1999. LNCS, vol. 1579, pp. 193–207. Springer, Heidelberg (1999). https://doi.org/10.1007/3-540-49059-0_14
6. Blanchette, J.C., Kaliszyk, C., Paulson, L.C., Urban, J.: Hammering towards QED. J. Formalized Reasoning **9**(1), 101–148 (2016)
7. The Coq Proof Assistant. http://coq.inria.fr
8. de Moura, L., Kong, S., Avigad, J., van Doorn, F., von Raumer, J.: The lean theorem prover (System Description). In: Felty, A.P., Middeldorp, A. (eds.) CADE 2015. LNCS (LNAI), vol. 9195, pp. 378–388. Springer, Cham (2015). https://doi.org/10.1007/978-3-319-21401-6_26
9. Devlin, J., Chang, M.-W., Lee, K., Toutanova, K.: BERT: pre-training of deep bidirectional transformers for language understanding. In: Proceedings of the 2019 Conference of the North American Chapter of the Association for Computational Linguistics: Human Language Technologies (Long and Short Papers), vol. 1, pp. 4171–4186 (2019)
10. Eén, N., Sörensson, N.: An extensible SAT-solver. In: Giunchiglia, E., Tacchella, A. (eds.) SAT 2003. LNCS, vol. 2919, pp. 502–518. Springer, Heidelberg (2004). https://doi.org/10.1007/978-3-540-24605-3_37
11. Fitting, M.: First-order Logic and Automated Theorem Proving. Springer, New York (2012). https://doi.org/10.1007/978-1-4612-2360-3
12. Garrabrant, S., Benson-Tilsen, T., Critch, A., Soares, N., Taylor, J.: Logical induction. arXiv preprint arXiv:1609.03543 (2016)
13. Gatys, L.A., Ecker, A.S., Bethge, M.: Image style transfer using convolutional neural networks. In: 2016 IEEE Conference on Computer Vision and Pattern Recognition, CVPR 2016, Las Vegas, NV, USA, 27–30 June 2016, pp. 2414–2423. IEEE Computer Society (2016)
14. Gauthier, T., Kaliszyk, C., Urban, J.: TacticToe: learning to reason with HOL4 tactics. In: Eiter, T., Sands, D. (eds.) LPAR-21, 21st International Conference on Logic for Programming, Artificial Intelligence and Reasoning, Maun, Botswana, 7–12 May 2017, EPiC Series in Computing, vol. 46, pp. 125–143. EasyChair (2017)
15. Gawehn, E., Hiss, J.A., Schneider, G.: Deep learning in drug discovery. Mol. Inform. **35**(1), 3–14 (2016)
16. Gonthier, G.: Formal proof-the four-color theorem. Not. AMS **55**(11), 1382–1393 (2008)

17. Gonthier, G., et al.: A machine-checked proof of the odd order theorem. In: Blazy, S., Paulin-Mohring, C., Pichardie, D. (eds.) ITP 2013. LNCS, vol. 7998, pp. 163–179. Springer, Heidelberg (2013). https://doi.org/10.1007/978-3-642-39634-2_14
18. Google's scalable supercomputers for machine learning, Cloud TPU Pods, are now publicly available in beta. https://bit.ly/2YkZh3i
19. Gordon, A., et al.: MorphNet: Fast & simple resource-constrained structure learning of deep networks. In: 2018 IEEE Conference on Computer Vision and Pattern Recognition, CVPR 2018, Salt Lake City, UT, USA, 18–22 June 2018, pp. 1586–1595. IEEE Computer Society (2018)
20. Grace, K., Salvatier, J., Dafoe, A., Zhang, B., Evans, O.: When will AI exceed human performance? evidence from AI experts. J. Artif. Intell. Res. **62**, 729–754 (2018)
21. Hadjeres, G., Pachet, F., Nielsen, F.: DeepBach: a steerable model for Bach chorales generation. In: Proceedings of the 34th International Conference on Machine Learning, vol. 70, pp. 1362–1371. JMLR (2017)
22. Hales, T., et al.: A formal proof of the Kepler conjecture. In: Forum of Mathematics, Pi, vol. 5. Cambridge University Press (2017)
23. Harrison, J.: HOL light: a tutorial introduction. In: Srivas, M., Camilleri, A. (eds.) FMCAD 1996. LNCS, vol. 1166, pp. 265–269. Springer, Heidelberg (1996). https://doi.org/10.1007/BFb0031814
24. He, K., Zhang, X., Ren, S., Sun, J.: Deep residual learning for image recognition. In: 2016 IEEE Conference on Computer Vision and Pattern Recognition, CVPR 2016, Las Vegas, NV, USA, 27–30 June 2016, pp. 770–778. IEEE Computer Society (2016)
25. Heule, M.J.H., Kullmann, O., Marek, V.W.: Solving and verifying the Boolean Pythagorean triples problem via cube-and-conquer. In: Creignou, N., Le Berre, D. (eds.) SAT 2016. LNCS, vol. 9710, pp. 228–245. Springer, Cham (2016). https://doi.org/10.1007/978-3-319-40970-2_15
26. Huang, D., Dhariwal, P., Song, D., Sutskever, I.: GamePad: a learning environment for theorem proving. In: 7th International Conference on Learning Representations, ICLR 2019, New Orleans, LA, USA, 6–9 May 2019. OpenReview.net (2019)
27. Kaliszyk, C., Urban, J.: HOL (y) hammer: online ATP service for HOL light. Math. Comput. Sci. **9**(1), 5–22 (2015)
28. Kaliszyk, C., Urban, J., Vyskočil, J.: Learning to parse on aligned corpora (Rough Diamond). In: Urban, C., Zhang, X. (eds.) ITP 2015. LNCS, vol. 9236, pp. 227–233. Springer, Cham (2015). https://doi.org/10.1007/978-3-319-22102-1_15
29. Kaliszyk, C., Urban, J., Vyskocil, J.: System description: statistical parsing of informalized Mizar formulas. In: Jebelean, T., Negru, V., Petcu, D., Zaharie, D., Ida, T., Watt, S.M., (eds.) 19th International Symposium on Symbolic and Numeric Algorithms for Scientific Computing, SYNASC 2017, Timisoara, Romania, 21–24 September 2017, pp. 169–172. IEEE Computer Society (2017)
30. Kocsis, L., Szepesvári, C.: Bandit based Monte-Carlo planning. In: Fürnkranz, J., Scheffer, T., Spiliopoulou, M. (eds.) ECML 2006. LNCS (LNAI), vol. 4212, pp. 282–293. Springer, Heidelberg (2006). https://doi.org/10.1007/11871842_29
31. Lample, G., Charton, F.: Deep learning for symbolic mathematics. In: 8th International Conference on Learning Representations, ICLR 2020, Addis Ababa, Ethiopia, 26–30 April 2020. OpenReview.net (2020)
32. Lample, G., Conneau, A., Denoyer, L., Ranzato, M.: Unsupervised machine translation using monolingual corpora only. In: 6th International Conference on Learning Representations, ICLR 2018, Vancouver, BC, Canada, 30 April–3 May 2018, Conference Track Proceedings. OpenReview.net (2018)

33. Lee, D., Szegedy, C., Rabe, M.N., Loos, S.M., Bansal, K.: Mathematical reasoning in latent space. In: 8th International Conference on Learning Representations, ICLR 2020, Addis Ababa, Ethiopia, 26–30 April 2020. OpenReview.net (2020)
34. Liu, Y., et al.: RoBERTa: a robustly optimized BERT pretraining approach. arXiv preprint arXiv:1907.11692 (2019)
35. Loos, S., Irving, G., Szegedy, C., Kaliszyk, C.: Deep network guided proof search. In: Eiter, T., Sands, D. (eds.) LPAR-21, 21st International Conference on Logic for Programming, Artificial Intelligence and Reasoning, Maun, Botswana, 7–12 May 2017, EPiC Series in Computing, vol. 46, pp. 85–105. EasyChair (2017)
36. McCarthy, J.: Computer programs for checking mathematical proofs. In: A Paper Presented at the Symposium on Recursive Function Theory, New York, April 1961
37. Megill, N.: Metamath. In: Wiedijk, F. (ed.) The Seventeen Provers of the World. LNCS (LNAI), vol. 3600, pp. 88–95. Springer, Heidelberg (2006). https://doi.org/10.1007/11542384_13
38. The Mizar Mathematical Library. http://mizar.org
39. Nisan, N., et al.: Introduction to mechanism design (for computer scientists). Algorithmic Game Theor. **9**, 209–242 (2007)
40. Paliwal, A., Loos, S., Rabe, M., Bansal, K., Szegedy, C.: Graph representations for higher-order logic and theorem proving. In: The Thirty-Fourth AAAI Conference on Artificial Intelligence, AAAI 2020, New York, NY, USA, 7–12 February 2020. AAAI Press (2020)
41. Peters, M.E., et al.: Deep contextualized word representations. In: Walker, M.A., Ji, H., Stent, A. (eds.) Proceedings of the 2018 Conference of the North American Chapter of the Association for Computational Linguistics: Human Language Technologies, NAACL-HLT 2018, New Orleans, Louisiana, USA, 1–6 June 2018, (Long Papers), vol. 1, pp. 2227–2237. Association for Computational Linguistics (2018)
42. Silver, D., et al.: A general reinforcement learning algorithm that masters chess, shogi, and go through self-play. Science **362**(6419), 1140–1144 (2018)
43. Silver, D., et al.: Mastering the game of go without human knowledge. Nature **550**(7676), 354 (2017)
44. Simon, D.L.: Checking number theory proofs in natural language. Ph.D thesis (1990)
45. Slind, K., Norrish, M.: A brief overview of HOL4. In: Mohamed, O.A., Muñoz, C., Tahar, S. (eds.) TPHOLs 2008. LNCS, vol. 5170, pp. 28–32. Springer, Heidelberg (2008). https://doi.org/10.1007/978-3-540-71067-7_6
46. Szegedy, C., et al.: Going deeper with convolutions. In: IEEE Conference on Computer Vision and Pattern Recognition, CVPR 2015, Boston, MA, USA, 7–12 June 2015, pp. 1–9. IEEE Computer Society (2015)
47. Tan, M., Le, Q.V.: EfficientNet: rethinking model scaling for convolutional neural networks. In: Chaudhuri, K., Salakhutdinov, R. (eds.) Proceedings of the 36th International Conference on Machine Learning, ICML 2019, Long Beach, California, USA, 9–15 June 2019, Proceedings of Machine Learning Research, vol. 97, pp. 6105–6114. PMLR (2019)
48. Urban, J.: Translating Mizar for first order theorem provers. In: Asperti, A., Buchberger, B., Davenport, J.H. (eds.) MKM 2003. LNCS, vol. 2594, pp. 203–215. Springer, Heidelberg (2003). https://doi.org/10.1007/3-540-36469-2_16
49. Urban, J.: MPTP 0.2: design, implementation, and initial experiments. J. Autom. Reasoning **37**(1–2), 21–43 (2006)

50. Urban, J.: MaLARea: a metasystem for automated reasoning in large theories. In: Sutcliffe, G., Urban, J., Schulz, S. (eds.) Proceedings of the CADE-21 Workshop on Empirically Successful Automated Reasoning in Large Theories, Bremen, Germany, 17th July 2007, CEUR Workshop Proceedings, vol. 257. CEUR-WS.org (2007)

51. Vaswani, A., et al.: Attention is all you need. In: Guyon, I., et al. (eds.) Advances in Neural Information Processing Systems 30: Annual Conference on Neural Information Processing Systems 2017, Long Beach, CA, USA, 4–9 December 2017, pp. 5998–6008 (2017)

52. Wang, M., Tang, Y., Wang, J., Deng, J.: Premise selection for theorem proving by deep graph embedding. In: Advances in Neural Information Processing Systems 30 (NIPS 2017), pp. 2786–2796 (2017)

53. Wenzel, M., Paulson, L.C., Nipkow, T.: The Isabelle framework. In: Mohamed, O.A., Muñoz, C., Tahar, S. (eds.) TPHOLs 2008. LNCS, vol. 5170, pp. 33–38. Springer, Heidelberg (2008). https://doi.org/10.1007/978-3-540-71067-7_7

54. Wu, Z., Pan, S., Chen, F., Long, G., Zhang, C., Philip, S.Y.: A comprehensive survey on graph neural networks. In: IEEE Transactions on Neural Networks and Learning Systems, pp. 1–21 (2020)

55. Yang, K., Deng, J.: Learning to prove theorems via interacting with proof assistants. In: Chaudhuri, K., Salakhutdinov, R. (eds.) Proceedings of the 36th International Conference on Machine Learning, ICML 2019, Long Beach, California, USA, 9–15 June 2019, Proceedings of Machine Learning Research, vol. 97, pp. 6984–6994. PMLR (2019)

56. Yang, Z., Dai, Z., Yang, Y., Carbonell, J.G., Salakhutdinov, R., Le, Q.V.: XLNet: generalized autoregressive pretraining for language understanding. In: Wallach, H.M., et al. (eds.) Advances in Neural Information Processing Systems 32: Annual Conference on Neural Information Processing Systems 2019, NeurIPS 2019, Canada, Vancouver, BC, 8–14 December 2019, pp. 5754–5764 (2019)

57. Yu, A.W., et al.: QANet: combining local convolution with global self-attention for reading comprehension. In: 6th International Conference on Learning Representations, ICLR 2018, Vancouver, BC, Canada, 30 April–3 May 2018, Conference Track Proceedings. OpenReview.net (2018)

58. Yuksel, S.E., Wilson, J.N., Gader, P.D.: Twenty years of mixture of experts. IEEE Trans. Neural Networks Learn. Syst. **23**(8), 1177–1193 (2012)

59. Zhu, J.-Y., Park, T., Isola, P., Efros, A.A.: Unpaired image-to-image translation using cycle-consistent adversarial networks. In: 2017 IEEE Conference on Computer Vision and Pattern Recognition, CVPR 2017, Honolulu, HI, USA, 21–26 July 2017, pp. 2223–2232. IEEE Computer Society (2017)

60. Zinn, C.: Understanding informal mathematical discourse. Ph.D thesis, Institut für Informatik, Universität Erlangen-Nürnberg (2004)

61. Zombori, Z., Csiszárik, A., Michalewski, H., Kaliszyk, C., Urban, J.: Towards finding longer proofs. arXiv preprint arXiv:1905.13100 (2019)

62. Zoph, B., Le, Q.V.: Neural architecture search with reinforcement learning. In: 5th International Conference on Learning Representations, ICLR 2017, Toulon, France, 24–26 April 2017, Conference Track Proceedings. OpenReview.net (2017)

Full Papers

Formal Adventures in Convex and Conical Spaces

Reynald Affeldt[1]⊙, Jacques Garrigue[2](✉)⊙, and Takafumi Saikawa[2]⊙

[1] National Institute of Advanced Industrial Science and Technology, Tsukuba, Japan
[2] Nagoya University, Nagoya, Japan
garrigue@math.nagoya-u.ac.jp

Abstract. Convex sets appear in various mathematical theories, and are used to define notions such as convex functions and hulls. As an abstraction from the usual definition of convex sets in vector spaces, we formalize in Coq an intrinsic axiomatization of convex sets, namely convex spaces, based on an operation taking barycenters of points. A convex space corresponds to a specific type that does not refer to a surrounding vector space. This simplifies the definitions of functions on it. We show applications including the convexity of information-theoretic functions defined over types of distributions. We also show how convex spaces are embedded in conical spaces, which are abstract real cones, and use the embedding as an effective device to ease calculations.

1 Introduction

The notion of convex sets appears in various mathematical theories. A subset X of a real vector space is called a convex set if, for any $x, y \in X$ and $p \in [0, 1]$, their *convex combination* $px + (1 - p)y$ is again in X. One basic use of it is to define the convexity of functions. A function f is said to be convex if $f(px + (1 - p)y) \leq pf(x) + (1 - p)f(y)$ for any convex combination $px + (1 - p)y$. Thus, convex sets are natural domains for convex functions to be defined on. Good examples of these notions can be found in information theory, where convexity is a fundamental property of important functions such as logarithm, entropy, and mutual information. Our INFOTHEO library [17] developed in the COQ proof assistant [29] has a formalization of textbook proofs [12] of such results.

In the course of formalizing such convexity results, we find that axiomatizing convex sets is a useful step which provides clarity and organizability in the results. We abstract the usual treatment of convex sets as subsets of some vector space and employ an algebraic theory of *convex spaces*, which was introduced by Stone [27]. The formalization uses the *packed class* construction [15,24], so as to obtain generic notations and lemmas, and more importantly, to be able to combine structures. Binary convex spaces are formalized in Sect. 2, and their multiary versions are formalized in Sect. 3, along with proofs of equivalence.

We also formalize an embedding of convex spaces into *conical spaces* (a.k.a. cones or real cones [31]), which we find an indispensable tool to formalize convex

© Springer Nature Switzerland AG 2020
C. Benzmüller and B. Miller (Eds.): CICM 2020, LNAI 12236, pp. 23–38, 2020.
https://doi.org/10.1007/978-3-030-53518-6_2

spaces. Examples in the literature avoid proving properties of convex spaces directly and choose to work in conical spaces. This is especially the case when their goal can be achieved either way [23,31]. Some authors suggest that the results in conical spaces can be backported to convex spaces [13,21]. We apply this method in Sect. 4 to enable additive handling of convex combinations. By formalizing the relationship between convex and conical spaces, we work out short proofs of a number of lemmas on convex spaces. Among them is Stone's key lemma [27, Lemma 2], whose proof is often omitted in the literature despite its fundamental role in the study of convex spaces.

We complete this presentation with applications of our formalization to convex hulls (Sect. 5) and to convex functions (Sect. 6).

While our proofs do not introduce extra axioms, some libraries used in our development, such as mathcomp-analysis [1], contain axioms which make parts of our work classical. In particular, our definition of convex sets is based on classical sets, assuming decidable membership.

2   Convex Spaces

Let us begin with the definition of convex spaces. As mentioned in the introduction, convex spaces are an axiomatization of the usual notion of convex sets in vector spaces. It has a long history of repeated reintroduction by many authors, often with minor differences and different names: barycentric algebra [27], semiconvex algebra [28], or, just, convex sets [19].

We define convex spaces following Fritz [14, Definition 3.1].

Definition 1 (Module ConvexSpace in [18]). *A convex space is a structure for the following signature:*

- *Carrier set X.*
- *Convex combination operations $(\_ \triangleleft_p \triangleright \_) : X \times X \to X$ indexed by $p \in [0,1]$.*
- *Unit law: $x \triangleleft_1 \triangleright y = x$.*
- *Idempotence law: $x \triangleleft_p \triangleright x = x$.*
- *Skewed commutativity law: $x \triangleleft_{1-p} \triangleright y = y \triangleleft_p \triangleright x$.*
- *Quasi-associativity law: $x \triangleleft_p \triangleright (y \triangleleft_q \triangleright z) = (x \triangleleft_r \triangleright y) \triangleleft_s \triangleright z$,*

  where $s = 1 - (1-p)(1-q)$ and $r = \begin{cases} p/s & \text{if } s \neq 0 \\ 0 & \text{otherwise} \end{cases}$.

  (Note that r is irrelevant to the value of $(x \triangleleft_r \triangleright y) \triangleleft_s \triangleright z$ if $s = 0$.)

We can translate this definition to COQ as a *packed class* [15] with the following mixin interface:

```
1   Record mixin_of (T : choiceType) : Type := Mixin {
2     conv : prob -> T -> T -> T where "a <| p |> b" := (conv p a b);
3     _ : forall a b, a <| 1%:pr |> b = a ;
4     _ : forall p a, a <| p |> a = a ;
5     _ : forall p a b, a <| p |> b = b <| p.~%:pr |> a;
6     _ : forall (p q : prob) (a b c : T),
7       a <| p |> (b <| q |> c) = (a <| [r_of p, q] |> b) <| [s_of p, q] |> c }.
```

There are some notations and definitions to be explained. The type `prob` in the above Coq code denotes the closed unit interval $[0, 1]$. The notation `r%:pr` is a notation for a real number `r` equipped with a canonical proof that $0 \leq r \leq 1$. The notation `p.~` is for $1 - p$. The notation `[s_of p, q]` is for $1 - (1-p)(1-q)$, and `[r_of p, q]` for $p/[s\_of\ p,\ q]$.

Intuitively, one can regard the convex combination as a probabilistic choice between two points. At line 3, the left argument is chosen with probability 1. The lines that follow correspond to idempotence, skewed commutativity, and quasi-associativity.

An easy example of convex space is the real line $\mathbb{R}$, whose convex combination is expressed by ordinary addition and multiplication as $pa + (1-p)b$. Probability distributions also form a convex space. In the formalization, the type `fdist` A of distributions over any finite type A (borrowed from previous work [6]) is equipped with a convex space structure, where the convex combination of two distributions d_1, d_2 is defined pointwise as $x \mapsto pd_1(x) + (1-p)d_2(x)$.

As a result of the packed class construction, we obtain the type `convType` of all types which implicitly carry the above axioms. Then, each example of convex space is declared to be canonically a member of `convType`, enabling the implicit inference of the appropriate convex space structure. These two implicit inference mechanisms combined make the statement of generic lemmas on convex spaces simple and applications easy.

3   Multiary Convex Combination

Convex spaces can also be characterized by multiary convex combination operations, which combine finitely many points $x_0, \ldots, x_{n-1}$ at once, according to some finite probability distribution d over the set $I_n = \{0, \ldots, n-1\}$, i.e., $d_i \geq 0$ and $\sum_{i<n} d_i = 1$. In this section we consider different axiomatizations, and their equivalence with the binary axioms.

3.1   Axiomatization

A definition of convex spaces based on multiary operations is given as follows (see for example [10, Definition 5] and [16, Sect. 2.1]).

Definition 2 (Convex space, multiary version). *A convex space based on multiary operations is a structure for the following signature:*

– *Carrier set X.*
– *Multiary convex combination operations, indexed by an arity n and a distribution d over I_n:*

$$X^n \quad \to \quad X$$
$$(x_i)_{i<n} \mapsto \underset{i<n}{\Diamond} d_i x_i$$

– *Projection law: if $d_j = 1$, $\underset{i<n}{\Diamond} d_i x_i = x_j$.*   (`ax_proj` *in [18]*)

– *Barycenter law:* $\underset{i<n}{\Diamond} d_i \left(\underset{j<m}{\Diamond} e_{i,j} x_j \right) = \underset{j<m}{\Diamond} \left(\sum_{i<n} d_i e_{i,j} \right) x_j.$ (**ax_bary** *in [18]*)

Note that in our CoQ code, $\Diamond_{i<n} d_i x_i$ appears as `<&>_d x` or `altConvn d x`, indicating more explicitly that the operation takes two arguments d and x.

This multiary convex structure and the binary one given in Sect. 2 are equivalent: the multiary and binary operators interpret each other satisfying the needed axioms, and the interpretations cancel out when composed. While the binary axiomatization is easy to instantiate, the multiary version exhibits the relationship to probability distributions. Therefore we want to establish this equivalence before working further on other constructions over convex spaces.

In the literature, this equivalence is justified without much detail by referring to the seminal article by Stone [27] (see, e.g., [19, Theorem 4], [10, Proposition 7]). Yet, what Stone gave is not an explicit axiomatization of the multiary convex operator, but a number of lemmas targeted at proving an embedding of (binary) convex spaces into vector spaces. These lemmas include the following one, that is seen as a justification for the barycenter law in the binary axiomatization.

Lemma 1 (Lemma 4 in [27]). *If the given masses and their associated points are partitioned into groups (of non-zero total masses) in any way, then the center of mass is identical with that of masses equal to the respective total masses for the various groups, each placed at the center of mass for the corresponding group.*

The relation to the barycenter law is implied if one sees a convex combination $\Diamond_{j<m} (\sum_{i<n} d_i e_{i,j}) x_j$ as a point defined in terms of a set of generating points $\{x_j\}_{j<m}$ (they generate their convex hull). Then $\Diamond_{i<n} d_i (\Diamond_{j<m} e_{i,j} x_j)$ corresponds to grouping the generating points by filtering through the distributions $\{e_i\}_{i<n}$. But this grouping is not necessarily a partition since there could be shared elements, hence the relation is not direct.

Beaulieu [8, Definition 3.1.4] proposed an alternative multiary axiomatization, which was actually presented as a model for countable probabilistic choice (rather than a definition of convex space). His partition law corresponds exactly to the statement of Stone's lemma.

Definition 3 (Convex space, Beaulieu style). *A convex space is a structure for the previous operations* $\Diamond_{i<n} d_i$ *and the following laws.*

– *Partition law:* $\underset{i \in I}{\Diamond} \lambda_i x_i = \underset{j \in J}{\Diamond} \rho_j \left(\underset{k \in K_j}{\Diamond} \frac{\lambda_k}{\rho_j} x_k \right)$ (**ax_part** *in [18]*)

  where $\{K_j \mid j \in J\}$ *is a partition of* I, *and* $\rho_j = \sum_{k \in K_j} \lambda_k \neq 0$.
– *Idempotence law:* $\underset{i \in I}{\Diamond} \lambda_i A_i = A$ *if* $A_i = A$ *for all* $\lambda_i > 0$. (**ax_idem** *in [18]*)

In the implementation, using sets as indexing domains of the combination operators would be cumbersome, so that the partition law is actually expressed as follows, using a map $\check{K}$ and Kronecker's δ.

$$\underset{i<n}{\Diamond} \lambda_i x_i = \underset{j<m}{\Diamond} \rho_j \left(\underset{k<n}{\Diamond} \delta_{j, \check{K}(k)} \frac{\lambda_k}{\rho_j} x_k \right) \quad \text{where } \check{K} : I_n \to I_m, \; K_j = \check{K}^{-1}(j)$$

We also have to separately show that $(\delta_{j,\check{K}(k)}\frac{\lambda_k}{\rho_j})_{k<n}$ and $(\rho_j)_{j<m}$ form probability distributions. As an exceptional case, $(\delta_{j,\check{K}(k)}\frac{\lambda_k}{\rho_j})_{k<n}$ is replaced by a uniform distribution if $\rho_j = 0$.

3.2   Equivalence of Axiomatizations

After considering the different axiomatizations, we decided to prove a triangular equivalence: between multiary convex structures in standard and Beaulieu style, and then with the binary convex structure given in Sect. 2. The relations we will explain in this section are depicted in Fig. 1.

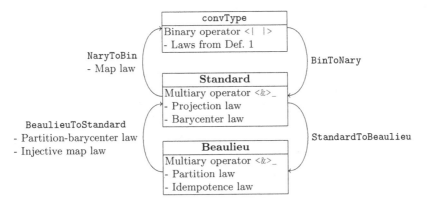

Fig. 1. Relations between the various formalizations of convex spaces

The first equivalence, between multiary convex axioms, is rather technical. The first direction, proving Beaulieu's axioms from the standard presentation (functor `StandardToBeaulieu` in [18]), is relatively easy, as the partition law is intuitively just a special case of the barycenter law, where supports[1] are disjoint, and the idempotence law can be derived as a combination of the two standard laws. However, the second direction (functor `BeaulieuToStandard`) is harder, and led us to introduce two derived laws:

- *Partition-barycenter law: barycenter law, with disjoint supports.* (`ax_bary_part`)
- *Injective map law:* $\underset{i<m}{\diamondsuit}\, d_i g_{u(i)} = \underset{j<n}{\diamondsuit}\sum_{\substack{i<m\\u(i)=j}} d_i g_j$ *with u injective.* (`ax_inj_map`)

The partition-barycenter law can be derived from the Beaulieu style axioms, and in turn is used to prove the injective map law. Together they allow to prove the barycenter law.

The equivalence between binary and multiary axiomatizations requires first to define their operators in terms of each other.

---

[1] The support of a probability distribution d is the set $\{i \mid d_i > 0\}$.

Definition 4 (Convn and binconv in [18])

(a) *Let* $d : I_n \to [0,1]$ *be a finite distribution, and* $x : I_n \to X$ *be points in a convex space* X. *Then the multiary convex combination of these points and distribution is defined from the binary operator by recursion on* n *as follows:*

$$\underset{i<n}{\diamond}\, d_i x_i = \begin{cases} x_0 & \text{if } d_0 = 1 \text{ or } n = 1 \\ x_0 \triangleleft_{d_0} \triangleright \left(\underset{i<n-1}{\diamond} d'_i x_{i+1} \right) & \text{otherwise} \end{cases}$$

where d' *is a new distribution:* $d'_i = d_{i+1}/(1 - d_0)$.

(b) *Let* p *be a probability and* x_0, x_1 *be points in a convex space. Then their binary combination is defined from the multiary operator as follows:*

$$x_0 \triangleleft_p \triangleright x_1 = \underset{i<2}{\diamond}\, d_i x_i \qquad \text{where } d_0 = p \text{ and } d_1 = 1 - p.$$

The first direction, functor `BinToNary` in [18], must prove that the first definition satisfies the multiary axioms, and indeed amounts to proving a variant of Stone's lemma. We will see in the next section that the original proof by Stone is better formalized by transporting the argument to conical spaces.

The opposite direction, functor `NaryToBin`, must prove the binary axioms from the multiary ones. While we start from the standard version, the idempotence law proved to be instrumental in this task, together with the following unrestricted map law.

– *Map law:* $\quad \underset{i<m}{\diamond}\, d_i g_{u(i)} = \underset{j<n}{\diamond} \underset{\substack{i<m \\ u(i)=j}}{\sum}\, d_i g_j$ *for any map* u. $\qquad$ (**ax_map** *in* [18])

Finally, one also needs to prove that the definitions we used for each operation in both directions are coherent.

Lemma 2 (equiv_conv and equiv_convn in [18]). *The constructions in Definition 4 (Convn and binconv) cancel each other. That is,*

– *If* $\diamond^*$ *is the operator induced by Definition 4(a), and* $\triangleleft\_\triangleright^\dagger$ *the one induced from it by Definition 4(b), we can derive* $a \triangleleft_p \triangleright^\dagger b = a \triangleleft_p \triangleright b$ *from the binary axioms.*
– *If* $\triangleleft\_\triangleright^*$ *the operator induced by Definition 4(b),* $\diamond^\dagger$ *is the one induced from it by Definition 4(a), we can derive* $\diamond^\dagger_{i<n}\, d_i x_i = \diamond_{i<n}\, d_i x_i$ *from the multiary axioms.*

4   Conical Spaces and Embedded Convex Spaces

The definition of multiary convex combination operator in the previous section (Definition 4(a)) relied on recursion. This makes the definition look complicated, and moreover, the algebraic properties of the combination difficult to see. If we consider the special case of convex sets in a vector space, the meaning of multiary combinations and the algebraic properties become evident:

$$\underset{i<n}{\diamond}\, d_i x_i = d_0 x_0 + \cdots + d_{n-1} x_{n-1}.$$

The additions on the right-hand side are of vectors, and thus are associative and commutative. This means that the multiary combination on the left-hand side is invariant under permutations or partitions on indices. We want to show that these invariance properties are also satisfied generally in any convex space.

However, the search for the proofs is painful if naively done. This is because binary convex combination operations satisfy associativity and commutativity only through cumbersome parameter computations. For example, a direct proof of the permutation case involves manipulations on the set I_n of indices and on the symmetry groups, which require fairly long combinatorics [27, Lemma 2].

We present a solution to this complexity by transporting the arguments on convex spaces to a closely related construction of conical spaces. Conical spaces are an abstraction of cones in real vector spaces just like convex spaces are an abstraction of convex sets. Like convex spaces, the definition of conical spaces appears in many articles. We refer to the ones by Flood (called semicone there) [13] and by Varacca and Winskel (called real cone there) [31]:

Definition 5 (Conical space). *A conical space is a semimodule over the semiring of non-negative reals. That is, it is a structure for the following signature:*

- *Carrier set X.*
- *Zero $\mathbf{0} : X$.*
- *Addition operation $\_ + \_ : X \times X \to X$.*
- *Scaling operations $c\_ : X \to X$ indexed by $c \in \mathbb{R}_{\geq 0}$.*
- *Associativity law for addition: $x + (y + z) = (x + y) + z$.*
- *Commutativity law for addition: $x + y = y + x$.*
- *Associativity law for scaling: $c(dx) = (cd)x$.*
- *Left-distributivity law: $(c + d)x = cx + dx$.*
- *Right-distributivity law: $c(x + y) = cx + cy$.*
- *Zero law for addition: $\mathbf{0} + x = x$.*
- *Left zero law for scaling: $0x = \mathbf{0}$.*
- *Right zero law for scaling: $c\mathbf{0} = \mathbf{0}$.*
- *One law for scaling: $1x = x$.*

We display this definition only to show that conical spaces have straightforward associativity and commutativity. In fact, the formalization is elaborated on the embedding of convex spaces into canonically constructed conical spaces, which appeared in the article by Flood [13]. We build on top of each convex space X, the conical space S_X of its "scaled points":

Definition 6 (scaled_pt, addpt, and scalept in [18]). *Let X be a convex space. We define a set S_X which becomes a conical space with the following addition and scaling operations.*

$$S_X := (\mathbb{R}_{>0} \times X) \cup \{\mathbf{0}\}.$$

That is, the points of S_X are either a pair $p * x$ of $p \in \mathbb{R}_{>0}$ and $x \in X$, or a new additive unit $\mathbf{0}$. Addition of points $a, b \in S_X$ is defined by cases to deal with $\mathbf{0}$:

$$a + b := \begin{cases} (r + q) * (x \triangleleft_{r/(r+q)} \triangleright y) & \text{if } a = r * x \text{ and } b = q * y \\ a & \text{if } b = \mathbf{0} \\ b & \text{if } a = \mathbf{0} \end{cases}$$

Scaling $a \in S_X$ *by* $p \in \mathbb{R}_{\geq 0}$ *is also defined by cases:*

$$pa := \begin{cases} pq * x & \text{if } p > 0 \text{ and } a = q * x \\ \mathbf{0} & \text{otherwise} \end{cases}$$

We omit here the proofs that S_X with these addition and scaling satisfies the conical laws. They are proved formally in [18] (see the lemmas addptC, addptA, scalept_addpt, etc.).

Properties of the underlying convex spaces are transported into and back from this conical space, through an embedding:

Definition 7 (S1 in [18])

$$\iota : X \longmapsto S_X$$
$$x \longmapsto 1 * x$$

Convex combinations in X are mapped by ι to additions in S_X.

Lemma 3 (S1_convn in [18])

$$\iota\left(\diamondsuit_{i<n} d_i x_i\right) = \sum_{i<n} d_i \iota(x_i).$$

The right-hand side of the lemma is a conical sum (Fig. 2), which behaves like an ordinary linear sum thanks to the conical laws, and enjoys good support from MATHCOMP's big operator library [9].

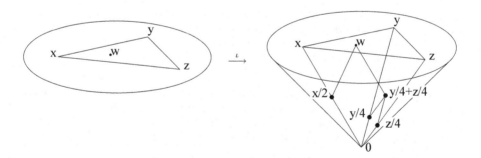

Fig. 2. Example of S1_convn: $1 * w = \frac{1}{2} * x + \frac{1}{4} * y + \frac{1}{4} * z$

With these preparations, properties such as [27, Lemma 2] can be proved in a few lines of COQ code:

Lemma 4 (Convn_perm in [18])

$$\diamondsuit_{i<n} d_i x_i = \diamondsuit_{i<n} (d \circ s)_i (x \circ s)_i,$$

where s *is any permutation on the set of indices* n.

The proof of the barycenter property [27, Lemma 4] from Sect. 3 is based on the same technique (see `Convn_convnfdist` in [18]).

A way to understand this conical approach is to start from Stone's definition of convex spaces [27]. He uses a quaternary convex operator $(x, y; \alpha, \beta)$ where x and y are points of the space, and α and β are non-negative coefficients such that $\alpha + \beta > 0$. Its values are quotiented by an axiom to be invariant under scaling, removing the need to normalize coefficients for associativity. This amounts to regarding a convex space as the projective space of some conical space.

The definition of S_X is a concrete reconstruction of such a conical space from a given convex space X. The benefit of this method over Stone's is the removal of quotients by moving the coefficients from operations to values. We can then use the linear-algebraic properties of conical sums such as the neutrality of zeroes, which had to be specially handled in Stone's proofs (e.g., [27, Lemma 2]).

Examples. We illustrate how ι is used in practice with the proof of the *entropic identity*. Let T be a `convType`; we want to show that

$$(a \triangleleft_q \triangleright b) \triangleleft_p \triangleright (c \triangleleft_q \triangleright d) = (a \triangleleft_p \triangleright c) \triangleleft_q \triangleright (b \triangleleft_p \triangleright d). \tag{1}$$

We could use the properties of convex spaces, but this will result in cumbersome computations, in particular because of quasi-associativity. Instead, we proceed by an embedding into the set of scaled points over T using ι. First, we observe that these scaled points form a convex space for the operator $p, a, b \mapsto pa + \bar{p}b$ and that $\iota(a \triangleleft_p \triangleright b) = \iota(a) \triangleleft_p \triangleright \iota(b)$. As a consequence, when we apply ι to Equation (1), its left-hand side becomes

$$p(q\iota(a) + \bar{q}\iota(b)) + \bar{p}(q\iota(c) + \bar{q}\iota(d)).$$

The main difference with Eq. (1) is that $+$ (Coq notation: `addpt`) enjoys (unconditional) associativity, making the rest of the proof easier. In the proof script below, line 4 performs the embedding by first using the injectivity of ι (lemma `S1_inj`), then using the fact that ι is a morphism w.r.t. $\_\triangleleft_p\triangleright\_$ (lemma `S1_conv`), and last by revealing the definition of the operator of the convex spaces formed by scaled points (lemma `convptE`). The proof can be completed by rewritings with properties of `addpt` and `scalept` until the left-hand side matches the right-hand side.

```
1  Lemma convACA (a b c d : T) p q :
2    (a <|q|> b) <|p|> (c <|q|> d) = (a <|p|> c) <|q|> (b <|p|> d).
3  Proof.
4    apply S1_inj; rewrite ![in LHS]S1_conv !convptE.
5    rewrite !scalept_addpt ?scalept_comp //.
6    rewrite !(mulRC p) !(mulRC p.~) addptA addptC (addptC (scalept (q * p) _)).
7    rewrite !addptA -addptA -!scalept_comp -?scalept_addpt //.
8    by rewrite !(addptC (scalept _.~ _)) !S1_conv.
9  Qed.
```

We conclude this section with an example that provides a closed formula for the multiary convex combination $\langle | \rangle_{i<n} e_i g_i$ (Coq notation: `<|>_e g`) in the case of the real line (seen as a convex space):

```
1   Definition scaleR x : R := if x is p *: y then p * y else 0.
2   Definition big_scaleR := big_morph scaleR scaleR_addpt scaleR0.
3   Lemma avgnRE n (g : 'I_n -> R) e : <|>_e g = \sum_(i < n) e i * g i.
4   Proof.
5   rewrite -[LHS]Scaled1RK S1_convn big_scaleR.
6   by under eq_bigr do rewrite scaleR_scalept // Scaled1RK.
7   Qed.
```

This corresponds to the following transformations of the left-hand side.

$$
\begin{aligned}
\Diamond_{i<n}\, e_i g_i &= \texttt{scaleR}(\iota(\Diamond_{i<n}\, e_i g_i)) & \text{by Scaled1RK} \\
&= \texttt{scaleR}(\textstyle\sum_{i<n} e_i \iota(g_i)) & \text{by S1\_convn} \\
&= \textstyle\sum_{i<n} \texttt{scaleR}(e_i \iota(g_i)) & \text{by big\_scaleR} \\
&= \textstyle\sum_{i<n} e_i \texttt{scaleR}(\iota(g_i)) & \text{by scaleR\_scalept} \\
&= \textstyle\sum_{i<n} e_i g_i & \text{by Scaled1RK}
\end{aligned}
$$

5 Formalization of Convex Sets and Hulls

Our first application of convex and conical spaces is the formalization of convex sets and convex hulls. Besides mathematics, they also appear in many applications of convex spaces such as program semantics [8,11].

Definition 8 (is_convex_set in [18]). *Let T be a convex space. A subset D in T is a convex set if, for any $p \in [0,1]$ and $x, y \in D$, $x \triangleleft_p \triangleright y \in D$.*

We use the predicate is_convex_set to define the type {convex_set T} of convex sets over T.

We can turn any set of points in a convex space into a convex set, namely, by taking *convex hulls*.

Definition 9 (hull in [18]). *For a subset X of T, its hull $\overline{X}$ is*

$$
\overline{X} = \left\{ \Diamond_{i<n} d_i x_i \ \middle|\ n \in \mathbb{N} \wedge d \text{ is a distribution over } I_n \wedge \forall i < n,\ x_i \in X \right\}.
$$

Example. The following example illustrates the usefulness of conical spaces when reasoning about convex hulls.

Our goal is to prove that for any $z \in \text{hull}\,(X \cup Y)$ ($X \neq \emptyset$, $Y \neq \emptyset$), there exist $x \in X$ and $y \in Y$ such that $z = x \triangleleft_p \triangleright y$ for some p (see the formal statement at line 1 below).

We first introduce two notations. Let scaled_set X be the set $\{p * x \mid x \in \texttt{X}\}$. For any $a \neq 0$, let [point of a0] (where a0 is the proof that $a \neq 0$) be the x such that $a = p * x$ for some p.

To prove our goal, it is sufficient to prove that there exist $a \in$ scaled_set X and $b \in$ scaled_set Y such that $\iota(z) = a + b$ (this reasoning step is the purpose of line 6). When $a = 0$ or $b = 0$, we omit easy proofs at lines 8 and 9. Otherwise, we can take x to be [point of a0] and y to be [point of b0] as performed by the four lines from line 10.

We now establish the sufficient condition (from line 14). Since z is in the hull, we have a distribution d and n points g_i such that $z = \diamond_{i<n} d_i g_i$. We then decompose $\iota(z)$ as follows:

$$\iota(z) = \sum_{i<n} d_i(\iota(g_i)) = \underbrace{\sum_{i<n, g_i \in X} d_i(\iota(g_i))}_{b} + \underbrace{\sum_{i<n, g_i \notin X} d_i(\iota(g_i))}_{c}.$$

We conclude by observing that b is in scaled_set X and that c is in scaled_set Y because $\{g_i | g_i \notin X\} \subseteq Y$.

```
1   Lemma hull_setU (z : T) (X Y : {convex_set T}) : X !=set0 -> Y !=set0 ->
2     hull (X `|` Y) z ->
3     exists2 x, x \in X & exists2 y, y \in Y & exists p, z = x <| p |> y.
4   Proof.
5   move=> [dx ?] [dy ?] [n -[g [d [gT zg]]]].
6   suff [a] : exists2 a, a \in scaled_set X & exists2 b, b \in scaled_set Y &
7       S1 z = addpt a b.
8     have [/eqP -> _ [b bY]|a0 aX [b]] := boolP (a == Zero) by ...
9     have [/eqP -> _|b0 bY] := boolP (b == Zero) by ...
10    rewrite addptE => -[_ zxy].
11    exists [point of a0]; first exact: (@scaled_set_extract _ a).
12    exists [point of b0]; first exact: scaled_set_extract.
13    by eexists; rewrite zxy.
14  move/(congr1 (@S1 _)): zg; rewrite S1_convn.
15  rewrite (bigID (fun i => g i \in X)) /=.
16  set b := \ssum_(i | _) _.
17  set c := \ssum_(i | _) _.
18  move=> zbc.
19  exists b; first exact: ssum_scaled_set.
20  exists c => //.
21  apply: (@ssum_scaled_set _ [pred i | g i \notin X]) => i /=.
22  move/asboolP; rewrite in_setE.
23  by case: (gT (g i) (imageP _ I)).
24  Qed.
```

6   Formalization of Convex Functions

In this section, we first (Sect. 6.1) formalize a generic definition of convex functions based on convex spaces; for that purpose, we introduce in particular *ordered convex spaces*. To demonstrate this formalization, we then apply it to the proof of the concavity of the logarithm function and to an information-theoretic function (Sect. 6.2).

6.1   Ordered Convex Spaces and Convex Functions

An ordered convex space extends a convex space with a partial order structure:

Definition 10 (Module `OrderedConvexSpace` in [18]). *An ordered convex space is a structure whose signature extends the one of convex spaces as follows:*

- *Convex space X.*
- *Ordering relation $(\_ \leq \_) \subset X \times X$.*
- *Reflexivity law: $x \leq x$.*
- *Transitivity law: $x \leq y \land y \leq z \Rightarrow x \leq z$.*
- *Antisymmetry law: $x \leq y \land y \leq x \Rightarrow x = y$.*

The above definition does not force any interaction between convexity and ordering. It would also be a natural design to include an axiom stating that convex combinations preserve ordering [21, Sect. 2]. We however do not need such interactions for defining convex functions, which is our purpose here.

Convexity of a function is defined if its codomain is an ordered convex space. In the following, let T be a convex space and U be an ordered convex space.

Definition 11 (`convex_function_at` in [18]). *A function $f : T \to U$ is convex at $p \in [0,1]$ and $x, y \in T$ if $f(x \triangleleft_p \triangleright y) \leq f(x) \triangleleft_p \triangleright f(y)$.*

Definition 12 (`convex_function` in [18]). *A function $f : T \to U$ is convex if it is convex at all $p \in [0,1]$ and $x, y \in T$.*

The above predicates expect total functions. For partial functions, we resort to convex sets (Definition 8).

Definition 13 (`convex_function_in` in [18]). *Let D be a convex set in T. A function $f : T \to U$ is convex in D if it is convex at any $p \in [0,1]$ and $x, y \in D$.*

Concave functions are defined similarly since f is concave for the order $\leq$ if it is convex for $\geq$. When the codomain of f is $\mathbb{R}$, the prototypical example of an ordered convex space, it is also easy to prove that f is concave if $-f$ is convex.

6.2   Examples of Convex Functions

As a first example, we prove that the real logarithm function is concave. The concavity of logarithm is frequently used in information theory, for example, properties of data compression depend on it [4].

The definition of logarithm we use in CoQ is the one of the standard library; it has the entire $\mathbb{R}$ as its domain by setting $\log(x) = 0$ for $x \leq 0$. The statement of concavity is then restricted to the subset $\mathbb{R}_{>0}$.[2]

---

[2] This way of restricting the domain of functions in their properties rather than in their definitions is a design choice often found in CoQ. It makes it possible for functions such as the logarithm to be composable without being careful about their domains and ranges, and leads to a clean separation between definitions and properties of functions in the formalization.

Lemma 5 (`log_concave` in [17, `probability/ln_facts.v`]). *The extended logarithm function*

$$x \mapsto \begin{cases} \log(x) & \text{if } x \in \mathbb{R}_{>0} \\ 0 & \text{otherwise} \end{cases}$$

is concave in $\mathbb{R}_{>0}$.

The statement in COQ of these lemmas is as follows:

```
Lemma log_concave : concave_function_in Rpos_interval log.
```

The predicate `concave_function_in` has been explained in Sect. 6.1. The object `Rpos_interval` is the set of positive numbers described as the predicate `fun x => 0 < x` equipped with the proof that this set is indeed convex. The heart of the proof is the fact that a function whose second derivative is non-negative is convex (`Section twice_derivable_convex` in [18]). Our proof proceeds by using the formalization of real analysis from the COQ standard library; our formalization of convex spaces can thus be seen as an added abstraction layer of convexity to this library.

Our second example of convex function is the *divergence* (a.k.a. relative entropy or Kullback-Leibler divergence) of two probability distributions: an important information-theoretic function. Let `P` and `Q` be two finite distributions (over some finite type `A`). Their divergence `div` is defined as follows:
`Variables (A : finType) (P Q : fdist A).`
`Definition div := \sum_(a in A) P a * log (P a / Q a).`
Actually, `div P Q` is defined only when `Q` *dominates* `P`, i.e., when `Q a = 0` implies `P a = 0` for all `a`. We call such a pair of probability distributions a *dominated pair*. Hereafter, we denote `div P Q` by `D(P || Q)` and the dominance of `P` by `Q` by `P `<< Q`.

We now show that the divergence function is convex over the set of dominated pairs. To formalize this statement using our definitions, we first need to show that dominated pairs form a convex space. To achieve this, it suffices to define the convex combination of the dominated pairs `a `<< b` and `c `<< d` as `a <| p |> c `<< b <| p |> d` (where we use the convex combination of probability distributions). This operator is easily shown to enjoy the properties of convex spaces (Sect. 2). Once this is done, one just needs to uncurry the divergence function to use the `convex_function` predicate:

`Lemma convex_div : convex_function (uncurry_dom_pair (@div A)).`

The proof follows the standard one [12, Theorem. 2.7.2] and relies on the log-sum inequality formalized in previous work [6].

In previous work [5], we applied above results to the proofs of convexity of other information-theoretic functions such as the entropy and the mutual information.

7   Related Work

Conical spaces have been known in the literature to work as a nice-behaving replacement of convex spaces when constructing models of nondeterministic computations. Varacca and Winskel [31] used convexity when building a categorical monad combining probability and nondeterminism, but they chose to avoid the problem of equational laws in convex spaces by instead working with conical spaces. There is a similar preference in the study of domain-theoretic semantics of nondeterminism, to a conical structure (d-cones [23]) over the corresponding convex structure (abstract probabilistic domain [20]). The problem is the same in this case: the difficulty in working with the equational laws of convex spaces [22,30].

Flood [13] proposed to use conical spaces to investigate the properties of convex spaces. He showed that for any convex space, there is an enveloping conical space and the convex space is embedded in it. (A version of the embedding for convex sets into cones in vector spaces was already present in Semadini's book [26].) Keimel and Plotkin [21] extended the idea for their version of ordered convex spaces and applied it in the proof of their key lemma [21, Lemma 2.8], which is an ordered version of the one proved by Neumann [25, Lemma 2].

Another aspect of convex spaces is the relationship to probabilistic distributions. From any set, one can freely generate a convex space by formally taking all finite convex combinations of elements of this set. The resulting convex space can be seen as a set of distributions over the original set, since the formal convex combinations are equivalent to distributions over the given points. By this construction, convex spaces serve as a foundation for the algebraic and category-theoretic treatments of probability. This allows for another application of our work to the semantics of probabilistic and nondeterministic programming [16,19]. We have also been investigating this topic [3,7]. Our most recent result [2] is based on the properties of convex sets and convex hulls, and deals with derived notions such as convex powersets. Its purpose is the formal study of program semantics from a category-theoretic point of view, rather than the formal study of the mathematical structure of convex spaces itself, which is rather the purpose of this paper.

8 Conclusion

In this paper, we formalized convex and conical spaces and developed their theories. In particular, we formally studied the various presentations of the convex combination operator, be it binary or multiary (Sect. 3). We provide formal proofs of the equivalence between several axiomatizations of both operators, where "proofs" in the literature were often only mere references to Stone's foundational paper [27], while it only contains a reduction of the multiary case to the binary one. Based on convex and conical spaces, we also developed a theory of convex functions and of convex hulls. We illustrated these developments with detailed examples from real analysis and information theory.

Acknowledgments. We acknowledge the support of the JSPS KAKENHI Grant Number 18H03204. We also thank Shinya Katsumata for his comments.

References

1. Affeldt, R., Cohen, C., Rouhling, D.: Formalization techniques for asymptotic reasoning in classical analysis. J. Formaliz. Reason. **11**(1), 43–76 (2018)
2. Affeldt, R., Garrigue, J., Nowak, D., Saikawa, T.: A trustful monad for axiomatic reasoning with probability and nondeterminism, March 2020, https://arxiv.org/abs/2003.09993
3. Affeldt, R., et al.: Monadic equational reasoning in Coq (2019). https://github.com/affeldt-aist/monae/, Coq scripts
4. Affeldt, R., Garrigue, J., Saikawa, T.: Examples of formal proofs about data compression. In: International Symposium on Information Theory and Its Applications (ISITA 2018), Singapore, 28–31 October 2018, pp. 665–669. IEICE, IEEE Xplore, October 2018
5. Affeldt, R., Garrigue, J., Saikawa, T.: Reasoning with conditional probabilities and joint distributions in Coq. Computer Software (2020, to appear). Japan Society for Software Science and Technology. https://staff.aist.go.jp/reynald.affeldt/documents/cproba_preprint.pdf
6. Affeldt, R., Hagiwara, M., Sénizergues, J.: Formalization of Shannon's theorems. J. Autom. Reason. **53**(1), 63–103 (2014)
7. Affeldt, R., Nowak, D., Saikawa, T.: A hierarchy of monadic effects for program verification using equational reasoning. In: Hutton, G. (ed.) MPC 2019. LNCS, vol. 11825, pp. 226–254. Springer, Cham (2019). https://doi.org/10.1007/978-3-030-33636-3_9
8. Beaulieu, G.: Probabilistic completion of nondeterministic models. Ph.D. thesis, University of Ottawa (2008)
9. Bertot, Y., Gonthier, G., Ould Biha, S., Pasca, I.: Canonical big operators. In: Mohamed, O.A., Muñoz, C., Tahar, S. (eds.) TPHOLs 2008. LNCS, vol. 5170, pp. 86–101. Springer, Heidelberg (2008). https://doi.org/10.1007/978-3-540-71067-7_11
10. Bonchi, F., Silva, A., Sokolova, A.: The power of convex algebras. In: Meyer, R., Nestmann, U. (eds.) 28th International Conference on Concurrency Theory (CONCUR 2017). Leibniz International Proceedings in Informatics (LIPIcs), vol. 85, pp. 23:1–23:18. Schloss Dagstuhl-Leibniz-Zentrum fuer Informatik (2017). https://doi.org/10.4230/LIPIcs.CONCUR.2017.23
11. Cheung, K.H.: Distributive interaction of algebraic effects. Ph.D. thesis, University of Oxford (2017)
12. Cover, T.M., Thomas, J.A.: Elements of Information Theory, 2nd edn. Wiley, Hoboken (2006)
13. Flood, J.: Semiconvex geometry. J. Aust. Math. Soc. **30**(4), 496–510 (1981). https://doi.org/10.1017/S1446788700017973
14. Fritz, T.: Convex spaces I: Definition and examples (2015). https://arxiv.org/abs/0903.5522, First version: 2009
15. Garillot, F., Gonthier, G., Mahboubi, A., Rideau, L.: Packaging mathematical structures. In: Berghofer, S., Nipkow, T., Urban, C., Wenzel, M. (eds.) TPHOLs 2009. LNCS, vol. 5674, pp. 327–342. Springer, Heidelberg (2009). https://doi.org/10.1007/978-3-642-03359-9_23
16. van Heerdt, G., Hsu, J., Ouaknine, J., Silva, A.: Convex language semantics for nondeterministic probabilistic automata. In: Fischer, B., Uustalu, T. (eds.) ICTAC 2018. LNCS, vol. 11187, pp. 472–492. Springer, Cham (2018). https://doi.org/10.1007/978-3-030-02508-3_25

17. Infotheo: A Coq formalization of information theory and linear error-correcting codes (2020). https://github.com/affeldt-aist/infotheo/, Coq scripts
18. Infotheo: probability/convex_choice.v. In: [17] (2020), Coq scripts
19. Jacobs, B.: Convexity, duality and effects. In: Calude, C.S., Sassone, V. (eds.) TCS 2010. IAICT, vol. 323, pp. 1–19. Springer, Heidelberg (2010). https://doi.org/10.1007/978-3-642-15240-5_1
20. Jones, C., Plotkin, G.D.: A probabilistic powerdomain of evaluations. In: [1989] Proceedings. Fourth Annual Symposium on Logic in Computer Science, pp. 186–195, June 1989. https://doi.org/10.1109/LICS.1989.39173
21. Keimel, K., Plotkin, G.: Mixed powerdomains for probability and nondeterminism. Log. Meth. Comput. Sci. **13**, December 2016. https://doi.org/10.23638/LMCS-13(1:2)2017
22. Keimel, K., Plotkin, G.D.: Predicate transformers for extended probability and non-determinism. Math. Struct. Comput. Sci. **19**(3), 501–539 (2009). https://doi.org/10.1017/S0960129509007555
23. Kirch, O.: Bereiche und Bewertungen. Master's thesis, Technischen Hochschule Darmstadt (1993)
24. Mahboubi, A., Tassi, E.: Canonical structures for the working coq user. In: Blazy, S., Paulin-Mohring, C., Pichardie, D. (eds.) ITP 2013. LNCS, vol. 7998, pp. 19–34. Springer, Heidelberg (2013). https://doi.org/10.1007/978-3-642-39634-2_5
25. Neumann, W.D.: On the quasivariety of convex subsets of affine spaces. Archiv der Mathematik **21**, 11–16 (1970)
26. Semadini, Z.: Banach Spaces of Continuous Functions. PWN (1971)
27. Stone, M.H.: Postulates for the barycentric calculus. Ann. Mat. Pura Appl. **29**(1), 25–30 (1949)
28. Świrszcz, T.: Monadic functors and convexity. Bulletin de l'Académie polonaise des sciences. Série des sciences mathématiques, astronomiques et physiques **22**(1) (1974)
29. The Coq Development Team: The Coq Proof Assistant Reference Manual. Inria (2019). https://coq.inria.fr. Version 8.11.0
30. Tix, R., Keimel, K., Plotkin, G.: Semantic domains for combining probability and non-determinism. Electron. Notes Theor. Comput. Sci. **222**, 3–99 (2009). https://doi.org/10.1016/j.entcs.2009.01.002
31. Varacca, D., Winskel, G.: Distributing probability over non-determinism. Math. Struct. Comput. Sci. **16**(1), 87–113 (2006)

Towards a Heterogeneous Query Language for Mathematical Knowledge

Katja Berčič[(✉)] [iD], Michael Kohlhase [iD], and Florian Rabe [iD]

Computer Science, FAU Erlangen-Nürnberg, Erlangen, Germany
katja.bercic@fau.de

Abstract. With more than 120.000 articles published annually in mathematical journals alone, mathematical search has often been touted as a killer application of computer-supported mathematics. But the artefacts of mathematics – e.g. mathematical documents, formulas, examples, algorithms, concrete data sets, or semantic web-style graph abstractions – that should be searched cover a variety of aspects. All are organized in complex ways and offer distinct challenges and techniques for search. Existing representation languages, the corresponding query languages and search systems usually concentrate on only one of these aspects. As a consequence, each system only partially covers the information retrieval needs of mathematical practitioners, and integrated solutions allowing multi-aspect queries are rare and basic.

We present an architecture for a generic multi-aspect search system and analyze the requirements on paradigmatic practical information retrieval needs.

1   Introduction and Related Work

Motivation. Computers and Humans have complementary strengths: Computers can handle large data and computations flawlessly at enormous speeds. Humans can sense the environment, react to unforeseen circumstances and use their intuitions to guide them through only partially understood situations. We speak of a **horizontal** task if it involves systematically sifting through large volumes of data or carrying out large computations. This contrasts with a **vertical** task, which involves intricately combining multiple previously unclear methods in a limited domain. In general, humans excel (only) at vertical tasks, while machines excel (only) at horizontal ones. For example, in mathematics humans explore mathematical theories and come up with novel insights/proofs but may delegate symbolic/numeric computation, proof checking/search, data storage, and typesetting of documents to computers.

A general goal is to develop solutions for horizontal problems in mathematics and dovetail the solutions into the vertical workflows of practicing mathematicians. One of the most important horizontal problems is Mathematical

The authors were supported by DFG grant RA-1872/3-1, KO 2428/13-1 OAF and EU grant Horizon 2020 ERI 676541 OpenDreamKit.

C. Benzmüller and B. Miller (Eds.): CICM 2020, LNAI 12236, pp. 39–54, 2020.
https://doi.org/10.1007/978-3-030-53518-6_3

Information Retrieval (MIR), i.e., finding mathematical objects with particular properties—e.g. a counterexample, a theorem that allows rewriting a formula into a more tractable form, an article that describes a method applicable to a current problem, or an algorithm that computes a particular value.

Despite significant efforts and successes, current MIR systems are far behind practical needs. It is not even clear how to best design a good MIR system. Many existing mathematical tools are highly specialized, e.g., into proof assistants, computer algebra systems, mathematical databases, or narrative languages like LATEX or HTML+MathML. Current MIR solutions often exploit this specialization by custom-fitting indexing and querying solutions to the data model of the tool, e.g., using substitution tree indexing for a set of theorems or SQL queries for a mathematical database. But MIR is often needed outside such a tool, e.g., imagine a mathematics-aware Google-like interface that finds semantically relevant results in the Coq library, the arXiv, and the OEIS. Thus, the question arises how to query heterogeneous mathematical knowledge, i.e., how to design representation and query languages that allow finding results in many different libraries using vastly different representation languages.

Contribution. We present the high-level design of an indexing and querying infrastructure that we believe to be an interesting candidate for a comprehensive solution. We cannot provide a detailed scalable solution at this point. In fact, we believe more conceptual and experimental research is needed before that would be feasible.

Concretely, our design is based on the ideas of [Car+20a], which classify mathematical libraries and objects by five aspects: deductive, computational, narrative, databases containing concrete objects, and organizational ontologies—a classification that matches existing tools and optimized indexing and querying solutions quite well. Our key ideas are: (i) While every library typically has one primary aspect (e.g., deductive for a Coq library), it may contain objects of any other aspect as well (e.g., narrative comments). (ii) Our solution is centered around a set of specialized indexes (one per aspect), and indexing a library generates entries in each of these indexes. (iii) For each index, existing solutions provide optimized querying support (e.g., SQL for concrete databases), and these supply the atomic queries of a comprehensive MIR system. (iv) Complex queries arise by combining atomic ones (e.g., intersection), and query evaluation is based on decomposing a query into atomic ones that are executed by the respective tools. This paper is a short version of [BKR20], which has more details and examples.

Related Work. **Information retrieval** (IR) is the activity of obtaining information relevant to an **information need** from a collection of resources. In MIR, both the resources and the information need are mathematical in nature. Current approaches to MIR have mostly been technology-oriented, focusing either on formula search or on adapting traditional IR techniques to include formula data. [GSC15] gives a survey and [Aiz+16] a description of the NTCIR MIR challenges. An exception to this is the work reported in [ST16, Sta+18] which concentrates on extracting semantic/mathematical information from mathematical documents and then use it for information retrieval.

Our architecture can be seen as a variant of the data integration system using a Global-as-View schema mapping in the sense of [DHI12], which combines different relational databases. They use a query language based on what they call the mediated global schema, which is induced as the union of the local schemas under a database view. That kind of heterogeneity problem is much simpler because it involves only mediating between different schemas in a fixed aspect (namely relational databases) whereas the MIR problem requires mediating across different aspects. It remains an open question whether such SQL-specific solutions can be applied directly to MIR: the awkwardness of encoding knowledge of the other aspects in SQL may be offset by the high levels of optimization in existing solutions such as Apache Drill [AD]; but also see [Cho+05].

Overview. In the next section we will show that mathematical resources and information needs have more aspects than the formulas and words used in MIR so far. In Sect. 3 we present an architecture for a generic multi-aspect representation and search system, in Sect. 4 we discus indexing concrete mathematical data, and in Sect. 5 we specify a cross-aspect query language for MIR. Section 6 concludes the paper.

A Multi-aspect Library. The Online Encyclopedia of Integer Sequences (OEIS) [Slo03, OEIS], a popular web portal that contains information on more than 300.000 integer sequences, is an example of a mathematical library whose contents range over multiple aspects.

Internally, the OEIS uses a line-based text format to represent this information. Listing 1.1 shows a fragment of the representation for the Fibonacci numbers. Lines are prefixed by a classifier letter (%I for identifiers, %S for a prefix of the sequence, %N for the "name", %C for comments, %D for references, %A for the OEIS author, and %F for formulae) that indicates the **item class**.

```
%I  A000045 M0692 N0256
%S  A000045 0,1,1,2,3,5,8,13,21,34,55,89,144,233,377,610,987
%N  A000045 Fibonacci numbers: F(n) = F(n−1) + F(n−2) with F(0) = 0 and F(1) =
      1.
%C  A000045 Also sometimes called Lamés sequence.
%D  A000045 V. E. Hoggatt, Jr., Fibonacci and Lucas Numbers. Houghton, Boston,
      MA, 1969.
%F  A000045 F(n) = ((1+sqrt(5))^n−(1−sqrt(5))^n)/(2^n∗sqrt(5))
%F  A000045 G.f.: Sum_{n>=0} x^n ∗ Product_{k=1..n} (k + x)/(1 + k∗x). − _Paul
      D. Hanna_, Oct 26 2013
%F  A000045 This is a divisibility sequence; that is, if n divides m, then a(n
      ) divides a(m)
%A  A000045 _N. J. A. Sloane_, Apr 30 1991
```

Listing 1.1. OEIS Sources for Sequence A000045 (Fibonacci Numbers)

The OEIS portal features a simple boolean search engine which allows to search for sequences by OEIS ID, name, keywords, and subsequence (this can contain anonymous wildcards for integers and subsequences). Additionally, atomic queries can be qualified by **prefixes** that restrict keywords to the various classes of items or change the sequence matching algorithm (e.g. from signed to unsigned equality on components). The query results of this query are a sequence of complete presentations of the sequence information ordered by "relevance", which combines match quality, sequence popularity and number. There is a variant called superseeker (an e-mail server) that "tries hard to find an explanation for a number sequence" combining information from the OEIS and other sources.

2   Aspects of Math Resources and Information Needs

In [Car+20a] we have identified the following five basic **aspects** of mathematics:

i) **Inference:** deriving statements by *deduction* (i.e., proving), *abduction* (i.e., conjecture formation from best explanations), and *induction* (i.e., conjecture formation from examples).

ii) **Computation:** algorithmic manipulation and simplification of mathematical expressions and other representations of mathematical objects.

iii) **Concretization:** generating, collecting, maintaining, and accessing collections of examples that suggest patterns and relations and allow testing of conjectures.

iv) **Narration:** bringing the results into a form that can be digested by humans, usually in mathematical documents like articles, books, or preprints, that expose the ideas in natural language but also in diagrams, tables, and simulations.

v) **Organization**, i.e., the modular structuring of mathematical knowledge.

These aspects—their existence and importance to mathematics—should be rather uncontroversial. Figure 1 illustrates their tight relation: we locate the organization aspect at the centre and the other four aspects at the corners of a tetrahedron, since the latter are all consumers and producers of the mathematical knowledge represented by the former. [Car+20b] gives a survey of paradigmatic mathematical software systems by the five aspects they address.

Fig. 1. Five aspects of math artefacts

We use the term **symbolic** to cover deductive (aspect Inference) or computational (aspect Computation) in this paper. While these libraries are pragmatically very different and are thus distinguished in the classification above they can be treated in the same way for the purpose of search. Coming back to OEIS, we see that it contains all five aspects of mathematical knowledge:

1. symbolic knowledge: the formulae, even though in this case they are informal ASCII art; there is also computer code,

2. concrete knowledge: the sequence prefix,
3. narrative knowledge: the name and comments,
4. organizational knowledge: the identifiers and references.

Mathematical information needs typically involve combinations of these five aspects. A paradigmatic example is the quest for *"all published integer sequences that are not (yet) listed in the OEIS"* of an OEIS editor who wants to extend OEIS coverage. Answering this information need will involve finding integer sequences in documents (a combination of concretized and narrative knowledge), determining whether these documents are published (i.e. part of the archival literature; this involves organizational metadata), and pruning out the OEIS sequences. An OEIS user might be interested in *"the integer sequences whose generating function is a rational polynomial in $\sin(x)$ that has a Maple implementation not affected by the bug in module M"*. This additionally involves symbolic knowledge about generating function (formula expressions), and Maple algorithms.

We take these examples as motivation to develop an approach for multi/cross-aspect information retrieval now.

3   Heterogeneous Indexing of Mathematical Libraries

We motivate and introduce some general concepts that can be seen as fundamental assumptions from which much of our proposed design is derived.

Fragments of a Library. We require that libraries of any aspect define document fragments and assign unique identifiers (URIs) to them. These fragments will be *used* critically in the interface specification for query engines. In particular, query results contain at least a set of fragments that match the query (plus possibly other information, e.g., how or how well they match the query).

Identifying and Producing the fragments is natural as individual libraries typically already have a corresponding concept, e.g.:

- An organizational library already focuses on introducing concepts with unique identifiers. Each such concept is a fragment, with the same id.
- A symbolic library is structured into files which contain a tree structure of nested theories/modules/etc. whose leaves are declarations for named types, functions, etc. Each node is a fragment with a qualified identifier. The underlying languages usually already define fragments and their identifiers in this way because they need them for intra-logical referencing.
- A concretized library is essentially a set of database tables (however the actual implementation may look like), and each table row is a fragment. In practice, typically one column serves as a key, and the triple of database, table name, and key provides the fragment identifier. For example, in many mathematical tables that contain enumerations of objects (e.g., in LMFDB [Lmf]), the key can be obtained by concatenating multiple properties of the object that, together, uniquely characterize it.

- A narrative library is structured both non-semantically into sections, paragraphs, etc. and semantically into statements like definitions and theorems. These are often numbered in the presentation, and internally labels are used to identify them. Those are the fragments, and their identifiers.

Thus, it is straightforward to extend an existing implementation of a language L in such a way that it can produce the list of fragment-id pairs in a L-libraries. This is the basic functionality of what we call a **harvester** for L below.

Findable Objects in a Fragment. Next, to describe what it means for a fragment to match a query, we assume that every fragment has some internal structure that allows defining *occurrences* of *objects* in the fragment. This is the main task of the harvester: it has to define what exactly an occurrence is and produces for each fragment the list of objects in it.

Most of the time, these objects have the same aspect as the containing library. For example, if L is a symbolic language, the most important objects are symbolic expressions such as the types of the declarations or the formulas in theorems. Similarly, in a narrative library, they are n-grams of words, and in a table-based database, they are the primitive database values in the table cells.

However, it is critical to observe that the same library may contain objects of many different aspects. In fact, libraries of any primary aspect can and in practice often do contain objects of the other aspects as well. Some of these objects work in the same way across libraries, although the concrete syntax may vary. Any library can contain:

- metadata attributing narrative or symbolic objects to a fragment,
- cross-references to fragments of any other library,
- contain narrative comments.

Other such cross-aspect objects are specific to the combination of aspects, e.g.:

- The text of a fragment of a narrative library may be interspersed with symbolic expressions. This occurs in virtually every scientific document.
- A table in a database can use a schema that declares some columns to contain objects of other aspects. These may be narrative objects represented as a string, or symbolic objects encoded as primitive database values (e.g., a polynomial encoded as a list of integer coefficients).
- An expression in a symbolic fragment may contain references to concrete objects stored externally, e.g., when using a database for persistent memorization. This can be useful in mathematical computation systems[1], which often need to handle complex pure functions.

Thus, it would be a mistake to assume that a library of aspect A is indexed in an A-index and queried with an A-query language. Instead, every library fragment F can contain objects O_i of any aspect A_i. We require that it be

---

[1] https://github.com/OpenDreamKit/OpenDreamKit/raw/master/WP6/D6.9/ report-final.pdf.

possible to find F as a result of queries in any aspect A_i. For example, a symbolic query (i.e., a symbolic expression with some free variables) can be matched against the symbolic objects found in F irrespective of the aspect of the library containing F.

Heterogeneous Indexing. While every library can contain objects of any aspect, the aspects of the objects may not be neglected: indexing and efficient querying differs vastly across aspects. For example, querying n-grams of words is different from querying symbolic expressions.

From the above, we can derive the general design of an indexing infrastructure. Figure 2 gives an overview. For every library, we need to run a harvester, which returns the set of findable objects, each consisting of (i) an aspect and an object of that aspect (ii) the identifier of the containing fragment, (iii) optionally, any other information about the occurrences of the object, e.g., the position within the fragment. The findable objects of all libraries are collected and stored in aspect-specific indexes, i.e., we use one index per aspect and arbitrarily many libraries. (If this runs into scalability issues, we can federate the individual indexes, but that is an implementation issue.)

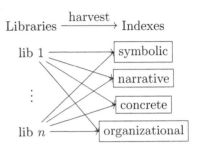

Fig. 2. Heterogeneous indexing

For example, these indexes could be

- a triple store like GraphDB [Eso] for *organizational* metadata and cross-references,
- a substitution tree index like MathWebSearch [HKP14] for *symbolic* objects,
- a text indexer like Elastic search [Eso] for *narrative* objects,
- a yet-to-be-developed index for *concrete* values that we discuss in Sect. 4.

The harvesters are specific to a library language and often integrated with the respective tool. For example, a Coq harvester could be integrated with Coq to harvest any library written in Coq while compiling it; a CSV harvester could be a stand-alone tool to harvest any concrete database represented as a CSV dump. Alternatively, if the language-specific part has already been abstracted away by exporting libraries in aspect-independent formats such as OMDoc, one can write language-independent harvesters once and for all.

In all cases, it may make sense to write four different harvesters (one for each index aspect) for the same language. For example, the Coq harvester for narrative objects may be written as a stand-alone parser of the Coq language that extracts all comments.

Indexing Induced Objects. Finally, we mention an optional concept that we expect to become relevant in practice as well even though it might not be present in the first implementations: harvesters that generate new objects that did not physically occur in the fragment but logically belong to it. We call these *induced* objects. There are many instances of induced objects, e.g.:

- In an organizational library, we can take the transitive closure of a relation.
- In a symbolic language that uses some kind of inheritance or logical imports, a fragment F might be a class/module etc., and we can index also objects logically occurring in F through inheritance. That is already done routinely in many documentation generation tools, especially for object-oriented programming languages. We also built a symbolic index like that for MMT in [IKP14].
- Sometimes, especially in deduction systems, the most feasible way to implement the harvester is to instrument the kernel. But the kernel may perform extensive normalization, in which case the index will contain the objects induced by normalization. Unfortunately, that also means it might not contain some objects originally in the library (because they are normalized away), which is a known problem with indexing deductive libraries.

4   Indexing Concrete Values

Motivation. Above we have described concrete values as being stored in relational databases. Conceptually, this fits well for all the datasets we have surveyed [MDT]. In practice, the situation may differ a bit. Sometimes the information is more efficiently retrieved by on demand computation. For example, the authors of the GAP small groups library [EBO] used computer algebra system integration to bring the average space demand down to less than two bits per group without significantly sacrificing the speed of retrieval. When computation is not feasible, custom compression is often needed to manage the size of large datasets like [FL]. All of these datasets could be stored as simple tables, but that has not been seen as advantageous so far.

Even if all libraries used relational tables, an indexing and querying solution should not necessarily be built on operations such as filters and joins. These are what SQL focuses on, and work for MIR needs where the user knows the data format and how to extract information from it. SQL is less useful for more exploratory MIR tasks, which is what we focus on in this paper. Relational database indexes usually focus on each index providing fast access to the rows in one table. This is not as suitable for the design from Sect. 3, where we require a single index holding all objects (i.e., the entries of all cells) searcheably.

It is therefore helpful to develop an indexing solution that goes beyond just taking the union of the individual datasets. We have already collected some initial experiences in the MathDataHub system [DMH], where datasets are broken down into parts that roughly correspond to mathematical properties (group order, number of triangles in a graph, ...). Such an approach supports indexing subsets of datasets and allows for building new datasets from old ones. Even though that work predates and is in fact not always consistent with the ideas developed in this paper, some parts of it can be seen as an ad-hoc prototype solution of a concrete index.

In the sequel, we follow our design from the previous section and specify how a relational database can be used to build an index of concrete objects. Note that in this design, the entire database serves as the index, and that use of the word "index" must be distinguished from any internal indexes kept by the database implementation.

The Symbolic-Concrete Spectrum. We use the following intuition to distinguish between symbolic and concrete objects: Symbolic objects include free names (constants, variables) and thus cannot always be reduced to a value. Concrete objects, on the other hand, are closed and fully evaluated. The distinction is not as clear-cut as one might think:

- A closed expression containing bound variables is a borderline case; we consider it symbolic.
- A polynomial (with evaluated coefficients) contains the variable name; but if we consider those names to be string values (which is done in many datasets), the whole polynomial can be seen as concrete.
- Irrational numbers such as e or $\sqrt{2}$ contain names but are still generally considered to be values.

The distinction is important because it leads to differences in indexing. The MIR needs for symbolic objects focus on their structure. Symbolic objects can be stored efficiently in a substitution tree index and queried by unification queries as done in MathWebSearch. However, the more desirable querying up to inferable/computable properties is difficult, e.g., search/unification up to associative and commutative properties is a well-known difficult problem. On the other hand, many interesting properties of concrete objects are (often efficiently) computable, e.g., it is easy to check if a finite prefix of an integer sequence contains a certain subsequence. Thus, it is desirable to index concrete objects and their properties in a way that supports such queries.

To make the distinction precise, we have introduced a rigorous treatment in [WKR17]. Firstly, we standardized a set of types (numbers, strings, lists, and tuples) for concrete objects commonly used in data representation languages such as JSON or CSV. Secondly, we standardized a notation of codecs that represent symbolic objects as concrete ones. This allows treating any mathematical object as a triple of its symbolic representation, a codec, and the corresponding encoded concrete object.

An Index Design. We use a relational database with one table for each type in our standardized language of concrete objects. Each table has a column "value" holding the object using a chosen standard encoding.

For each type we define a set of operations that are precomputed and stored with the objects (e.g., the factorization of an integer or the roots of a polynomial), and their results are stored in additional columns. However, these columns do not hold the actual result objects; instead, the results are concrete objects that are themselves stored in the index, and the columns just hold references to them. (A recursion threshold is used in case this process does not terminate.)

In practice, we must distinguish between different kinds of precomputed operations. Some will require so much mathematical knowledge that they can only be computed by computer algebra systems. Those computations may or may not be linkable via the database's foreign function interface. On the other end of the spectrum, some computations will be so easy that they can be carried out by the database on the fly, e.g., in a function-based SQL index.

Overall, this design has the advantage of being extensible. We can easily add new types (i.e., tables) and new precomputed operations (i.e., columns). This results in a formal language of types, constructors for objects of these types, and operations on such objects, which we call MDDL (for mathematical data description language).

Concrete Queries. A concrete query over this index is of the form SELECT X_1 : $T_1, \ldots, X_n : T_n$ WHERE $P(X_1, \ldots, X_n)$. Here the T_i are types and P is a computable MDDL-expression of boolean type. The X_i represent objects in the index of type T_i and are bound in P. The intended semantics is that it returns all substitutions to the X_i for which P is true.

It is straightforward to develop more complex query languages, but even this simple form is quite difficult to implement. Most critically, even if P is computable, it may not be efficiently computable. And even if it is, it may not be practical to program the computation inside an SQL database.

On the other hand, many simple forms of P can be directly translated to SQL queries. For example, if f is one of the precomputed values for T, then SELECT X : T WHERE $f(X) = 5$ becomes the SQL query SELECT value FROM T WHERE $f = 5$.

Open Problems. While we are convinced in general of the utility of this design, several open problems remain, for which further research is needed. We discuss these in the remainder.

In some cases, our design will explode. For example, storing all subsequences of an OEIS sequence may become infeasible quickly even if attention is restricted to fixed-length prefixes of sequences. Thus, special indexing techniques must be developed for individual types and operations.

Another issue is the choice of codec in the index. For each type, we can choose a standard codec and use it to represent the objects in that type's table. Then harvesters that find encoded objects in different encodings must transcode them into the standard encoding. However, in some cases this will be inefficient—the most common example is the trade-off between sparse and dense encodings of lists.

But even in the seemingly trivial case of integers, this can become an issue: For example, in [WKR17], we encountered multiple different encodings of unlimited precision integers transcoding between which was not always trivial. This is aggravated in connection with the next issue discussed below: different codecs may commute more easily with different mathematical operations. Therefore, it may be necessary to use multiple tables for the same type—one per codec. This will make retrieval harder as results from all tables have to be considered; moreover, the same object might exist in multiple tables.

Finally, if an index is hosted by a relational database, it is desirable to match mathematical operations to primitive database operations. But this is difficult because the database only sees the encoding. For example, computing the degree of a univariate polynomial encoded as a list of coefficients can easily be done by the database by taking the length of the list. But computing its roots requires decoding it, computing the roots in custom code, presumably in a computer algebra system, and then encoding the results.

5 A Heterogeneous Query Language

Overview. Figure 3 shows the general search architecture we propose. On the left we have any number of libraries, which are harvested into four aspect-specific indexes as described above. A user query Q is expressed in a cross-aspect query language described below. It is passed to a query engine that separates Q into a set of aspect-specific atomic queries Q_i, for which the respective

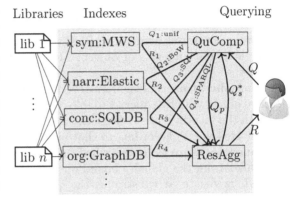

Fig. 3. The search architecture

database returns result R_i. These are then aggregated into the overall result R that is returned to the user. Note that our drawing uses exactly one query Q_i per aspect—that is just an example, and there can be any number of queries (including zero) per index. It is also straightforward to extend the design with additional indexes if new kinds of indexes are conceived.

In this paper, we focus on a relatively simple format for the queries: Every query Q consists of

- a list of query variables $X_1, \ldots, X_n$, we use upper case letters for them,
- a list of atomic queries $Q_i(X_1, \ldots, X_n)$.

Each atomic query is aspect-specific and resolved by lookup in the respective index. The intuition of the overall result R is to return the intersection of the atomic queries Q_i. More formally, the results R_i and R of the queries are substitutions for the query variables. The atomic queries are evaluated sequentially; each time some query variables may already have been instantiated by previous atomic queries, and the results are substitutions for the remaining ones.

More complex queries can easily be conceived, but this simple fragment captures not only the most practically relevant cases but also one of the biggest difficulties of heterogeneous queries: How can queries of different aspects meaningfully share query variables? The latter is what we discuss in the remainder.

Atomic Queries with Shared Variables. To specify our query language in detail, we have to spell out the structure of the atomic queries. Here, we are mostly bound by the capabilities of the existing aspect-specific indexes except for occasionally deriving improvement suggestions for them.

All atomic queries are relative to a set of query variables ranging over formal objects. All query variables may by typed with MDDL types. The results are substitutions of the query variables with formal objects. Here the set of formal objects should be a large enough to subsume content MathML but should also allow any URI as an identifier even if it is not declared in some content dictionary (e.g., any identifier of a paper, author, etc.) as well as sufficient literals as needed to build concrete objects.

Concretely, we assume the following:

– An **organizational atom** is an RDF triple $s\ p\ o$ possibly containing a query variable as the subject s or object o. It instantiates these with identifiers or literals.
– A **symbolic atom** is of the form $F \in \texttt{Symb}(S(X_1, \ldots, X_n))$ where S is some formal object with free query variables and F is a query variable. It substitutes F with the identifier of the fragment that contains an object matching S and substitutes the X_i according to that match.
– A **concrete atom** is as described in Sect. 4 except that the free variables are taken from the globally bound query variables X_i. Thus, it is simply an MDDL predicate. It substitutes the query variables with pairs of concrete object and codec.
– A **narrative atom** is of the form $F \in \texttt{Narr}(W_1, \ldots, W_m)$ where F is a query variable and each W_i is a string-valued object. The query instantiates F with the identifier that matches the bag of words containing the W_i. Due to the nature of implementations of narrative queries, the bag of words may not contain any free variables when sent to the narrative index, i.e., any W_i that are query variables must have been instantiated previously (with a string value) by some other atoms.

Both SPAQRL and MDDL queries naturally use a **SELECTWHERE** form with the **WHERE** clause containing a conjunction of atoms. This inspires our overall syntax for heterogeneous queries: **SELECT** V^* **WHERE** A^* where each V declares a query variable X as $X : T$, and each A is one of the four atoms. For convenience, we also allow undeclared query variables—these are simply dropped from the returned substitutions.

Notably, stand-alone symbolic query engines only use S as the query (rather than $F \in \texttt{Symb}(S)$) and return pairs of fragment identifiers and substitutions. Similarly, stand-alone narrative query engines usually only use the bag of words as the query. But in heterogeneous queries, we may want to use the fragment identifier in other atoms of the query. Therefore, we have extended the syntax for symbolic and narrative atoms with an explicit query variable referring to the fragment. The corresponding extension is not needed for organizational and concrete atoms.

A key difficulty is that atoms of different aspects instantiate variables with different kinds of objects, and these cannot always be directly substituted into atoms of other aspects. For example, consider a symbolic atom $F \in \mathtt{Symb}(X^2)$ that substitutes X with some identifier MathML symbol s. We can still use the variable X is a subsequent narrative atom by converting it to a string, e.g., by using the name of s. But if X is substituted with a composite MathML object, we have to first evaluate it into a string, which may or may not be possible or easy. Similarly, we can still use X in a subsequent concrete atom, but only if we infer a codec that should be used to encode X into a concrete object; this codec can be inferred from the type declared for X in the query or in some cases simply from the shape of X. Therefore, for each pair (a, b) of aspects, we need conversion rules that allow converting objects substituted by a-atoms to objects usable in b-atoms. Figure 4 gives an overview of possible conversions for column heads a and row head b.

instantiating query[*] instantiates with	organizational id or literal	symbolic symb. obj.	concrete conc. obj.+codec
used by … queries via …			
organizational	as is	ids, literals: as is other: evaluate	
symbolic	as is	as is	decode
concrete	literals: as codes ids: fail	encode[P]	as is
narrative	ids: name as string literals: as string other: evaluate		value as string

[*]: narrative queries never instantiate variables; [P] marks partial conversions

Fig. 4. Conversions of objects across queries of different aspects

Of course, if a query contains multiple atoms of the same aspects, it may be reasonable to merge them. Multiple organizational atoms can be directly joined into a SPARQL query, and similarly, multiple concrete atoms can be translated jointly into a single SQL query. However, two additional and conflicting implementations strategies must be considered: On the one hand, it is desirable to first execute those atomic queries that fill in many query variables. That makes later queries more specific and thus more efficient. On the other hand, it is desirable to first execute those atomic queries that return the fewest results. Because every result leads to a different substitution, all subsequent atomic queries using those query variables must be duplicated for each result. It remains an open question which strategy works best in practice, and it is unlikely that a single best strategy exists. But there is a large databases literature to draw experience from.

While it is, in our experience, not very common to find queries that naturally combine all four index types, combinations of two or three are quite common.

Example 1. Consider a concrete library of graphs in a table that additionally stores human-recognizable names and arc-transitivity for each graph (for example, [EET]). These are harvested into a concrete index with a type and codec for graphs, e.g., the `sparse6` format [McF], a Boolean computed property for the arc-transitivity, and a string property for the name. Additionally, consider all papers from the Cornell e-Print arXiv harvested into the same narrative index [SK08], and an organizational index that stores triples for the BIBO publication and SPAR semantic publishing ontologies.

Q1: Find arc-transitive graphs that are mentioned by name in articles in journals with h-index greater than 50.

can be encoded in the following query using the concrete, narrative, and organizational aspects:

SELECT $G : Graph$ WHERE
$\mathtt{arcTransitive}(G), F \in \mathtt{Narr}(\mathtt{Name}(G), \text{"graph"}),$
$F \mathtt{\ partOf\ } P, P \mathtt{\ bibo : publishedIn\ } J, J \mathtt{\ spar : hasHindex\ } H, H > 50$

The first atom in the WHERE-clause returns all arc-transitive graphs G in the concrete index.

The second atom retrieves the names of these graphs and runs a narrative query for them. This includes evaluating the expression $\mathtt{Name}(G)$ into a string by retrieving the corresponding value from the concrete index. To avoid false-positives, we include the word "`graph`" in the narrative atom. It instantiates F with the identifier of the matching fragment, presumably a part of a paper.

The next three atoms are organizational atoms that perform a SPARQL query retrieving first the identifier P of the paper containing F, the identifiers J of the journal it appeared in, and its h-index H. H is a concrete value that is reused in the final concrete query on the size of H.

Finally, we throw away all variables from the obtained substitutions except for the graphs G. Alternatively, we could include P in the SELECT-clause to also return the paper.

In the above example, we see how a query compiler should consider merging consecutive organizational atoms into a single SPARQL query. In that case, the last concrete atom of the example could, because it is so simple, alternatively and more efficiently be included in that SPARQL query as well. Moreover, the atoms in the WHERE-clause were ordered in a way that previous queries restrict the scope of the subsequent ones. More generally, the query compilers should reorder the atoms automatically.

6   Conclusion and Future Work

We have presented a high-level design for a cross-aspect query language and search engine for mathematical information retrieval. The crucial observation is that mathematical information needs address multiple aspects and even though mathematical libraries often have a primary aspect, they usually also contain or reference material of other aspects as well. Our cross-aspect search architecture proposes to harvest all objects into aspect-specific indexes. Correspondingly, the proposed query language combines atomic queries from existing aspect-specific query languages and a query compiler distributes them to the respective indices. The query language is more than just a sum of the four parts as it allows to share variables between the aspect-specific sub-queries and compute non-trivial joins.

We have conducted a requirement analysis on the respective basis technologies and have confirmed the principal adequacy of the query language on paradigmatic, cross-aspect information needs. This shows that existing search/indexing technologies are essentially sufficient for cross-aspect search except for the concrete aspect, where our previous work in MathDataHub provides a good first step.

The obvious next step is an implementation of a distributed cross-aspect search engine as sketched as part of the MathHub system. MathHub already has already collected most of the largest theorem prover libraries (symbolic), the 1.5M preprints of the arXiv, and several large collections of concrete mathematical objects in a common representation format and assigned uniform identifiers to their fragments. MathHub already integrates symbolic and narrative indices, and the MMT system which MathHub employs for knowledge management – while not a dedicated index – can already answer complex symbolic and organizational queries [Rab12].

References

[AD] Apache Drill - Schema-free SQL Query Engine for Hadoop, NoSQL and Cloud Storage. https://drill.apache.org. Accessed 03 Feb 2020

[Aiz+16] Aizawa, A., et al.: NTCIR-12 MathIR task overview. In: Kando, N., Sakai, T., Sanderson, M. (ed.) Proceedings of the 12th NTCIR Conference on Evaluation of Information Access Technologies, Tokyo, Japan: NII, Tokyo, pp. 299–308 (2016). https://tinyurl.com/sofcxjs

[BKR20] Berčič, K., Kohlhase, M., Rabe, F.: Towards a Heterogeneous Query Language for Mathematical Knowledge - Extended Report (2020). http://kwarc.info/kohlhase/papers/tetrasearch.pdf. Accessed 27 Mar 2020

[Car+20a] Carette, J., et al.: Big math and the one-brain barrier - the tetrapod model of mathematical knowledge. In: Mathematical Intelligencer (2020, in press). https://arxiv.org/abs/1904.10405

[Car+20b] Carette, J., et al.: The space of mathematical software systems - a survey of paradigmatic systems. preprint; http://arxiv.org/abs/2002.04955 (2020)

[Cho+05] Chong, E.I., et al.: An efficient SQL-based RDF querying scheme. In: Proceedings of the 31st VLDB Conference (2005)

[DHI12] Doan, A.H., Halevy, A., Ives, Z.: Principles of Data Integration. Elsevier, Amsterdam (2012)

[DMH] Datasets on MathHub.info. https://data.mathhub.info. Accessed 24 Sept 2019

[EBO] Eick, B., Besche, H.U., O'Brien, E.: SmallGrp - The GAP Small Groups Library. https://www.gap-system.org/Manuals/pkg/SmallGrp-1.3/doc/chap1.html. Accessed 13 Oct 2018

[EET] Wilson, S., Potočnik, P.: A Census of edge-transitive tetravalent graphs. https://jan.ucc.nau.edu/~swilson/C4FullSite/index.html. Accessed 23 Jan 2019

[Eso] Elastic Search, 20 February 2014. http://www.elasticsearch.org/. Accessed 20 Feb 2014

[FL] Kohonen, J.: Lists of finite lattices (modular, semimodular, graded and geometric). https://www.shsu.edu/mem037/Lattices.html. Accessed 25 Jan 2019

[GSC15] Guidi, F., Sacerdoti Coen, C.: A survey on retrieval of mathematical knowledge. In: Kerber, M., Carette, J., Kaliszyk, C., Rabe, F., Sorge, V. (eds.) CICM 2015. LNCS (LNAI), vol. 9150, pp. 296–315. Springer, Cham (2015). https://doi.org/10.1007/978-3-319-20615-8_20

[HKP14] Hambasan, R., Kohlhase, M., Prodescu, C.: MathWeb-search at NTCIR-11. In: Kando, N., Joho, H., Kishida, K. (ed.) NTCIR 11 Conference, Tokyo, Japan: NII, Tokyo, pp. 114–119 (2014). https://tinyurl.com/wzj7mcg

[IKP14] Iancu, M., Kohlhase, M., Prodescu, C.: Representing, archiving, and searching the space of mathematical knowledge. In: Hong, H., Yap, C. (eds.) ICMS 2014. LNCS, vol. 8592, pp. 26–30. Springer, Heidelberg (2014). https://doi.org/10.1007/978-3-662-44199-2_5

[Lmf] The L-functions and Modular Forms Database. http://www.lmfdb.org. Accessed 27 Aug 2016

[McF] McKay, B.: Description of graph6, sparse6 and digraph6 encodings. http://users.cecs.anu.edu.au/~bdm/data/formats.txt. Accessed 22 Mar 2019

[MDT] Berčič, K.: Math Databases Table. https://mathdb.mathhub.info/. Accessed 15 Jan 2020

[OEIS] The On-Line Encyclopedia of Integer Sequences. http://oeis.org. Accessed 28 May 2017

[Rab12] Rabe, F.: A query language for formal mathematical libraries. In: Jeuring, J., et al. (eds.) CICM 2012. LNCS (LNAI), vol. 7362, pp. 143–158. Springer, Heidelberg (2012). https://doi.org/10.1007/978-3-642-31374-5_10

[SK08] Stamerjohanns, H., Kohlhase, M.: Transforming the arXiv to XML. In: Autexier, S., et al. (eds.) CICM 2008. LNCS (LNAI), vol. 5144, pp. 574–582. Springer, Heidelberg (2008). https://doi.org/10.1007/978-3-540-85110-3_46

[Slo03] Sloane, N.J.A.: The on-line encyclopedia of integer sequences. In: Notices of the AMS, vol. 50, no. 8, p. 912 (2003)

[ST16] Stathopoulos, Y., Teufel, S.: Mathematical information retrieval based on type embeddings and query expansion. In: Proceedings of COLING 2016, ACL, pp. 2344–2355 (2016). https://www.aclweb.org/anthology/C16-1221

[Sta+18] Stathopoulos, Y., et al.: Variable typing: assigning meaning to variables in mathematical text. In: NAACL 2018 Proceedings, ACL, pp. 303–312 (2018). https://doi.org/10.18653/v1/N18-1028

[WKR17] T. Wiesing, M. Kohlhase, and F. Rabe. "Virtual Theories - A Uniform Interface to Mathematical Knowledge Bases". In: Mathematical Aspects of Computer and Information Sciences. Ed. by J. Blömer et al. Springer, 2017, pp. 243–257

Leveraging the Information Contained in Theory Presentations

Jacques Carette, William M. Farmer, and Yasmine Sharoda$^{(\boxtimes)}$

Computing and Software, McMaster University, Hamilton, Canada
{carette,wmfarmer,sharodym}@mcmaster.ca
http://www.cas.mcmaster.ca/research/mathscheme/

Abstract. A theorem prover without an extensive library is much less useful to its potential users. Algebra, the study of algebraic structures, is a core component of such libraries. Algebraic theories also are themselves structured, the study of which was started as Universal Algebra. Various constructions (homomorphism, term algebras, products, etc.) and their properties are both universal and constructive. Thus they are ripe for being automated. Unfortunately, current practice still requires library builders to write these by hand. We first highlight specific redundancies in libraries of existing systems. Then we describe a framework for generating these derived concepts from theory definitions. We demonstrate the usefulness of this framework on a test library of 227 theories.

Keywords: Formal library · Algebraic hierarchy

1 Introduction

A theorem prover on its own is not nearly as useful for end-users as one equipped with extensive libraries. Most users have tasks to perform that are not related to new ideas in theorem proving. The larger the library of standard material, the faster that users can just get to work. However building large libraries is currently very labor intensive. Although some provers provide considerable automation for proof development, they do not the same for theory development.

This is the problem we continue [1,6,8,9] to tackle here, and that others [11] have started to look at as well. It is worthwhile noting that some programming languages already provide interesting features in this direction. For example, Haskell [22] provides the *deriving* mechanism that lets one get instances for some classes "for free"; recently, the *Deriving Via* mechanism [2] has been introduced, that greatly amplifies these features. Some libraries, such as the one for *Lens* [24], use *Template Haskell* [33] for the same purpose.

Libraries of algebra define algebraic structures, constructions on these, and properties satisfied by the structures and constructions. While structures like Semigroup, Monoid, AbelianGroup, Ring and Field readily come to mind, a look at compendiums [21,23] reveals a much larger zoo of hundreds of structures.

© Springer Nature Switzerland AG 2020
C. Benzmüller and B. Miller (Eds.): CICM 2020, LNAI 12236, pp. 55–70, 2020.
https://doi.org/10.1007/978-3-030-53518-6_4

Haskell
```
class Semiring a => Monoid a
  where
    mempty :: a
    mappend :: a -> a -> a
    mappend = (<>)
    mconcat :: [a] -> a
    mconcat =
      foldr mappend mempty
```

Coq
```
class Monoid {A : type}
  (dot : A → A → A)
  (one : A) : Prop := {
  dot_assoc : forall x y z : A,
  (dot x (dot y z)) =
  dot (dot x y) z
  unit_left : forall x,
  dot one x = x
  unit_right : forall x,
  dot x one = x
}
```

Alternative Definition:
```
Record monoid := {
  dom : Type;
  op : dom -> dom -> dom
    where "x * y" := op x y;
  id : dom where "1" := id;
  assoc : forall x y z,
    x * (y * z) = (x * y) * z;
  left_neutral : forall x,
    1 * x = x;
  right_neutal : forall x,
    x * 1 = x;
}
```

MathScheme
```
Monoid := Theory {
  U : type;
  * : (U,U) → U;
  e : U;
  axiom right_identity_*_e :
    forall x : U · (x * e) = x;
  axiom left_identity_*_e :
    forall x : U · (e * x) = x;
  axiom associativity_* :
    forall x,y,z : U ·
  (x * y) * z = x * (y * z);
}
```

Agda
```
record Monoid c ℓ :
    Set (suc (c ⊔ ℓ)) where
  infixl 7 _•_
  infix 4 _≈_
  field
    Carrier : Set c
    _≈_ : Rel Carrier ℓ
    _•_ : Op2 Carrier
    isMonoid : IsMonoid _≈_ _•_ ε
where IsMonoid is defined as
record IsMonid (• : Op2) (ε : A)
  : Set (a ⊔ ℓ) where
  field
    isSemiring : IsSemiring •
    identity : Identity ε
    identity$^l$ : LeftIdentity ε •
    identity$^l$ : proj₁ identity
    identity$^r$ : Rightdentity ε •
    identity$^r$ : proj₂ identity
```

MMT
```
theory Semigroup : ?NatDed =
u : sort
comp : tm u → tm u → tm u
  # 1 * 2 prec 40
assoc : ⊢ ∀ [x, y, z]
  (x * y) * z = x * (y * z)
assocLeftToRight :
  {x,y,z} ⊢ (x * y) * z
          = x * (y * z)
  = [x,y,z]
    allE (allE (allE assoc x) y) z
assocRightToLeft :
  {x,y,z} ⊢ x * (y * z)
          = (x * y) * z
  = [x,y,z] sym assocLR
theory Monoid : ?NatDed
includes ?Semigroup
unit : tm u # e
unit_axiom : ⊢ ∀ [x] = x * e = x
```

Fig. 1. Representation of `Monoid` theory in different languages.

Picking `Monoid` as an example, it is a structure with a carrier set, an associative binary operation and an identity element for the binary operation. Different systems implement `Monoid` in different ways (see Fig. 1). Other than layout and vocabulary, different libraries also make more substantial choices:

- Whether declarations are arguments or fields.
- The packaging structure — whether theory, record, locale, etc.
- The underlying notion of equality.

Some of these choices are mathematically irrelevant—in the sense that the resulting theories can be proved to be equivalent, internally or externally—while others are more subtle, such as the choice of equality.

A useful construction on top of `Monoid` is the homomorphism between two of its instances, which maps elements of the carrier of the first instance to that of the second one such that structure is preserved. For an operation `op` and a function `hom`, the preservation axiom has the form

```
hom (op x₁ .. xₙ) = op (hom x₁) .. (hom xₙ)
```

One can see that this definition can be "derived" from that of `Monoid`. And that, in fact, this derivation is uniform in the "shape" of the definition of `Monoid`, so that this construction applies to any single-sorted equational theory. This observation is one of the cornerstones of Universal Algebra [35].

There are other classical constructions that can also be generated. This poses a number of questions:

- What other information can be generated from theory presentations?
- How would this affect the activity of library building?
- What pieces of information are needed for the system to generate particular constructions?

Theories written in equational logic that describe algebraic structures are rich in implicit information that can be extracted automatically.

There are obstacles to this automation. For example, definitional and "bundling" choices can make reuse of definitions from one project in another with different aims difficult. Thus users resort to redefining constructs that have already been formalized. We then end up with multiple libraries for the same topic in the same system. For example, there are at least four algebra libraries in Coq [17,18,30,34], and even more for Category Theory [19]. In [17], the authors mention, referring to other libraries:

> "In spite of this body of prior work, however, we have found it difficult to make practical use of the algebraic hierarchy in our project to formalize the Feit-Thompson Theorem in the Coq system."

Universal Algebra [29,31,35] provides us with tools and abstractions well-suited to this task. It is already used in providing semantics and specifications of computer systems [14,15,32] and has been formalized in Coq [3] and Agda [20]. We use Universal Algebra abstractions as basis for our framework to automate the generation of useful information from the definition of a theory. We use Tog to realize our framework[1]. Tog is a small implementation of a dependent type theory, in the style of Agda, Idris and Coq. It serves well as an abstraction over the design details of different systems. Studying theory presentations at this level of abstraction is the first step to generating useful constructions for widely used systems, like Agda, Coq, Isabelle and others.

In Sect. 2 we highlight some of the redundancies in current libraries. We present our framework for mechanizing the generation of this information in Sect. 3. We follow this with a discussion of related work in Sect. 4 and a conclusion and future work in Sect. 5.

2   Algebra in Current Libraries

Our first observation is that current formalizations of Algebra contain quite a bit of information that is "free" in the sense that it can be mechanically generated from basic definitions. For example, given a theory X, it is mechanical to define X-homomorphisms. To do this within a system is extremely difficult, as it would require introspection and for theory *definitions* to be first-class citizens, which is not the case for any system based on type-theory that we are aware of. Untyped systems in the Lisp tradition do this routinely, as does Maude [10], which is based on *rewriting logic*; the downside is that there is no difference between meaningful and meaningless transformations in these systems, only between "runs successfully" and "crashes". However, these constructions are fully typeable and, moreover, are not system-specific (as they can be phrased meta-theoretically within Universal Algebra), even though an implementation has to be aware of the syntactic details of each system.

Lest the reader think that our quest is a little quixotic, we first look at current libraries from a variety of systems, to find concrete examples of human-written code that could have been generated. We look at Agda, Isabelle/HOL and Lean in particular. More specifically, we look at version 1.3 of the Agda standard library, the 2019 release of the Isabelle/HOL library and Lean's mathlib, where we link to the proper release tag.

We use the theory `Monoid` as our running example, and we highlight the reusable components that the systems use to make writing the definitions easier and more robust.

2.1   Homomorphism

How do the libraries of our three systems[2] represent homomorphism?

Agda defines `Monoid` homomorphism, indirectly, in two ways. First, a predicate encapsulating the proof obligations is defined, which is layered on top of the

---

[1] The implementation is available at https://github.com/ysharoda/tog.

[2] We do not have enough room to give an introduction to each system; hopefully each system's syntax is clear enough for the main ideas to come through.

predicate for Semigroup homomorphism. This is then used to define homomorphisms themselves.

```
module _ {c₁ ℓ₁ c₂ ℓ₂}
          (From : Monoid c₁ ℓ₁)
          (To   : Monoid c₂ ℓ₂) where

 private
  module F = Monoid From
  module T = Monoid To

 record IsSemigroupMorphism (⟦_⟧:Morphism)
         : Set(c₁ ⊔ ℓ₁ ⊔ c₂ ⊔ ℓ₂) where
  field
   ⟦⟧-cong : ⟦_⟧ Preserves F._≈_ → T._≈_
   ·-homo  : Homomorphic₂ ⟦_⟧ F._·_ T._·_
   ···
 record IsMonoidMorphism (⟦_⟧:Morphism)
         : Set(c₁ ⊔ ℓ₁ ⊔ c₂ ⊔ ℓ₂) where
  field
   sm-homo : IsSemigroupMorphism F.semigroup T.semigroup ⟦_⟧
   ε-homo  : Homomorphic₀ ⟦_⟧ F.ε T.ε

open IsSemigroupMorphism sm-homo public
```

There are many design decisions embedded in the above definitions. These decisions are not canonical, so we need to understand them to later be able to both abstract them out and make them variation points in our generator. Namely, these decisions are:

- The choice of which declarations are parameters and which are fields. The monoids (From and To) over which we define homomorphism are parameters, not fields, as is the function ⟦_⟧.
- The preservation axioms can be defined based on their arity patterns, as type-level function such as Homomorphic₂:

  ```
  Homomorphic₂ : (A → B) → Op₂ A → Op₂ B → Set _
  Homomorphic₂ ⟦_⟧ _·_ _∘_ =
    ∀ x y → ⟦ x · y ⟧ ≈ (⟦ x ⟧ ∘ ⟦ y ⟧)
  ```

  The library also provides shortcuts for 0-ary and 1-ary function symbols, the most common cases.
- The definition of structures over setoids. Thus equalities need to be preserved, and that is what the ⟦⟧-cong axiom states.

Isabelle/HOL provides the following definition of monoid homomorphism:

```
definition
hom :: "_ ⇒ _ ⇒ ('a ⇒ 'b) set" where
  "hom G H =
  {h . h ∈ carrier G → carrier H ∧
```

```
(∀ x ∈ carrier G · ∀ y ∈ carrier G ·
   h (x ⊕_G y) = h x ⊕_H h y)}"
```

The reader might notice a discrepancy in the above: unit preservation is missing. The Isabelle library does not provide this version. There is, however, a proof that such a multiplication-preserving homomorphism necessarily maps the source unit to a unit of the image (sub)monoid, but that unit is not necessarily that of the full image. The above definition is also used to define group homomorphism and other structures. We consider this to be missing information in the library.

Lean's definition of monoid homomorphism is the one that most resembles the one found in textbooks.

```
structure monoid_hom (M : Type*) (N : Type*)
  [monoid M] [monoid N] :=
  (to_fun : M → N)
  (map_one' : to_fun 1 = 1)
  (map_mul' : ∀ x y, to_fun (x * y) = to_fun x * to_fun y)
```

However, in the same file, there is another definition of add_monoid_hom that looks "the same" up to renaming. This points to a weakness of Lean: there is no renaming operation on structure, and for a Ring to contain two "monoids", one is forced to duplicate definitions. This redundancy is unpleasant.

2.2 Term Language

The "term language" of a theory is the (inductive) data type that represents the syntax of well-formed terms of that theory, along with an interpretation function from *expressions* to the carrier of the (implicitly single-sorted) given theory, i.e. its denotational semantics.

In Agda, the definition of Monoid term language is straightforward:

```
data Expr (n : ℕ) where
  var : Fin n → Expr n
  id  : Expr n
  _⊕_ : Expr n → Expr n → Expr n
```

Defining the interpretation function requires the concept of an environment. An environment associates a value to every variable, and the semantics associates a value (of type Carrier) to each expression of Expr.

```
Env : Set _
Env = λ n → Vec Carrier n

[_] : ∀ {n} → Expr n → Env n → Carrier
[ var x ] ρ = lookup ρ x
[ id ] ρ = ε
[ e₁ ⊕ e₂ ] ρ = [ e₁ ] ρ · [ e₂ ] ρ
```

In Agda, these definitions are not found with the definitions of the algebraic structures themselves, but rather as part of the *Solver* for equations over that theory. Here, we find more duplication, as the above definitions are repeated for the following three highly related structures: `Monoid`, `CommutativeMonoid` and `IdempotentCommutativeMonoid`.

Despite its usefulness, we were not able to find the definition of the term language of a theory in Isabelle/HOL or Lean.

2.3   Product

Until recently, there was no definition of the product of algebraic structures in the Agda library. A recent pull request has suggested adding these, along with other constructions. The following hand-written definition has now been added:

```
rawMonoid : RawMonoid c cℓ → RawMonoid d dℓ →
RawMonoid (c ⊔ d) (cℓ ⊔ dℓ)
rawMonoid M N = record
  { Carrier = M.Carrier × N.Carrier
  ; _≈_ = Pointwise M._≈_ N._≈_
  ; _·_ = zip M._·_ N._·_
  ; ε = M.ε , N.ε
  }
  where
  module M = RawMonoid M
  module N = RawMonoid N
```

These could have been mechanically generated from the definition of `Monoid`.

Both Isabelle/HOL and Lean provide definitions of product algebras for monoids, which we omit for space. It is worth mentioning that the Lean library has 15 definitions for products of structures that look very similar and could be generated.

2.4   More Monoid-Based Examples

We have presented three concrete examples, based on monoid, of human-written code in current libraries that could have instead been generated. There are many more that could be, although these are sparsely found in current libraries. We continue to use monoid as our guiding example, and also briefly discuss how they can be generalized to a larger algebraic context and why they are useful. These are presented in a syntax that closely resembles that of Agda (and is formally Tog syntax), which should be understandable to anyone familiar with dependently-typed languages.

Trivial Submonoid. Given a monoid `M`, we can construct the trivial monoid, also called the zero monoid[3] (containing only the identity element) in the same language as `M`.

---

[3] As it is both initial and terminal in the corresponding Category.

```
record TrivialSubmonoid {A : Set} (M : Monoid A) : Set
where
  constructor trivialSubmonoid
  field
    singleton : {x : A} → x == M.e
```

One can easily proceed to show that this predicate on a monoid induces a new (sub)monoid. In fact, we do not need associativity for this; in other words, already a unital magma induces a trivial monoid.

Flipped Monoid. Given a monoid M, we can construct a new monoid where the binary operation is that of M but applied in reverse order.

The construction here is direct, in that the result is a Monoid.

```
record FlippedMonoid : {A : Set} → Monoid A → Monoid A
record FlippedMonoid m = {
  A = M.A,
  e = M.e,
  op = (x y : A) → M.op y x,
  lunit = M.runit,
  runit = M.lunit,
  assoc = sym M.assoc
}
```

This example can be generalized from a monoid to a magma.

Monoid Action. This example constructs, from a Monoid M and a set B, a monoid action of M on B.

```
record MonoidAction {A : Set} (M : Monoid A)
                    (B : Set) : Set where
  constructor monoidAction
  field
    act     : A → B → B
    actunit : {b : B} → (act M.e b) == b
    actop   : {x y : A} → {b : B} →
              (act (M.op x y) b) == (act x (act y b))
```

Monoid actions are extremely useful for expressing ideas in group theory, and in automata theory. They are only defined in the presence of a monoid structure, which can be easily checked at the meta level.

Subsets Action. The fourth example construct, from a Monoid M, the monoid on the subsets of M. Note that the following is pseudo-code written in an imagined Set-theoretic extension of dependent type theory.

```
record SubsetsAction {A : Set} (M : Monoid A) : Set
where
  constructor subsetsAction
```

```
field
   S       : (powerset A)
   e'      : S
   op'     : S → S → S
   e'def   : e' == {M.e}
   op'def  : {x y : S} → (op' x y)
             == {(M.op a b) | a ∈ x and b ∈ y}
```

The subsets monoid is used extensively in automata theory and group theory.

The above can also be written as a construction of a new monoid, in dependent type theory, where the carrier is the set of unary relations on A.

Monoid Cosets. The next example constructs, from a Monoid M, the cosets of M. This is also pseudo-code, as above.

```
record MonoidCosets {A : Set} (M : Monoid A) : Set
where
   constructor monoidCosets
   field
      S       : (powerset A)
      e'      : S
      op'     : A → S → S
      e'def   : e' == {M.e}
      op'def  : {a : A} → {x : S} → (op' a x)
                == {(M.op a b) | b ∈ x}
```

Monoid cosets are extensively used in group theory.

3   Constructions for Free!

A meta-theory (either a logic or a type theory) provides us with a concrete language in which to represent axiomatic theories. Through having a uniform syntactic representation of the components of axiomatic theories, we can manipulate them, and eventually generate new ones from them.

Our meta-theory is Martin-Löf Type Theory, as implemented in Tog [27]. Tog is developed by the implementors of Agda for the purpose of experimenting with new ideas in (implementations of) dependent type theories. It has mainly been used to experiment with type checking through unification [26]. Tog is minimalistic, and serves our purpose of being independent of the design details of many of the large proof languages. It also gives us a type checker.

The following implementation details of Tog are worth pointing out:

- It has one universe Set, which is the kind of all sorts.
- Functions are represented as curried lambda expressions: Fun Expr Expr.
- Axioms are represented as Π-types: Pi Telescope Expr. They use the underlying propositional equality: Eq Expr Expr.
- Theories are represented as parameterized dependent records, Σ-types.

- A parameter to the record has the type `Binding`. It can be hidden using `HBind [Arg] Expr`, or explicit using `Bind [Arg] Expr`.
- A declaration within the record has the type `Constr Name Expr`.

In Universal Algebra, an algebraic theory consists of sorts, function symbols (with their arities) and a list of axioms, often denoted as a theory T having three components (S,F,E). We assume a single sort. This can be internalized, in the Haskell implementation of Tog, as

```
data EqTheory = EqTheory  {
   thryName    :: Name_   ,
   sort        :: Constr  ,
   funcTypes   :: [Constr],
   axioms      :: [Constr],
   waist       :: Int      }
```

where:

- `sort`, `funcTypes`, and `axioms` are treated as elements of a telescope [13]. Therefore, the order in which they are defined matters.
- The `waist` is a number referring to how many of the declarations within the telescope are parameters. The notation is taken from [1]. This information is needed in generating some constructions, like homomorphism.

Given a Tog record type that exhibits an equational theory structure, like that of `Monoid` in Sect. 1, we convert it into an instance of `EqTheory`. We, then, proceed with generating useful information from the theory. Finally, we convert this information into Tog records and data types, so they can be type checked by Tog, i.e. our approach builds on Tog, without changing its syntax or type checker. In the sequel of this section, we describe the constructions we generate.

3.1 Signature

Given a theory T = (S,F,E), the signature of the theory is Sig(T) = (S,F). A signature is obtained from an `EqTheory` as follows:

```
signature_ :: Eq.EqTheory -> Eq.EqTheory
signature_ =
   over Eq.thyName (++ "Sig") . set Eq.axioms [] .   gmap ren
```

For a theory with name X, the signature is an `EqTheory` with the name `XSig` and an empty axioms list. The theory and its signature exists in the same module. Tog requires that they have different field names. We use `gmap ren` to apply this renaming. We discuss this in more details in Sect. 3.5.

3.2 Product Algebra

Given a theory T = (S,F,E), we obtain the product theory Prod(T) = (S×S, F', E') by replacing each occurrence of the type S by S×S. The modification to the function symbols and axioms is straightforward.

```
productThry :: Eq.EqTheory -> Eq.EqTheory
productThry t =
  over Eq.thyName (++ "Prod") $
  over Eq.funcTypes (map mkProd) $
  over Eq.axioms (map mkProd) $
  gmap ren t
```

Similar to what we did with signatures, the `ren` function renames the fields of the input theory. `mkProd` changes the sort to be an instance of `Prod`, with the sort of the input theory as the type parameter.

3.3   Term Language

For a theory `T = (S,F,E)`, the closed term language is generated by converting every function symbol to a constructor, with the same arity. The axioms are dropped.

```
termLang t =
 let constructors =
  gmap (ren (getConstrName $ t^.Eq.sort) nm) $ t^.Eq.funcTypes
 in Data (mkName $ t^.thyName ++ "Lang") NoParams $
  DataDeclDef setType constructors
```

Constructors are generated by substituting the name of the language type for a sort `A`. Term languages are realized as Tog data declarations using the constructor `Data`.

Generating the closed term language is a first step to generating an open term language (i.e. a term language parametrized by a type of variables), and an interpreter.

For some kinds of axioms, namely those that can be *oriented*, we can turn these into *simplification rules*, i.e. into (unconditional) rewrite rules. The resulting simplifier can be shown to be meaning preserving. These two pieces, the evaluator and simplifier, can be attached to each other to form a *partial evaluator*, using the "finally tagless" [7] method. Eventually, we would like to be able to automate the majority of the hand-written code for a generative geometry library [4], which is indeed quite amenable to such techniques. Unfortunately, the details will have to wait for a future paper.

3.4   Homomorphism

For a theory `T = (S,F,E)`, with instances T_1 and T_2, the homomorphism of `T` consists of

1. a function mapping the carrier of T_1 to that of T_2,
2. a set of axioms asserting that operations (i.e. elements of `F`) are preserved.

Our definition of homomorphism is parameterized by the instances T_1 and T_2. The parameters of `T`, if `waist` > 0, are lifted out as parameters to the resulting homomorphism, and used to define the instances of the theory.

```
homomorphism :: Eq.EqTheory -> Decl
homomorphism t =
  let nm = t ^. Eq.thyName ++ "Hom"
      a = Eq.args t
      (psort,pfuncs,_) = mkPConstrs t
      ((i1, n1), (i2, n2)) = createThryInsts t
      homFnc = genHomFunc psort n1 n2
      axioms = map (oneAxiom fnc psort n1 n2) pfuncs
  in Record (mkName nm)
     (mkParams $ (map (recordParams Bind) a) ++ [i1,i2])
     (RecordDeclDef setType
                    (mkName $ nm ++ "C")
                    (mkField $ fnc : axioms))
```

The genHomFunc function generates the homomorphism function. Each preservation axiom is created using the oneAxiom function.

Other kinds of morphisms can also be generated by providing more axioms to describe properties of the functions. For example a monomorphism would have the same definition with one more axiom stating that the function is injective. An endomorphism is a self-homomorphism, and thus can be parametrized by a single theory.

3.5 Discussion

The above are a small sample of what can be done. We've found at least 30 constructions that should be amenable to such a treatment and are currently implementing them, including quotient algebras and induction axioms. Figure 2 shows the generated constructions. The input is the theory of Monoid represented as a Tog record type (illustrated on the left with the blue background). For this, we generate the four constructions discussed above (illustrated with pink background). The names of carriers A_1 and A_2, names of instances Mo_1 and Mo_2 are machine generated based on the names used by the input theory, which are given by the user. A somehow unpleasant restriction is that all field names need to be distinct, even if the fields belong to different records. That is the reason we have names like eL in MonoidLang and eS in MonoidSig. This is still a minor inconvenience, given that we are working on an abstract level, from which more readable and usable code will be generated.

4 Related Work

Many algebraic hierarchies have been developed before. [18] documents the development of the algebra needed for proving the fundamental theorem of algebra. [17] formalizes the same knowledge in Coq, but suggests a packaging structure alternative to telescopes, to support multiple inheritance. [11] addresses the important problem of library maintainability, especially when dealing with changes to the hierarchy. We have proposed an alternate solution in [9], based on the categorical structures already present in dependent type theories.

```
record Monoid (A : Set) : Set
where
  constructor monoid
  field
    e  : A
    op : A → A → A
    lunit : {x : A} → (op e x) == x
    runit : {x : A} → (op x e) == x
    assoc : {x y z : A} →
      op x (op y z) == op (op x y) z


record MonoidHom
      (A1 : Set) (A2 : Set)
.     (Mo1 : Monoid A1)
      (Mo2 : Monoid A2) : Set where
  constructor MonoidHomC
  field
    hom : A1 → A2
    pres-e : hom (e Mo1) == e Mo2
    pres-op :
      (x1 : A1) (x2 : A1) →
      hom (op Mo1 x1 x2)
      == op Mo2 (hom x1) (hom x2)
```

```
data MonoidLang : Set where
  eL : MonoidLang
  opL : MonoidLang → MonoidLang
      → MonoidLang


record MonoidSig (AS : Set) : Set
where
  constructor MonoidSigSigC
  field
    eS : AS
    opS : AS → AS → AS


record MonoidProd (AP : Set)
    : Set
where
  constructor MonoidProdC
  field
    eP : Prod AP AP
    opP : Prod AP AP → Prod AP AP
        → Prod AP AP
    lunit_eP : (xP : Prod AP AP)
        → opP eP xP == xP
    runit_eP : (xP : Prod AP AP)
        → opP xP eP == xP
    associative_opP :
        (xP : Prod AP AP)
        (yP : Prod AP AP)
        (zP : Prod AP AP)
        → opP (opP xP yP) zP
        == opP xP (opP yP zP)
```

Fig. 2. The generated constructions from `Monoid` theory (Color figure online)

The algebraic library of Lean [12] is of particular interest, as its developers are quite concerned with automation. But this automation, also done via meta-programming, is largely oriented to proof automation via tactics. We instead focus on automating the generation of structures.

Universal Algebra constructions are grounded in set theory, yet is nevertheless quite constructive. It has been formalized in Coq [3,34] and Agda [20]. [34] is notable for the use of type classes to formalize the algebraic hierarchy.

While the work in interactive provers has been mainly manual, the programming languages community has been actively investigating the generation of various utilities derived from the definition of algebraic data types. Haskell's *deriving* mechanism has already been mentioned. This has been greatly extended twice, first in [25], to allow more generic deriving, and then in [2] allowing the users to define new patterns. The usefulness of these mechanisms has been of great inspiration to us. We would like to provide similar tools for library developers of interactive proof systems.

5   Conclusion and Future Work

Building large libraries of mathematical knowledge can greatly enhance the usefulness of interactive proof systems. Currently, the larger the library, the more labor intensive it becomes. We suggest automating some of the definitions of concepts derivable via known techniques. We have tested our implementation on a library of 227 theories, including `Ring` and `BoundedDistributedLattice`, built using the tiny theories approach [5] and the combinators of [9]. A theory defined declaratively using the combinators elaborate into a Tog record, which is then manipulated to generate the constructions presented in Sect. 3. From the declarative description of the 227 theories, we were able to generate a much larger library which contains 1132 definitions and, when pretty-printed, spanned 14811 lines, containing theories and data types representing the structures we discussed in Sect. 3. We are adding more derived theories, and can then get a multiplicative factor, as each time we do, we get 227 new theories.

While the knowledge representable in single-sorted equational logic is still impressive (e.g. it covers most of Algebra), we are also interested in generating the same structures (and more) for theories represented in more sophisticated logics [28], such as category theory represented in dependent type theory.

We currently generate all constructions for all theories in a given library. As more structures get generated, we would want to give developers more control over what to generate. Thus we intend to provide a scripting language for referring to theories, or groups of theories, and specifying what constructions to apply. This could also include an "on demand" version, similar to how the deriving mechanism of Haskell works. We are also interested in generating morphisms, as explained in [16], between theories. Even for our constructions, some of these morphism are not obvious, but are needed to transport results.

We envision using our current implementation as a meta-language to generate definitions for existing, full-featured systems, such as Isabelle/HOL and Agda. To achieve this, we will need to reintroduce certain details (such as notations) that we elided. The scripting language described above will need to be extended to cover different kinds of *design decisions*.

We envision a framework in which the contents of the library can be defined succinctly, and elaborated to a large reusable and flexible body of standardized mathematics knowledge.

References

1. Al-hassy, M., Carette, J., Kahl, W.: A language feature to unbundle data at will (short paper). In: Proceedings of the 18th ACM SIGPLAN International Conference on Generative Programming: Concepts and Experiences, GPCE 2019, pp. 14–19. ACM, New York (2019)
2. Blöndal, B., Löh, A., Scott, R.: Deriving via: or, how to turn hand-written instances into an anti-pattern. In: Proceedings of the 11th ACM SIGPLAN International Symposium on Haskell, Haskell 2018, pp. 55–67. Association for Computing Machinery, New York (2018)

3. Capretta, V.: Universal algebra in type theory. In: Bertot, Y., Dowek, G., Théry, L., Hirschowitz, A., Paulin, C. (eds.) TPHOLs 1999. LNCS, vol. 1690, pp. 131–148. Springer, Heidelberg (1999). https://doi.org/10.1007/3-540-48256-3_10
4. Carette, J., Elsheikh, M., Smith, S.: A generative geometric kernel. In: Proceedings of the 20th ACM SIGPLAN Workshop on Partial Evaluation and Program Manipulation, pp. 53–62. ACM (2011)
5. Carette, J., et al.: The MathScheme library: Some preliminary experiments. arXiv preprint arXiv:1106.1862, June 2011
6. Carette, J., Farmer, W.M., Kohlhase, M., Rabe, F.: Big math and the one-brain barrier a position paper and architecture proposal. arXiv preprint arXiv:1904.10405 (2019)
7. Carette, J., Kiselyov, O., Shan, C.: Finally tagless, partially evaluated: tagless staged interpreters for simpler typed languages. J. Funct. Program. **19**(5), 509–543 (2009)
8. Carette, J., O'Connor, R.: Theory presentation combinators. In: Jeuring, J., Campbell, J.A., Carette, J., Dos Reis, G., Sojka, P., Wenzel, M., Sorge, V. (eds.) CICM 2012. LNCS (LNAI), vol. 7362, pp. 202–215. Springer, Heidelberg (2012). https://doi.org/10.1007/978-3-642-31374-5_14
9. Carette, J., O'Connor, R., Sharoda, Y.: Building on the diamonds between theories: theory presentation combinators. arXiv preprint arXiv:1812.08079 (2018)
10. Clavel, M., Eker, S., Lincoln, P., Meseguer, J.: Principles of Maude. In: Meseguer, J. (ed.) Proceedings of the First International Workshop on Rewriting Logic, vol. 4, pp. 65–89 (1996)
11. Cohen, C., Sakaguchi, K., Tassi, E.: Hierarchy builder: algebraic hierarchies made easy in Coq with Elpi. https://hal.inria.fr/hal-02478907 (2020). working paper or preprint
12. The Mathlib Community. The lean mathematical library. arXiv preprint arXiv: 1910.09336 (2019).
13. de Bruijn, N.G.: Telescopic mappings in typed lambda calculus. Inf. Comput. **91**(2), 189–204 (1991)
14. Denecke, K., Wismath, S.L.: Universal Algebra and Applications in Theoretical Computer Science. Taylor & Francis, New York (2002)
15. Ehrig, H., Mahr, B.: Fundamentals of Algebraic Specification 1: Equations and Initial Semantics. Monographs in Theoretical Computer Science. An EATCS Series. Springer, Heidelberg (2012). https://doi.org/10.1007/978-3-642-69962-7
16. Farmer, W.M., Guttman, J.D., Javier Thayer, F.: Little theories. In: Kapur, D. (ed.) CADE 1992. LNCS, vol. 607, pp. 567–581. Springer, Heidelberg (1992). https://doi.org/10.1007/3-540-55602-8_192
17. Garillot, F., Gonthier, G., Mahboubi, A., Rideau, L.: Packaging mathematical structures. In: Berghofer, S., Nipkow, T., Urban, C., Wenzel, M. (eds.) TPHOLs 2009. LNCS, vol. 5674, pp. 327–342. Springer, Heidelberg (2009). https://doi.org/10.1007/978-3-642-03359-9_23
18. Geuvers, H., Pollack, R., Wiedijk, F., Zwanenburg, J.: A constructive algebraic hierarchy in Coq. J. Symb. Comput. **34**(4), 271–286 (2002)
19. Gross, J., Chlipala, A., Spivak, D.I.: Experience implementing a performant category-theory library in Coq. In: Klein, G., Gamboa, R. (eds.) ITP 2014. LNCS, vol. 8558, pp. 275–291. Springer, Cham (2014). https://doi.org/10.1007/978-3-319-08970-6_18
20. Gunther, E., Gadea, A., Pagano, M.: Formalization of universal algebra in Agda. Electron. Not. Theor. Comput. Sci. **338**, 147–166 (2018). The 12th Workshop on Logical and Semantic Frameworks, with Applications (LSFA 2017)

21. Halleck, J.: Logic system interrelationships. http://www.horizons-2000.org/2.%20Ideas%20and%20Meaning/John%20Halleck%27s%20Logic%20System%20Interrelationships.html. Accessed 20 Mar 2020

22. Haskell; an advanced, purely functional programming language. https://www.haskell.org/. Accessed 22 Mar 2020

23. Jipsen, P.: List of mathematical structures. http://math.chapman.edu/~jipsen/structures/doku.php. Accessed 20 Mar 2020

24. Haskell lens library. https://hackage.haskell.org/package/lens. version 4.19.1. Accessed 22 Mar 2020

25. Magalhães, J.P., Dijkstra, A., Jeuring, J., Löh, A.: A generic deriving mechanism for Haskell. ACM SIGPLAN Not. **45**(11), 37–48 (2010)

26. Mazzoli, F., Abel, A.: Type checking through unification. arXiv preprint arXiv:1609.09709 (2016)

27. Mazzoli, F., Danielsson, N.A., Norell, U., Vezzosi, A., Abel, A.: Tog, a prototypical implementation of dependent types. https://github.com/bitonic/tog

28. Meinke, K.: Universal algebra in higher types. Theor. Comput. Sci. **100**(2), 385–417 (1992)

29. Meinke, K., Tucker, J.V.: Universal algebra. University of Wales (Swansea). Mathematics and Computer Science Division (1991)

30. Pottier, L.: Coq user contributions - algebra library. https://github.com/coq-contribs/algebra

31. Sankappanavar, H.P., Burris, S.: A Course in Universal Algebra. Graduate Texts Math, vol. 78. Springer, New York (1981)

32. Sannella, D., Tarlecki, A.: Universal algebra. In: Foundations of Algebraic Specification and Formal Software Development. Monographs in Theoretical Computer Science. An EATCS Series, pp. 15–39. Springer, Heidelberg (2011). https://doi.org/10.1007/978-3-642-17336-3_1

33. Sheard, T., Jones, S.P.: Template meta-programming for Haskell. In: Proceedings of the 2002 ACM SIGPLAN Workshop on Haskell, Haskell 2002, pp. 1–16. Association for Computing Machinery, New York (2002)

34. Spitters, B., van der Weegen, E.: Developing the algebraic hierarchy with type classes in Coq. In: Kaufmann, M., Paulson, L.C. (eds.) ITP 2010. LNCS, vol. 6172, pp. 490–493. Springer, Heidelberg (2010). https://doi.org/10.1007/978-3-642-14052-5_35

35. Whitehead, A.N.: A Treatise on Universal Algebra: With Applications. Cornell University Library Historical Math Monographs. The University Press (1898)

Metamath Zero: Designing a Theorem Prover Prover

Mario Carneiro$^{(\boxtimes)}$ (iD)

Carnegie Mellon University, Pittsburgh, PA, USA
mcarneir@andrew.cmu.edu

Abstract. As the usage of theorem prover technology expands, so too does the reliance on correctness of the tools. Metamath Zero is a verification system that aims for simplicity of logic and implementation, without compromising on efficiency of verification. It is formally specified in its own language, and supports a number of translations to and from other proof languages. This paper describes the abstract logic of Metamath Zero, essentially a multi-sorted first order logic, as well as the binary proof format and the way in which it can ensure essentially linear time verification while still being concise and efficient at scale. Metamath Zero currently holds the record for fastest verification of the set.mm Metamath library of proofs in ZFC (including 71 of Wiedijk's 100 formalization targets), at less than 200 ms. Ultimately, we intend to use it to verify the correctness of the implementation of the verifier down to binary executable, so it can be used as a root of trust for more complex proof systems.

Keywords: Metamath zero · Mathematics · Formal proof · Verification · Metamathematics

1 Introduction

The idea of using computers to check mathematical statements has been around almost as long as computers themselves, but the scope of formalizations have grown in recent times, both in pure mathematics and software verification, and it now seems that there is nothing that is really beyond our reach if we aim for it. But at the same time, software faces a crisis of correctness, where more powerful systems lead to more reliance on computers and higher stakes for failure. Software verification stands poised to solve this problem, providing a high level of certainty in correctness for critical components.

But software verification systems are themselves critical components, particularly the popular and effective ones. A proof in such a system is only as good as the software that checks it. How can we bootstrap trust in our systems?

This paper presents a formal system, called Metamath Zero (MM0), which aims to fill this gap, having both a simple extensible logical theory and a straightforward yet efficient proof format. Work to prove the correctness theorem is

© Springer Nature Switzerland AG 2020
C. Benzmüller and B. Miller (Eds.): CICM 2020, LNAI 12236, pp. 71–88, 2020.
https://doi.org/10.1007/978-3-030-53518-6_5

ongoing, but this paper explains the design of the system and how it relates to other theorem provers, as well as general considerations for any bootstrapping theorem prover.

1.1 Who Verifies the Verifiers?

There are two major sources of untrustworthiness in a verification system: the logic and the implementation. If the logic is unsound, then it may be able to prove absurd statements. This is bad, but there are a number of axiomatic foundations such as ZFC that are widely believed to be consistent, and this is sufficient for our purpose. Much more concerning is implementation correctness. Implementation bugs can exist in the theorem prover itself, the compiler for the language, any additional components used by the compiler (the preprocessor, linker, and assembler, if applicable), as well as the operating system, firmware, and hardware. In this area, mathematics and logic holds little sway, and it is "common knowledge" that no nontrivial program is or can be bug-free. The argument for correctness of these systems is largely a social one: the compiler has compiled many programs without any bugs (that we noticed) (except when we noticed and fixed the bugs), so it must work well enough.

What can we do? Our strategy is to start from the ground up, defining all the properties that the verifier system of our dreams should have, and then start building it. With the right set-up, this turns out to be surprisingly achievable, and we believe we have come within striking distance of all targeted goals. Here are some dream goals:

1. It should be proven correct down to the lowest possible level. Some options for the lowest level include:
   (a) a logical rendering of the code;
   (b) the code itself, inside a logical rendering of the language;
   (c) the machine code, specified given an ISA (instruction set architecture);
   (d) the computer, down to the logic gates that make it up;
   (e) the fabrication process relative to some electrical or physical model.
2. It should permit the user to prove any theorem they like (including specifying the axiom system of interest).
3. It should permit the user to write any program they like and prove any theorem about that program.
4. There should be no practical upper limit on the complexity of the target programs, and they should be able to run as fast as the machine is capable.
5. It should be fast.
6. It should be easy to use.

While there is no theoretical reason not to push (1) all the way to level (e), the drawback of the most aggressive levels (d) and (e) is that it limits redistribution capabilities. If you prove a system correct at level (e), the proof only holds if you use the given fabrication process, and similarly (d) only holds if you use the given chip design. A proof relative to (c) holds as long as the "reader" has the same ISA as the author, so if we pick a relatively popular ISA then we can write proofs that are independently verifiable by a large segment of the population. For the MM0 project, we target (c) with the Intel x86-64 architecture on Linux. (This does put the OS in the trusted base, but it is not possible to do otherwise for a regular, user-mode application, which is again important for distribution. We can at least keep interaction with the OS to a minimum and formally specify what we expect from the OS, such that a "bare-metal" version of the verifier is largely the same.)

To satisfy (2), MM0 is a logical framework, with "pluggable axioms" to support any desired mathematical foundation. To satisfy (3) and (4), we implemented, in MM0, a specification for x86-64, so that users can write any program they like. To satisfy (5), proofs will be laid out such that checking them is as straightforward as possible, roughly linear time, while keeping the de Bruijn factor down.

(6) is a subjective criterion, and also one we are willing to compromise on in favor of the others. Nevertheless some degree of ease of use is needed in order to get enough done to achieve the other goals. To that end, MM0 the verifier has a front end MM1, which provides some ITP (interactive theorem prover) features, in an *unverified* setting. This is an extension of the LCF-style prover architecture to completely separate and isolate the verifier from the prover.

In particular, a compiler for producing verified programs would sit at this unverified prover level, producing machine code from high level code so that users don't have to write machine code. This compromises (4) to some extent if the compiler produces poor code, but that has an obvious mitigation.

1.2 Efficiency Matters

Why should it matter if a proof takes hours or days to compile? Sometimes, performance is about more than just getting work done a little faster. When something takes *a lot* less time, it changes the way you interact with the computer. A process that takes hours goes on the nightly build server; a process that takes minutes might be a compile that runs on your local machine; a process that takes seconds is a progress bar; and a process that takes milliseconds might happen in an editor between keystrokes.

A verifier is a *component* in a larger system. People have a tendency to stack libraries on top of libraries, so the cost of the thing at the base of the stack will ripple into every downstream use. It is easy to think that a proof that runs in 1 second is not so bad, and a factor of ten improvement is not noticeable, but a math library that has tens of thousands of these proofs will take hours, and a factor of ten improvement here is massive.

The set.mm Metamath library of theorems in ZFC contains over 34000 proofs, and MM0 can check a translation of it in 195 ± 5 ms. This can be (unfairly) compared to libraries in other systems such as Isabelle, Coq, or Lean that take over an hour to compile their standard library and sometimes much more, a difference of 4–5 orders of magnitude. While this is not definitive evidence, such a vast discrepancy indicates that architectural differences matter, and significant gains are possible over the status quo.

To be clear, it is not that these systems are implemented inefficiently – this can account for 1–2 orders of magnitude at most. The primary architectural difference is that Metamath does not put the running of tactics on the "critical path" of verification. The set.mm distributable artifact contains already fully elaborated compressed proofs, which makes loading and verification much faster. Tactics are ephemeral mechanisms in proof production that are not stored in the public repository. This approach has drawbacks for replaying or modifying heavily tactic-based proofs, though, and we will show how MM0 bridges this gap by enabling a range of caching strategies.

Most of the major theorem provers have some approximation to a "compiled proof" format. Coq's .vo files, and Lean's .olean files, were originally designed to be used to cache the result of compiling a source file, and so while they bear a passing resemblance to our .mmb format, because they are not actually intended as a substitute for verification, they quite unstable across versions, and undocumented. Isabelle and HOL systems usually use a memory dump for this purpose, which is even more obviously unstable and non-portable.

These systems also may have a "proof export" function [3,22], but these often do significant (and sometimes expensive in time and/or space) alterations to the kernel data structures, making it difficult for any external checker to be able to compete with the built-in checker. They are also not viewed as a high priority, and so they tend to be neglected and fall out of support.

1.3 The Metamath Zero Architecture

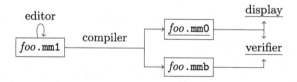

Fig. 1. The MM0 workflow. <u>Underlined</u> components are trusted.

At this point, we have what we need to explain the overall architecture, depicted in Fig. 1. The user writes proofs and programs in MM1, receiving feedback on their proof. This live feedback is implemented in MM1 and is not necessarily reliable, but the quick feedback loop helps with producing the proof. Once it is done, the MM1 compiler produces an .mmb (proof) file, and either produces an .mm0 (specification) file or checks the result against a given .mm0 file. The .mm0 file is a human readable file containing the statements of axioms and target theorems, while the .mmb file is a binary artifact containing the proof. The trusted MM0 verifier then reads the .mm0 and .mmb files, and reports success if the .mmb file is a proof of the .mm0 statements.

The trusted components in this architecture are the verifier, and the .mm0 file containing the statements of the theorems. Additionally one has to trust that the text file is faithfully shown to the reader, and the reader understands the content of the file. As such, the .mm0 file format balances human-readability with simplicity of the verifier implementation required to parse it and validate it against the data in the proof file.

The remainder of the paper discusses the various components of this process. Section 2 describes the logical framework in which theorems are proved, Sect. 2.1 describes the specification format, Sect. 3 describes the proof format, and Sect. 4 discusses how MM0 proof objects can be generated. Section 5 shows work done to connect MM0 to other proof languages. Section 6 discusses progress towards proving the verifier implementation correctness theorem.

2   The Metamath Zero Logic

As its name suggests, Metamath Zero is based on Metamath [18], a formal system developed by Norman Megill in 1990. Its largest database, set.mm, is the home of over 34000 proofs in ZFC set theory. In the space of theorem prover languages, it is one of the simplest, by design. The main difference is that MM0 has a native concept of definitions, rather than using axioms and trusting that those axioms are set up correctly. This is necessary in order to support the architecture in Sect. 1.3, because the .mmb proof file may introduce definitions that were not in the original specification, and the verifier must be able to validate these without adding to the trust base. Most of the other changes are knock-on effects of this. More detail on Metamath vs. MM0 can be found in [5].

MM0 is intended to act as a schematic metatheory over multi-sorted first order logic. This means that it contains *sorts*, two kinds of *variables*, *expressions* constructed from *term constructors* and *definitions*, and *axioms* and *theorems* using expressions for their hypotheses and conclusion. Theorems have *proofs*, which involve applications of other theorems and axioms. The remaining sections will go into more detail on each of these points.

Sorts. An MM0 file declares a (finite) collection of sorts. Every expression has a unique sort, and an expression can only be substituted for a variable of the same sort. There are no type constructors or function types, so the type system is finite. (Higher order functions are mimicked using open terms, see Sect. 2.)

Variables. MM0 distinguishes between two different kinds of variables. One may variously be called names, first order variables or bound/binding variables. These play the role of "variable variables" from Metamath, and will be denoted in this paper with letters $x, y, z, \ldots$. They are essentially names that may be bound by quantifiers internal to the logic. "Substitution" of names is α-conversion; expressions cannot be substituted directly for names, although axioms may be used to implement this action indirectly. The other kind of variable may be called

$$x, \varphi, s, f ::= \langle\text{ident}\rangle \qquad \text{names, metavariables, sort names, constructor names}$$

$$\Gamma ::= \cdot \mid \Gamma, x : s \mid \Gamma, \varphi : s\,\overline{x} \qquad\qquad\qquad \text{contexts}$$

$$e ::= x \mid \varphi \mid f\,\overline{e} \qquad\qquad\qquad\qquad\qquad \text{expressions}$$

$$A ::= e, \quad \Delta ::= \overline{A} \qquad\qquad\qquad\qquad\qquad \text{statements}$$

$$\delta ::= \mathsf{sort}\, s \qquad\qquad\qquad \text{sorts} \qquad \text{declarations}$$

$$\mid \mathsf{term}\, f(\Gamma) : s\,\overline{x} \qquad\qquad \text{constructors}$$

$$\mid \mathsf{def}\, f(\Gamma) : s\,\overline{x} = \overline{y : s'}.\, e \quad \text{definitions}$$

$$\mid \mathsf{axiom}\,(\Gamma; \Delta \vdash A) \qquad \text{axioms}$$

$$\mid \mathsf{thm}\,(\Gamma; \Delta \vdash A) \qquad \text{theorems}$$

$$E ::= \overline{\delta} \qquad\qquad\qquad\qquad\qquad\qquad\qquad \text{environment}$$

$$\boxed{(E)\ \Gamma\ \mathsf{ctx}} \qquad \frac{}{\cdot\ \mathsf{ctx}} \qquad \frac{\mathsf{sort}\, s \in E \quad \Gamma\ \mathsf{ctx}}{\Gamma, x : s\ \mathsf{ctx}} \qquad \frac{\mathsf{sort}\, s \in E \quad \Gamma\ \mathsf{ctx} \quad \overline{x \in \Gamma}}{\Gamma, \varphi : s\,\overline{x}\ \mathsf{ctx}}$$

$$\boxed{(E)\ \Gamma \vdash e : s} \qquad \frac{(x : s) \in \Gamma}{\Gamma \vdash x : s} \qquad \frac{(\varphi : s\,\overline{x}) \in \Gamma}{\Gamma \vdash \varphi : s} \qquad \frac{(f(\Gamma') : s\,\overline{x}) \in E \quad \Gamma \vdash \overline{e} :: \Gamma'}{\Gamma \vdash f\overline{e} : s}$$

$$\boxed{(E)\ \Gamma \vdash \overline{e} :: \Gamma'} \qquad \frac{}{\Gamma \vdash \cdot :: \cdot} \qquad \frac{\Gamma \vdash \overline{e} :: \Gamma' \quad (y : s) \in \Gamma}{\Gamma \vdash (\overline{e}, y) :: (\Gamma', x : s)} \qquad \frac{\Gamma \vdash \overline{e} :: \Gamma' \quad \Gamma \vdash e' : s}{\Gamma \vdash (\overline{e}, e') :: (\Gamma', \varphi : s\,\overline{x})}$$

$$\boxed{(E)\ \delta\ \mathsf{ok}} \qquad \frac{}{\mathsf{sort}\, s\ \mathsf{ok}} \qquad \frac{\mathsf{sort}\, s \in E \quad \Gamma\ \mathsf{ctx} \quad \overline{x \in \Gamma}}{\mathsf{term}\, f(\Gamma) : s\,\overline{x}\ \mathsf{ok}}$$

$$\frac{\mathsf{sort}\, s \in E \quad \Gamma, \overline{y : s'}\ \mathsf{ctx} \quad \overline{x \in \Gamma} \quad \Gamma, \overline{y : s'} \vdash e : s \quad \mathrm{FV}_{\Gamma, \overline{y : s'}}(e) \subseteq \overline{x}}{\mathsf{def}\, f(\Gamma) : s\,\overline{x} = \overline{y : s'}.\, e\ \mathsf{ok}}$$

$$\frac{\Gamma\ \mathsf{ctx} \quad \overline{\Gamma \vdash A : s} \quad \Gamma \vdash B : s'}{\mathsf{axiom}\,(\Gamma; \overline{A} \vdash B)\ \mathsf{ok}} \qquad \frac{\mathsf{axiom}\,(\Gamma; \overline{A} \vdash B)\ \mathsf{ok} \quad \Gamma, \overline{y : s'}; \overline{A} \vdash B}{\mathsf{thm}\,(\Gamma; \overline{A} \vdash B)\ \mathsf{ok}}$$

$$\boxed{E\ \mathsf{env}} \qquad \frac{}{\cdot\ \mathsf{env}} \qquad \frac{E\ \mathsf{env} \quad E \vdash \delta\ \mathsf{ok}}{E, \delta\ \mathsf{env}}$$

$$\mathrm{V}(x) = \{x\} \qquad \mathrm{FV}(x) = \{x\}$$

$$\mathrm{V}_\Gamma(\varphi) = \overline{x} \qquad \mathrm{FV}_\Gamma(\varphi) = \overline{x} \qquad\qquad\qquad \text{where } (\varphi : s\,\overline{x}) \in \Gamma$$

$$\mathrm{V}(f\,\overline{e}) = \bigcup_i \mathrm{V}(e_i) \quad \mathrm{FV}(f\,\overline{e}) = \underline{\mathrm{FV}}(\overline{e} :: \Gamma') \cup \{e_i \mid \Gamma'_i \in \overline{x}\} \quad \text{where } f(\Gamma') : s\,\overline{x}$$

$$\underline{\mathrm{FV}}(\cdot :: \cdot) = \emptyset$$

$$\underline{\mathrm{FV}}((\overline{e}, y) :: (\Gamma', x : s)) = \underline{\mathrm{FV}}(\overline{e} :: \Gamma')$$

$$\underline{\mathrm{FV}}((\overline{e}, e') :: (\Gamma', \varphi : s\,\overline{x})) = \underline{\mathrm{FV}}(\overline{e} :: \Gamma') \cup (\mathrm{FV}(e') \setminus \{e_i \mid \Gamma'_i \in \overline{x}\})$$

Fig. 2. MM0 syntax and well formedness judgments. $\bar{}$ denotes iteration or lists, and e_i denotes the ith element of $\overline{e}$. The Γ ctx, $\Gamma \vdash e : s$, $\Gamma \vdash \overline{e} :: \Gamma'$, and δ ok judgments are parameterized over a fixed global environment E. $(f(\Gamma') : s\,\overline{x}) \in E$ means there is a term or def in E with this signature. See Fig. 3 for the definition of $\Gamma; \overline{A} \vdash B$.

$$\boxed{(E;\Gamma;\Delta) \vdash A} \qquad \frac{A \in \Delta}{\vdash A} \qquad \frac{\vdash A \equiv B \quad \vdash A}{\vdash B}$$

$$\frac{(\Gamma';\overline{A} \vdash B) \in E \quad \Gamma \vdash \overline{e} :: \Gamma' \quad \forall i, \vdash A_i[\Gamma' \mapsto \overline{e}]}{\vdash B[\Gamma' \mapsto \overline{e}]}$$

$$\frac{\forall i \, j \, x, \; \Gamma_i = x \notin V_{\Gamma'}(\Gamma_j) \to e_i \notin V_{\Gamma}(e_j)}{\vdash B[\Gamma' \mapsto \overline{e}]}$$

$$\boxed{(E;\Gamma;\Delta) \vdash e \equiv e'} \qquad \frac{}{\vdash e \equiv e} \qquad \frac{\vdash e \equiv e'}{\vdash e' \equiv e} \qquad \frac{\vdash e_1 \equiv e_2 \quad \vdash e_2 \equiv e_3}{\vdash e_1 \equiv e_3}$$

$$\frac{\forall i, \vdash e_i \equiv e_i'}{\vdash f \, \overline{e} \equiv f \, \overline{e'}} \qquad \frac{(\mathsf{def}\, f(\Gamma') : s\,\overline{x} = \overline{y : s'}.\, e') \in E \quad \Gamma \vdash (\overline{e}, \overline{z}) :: (\Gamma', \overline{y : s'})}{\vdash f \, \overline{e} \equiv e'[\Gamma', \overline{y : s'} \mapsto \overline{e}, \overline{z}]}$$

$$\frac{\forall i \, j, \; z_i \notin V_{\Gamma}(e_j) \quad \forall i \, j, \; i \neq j \to z_i \neq z_j}{}$$

$$x[\Gamma' \mapsto \overline{e}] = e_i \qquad\qquad \text{where } x = \Gamma_i'$$
$$\varphi[\Gamma' \mapsto \overline{e}] = e_i \qquad\qquad \text{where } \varphi = \Gamma_i'$$
$$(f \, \overline{e'})[\Gamma' \mapsto \overline{e}] = f \, \overline{e'[\Gamma' \mapsto \overline{e}]}$$

Fig. 3. MM0 proof and convertibility judgments $\Gamma; \Delta \vdash A$ and $\Gamma; \Delta \vdash e \equiv e'$. The arguments E, Γ, Δ are fixed and hidden. $(\Gamma'; \overline{A} \vdash B) \in E$ means that an axiom or theorem with this signature is in E, that is, $\mathsf{axiom}\,(\Gamma'; \overline{A} \vdash B) \in E$ or $\mathsf{thm}\,(\Gamma'; \overline{A} \vdash B) \in E$.

a (schematic) metavariable or second order variable, and these may *not* be bound by quantifiers; they are always implicitly universally quantified and held fixed within a single theorem, but unlike names, they may be directly substituted for an expression. We use $\varphi, \psi, \chi, \ldots$ to denote schematic metavariables.

In FOL, notations like $\varphi(\overline{x})$ are often used to indicate that a metavariable is explicitly permitted to depend on the variables $\overline{x}$, and sometimes but not always additional "parameter" variables not under consideration. In MM0, we use a binder $\varphi : s\,\overline{x}$, where s is the sort and $\overline{x}$ are the *dependencies* of φ, to indicate that φ represents an open term that may reference the variables $\overline{x}$ declared in the context. Such a variable may also be glossed as a pre-applied higher order variable; for example a variable of type $\varphi : \mathsf{wff}\ x$ can be interpreted as a predicate $P : U \to \mathsf{bool}$ where every occurrence of φ in the statement is replaced with $P\,x$.

Term Constructors. Term constructor declarations are represented in Fig. 2 by $\mathsf{term}\,f(\Gamma) : s\,\overline{x}$. A term constructor is like a function symbol in FOL, except that it can bind variables if names are used in the arguments. Examples of term constructors are $\mathsf{imp}(\_ : \mathsf{wff}, \_ : \mathsf{wff}) : \mathsf{wff}$, which defines implication as a binary operator on the sort wff (which can be shortened to $\mathsf{imp} : \mathsf{wff} \Rightarrow \mathsf{wff} \Rightarrow \mathsf{wff}$), and $\mathsf{all}\,(x : \mathsf{var}, \varphi : \mathsf{wff}\,x) : \mathsf{wff}$, which defines the forall binder—all $x\ \varphi$ represents the FOL expression $\forall x, \varphi(x)$.

Using the rules in Fig. 2, we can calculate that $\mathrm{FV}(\mathsf{all}\,y\,\psi) = \mathrm{FV}(\psi) \setminus \{y\}$ (which accords with the usual FOL definition of the free variables of $\forall y, \psi(y)$), and $\mathrm{V}(\mathsf{all}\, y\, \psi) = \{y\} \cup \mathrm{V}(\psi)$. It is easy to see that $\mathrm{FV}(e) \subseteq \mathrm{V}(e)$ generally; that is, every free variable in an expression e is present in e. Metamath, and Metamath Zero, take the somewhat unorthodox approach of using V instead of FV in the definition of an admissible substitution (the side condition $\forall i\, j\, x$, $\Gamma_i = x \notin \mathrm{V}_{\Gamma'}(\Gamma_j) \rightarrow e_i \notin \mathrm{V}_\Gamma(e_j)$ in the theorem application rule in Fig. 3, which says in words that if Γ_j is a variable in the context that is not declared to depend on x, then the substitution for Γ_j cannot contain the name that is being substituted for x), but this is sound because if e does not contain any occurrence of x then it clearly does not contain a free occurrence of x. This is done because V is faster to compute than FV, and α-conversion in the logic can make up the difference.

Definitions. Definitions, denoted by $\mathsf{def}\, f(\Gamma) : s\,\overline{x} = \overline{y : s'}.\ e$ in Fig. 2, are similar to term constructors, but definitions can be unfolded by the convertibility judgment $\vdash e \equiv e'$.

Axioms and Theorems. Provable assertions are simply expressions of designated sorts. A general axiom or theorem is really an inference rule $\Gamma; \Delta \vdash A$, where Δ is a list of hypotheses and A is a conclusion, and Γ contains the variable declarations used in Δ and A. For example, the Łukasiewicz axioms for propositional logic in this notation are:

$$\varphi\, \psi : \mathsf{wff}; \cdot \vdash \varphi \rightarrow \psi \rightarrow \varphi$$
$$\varphi\, \psi\, \chi : \mathsf{wff}; \cdot \vdash (\varphi \rightarrow \psi \rightarrow \chi) \rightarrow (\varphi \rightarrow \psi) \rightarrow (\varphi \rightarrow \chi)$$
$$\varphi\, \psi : \mathsf{wff}; \cdot \vdash (\neg\varphi \rightarrow \neg\psi) \rightarrow (\psi \rightarrow \varphi)$$
$$\varphi\, \psi : \mathsf{wff}; \ \varphi \rightarrow \psi,\ \varphi \vdash \psi$$

Things get more interesting with the FOL axioms:

$$x : \mathsf{var}, \varphi\, \psi : \mathsf{wff}\, x; \cdot \vdash \forall x\, (\varphi \rightarrow \psi) \rightarrow (\forall x\, \varphi \rightarrow \forall x\, \psi)$$
$$x : \mathsf{var}, \varphi : \mathsf{wff}; \cdot \vdash \varphi \rightarrow \forall x\, \varphi$$

Notice that φ has type $\mathsf{wff}\, x$ in the first theorem and wff in the second, even though x appears in both statements. This indicates that in the first theorem φ may be substituted with an open term such as $x < 2$, while in the second theorem φ must not contain an occurrence of x (not even a bound occurrence).

Proofs and Convertibility. Metamath has only the first and third rules of Fig. 3: the hypothesis rule, and the application of a theorem after (direct) admissible substitution. Metamath Zero adds the second rule, which consists only of definition unfolding and compatibility rules.

The rule for $\mathsf{thm}\, (\Gamma; \overline{A} \vdash B)$ ok allows additional dummy variables $\overline{y : s'}$ to be used in the proof, as long as they do not appear in the statement ($\overline{A}$ and B must not mention $\overline{y}$). This in particular implies that all sorts are nonempty. (The free sort modifier allows us to relax this constraint; see [5].)

2.1   The .mm0 Specification Format[1]

The .mm0 file is responsible for explaining to the reader what the statement of each relevant theorem is. It closely resembles the axiomatic description of Sect. 2, but with a concrete syntax. The two FOL axioms above are rendered like so:

```
axiom all_mono {x: var} (P Q: wff x):
  $ A. x (P -> Q) -> A. x P -> A. x Q $;
axiom all_vacuous {x: var} (p: wff): $ p -> A. x p $;
```

assuming the sorts var, wff, the terms imp and all, and notations -> and A. for them have been previously declared.

As its name implies, the .mm0 specification file is only about specifying axioms and theorems, so it does not contain any proofs. Axioms and theorems look exactly the same except for the keyword used to introduce them. This is an unusual choice for a theorem prover, although some systems like Mizar and Isabelle support exporting an "abstract" of the development, with proofs omitted. We do this so that there is a clean separation between the trusted part (the statements of the theorems) and the verified part (the proofs of the theorems).

We can do something similar with definitions. A definition requires a definiens in Fig. 2, but we can instead write a definition with no definiens, so that it looks just like a term declaration. This allows us to assert *the existence* of a term constructor which satisfies any theorems that follow, which gives us a kind of abstraction. Sometimes it is easier to write down characteristic equations for a function rather than an explicit definition, especially in the case of recursive functions.

Once one is committed to not proving theorems in the specification file, it is able to shrink dramatically, because theorems never reference each other, and only reference terms and definitions involved in their statements. So if focus is given to one theorem, then almost everything else goes away, and even in extreme cases it becomes quite feasible to write down everything up to and including the axiomatic framework. For example, if we specify Fermat's last theorem, we must define the natural numbers and exponentiation in the specification file, but certainly not modular forms, which are properly the domain of the proof file.

Notation. The notation system was crafted so as to make parsing as simple as possible to implement, while still ensuring unambiguity, and allowing some simple infix and bracketing notations. Notations are enclosed in $ sentinels (as in LaTeX) so that parsing can be separated into a static part (containing the top level syntax of the language) and a dynamic part (containing user notations for mathematical operations that have been defined).

The dynamic parser is a precedence parser, with a numeric hierarchy of precedence levels $0, 1, 2, \ldots$ with an additional level max, forming the order $\mathbb{N} \cup \{\infty\}$. (max is the precedence of atoms and parenthesized expressions.) Infix constants are declared with a precedence, and left/right associativity.

---

[1] https://github.com/digama0/mm0/blob/master/mm0.md.

General notations are also permitted; these have an arbitrary sequence of constants and variables, and can be used to make composite notations like sum_ i < n ai as an approximation of $\sum_{i<n} a_i$. The only restriction on general notations to make them unambiguous is that they must begin with a unique constant, in this case sum_. This is restrictive, but usually one can get away with a subscript or similar disambiguating mark without significantly hampering readability. (This may be relaxed in higher level languages, but recall that we are still in the base of the bootstrap here, so every bit of simplicity matters.)

Coercions are functions from one sort to another that have no notation. For example, if we have a sort of set expressions and another sort of class expressions, we might register a coercion set → class so that $x \in y$ makes sense even if x and y are sets and $x \in A$ is a relation between a set and a class. For unambiguity, the verifier requires that the coercion graph have at most one path from any sort to any other. (This is quite limitative of the type system. The intent is for more complex typing schemes to be implemented through explicit typing proofs generated by a front-end with a more robust type system. The sorts here are more like syntactic classes than true types.)

3   The .mmb Binary Proof File[2]

Having a precise language for specifying formal statements is nice, but it is most powerful when coupled with a method for proving those formal statements. We have indicated several times now design decisions that were made for efficiency reasons. By spoon-feeding the verifier a very explicit proof, we end up doing a lot less computation, and by deduplicating and working directly with dag-like expressions at all stages, we can avoid all the exponential blowups that happen in unification. (As we will see in Sect. 4, the user does not have to write these proofs directly. It is expected that they are compiled from a more human-friendly input.) Using these techniques, we managed to translate set.mm into MM0 (see Sect. 5) and verify the resulting binary proof file in 195 ± 5 ms (Intel i7 3.9 GHz, single threaded). While set.mm is formidable, at 34 MB/590 kLOC, we are planning to scale up to larger or less optimized formal libraries to see if it is competitive even on more adversarial inputs.

The proof file is designed to be manipulated in situ; it does not need to be processed into memory structures, as it is already organized like one. It contains a header, the term and theorem tables, and the declaration stream, followed by debugging data.

The term table and theorem table contain the statements of all theorems and the types of all term constructors. These tables are consulted during typechecking, and the verifier uses a counter as a sliding window into the table to mark what part of the table has been verified (and thus is usable). This means that a term lookup is generally a single indexed memory access, usually in cache, which makes type checking for expressions extremely fast in practice.

---

[2] https://github.com/digama0/mm0/tree/master/mm0-c

After the term and theorem tables is the declaration stream, which validates each declaration in the .mm0 file, possibly interspersed with additional definitions and theorems. This data is processed in a single pass, and contains in particular proofs of theorems. A proof stream is a sequence of opcodes (see [5] for the full grammar) with associated data. Each instruction changes the state of the verifier, roughly in one-to-one correspondence with the proof rules in Fig. 3, and at the end the verifier should have a state indicating that the desired theorem has been proven.

During a proof, the verifier state consists of a store (a write-once memory arena that is cleared after each proof) which builds up pointer data structures for constructed expressions, a heap H, and a stack S. A stack element can be either an expression e or a proof $\vdash A$, both of which are simply pointers into the store where the relevant expression is stored. (There are also stack elements corresponding to convertibility proofs, which we will not discuss.)

At the beginning of a proof, the heap is initialized with expressions for all the variables. An opcode like Term f will pop n elements $\bar{e}$ from the stack, and push $f\ \bar{e}$, while Ref i will push $H[i]$ to the stack. The verifier is arranged such that an expression is always accessed via backreference if it is required more than once, so equality testing is always $O(1)$.

The opcode Thm T pops $\bar{e}$ from the stack (the number of variables in the theorem), pops B' from the stack (the substituted conclusion of the theorem), then calls a *unifier* for T, stored in the theorem table for T, which is another sequence of opcodes. This will pop some number of additional $\vdash A'$ assumptions from the stack, and then $\vdash B'$ is pushed on the stack.

The unifier is responsible for deconstructing B' and proving that $B[\Gamma \mapsto \bar{e}] = B'$, where B and Γ are fixed from the definition of T, and $\bar{e}$ and B' are provided by the theorem application. It has its own stack K and heap U; the unify heap is the incoming substitution, and the unify stack is the list of unification obligations. For example URef i pops e from the stack and checks that $U[i] = e$, while UTerm f pops an expression e from the unify stack, checks that $e = f\ \bar{e'}$, and then pushes $\bar{e'}$ on the stack (in reverse order). The appropriate list of opcodes can be easily constructed for a given expression by reading the term in prefix order, with UTerm at each term constructor and URef for variables. The UHyp instruction pops $\vdash A'$ from the main stack S and pushes A' to the unify stack K; this is how the theorem signals that it needs a hypothesis.

The handling of memory is interesting in that all allocations are controlled by the compiler in the sense that they happen only on Term f and Dummy s steps (Dummy s puts a new variable on the heap and stack). There is no "auto-allocation" during substitution because unification only deconstructs expressions, it does not create new ones. This means that the compiler can preprocess the proof to ensure that every equality test is a pointer equality, by only constructing the term on first use and referring back to it on subsequent uses. So the verifier can assume that the compiler has already done so and reject files that aren't prepared in this way, achieving the aforementioned $O(1)$ comparison.

Verification is not quite linear time, because each Thm T instruction causes the verifier to read the unifier for T, which may be large if T has a long statement. It is $O(mn)$ where n is the length of the proof and m is the length of the longest theorem statement. In practice this is essentially linear time, because it is rare to have theorems with long statements, and even rarer to use them so many times in a single proof.

One may think that the compilation process for such an intricately prepared proof would be difficult, but assuming that proof trees are stored as tree data structures in the usual way, the process is essentially hash-consing to deduplicate the tree, followed by a postorder traversal of the proof to produce the proof stream and a preorder traversal of the statement to produce the unify stream for the theorem. (See [5] for an example.)

4   The .mm1 Proof Authoring File[3]

In order to make the MM0 pipeline useful, we need a way to produce formal proofs, and that means a front end to complement the MM0 back end. The MM1 language has a syntax which is mostly an extension of MM0 which allows providing proofs of theorems. There are currently two MM1 compilers, mm0-hs written in Haskell and mm0-rs written in Rust, both of which provide verification, parsing and translation for all the MM0 family languages (the three formats mentioned in this paper, plus some debugging formats), compilation of MM1 files to MMB, and a server compliant with the Language Server Protocol to provide editing support (syntax highlighting, live diagnostics, go-to-definition, hovers, etc.) for Visual Studio Code, extensible to other editors in the future.

For the bootstrapping project, we used MM0 to specify (a conservative extension of) first order Peano Arithmetic (PA), and within this axiomatic system we defined the x86 instruction set architecture [6] and the MM0 formal system as defined in Sect. 2.1, to obtain an end-to-end specification from input strings, through lexing, parsing, specification well-formedness, type checking, and proof checking, relating it to the operation of an ELF binary file.

The PA formalization[4] contains about 1000 theorems and is written in MM1. Some of it is ported from set.mm, particularly in propositional logic and FOL, but PA has not otherwise been worked out in Metamath before. It goes as far as the construction of finite set theory and inductive types, needed for doing the requisite metamathematics. But it is enough to get the sense of the scalability of the approach. After compilation, verification takes 2 ± 0.05 ms using mm0-c, which makes sense since it is only a small fraction of the size of set.mm. Compilation is also quite competitive, at 306 ± 4 ms using mm0-rs. Based on the current proof sketch, we don't anticipate the x86 verification part to be more than 100 times larger than this project (and that's a generous bound – a more accurate estimate is about 8–20 times the size of **peano.mm1**), except possibly the compiler execution itself, which can skip the MM1 interface and produce

---

[3] https://github.com/digama0/mm0/tree/master/mm0-c.
[4] https://github.com/digama0/mm0/blob/master/examples/peano.mm1.

.mmb directly. (Note that tactics can make this number much less favorable, depending on how complex and expensive they are. Our aim is to get a compiler roughly comparable to a simple unoptimizing C compiler, so that execution time is reasonable even with proof production.)

Here we see an important reason for speed: the faster the server can read and execute the file, the faster the response time to live features like diagnostics that the user is relying on for making progress through the proof. The MM1 language also contains a Turing-complete meta-programming language based on Scheme. It is intended for writing small "tactics" that construct proofs. Besides a few small quality-of-life improvements, we used it to implement a general algorithm for proving congruence lemmas (theorems of the form $A = B \rightarrow f(A) = f(B)$) for all new definitions.

Support for multi-file developments is as yet nascent, but it is worth mentioning that besides other .mm1 files, an .mm1 file can import "compiled" .mmb files (from an .mm1 source or even generated from another source, such as a large scale tactic), which provides a way to isolate components and only compile as needed. It is possible to do much more in this direction, but the need is not pressing as end-to-end compiles are fast enough for interactive use.

While MM1 has a long way to go to compete with heavyweights in the theorem proving world like Coq, Isabelle, or Lean, we believe this to be an effective demonstration that even a parsimonious language like Metamath or MM0 can be used as the backend to a theorem prover, and "all" that is necessary is a bit of UI support to add features like a type system, a tactic language, unification, and inference.

5   MM0 as an Interchange Format

MM0 is a *logical framework* in the sense that it doesn't prescribe any particular axioms or semantics. This makes it well suited for translations to and from other systems. A downside of this approach is that while correctness is well defined, *soundness* is not, absent a fixed foundation. Instead, one gets several soundness theorems depending on what axioms are chosen and what semantics is targeted.

However, proof translation can function as a substitute for a soundness proof, and indeed, a proof translation amounts to building a class model of the source system in the target system. To that end, we have developed a translation from Metamath to MM0, as well as from MM0 to HOL-like systems. The latter can be used to give a proof of soundness relative to HOL, although each MM0 axiom produces an axiom on the HOL side and these must be manually inspected and either accepted or proven from HOL axioms.

The Haskell verifier mm0-hs contains a from-mm subcommand that will convert Metamath proofs to MM0. We used this tool to create the MM0 version of set.mm, and this has been very helpful for performance testing, although we are not using set.mm0 for the bootstrapping theorem. Translation is mostly cosmetic, but variable handling is a bit different so some theorems have to be duplicated as part of the "unbundling" transformation that is required to translate Metamath theorems into FOL-like systems. (See [5].)

The `to-hol` subcommand translates MM0 into a subset of HOL. A metavariable $\varphi : s\,\overline{x}$ becomes an n-ary variable $\varphi : s_1 \to \ldots \to s_n \to s$, where $x_i : s_i$, and all occurrences of φ in statements are replaced by $\varphi\,\overline{x}$. All hypotheses and the conclusion, are universally closed over the names, and the entire implication from hypotheses to conclusion is universally quantified over the metavariables. For example, the MM0 statement $x : \mathsf{var}, \varphi : \mathsf{wff}\,x;\;\; \varphi \vdash \mathsf{all}\,x\,\varphi$ becomes

$$\forall \varphi : \mathsf{var} \to \mathsf{wff},\; (\forall x : \mathsf{var}, \vdash \varphi\,x) \Rightarrow\; \vdash \mathsf{all}\,(\lambda x : \mathsf{var},\; \varphi\,x).$$

The actual output of `mm0-hs to-hol` is a bespoke intermediate language (although it has a typechecker), which is used as a stepping-off point to OpenTheory and Lean. One of the nice side effects of this work was that Metamath theorems in `set.mm` finally became available to other theorem provers. We demonstrate the utility of this translation by proving Dirichlet's theorem in Lean[5], using the number theory library in Metamath for the bulk of the proof and post-processing the statement so that it is expressed in idiomatic Lean style. The raw translation produces a proof in Lean of the Metamath library relative to the axioms of ZFC, which are then manually replaced with a proof of those axioms relative to Lean's standard axioms (note that Lean has higher consistency strength than ZFC), so the final statement as good as a regular Lean theorem.

6   Bootstrapping

There are a few components that go into bootstrapping a theorem prover. In short, what we want to do is prove a theorem of the form $\vdash$ 'mm0.exe is a piece of machine code that when executed given input E, terminates with exit code 0 only if E env'. In order to even write this statement down, we need:

1. The definition of E env, that is, the formalization of Sect. 2.
2. The definition of `mm0.exe`, that is, a compiled executable artifact that can act as a verifier in the manner of `mm0-c`.
3. The definition of executing a piece of machine code, which requires the formalization of the semantics of the target architecture, in this case x86-64 Linux. (It's not actually a `.exe` file, it is an ELF file.)

We have done part 1 in mm0.mm0[6] and part 3 in x86.mm0[7]. These parts are brought together into x86_mm0.mm0[8], containing the short final theorem. We use def Verifier: string; to declare an abstract definition of the verifier code itself (part 2), assert that it parses to a valid ELF file `VerifierElf`, and then the main theorems to prove are:

---

[5] https://github.com/digama0/mm0/blob/master/mm0-lean/mm0/set/post.lean.
[6] https://github.com/digama0/mm0/blob/master/examples/mm0.mm0.
[7] https://github.com/digama0/mm0/blob/master/examples/x86.mm0.
[8] https://github.com/digama0/mm0/blob/master/examples/x86_mm0.mm0.

```
theorem Verifier_terminates (k s: nat):
  $ initialConfig VerifierElf k -> alwaysTerminates k s 0 $;
theorem Verifier_Valid (k s: nat):
  $ initialConfig VerifierElf k /\ succeeds k s 0 -> Valid s $;
```

which assert that if the operating system loads `VerifierElf` into memory, resulting in initial state k, then on any input s, the program always terminates with no output (this is a bare verifier, which only produces success as an exit code), and if it succeeds, then s is `Valid`, meaning that it parses as a MM0 file which is well formed, and all the theorems in the file are provable.

This is a statement, but the proof is ongoing. [5] contains a discussion of the design of the proof, which requires writing a proof producing compiler.

7 Related Work

The idea of a bootstrapping theorem prover is not new. There are a number of notable projects in this space, many of which have influenced the design of MM0. However, none of these projects seem to have recognized (in words or actions) the value of parsimony, specifically as it relates to bootstrapping.

At its heart, a theorem prover that proves it is correct is a type of circular proof. While a proof of correctness can significantly amplify our confidence that we haven't missed any bugs, we must eventually turn to other methods to ground the argument, and direct inspection is always the fallback. But the effectiveness of direct inspection is inversely proportional to the size of the artifact, so the only way to make a bootstrap argument more airtight is to make it smaller.

The most closely related projects, in terms of bootstrapping a theorem prover down to machine code, are CakeML and Milawa.

- CakeML [15] is a compiler for ML that is written in the logic of HOL4 [23], and HOL4 is a theorem prover written in ML. Unfortunately, the ML that CakeML supports is not sufficient for HOL4, and while a simpler kernel, called Candle, has been implemented in CakeML, it supports a variant of HOL Light, not HOL4.
- Milawa [8] is a theorem prover based on ACL2, which has a sequence of verifiers $A_i \vdash A_{i+1}$ with $A_{12} \vdash$ 'A_0 is correct'. This project was later extended by Magnus Myreen to *Jitawa* [20], a Lisp runtime that was verified in HOL4 down to the machine code and can run Milawa.

There are a few other projects that have done bootstraps at the logic level:

- "Coq in Coq" (1996) [2] is a formalization of Calculus of Constructions and a typechecker thereof in Coq. Unfortunately, this lacks inductive types, so it fails to "close the loop" of the bootstrap.
- "Towards self-verification of HOL Light" (2006) [11] writes down a translation of the HOL Light kernel (written in OCaml) in HOL Light, and proves soundness given additional axioms. This leaves off verification of OCaml (in fact OCaml is known to break soundness), and the translation from OCaml code to HOL Light definitions is unverified and slightly nontrivial in places.

– "Coq Coq Correct!" (2019) [24] improves on "Coq in Coq" by verifying a typechecker for PCUIC, which is a much closer approximation to Coq, and expressive enough to contain the formalization itself. Sadly, the typechecker is not fast enough in practice to be able to typecheck its own formalization.

The MM0 project draws from ideas in a number of fields, most of which have long histories and many contributors.

– Code extraction [10,17] is a popular way to get verified binaries; however, as argued in [14], we believe that this leaves large gaps in the verified part.
– ISA specification: [7] is a complete formal specification of Intel x86-64 in the K framework [21]; Sail [1] is a language specifically for specifying ISAs. Our x86.mm0 specification is based on a port of the Sail x86 spec. Centaur [9] is using an x86 specification to build a provably correct chip design.
– Machine code verification using separation logic [19]
– Verified compilers such as CompCert [16] and CakeML [15]
– VST [4], a tool for proving correctness of C programs in Coq
– RustBelt [12] is a project to prove soundness of the Rust type system using Iris [13], a higher order concurrent separation logic.

8   Conclusion

Metamath Zero is a theorem prover built to solve the problem of bootstrapping trust into a system. It is general purpose, so it can support all common formal systems (ZFC, HOL, DTT, PA, really anything recursively enumerable). It is extremely fast, at least on hand-written inputs like `set.mm`, and is built to handle computer-science-sized problems.

Although the correctness theorem for MM0 is still ongoing, we believe there is value added in clearly delineating the necessary components for a system that pushes the boundaries of formal verification to cover as much as possible, so that we can have programs that are both fast and correct.

We hope to see a future where all the major theorem provers are either proven correct or can export their proofs to systems that are proven correct, so that when we verify our most important software, we bequeath the highest level of confidence we are capable of providing. It's not an impossible dream—the technology is in our hands; we need only define the problem, and solve it.

Acknowledgments. I would like to thank Norman Megill for writing Metamath, and André Bacci, Wolf Lammen, David A. Wheeler, Giovanni Mascellani, Seul Baek, and Jeremy Avigad for their input and suggestions during the design phase of MM0. I thank Jeremy Avigad, Jesse Han, Benoît Jubin, and the anonymous reviewers for their reviews of early versions of this work.

This work was supported in part by AFOSR grant FA9550-18-1-0120 and a grant from the Sloan Foundation.

References

1. Armstrong, A., et al.: ISA semantics for ARMv8-A, RISC-V, and CHERI-MIPS. In: Proceedings of 46th ACM SIGPLAN Symposium on Principles of Programming Languages, January 2019. https://doi.org/10.1145/3290384. Proc. ACM Program. Lang. **3**(POPL), Article 71

2. Barras, B.: Coq en coq (1996)

3. Berghofer, S., Nipkow, T.: Proof terms for simply typed higher order logic. In: Aagaard, M., Harrison, J. (eds.) TPHOLs 2000. LNCS, vol. 1869, pp. 38–52. Springer, Heidelberg (2000). https://doi.org/10.1007/3-540-44659-1_3

4. Cao, Q., Beringer, L., Gruetter, S., Dodds, J., Appel, A.W.: VST-FLOYD: a separation logic tool to verify correctness of C programs. J. Autom. Reason. **61**(1–4), 367–422 (2018)

5. Carneiro, M.: Metamath Zero: The Cartesian Theorem Prover (2019, preprint)

6. Carneiro, M.: Specifying verified x86 software from scratch. In: Workshop on Instruction Set Architecture Specification (SpISA 2019) (2019). https://www.cl.cam.ac.uk/~jrh13/spisa19/paper_07.pdf

7. Dasgupta, S., Park, D., Kasampalis, T., Adve, V.S., Roşu, G.: A complete formal semantics of x86-64 user-level instruction set architecture. In: Proceedings of the 40th ACM SIGPLAN Conference on Programming Language Design and Implementation (PLDI 2019), pp. 1133–1148. ACM, June 2019. https://doi.org/10.1145/3314221.3314601

8. Davis, J.C., Moore, J.S.: A self-verifying theorem prover. Ph.D. thesis, University of Texas (2009)

9. Goel, S., Slobodova, A., Sumners, R., Swords, S.: Verifying x86 instruction implementations. In: Proceedings of the 9th ACM SIGPLAN International Conference on Certified Programs and Proofs, pp. 47–60 (2020)

10. Haftmann, F.: Code generation from Isabelle/HOL theories

11. Harrison, J.: Towards self-verification of HOL light. In: Furbach, U., Shankar, N. (eds.) IJCAR 2006. LNCS (LNAI), vol. 4130, pp. 177–191. Springer, Heidelberg (2006). https://doi.org/10.1007/11814771_17

12. Jung, R., Jourdan, J.H., Krebbers, R., Dreyer, D.: Rustbelt: securing the foundations of the rust programming language. Proc. ACM Program. Lang. **2**(POPL), 1–34 (2017)

13. Jung, R., Krebbers, R., Jourdan, J.H., Bizjak, A., Birkedal, L., Dreyer, D.: Iris from the ground up: a modular foundation for higher-order concurrent separation logic. J. Funct. Program. **28** (2018)

14. Kumar, R., Mullen, E., Tatlock, Z., Myreen, M.O.: Software verification with ITPs should use binary code extraction to reduce the TCB. In: Avigad, J., Mahboubi, A. (eds.) ITP 2018. LNCS, vol. 10895, pp. 362–369. Springer, Cham (2018). https://doi.org/10.1007/978-3-319-94821-8_21

15. Kumar, R., Myreen, M.O., Norrish, M., Owens, S.: CakeML: a verified implementation of ML. SIGPLAN Not. **49**(1), 179–191 (2014). https://doi.org/10.1145/2578855.2535841

16. Leroy, X., et al.: The compcert verified compiler. Documentation and user's manual. INRIA Paris-Rocquencourt 53 (2012)

17. Letouzey, P.: Extraction in Coq: an overview. In: Beckmann, A., Dimitracopoulos, C., Löwe, B. (eds.) CiE 2008. LNCS, vol. 5028, pp. 359–369. Springer, Heidelberg (2008). https://doi.org/10.1007/978-3-540-69407-6_39

18. Megill, N., Wheeler, D.A.: Metamath: A Computer Language for Mathematical Proofs. Lulu Press, Morrisville (2019)
19. Myreen, M.O.: Formal verification of machine-code programs. Technical report, University of Cambridge, Computer Laboratory (2009)
20. Myreen, M.O., Davis, J.: A verified runtime for a verified theorem prover. In: van Eekelen, M., Geuvers, H., Schmaltz, J., Wiedijk, F. (eds.) ITP 2011. LNCS, vol. 6898, pp. 265–280. Springer, Heidelberg (2011). https://doi.org/10.1007/978-3-642-22863-6_20
21. Roşu, G., Şerbănuţă, T.F.: An overview of the K semantic framework. J. Logic Algebraic Program. **79**(6), 397–434 (2010). https://doi.org/10.1016/j.jlap.2010.03.012
22. Sacerdoti Coen, C.: A plugin to export Coq libraries to XML. In: Kaliszyk, C., Brady, E., Kohlhase, A., Sacerdoti Coen, C. (eds.) CICM 2019. LNCS (LNAI), vol. 11617, pp. 243–257. Springer, Cham (2019). https://doi.org/10.1007/978-3-030-23250-4_17
23. Slind, K., Norrish, M.: A brief overview of HOL4. In: Mohamed, O.A., Muñoz, C., Tahar, S. (eds.) TPHOLs 2008. LNCS, vol. 5170, pp. 28–32. Springer, Heidelberg (2008). https://doi.org/10.1007/978-3-540-71067-7_6
24. Sozeau, M., Forster, Y., Winterhalter, T.: Coq Coq correct!

Adding an Abstraction Barrier to ZF Set Theory

Ciarán Dunne$^{(\boxtimes)}$, J. B. Wells, and Fairouz Kamareddine

Heriot-Watt University, Edinburgh, Scotland
cmd11@hw.ac.uk

Abstract. Much mathematical writing exists that is, explicitly or implicitly, based on set theory, often Zermelo-Fraenkel set theory (ZF) or one of its variants. In ZF, the domain of discourse contains only sets, and hence every mathematical object must be a set. Consequently, in ZF with the usual encoding of an ordered pair $\langle a, b \rangle$, formulas like $\{a\} \in \langle a, b \rangle$ have truth values, and operations like $\mathcal{P}(\langle a, b \rangle)$ have results that are sets. Such 'accidental theorems' do not match how people think about the mathematics and also cause practical difficulties when using set theory in machine-assisted theorem proving. In contrast, in a number of proof assistants, mathematical objects and concepts can be built of type-theoretic stuff so that many mathematical objects can be, in essence, terms of an extended typed λ-calculus. However, dilemmas and frustration arise when formalizing mathematics in type theory.

Motivated by problems of formalizing mathematics with (1) purely set-theoretic and (2) type-theoretic approaches, we explore an option with much of the flexibility of set theory and some of the useful features of type theory. We present ZFP: a modification of ZF that has ordered pairs as primitive, non-set objects. ZFP has a more natural and abstract axiomatic definition of ordered pairs free of any notion of representation. This paper presents axioms for ZFP, and a proof in ZF (machine-checked in Isabelle/ZF) of the existence of a model for ZFP, which implies that ZFP is consistent if ZF is. We discuss the approach used to add this abstraction barrier to ZF.

Keywords: Set theory · Formalisation of mathematics · Theorem proving

1 Introduction

1.1 Background: Set Theory and Type Theory as Foundations

A large portion of the mathematical literature is based on set theory, explicitly or implicitly, directly or indirectly. Set theory is pervasive in mathematical culture. University mathematics programmes have introductory courses on set theory and many other courses that rely heavily on set-theoretic concepts (sets, classes, etc.), notation (comprehensions a.k.a. set-builders, power set, etc.), and reasoning.

© Springer Nature Switzerland AG 2020
C. Benzmüller and B. Miller (Eds.): CICM 2020, LNAI 12236, pp. 89–104, 2020.
https://doi.org/10.1007/978-3-030-53518-6_6

Formal foundations for mathematics have been developed since the early 20th century, with both set-theoretic and type-theoretic approaches being considered. Although there are a number of set-theoretic foundations, for this paper it is sufficient to consider Zermelo-Fraenkel set theory (ZF), which anyway seems to be broadly accepted and reasonably representative of the strengths and weaknesses of set theory in actual practice. The core concept of ZF is the *set membership relation* ∈, which acts on a domain of objects called *sets*. The theory is a collection of formulas (known as *axioms*) of first-order logic which characterise the membership relation. Logical deduction from these axioms yields a rich theory of sets. Moreover, mathematical objects such as ordered pairs, functions, and numbers can be represented as sets in ZF.

At roughly the same time as Zermelo was formulating his axiomatic set theory, Russell introduced the first type theory. Both Zermelo and Russell had the goal of rigorous, formal, logical reasoning free from the paradoxes that plagued the earlier systems of Cantor and Frege. Most modern type theories are descendants of Church's typed λ-calculus [9]. Many of the methods of modern type theory have been developed by computer scientists to solve problems in programming languages and formal verification. Types add layers of reasoning that help with soundness and representation independence. Some type theories have been used to formulate foundations of mathematics in which mathematical objects (e.g., groups, rings, etc.) are represented by terms and types of what is essentially a very fancy typed λ-calculus.

Formalizing mathematics that has been developed in a set-theoretic culture using a type-theoretic foundation can lead to dilemmas and frustration [6]. Subtyping may not work smoothly when formalising chains of structures such as the number systems and those belonging to universal algebra. There are also design choices in how to model predicates which can make proving some things easier but other things much harder. The rules of powerful type systems are also very complicated, so users require machine assistance to follow the typing rules, and even with machine support it can be quite challenging. In contrast, ZF-like set theories typically have very few 'types', e.g., there might be a type of sets and a type of logical formulas or perhaps a type of classes. When nearly every mathematical object you need is of 'type set' it is easy to obey the typing rules.

There are problems formalizing mathematics in pure ZF set theory also. When everything is of 'type set', a computer proof system has no easy way to know that it would be wasting its time to try to prove a theorem about ordinal numbers using lemmas and tactics for groups or rings, so automated support is more challenging. When representing mathematical objects (e.g., numbers) as sets, the bookkeeping of the intended 'type' of these objects is not avoided, but must be managed by the user outside the realm of a type system. In many not-too-tricky cases, a type inference algorithm can automatically infer type information that represents necessary preconditions for successful use of theorems and lemmas, but in pure set theory such automated inference is not very useful when the only type is 'set'.

Furthermore, practical computerisation in ZF requires abbreviation and definition mechanisms which first-order logic does not provide. Two contrasting examples of how this can be done are Metamath and Isabelle/ZF. Metamath [10] is mostly string based, and has 'syntax definitions' to introduce new constants, or syntax patterns. These definitions are given meaning by 'defining axioms' (whose correctness is not checked by the verifier). Isabelle/ZF is built on top of Isabelle/Pure, which is a fragment of intuitionistic higher-order logic that is based on Church's typed λ-calculus [11]. This means that meta-level activities such as variable binding, definitions, and abbreviations are handled by Isabelle/ZF in a type theory, albeit a very simple type theory. Isabelle also handles proof tactics in SML, which can be seen as another typed λ-calculus.

1.2   The Issue of Representation and the Case of the Ordered Pair

As discussed above, set theory can represent a multitude of mathematical objects as sets, but in some cases the user might prefer that some of their mathematical objects are genuinely not sets. The alternative of using a sophisticated type-theoretic foundation might not be the right solution, for a variety of reasons, some of which are mentioned above. So the user might ask: "May I please have a set theory which has genuine non-sets that I can use for purpose XYZ?"

There are indeed set theories with non-set objects [7], which are generally known as *urelements*, so named because they are often considered to be primordial, existing independently of and before the sets. A popular use for urelements is as 'atoms' whose only properties are being distinct from everything else and existing in large enough multitudes. Adding genuine non-sets takes some work, because the assumption that 'everything is a set' is deeply embedded in ZF's axioms. One example is the axiom of Extensionality,

$$\forall x, y : (\forall a : a \in x \leftrightarrow a \in y) \rightarrow x = y$$

which asserts that any two objects are equal if they have exactly the same set members. Because non-set objects of course have no set members, this ZF axiom forces them all to equal the empty set, meaning there can not be any.

Existing set theories with urelements generally (except see GST below) do not consider urelements with 'internal' structure that might include sets. The *ordered pair* is a simple and important example of a mathematical object with 'internal' structure which is not usually intended to be viewed as a set. Ordered pairs have been of enormous value in building theories of relations, functions, and spaces. The most widely used set-theoretical definition, by Kuratowski, defines the ordered pair $\langle a, b \rangle$ to be the set $\{\{a\}, \{a, b\}\}$. Because a is in all sets in $\langle a, b \rangle$ and b is only in one, a first-order logic formula using only the membership relation can check if an object is the first (or second) projection of an ordered pair. Kuratowski pairs satisfy the characteristic property of ordered pairs:

$$\langle a, b \rangle = \langle c, d \rangle \leftrightarrow (a = c \wedge b = d)$$

Like for any ZF representation of mathematical objects not thought of as sets, Kuratowski pairs have 'accidental theorems' such as $\{b\} \in \langle b, c \rangle$, and $\{\langle b, b \rangle\} = \{\{\{b\}\}\} = \langle \{b\}, \{b\} \rangle$, and $\{\langle 0, 0 \rangle\} = \langle 1, 1 \rangle$ with Von Neumann numbers.

The set representation of conceptually non-set objects raises issues. There are places in the literature where some mathematical objects are thought of as (or even explicitly stated to be) non-sets with no set members. One can find definitions or proofs by cases on 'type' that assume the case of sets never overlaps with the cases of pairs, numbers, etc. To view such writing as being founded on pure set theory requires either proving that none of the sets used overlap with the set representations used for abstract objects or inserting many tagging and tag-checking operations (see, e.g., the translation we give in Definition 4.7 as part of proving a model for our system ZFP can be built in the pure set theory ZF). When formalizing and machine-checking mathematics, additional difficulties arise, some of which are mentioned above.

1.3   ZFP: Extending ZF Set Theory with Primitive Ordered Pairs

We aim to go beyond previous set theories with urelements to develop methods for extending set theories with genuine non-set objects whose internal structure can contain other objects including the possibility of sets. As a first instance of this aim, we achieve the objective of ZFP, a set theory with primitive non-set ordered pairs such that there is no limit on the 'types' of objects that sets and ordered pairs may contain. We axiomatise ZFP and prove its consistency relative to ZF. We hope that our explanation of how we did this will be useful guidance for other work extending set theories.

ZFP extends $\in$ with two new binary predicate symbols, π_1 and π_2, whose intended meanings are 'is first projection of' and 'is second projection of'. We define abbreviations for formulas $\mathsf{Set}(x)$ and $\mathsf{Pair}(x)$ that distinguish sets and ordered pairs by the rule that an ordered pair has a first projection and a set does not. ZFP's axioms are in two groups, one for sets and one for ordered pairs. We were able to generate nearly all of ZFP's axioms for sets by modifying the axioms of ZF by restricting quantifiers using $\mathsf{Set}(x)$ in the right places. The axiom of Foundation needed to be modified to handle sets and ordered pairs simultaneously. ZFP's axioms for ordered pairs specify the expected abstract properties, including that ordered pairs have no set members.

To prove ZFP is consistent if ZF is, we construct in ZF a model and prove it satisfies ZFP's axioms [4]. Building a model for a set theory with non-set objects with 'internal' structure that can include sets differs from building a model for a set theory with no urelements or with only simple urelements, because there can be new non-set objects at each stage of the construction. $\mathbf{W}$, the domain of our model, is similar to the domain $\mathbf{V}$ of the Von Neumann hierarchy. Each tier of $\mathbf{V}$ is constructed by taking the power set of the previous tiers. In contrast, when building the tiers of $\mathbf{W}$, each successor tier $W_{\alpha+}$ is formed by taking the disjoint sum of the power set $\mathcal{P}(W_\alpha)$ and the cartesian product $(W_\alpha)^2$. Hence every object in $\mathbf{W}$ has a tag that tells whether it is intended to model a set or an ordered pair. This supports defining relations that model ZFP's $\in$, π_1, and π_2

which may only return true when their second argument is of the correct 'type'. This proof has been machine-checked in Isabelle/ZF.[1]

Although our model for ZFP is built purely of sets and implements ordered pairs as sets, another model could use other methods (e.g., type-theoretic) and implement ordered pairs differently. Hence, we have put an 'abstraction barrier' between the user of ZFP and the implementation of ordered pairs.

1.4 Related Work

Harrison [6] details the challenges that face both type-theoretic and set-theoretic foundations for formalised mathematics. Harrison makes the case for using set theory as 'machine code', leaving theorem proving to layers of code. Harrison suggests using a set theory with urelements to avoid the issue of 'accidental theorems'. Weidijk [13] formulates axiomatic set theories and type theories in AutoMath in order to compare them and assess their relative complexity.

A significant work aiming to make computer formalisation of set-theoretical mathematics practical is Farmer's Chiron [5], a conservative extension of the set theory NBG (itself a conservative extension of ZF). Chiron has additional features such as support for undefinedness, definite descriptions, quotation and evaluation of expressions, and a kind of types.

Aczel and Lunnon worked on Generalised Set Theory (GST) [1] with the aim of better supporting work in situation theory. GST extends set theory with a mechanism for primitive functions, as well as a number of other features. It appears that GST assumes the Anti-Foundation axiom instead of Foundation which ZF uses. Unfortunately, we failed to find a specification of the axioms of GST. Part of GST seems similar to our work but a technical comparison is difficult without the axioms.

Although ordered pairs now seem obvious, Kanamori's excellent history [8] shows a sequence of conceptual breakthroughs were needed to reach the modern ordered pair. How we built a model for ZFP was heavily inspired by the way Barwise [2] interprets KPU (Kripke-Platek set theory with Urelements) in KP.

1.5 Outline

Section 2 presents and discusses the first-order logic we use and definitions and axioms of ZF. Section 3 presents and discusses ZFP in the form of definitions and two collections of axioms, one for sets, and one for ordered pairs. Section 4 proves the existence in ZF of a model for the axioms of ZFP (which implies that ZFP is consistent if ZF is). Section 5 discusses the significance of these results, and how they will be used in further investigation.

2 Formal Machinery

Let $X := Y$ be meta-level notation meaning that X stands for Y.

---

[1] See http://www.macs.hw.ac.uk/~cmd1/cicm2020/ZFP.thy for the source, and http://www.macs.hw.ac.uk/~cmd1/cicm2020/ZFPDoc/index.html for the HTML.

2.1 First-Order Logic with Equality

We use a fragment of first-order logic (FOL) with equality sufficient for defining ZF and ZFP. We consider only four binary infix *predicate symbols* including equality. The MBNF [12] specification of the syntax is:

$$a, \dots, z \doteq \mathsf{Var} ::= \mathsf{v0} \mid \mathsf{v1} \mid \cdots \qquad \sim \,\doteq\, \mathsf{Pred} ::= \,\in\, \mid \pi_1 \mid \pi_2 \mid\, =$$
$$A, \dots, Z \doteq \mathsf{Term} ::= x \mid \imath x : \varphi \qquad \varphi, \psi \doteq \mathsf{Form} ::= X \sim Y \mid \varphi \to \psi \mid \neg\varphi \mid \forall x : \varphi$$

We work with terms and formulas modulo α-conversion where $\forall x$ and $\imath x$ bind x. Except where explicitly specified otherwise, we require metavariables ranging over the set Var to have the attribute of *distinctness*. Two different metavariables with the distinctness attribute can not be equal. For example, $x = \mathsf{v9}$ and $x_1 = \mathsf{v27}$ and $y = \mathsf{v53}$ could hold simultaneously, but neither $x = \mathsf{v9} = x_1$ nor $x = \mathsf{v53} = y$ are allowed. This restriction applies only to metavariables: the same object-level variable can be used in nested scopes, e.g., the formula $(\forall \mathsf{v7} : \forall \mathsf{v7} : \mathsf{v7} \in \mathsf{v7})$ is fine and equal to $(\forall \mathsf{v0} : \forall \mathsf{v1} : \mathsf{v1} \in \mathsf{v1})$. We assume the usual abbreviations for logical connectives ($\wedge, \vee, \leftrightarrow$), for quantifiers ($\exists, \exists!$, $\forall x_1, \dots, x_n, \exists x_1, \dots, x_n$), and for predicate symbols ($\neq, \notin, \ni$).

A term can be a *definite description* ($\imath x : \varphi$) which, if there is exactly one member x of the domain of discourse such that the formula φ is true, evaluates to that member and otherwise evaluates to a special value $\bot$ outside the domain of discourse such that any predicate symbol (including equality) with $\bot$ as an argument evaluates to false.[2] A term is said to be *undefined* or to *have no value* iff it evaluates to $\bot$. An alternative specification of definite descriptions that gives formulas the same meanings is eliminating them by the following rule (only the left case is given; the right case is similar):

$$((\imath x : \varphi) \sim Y) := (\exists x : x \sim Y \wedge \varphi) \wedge \exists! x : \varphi \text{ where } x \text{ is not free in } Y$$

2.2 Zermelo-Fraenkel Set Theory

The only predicate symbols ZF uses are the *membership relation* $\in$ and equality. ZF makes no use of the FOL predicate symbols π_1 and π_2, but instead we define these symbols as parts of abbreviations in Sect. 2.3. We use the following abbreviations where $n \geq 3$ and a, c, x, y, and z are not free in the other arguments and b is not free in X:

$$(\forall b \in X : \varphi) := (\forall b : b \in X \to \varphi) \qquad\qquad (\exists b \in X : \varphi) := (\exists b : b \in X \wedge \varphi)$$
$$\cup X := (\imath y : \forall a : a \in y \leftrightarrow \exists z \in X : a \in z) \qquad X \subseteq Y := (\forall c \in X : c \in Y)$$
$$\{A, B\} := (\imath x : \forall c : c \in x \leftrightarrow (c = A \vee c = B)) \quad X \cup Y := \cup\{X, Y\}$$
$$\mathcal{P}(X) := (\imath y : \forall z : z \in y \leftrightarrow z \subseteq X) \qquad\qquad \{A\} := \{A, A\}$$
$$\{A_1, \dots, A_n\} := \{A_1\} \cup \{A_2, \dots, A_n\} \qquad\qquad \emptyset := (\imath x : \forall a : a \notin x)$$
$$\{b \in X \mid \varphi\} := (\imath y : \forall b : b \in y \leftrightarrow (b \in X \wedge \varphi)) \quad X^+ := X \cup \{X\}$$

These abbreviations are defined if their arguments are defined due to the axioms.

---

[2] When working with functions that might be applied outside their domain, one might prefer to have $\bot = \bot$, but this is a bit more complex and not needed for this paper.

Definition 2.1. *The axioms of ZF are all the instances of the following formulas for every formula φ with free variables at most a, b, c_1 and c_2.*

1. *Extensionality:* $\forall x, y : (\forall a : a \in x \leftrightarrow a \in y) \rightarrow x = y$
2. *Union:* $\forall x : \exists y : \forall a : a \in y \leftrightarrow (\exists z \in x : a \in z)$
3. *Power Set:* $\forall x : \exists y : \forall z : z \in y \leftrightarrow z \subseteq x$
4. *Infinity (ugly version; pretty version below):* $\exists y : (\exists z \in y : \forall b : b \notin z) \wedge (\forall x \in y : \exists s \in y : \forall c : c \in s \leftrightarrow (c \in x \vee c = x))$
5. *Replacement:* $\forall c_1, c_2, x : (\forall a \in x : \exists! b : \varphi) \rightarrow (\exists y : \forall b : b \in y \leftrightarrow \exists a \in x : \varphi)$
6. *Foundation:* $\forall x : x = \emptyset \vee (\exists y \in x : \neg \exists b \in x : b \in y)$

The axioms are due to Zermelo, except for Replacement which is due to Fraenkel and Skolem [3] and Foundation which is due to Von Neumann. Extensionality asserts that sets are equal iff they contain the same members. Union and Power Set state that $\cup X$ and $\mathcal{P}(X)$ are defined if X is defined; this implies the domain of discourse is closed under $\cup$ and $\mathcal{P}$. Infinity states that there exists a set containing $\emptyset$ which is closed under the ordinal successor operation; from this we can extract the Von Neumann natural numbers $\mathbb{N}$. Here is a prettier presentation of Infinity that we do not use as the axiom to avoid bootstrap confusion[3]:

$$\exists y : \emptyset \in y \wedge (\forall x \in y : x^+ \in y)$$

The powerful infinite axiom schema Replacement asserts the existence of the range of a function determined by any formula φ where the values of the variables a and b that make φ true have a functional dependency of b on a and where the domain of the function exists as a set. Foundation enforces the policy that there are no infinite descending chains of the form $X_0 \ni X_1 \ni \cdots$.

Lemma 2.2. *The following theorems of ZF are often presented as axioms. For every formula φ such that any free variable must be a, the following hold in ZF:*

1. *Empty Set:* $\exists x : \forall b : b \notin x$
2. *Pairing:* $\forall a, b : \exists x : \forall c : (c \in x \leftrightarrow (c = a \vee c = b))$
3. *Specification:* $\forall x : \exists y : \forall a : (a \in y \leftrightarrow (a \in x \wedge \varphi))$

2.3   Ordered Pairs in ZF

We define the Kuratowski ordered pair $\langle A, B \rangle$ and related operations as follows where a, b, p, and x are not free in A, B, and Q:

$$\langle A, B \rangle := \{\{A\}, \{A, B\}\}$$
$$A \, \pi_1 \, Q := (\forall x \in Q : A \in x) \qquad B \, \pi_2 \, Q := (\exists! x \in Q : B \in x)$$
$$A \times B := (\imath x : \forall p : p \in x \leftrightarrow (\exists c \in A, d \in B : p = \langle c, d \rangle))$$

---

[3] Provided *some* object exists, Replacement can build $\emptyset$, and then further axiom use can build operations like $\{B, C\}$, $\{B\}$, $X \cup Y$, and X^+, thus ensuring the terms $\emptyset$ and x^+ are defined in the pretty version of Infinity. We prefer getting that initial object from an axiom over using the FOL assumption that the domain of discourse is non-empty. The only axiom giving an object for free is Infinity. We find it confusing to use Infinity in proving the definedness of subterms of itself, so we don't.

We call a and b the *first* and *second projections* of $\langle a, b \rangle$ respectively. The first projection of an ordered pair q is in all sets in q, whereas the second is only in one.[4] The projection relations π_1 and π_2 only give meaningful results when the set Q on the right side of the relation is an ordered pair, i.e., this holds:

$$(\exists c, d : Q = \langle c, d \rangle) \to (\forall a, b : (a\ \pi_1\ Q \wedge b\ \pi_2\ Q) \leftrightarrow Q = \langle a, b \rangle)$$

Kuratowski ordered pairs are sets and have set members that are distinct from their projections. In fact, no matter which representation we use, there will always exist some x such that $x \in \langle a, b \rangle$ (for all but at most one ordered pair which can be represented by $\emptyset$). If A and B are defined, we can show the cartesian product $A \times B$ is defined using Replacement nested inside Replacement[5]:

$$A \times B = \cup \{ z \mid \exists c \in A : z = \{ p \mid \exists d \in B : p = \langle c, d \rangle \} \}$$

3   Extending ZF to ZFP

This section introduces Zermelo-Fraenkel Set Theory with Ordered Pairs (ZFP), a set theory with primitive non-set ordered pairs. ZFP axiomatises the membership predicate symbol $\in$ similarly to ZF. The ordered pair projection predicate symbols π_1 and π_2 are axiomatised in ZFP instead of being abbreviations that use $\in$ as in ZF. Ordered pairs in ZFP qualify as urelements because they contain no members via the set membership relation $\in$, but they are unusual urelements because they can contain arbitrary sets via the π_1 and π_2 relations.

3.1   Definitions and Axioms of ZFP

We use the metavariables p, q, P, and Q where it might help the reader to think 'ordered pair', and the metavariables s, x, y, z, X, Y, and Z where it might help the reader to think 'set'; this convention has no formal status and all FOL variables continue to range over all objects in the domain of discourse. We call b a *member* of x iff $b \in x$. We call b a *projection* of q iff $b\ \pi_1\ q$ or $b\ \pi_2\ q$. An *ordered pair* is any object with a projection, and a *set* is any object that is not an ordered pair. We use the following abbreviations where b is not free in Q and X and q is not free in A and B:

$$
\begin{aligned}
&\mathsf{Pair}(Q) &&:= \exists b : b\ \pi_1\ Q &\qquad& \mathsf{Set}(X) &&:= \neg \mathsf{Pair}(X) \\
&\forall_{\mathsf{Pair}} p : \varphi &&:= \forall p : \mathsf{Pair}(p) \to \varphi && \forall_{\mathsf{Set}} x : \varphi &&:= \forall x : \mathsf{Set}(x) \to \varphi \\
&\exists_{\mathsf{Pair}} p : \varphi &&:= \exists p : \mathsf{Pair}(p) \wedge \varphi && \exists_{\mathsf{Set}} x : \varphi &&:= \exists x : \mathsf{Set}(x) \wedge \varphi \\
&\iota_{\mathsf{Pair}} p : \varphi &&:= \iota p : \mathsf{Pair}(p) \wedge \varphi && \iota_{\mathsf{Set}} x : \varphi &&:= \iota x : \mathsf{Set}(x) \wedge \varphi \\
&(A, B) &&:= (\iota q : A\ \pi_1\ q \wedge B\ \pi_2\ q)
\end{aligned}
$$

---

[4] This holds even in the case of $\langle a, a \rangle = \{\{a\}, \{a, a\}\} = \{\{a\}\}$.

[5] The traditional construction of $A \times B$ as $\{ p \in \mathcal{P}(\mathcal{P}(A \cup B)) \mid \exists c \in A, d \in B : p = \langle c, d \rangle \}$ is only needed if the weaker Specification is preferred over Replacement. We avoid the traditional construction because it depends on a set representation of ordered pairs and thus will not work for ZFP.

We reuse the text of the abbreviation definitions for ZF for $\{A, B\}$, $X \cup Y$, $\{A\}$, and $\{A_1, \ldots, A_n\}$ where $n \geq 3$. We redefine the following abbreviations a bit differently for ZFP, where a, b, c, p, x, y, and z are not free in A, B, X and Y:

$$
\begin{aligned}
X \subseteq Y &:= \mathsf{Set}(X) \wedge \mathsf{Set}(Y) \wedge (\forall c \in X : c \in Y) \\
\cup X &:= (\imath_{\mathsf{Set}}\, y : \forall a : a \in y \leftrightarrow \exists z \in X : a \in z) \\
\mathcal{P}(X) &:= (\imath_{\mathsf{Set}}\, y : \forall z : z \in y \leftrightarrow z \subseteq X) \\
\emptyset &:= (\imath_{\mathsf{Set}}\, x : \forall a : a \notin x) \\
\{b \in X \mid \varphi\} &:= (\imath_{\mathsf{Set}}\, y : \forall b : b \in y \leftrightarrow (b \in X \wedge \varphi)) \\
A \times B &:= (\imath x : \forall p : p \in x \leftrightarrow (\exists c \in A, d \in B : p = (c, d)))
\end{aligned}
$$

These abbreviations are defined if their arguments are defined due to the axioms.

Definition 3.1. *The axioms of ZFP are all the instances of the following formulas for every formula φ with free variables at most a, b, c_1, c_2.*

- **Sets**
  S1. *Set Extensionality:* $\forall_{\mathsf{Set}}\, x, y : (\forall a : a \in x \leftrightarrow a \in y) \to x = y$
  S2. *Union:* $\forall_{\mathsf{Set}}\, x : \exists y : \forall a : a \in y \leftrightarrow (\exists z \in x : a \in z)$
  S3. *Power Set:* $\forall_{\mathsf{Set}}\, x : \exists y : \forall z : z \in y \leftrightarrow z \subseteq x$
  S4. *Infinity (ugly version):* $\exists y : (\exists_{\mathsf{Set}}\, z \in y : \forall b : b \notin z) \wedge (\forall x \in y : \exists s \in y : \forall c : c \in s \leftrightarrow (c \in x \vee c = x)).$
  S5. *Replacement:* $\forall c_1, c_2, x : (\forall a \in x : \exists! b : \varphi) \to (\exists_{\mathsf{Set}}\, y : \forall b : b \in y \leftrightarrow \exists a \in x : \varphi)$
  S6 *Foundation:* $\forall_{\mathsf{Set}}\, x : x = \emptyset \vee (\exists a \in x : \neg \exists b \in x : b\, \pi_1\, a \vee b\, \pi_2\, a \vee b \in a)$
- **Ordered Pairs**
  P1. *Ordered Pair Emptiness:* $\forall_{\mathsf{Pair}}\, p : \forall a : a \notin p$
  P2. *Ordered Pair Formation:* $\forall a, b : \exists p : a\, \pi_1\, p \wedge b\, \pi_2\, p$
  P3. *Projection Both-Or-Neither:* $\forall p : (\exists a : a\, \pi_1\, p) \leftrightarrow (\exists b : b\, \pi_2\, p)$
  P4. *Projection Uniqueness:* $\forall_{\mathsf{Pair}}\, p : (\exists! a : a\, \pi_1\, p) \wedge (\exists! b : b\, \pi_2\, p)$
  P5. *Ordered Pair Extensionality:*
  $\forall_{\mathsf{Pair}}\, p, q : (\forall a : (a\, \pi_1\, p \leftrightarrow a\, \pi_1\, q) \wedge (a\, \pi_2\, p \leftrightarrow a\, \pi_2\, q)) \to p = q$

Lemma 3.2. *For every formula φ such that any free variable must be a, the following hold in ZFP:*

1. *Unordered/Set Pairing:* $\forall a, b : \exists x : \forall c : c \in x \leftrightarrow (c = a \vee c = b)$
2. *Specification:* $\forall_{\mathsf{Set}}\, x : \exists_{\mathsf{Set}}\, y : \forall a : a \in y \leftrightarrow (a \in x \wedge \varphi)$
3. *Cartesian Product Existence:*
   $\forall_{\mathsf{Set}}\, x, y : \exists_{\mathsf{Set}}\, z : \forall p : p \in z \leftrightarrow (\exists a \in x, b \in y : a\, \pi_1\, p \wedge b\, \pi_2\, p)$

For Lemma 3.2 (3), note that the cartesian product $A \times B$ can be built in ZFP using the same construction given for ZF in Sect. 2.3, which does not depend on any set representation of ordered pairs.

3.2   Discussion

Axioms for Sets. Each ZF axiom was transformed to make a ZFP axiom. First, because we use abbreviations for more readable axioms, those used in axioms needed to be modified for ZFP. The definition of $\subseteq$ (used in Power Set) was changed to ensure an ordered pair is neither a subset nor has a subset. The definition of $\emptyset$ (used in Foundation) was changed to ensure a defined result.

Second, some occurrences of $(\forall b : \psi)$ and $(\exists b : \psi)$ needed to enforce that ψ can be true only when b stands for a set. Where needed, such occurrences were changed to $(\forall_{\mathsf{Set}} b : \psi)$ respectively $(\exists_{\mathsf{Set}} b : \psi)$. Each quantifier needed individual consideration. If the sethood of b was already enforced by ψ only being true when b has at least 1 set member, there was no need for a change but a change might also clarify the axiom. If the truth of ψ was unaffected by any set members of b, there was no need for a change and this generally indicated that a change would go against the axiom's intention. We needed to understand the axiom's *intention* and *expected usage* because it was not written to specify where it is expected that 'X is a set' (because this always holds in ZF).

Finally, Foundation was extended to enforce a policy of no infinite descending chains through not just $\in$ but also π_1 and π_2, so that ZF proofs using Kuratowski ordered pairs (having no such chains) would continue to work in ZFP.

Consider the example of Power Set which states that for any set X there exists a set Y containing all of the subsets of X and nothing else, i.e., $\mathcal{P}(X)$:

$$\forall_{\mathsf{Set}} x : \exists y : \forall z : (z \in y \leftrightarrow z \subseteq x)$$

We could have left $\forall_{\mathsf{Set}} x$ as $\forall x$, because when x is an ordered pair it would act like $\emptyset$ and this would only add another reason that $\mathcal{P}(\emptyset)$ exists. However, we thought this would be obscure. It would not hurt to change $\exists y$ to $\exists_{\mathsf{Set}} y$ but there is no need to do so because the body forces y to contain a set member and hence rejects y being an ordered pair. We did not change $\forall z$ to $\forall_{\mathsf{Set}} z$ because this would allow y to contain extra junk ordered pairs that proofs expecting to get $\mathcal{P}(x)$ would have to do extra work using Replacement to filter out.

Axioms for Ordered Pairs. The ZFP axioms for ordered pairs specify the abstract properties of ordered pairs via the relations π_1 and π_2. These ordered pairs have no 'type' restrictions, i.e., each pair projection can be either a set or an ordered pair. Ordered Pair Emptiness (P1) ensures that no object has both a projection (ordered pairs only) and a set member (sets only). Ordered Pair Formation (P2) ensures that for every two objects b and c there exists an ordered pair with b as first projection and c as second. Projection Both-Or-Neither (P3) ensures that every object either has no projections (sets) or both projections (ordered pairs). Projection Uniqueness (P4) ensures each ordered pair has exactly one first projection and one second projection. Ordered Pair Extensionality (P5) ensures that for every choice of first and second projections, there is exactly one ordered pair.

Comparing the Objects and Theorems of ZF and ZFP. A set is *pure* iff all its members are pure sets. Each ZF object is a pure set and is also a pure set of ZFP, but ZFP has additional impure sets which have members that are primitive ordered pairs or impure sets, and ZFP also has primitive ordered pairs. The set membership relation $\in$ of ZF is the restriction of the relation $\in$ of ZFP to pure sets. Let $\mathsf{Pure}(x)$ be a formula (implemented with transfinite recursion) that holds in ZFP when x is a pure set. For every ZF formula φ, let $\mathsf{PRestrict}(\varphi)$ be the ZFP formula obtained from φ by changing each subformula $(\forall\, x : \psi)$ to $(\forall\, x : \mathsf{Pure}(x) \to \psi)$. Then φ is a ZF theorem iff $\mathsf{PRestrict}(\varphi)$ is a ZFP theorem. If one wants to go the other direction and take a ZFP formula ψ and find a ZF formula ψ' that 'does the same thing', one must represent as ZF sets both (1) the primitive ordered pairs *and* (2) the sets of ZFP, and then one must either prevent or somehow manage the possible confusion between the representations of (1) and (2). Section 4.2 is an example of doing this rigorously.

Design Alternatives. We considered having the projections π_1 and π_2 be unary FOL function symbols, but this would require the term $\pi_1(x)$ to denote an object within the domain of discourse for every set x, so we avoided this. We considered having the pairing operator $(\cdot, \cdot)$ be a binary FOL function symbol. Using a binary function symbol would mean the graph model would have hyper-edges (i.e., connecting 3 or more nodes) which is more difficult to think about. Because we used two separate binary predicate symbols, one for each projection, we get a fairly standard-looking directed-graph model with ordinary edges. If we used a binary FOL function symbol $(\cdot, \cdot)$ for pairing, we could replace our axioms P2, P3, P4, and P5 by the characteristic property of ordered pairs:

$$\forall\, a, b, c, d : (a, b) = (c, d) \to (a = b \wedge c = d)$$

Our axioms can be seen as the result of applying a function-symbol-elimination transformation to this alternative.

Very early on, we considered simply using ZF's axioms as they are, adding a binary pairing function symbol, and adding the characteristic property of ordered pairs as an axiom. In this theory, formulas such as $\{b\} \in \langle b, c \rangle$ would be independent, because the representation of ordered pairs would be unknown (and need not even be definable in ZF), so some 'junk theorems' would no longer hold. We avoided this alternative for many reasons. First, Extensionality would force all but one ordered pair (which could be $\emptyset$) to have set members, so there would be 'junk theorems' such as $(a, b) \neq (c, d) \to \exists e : e \in (a, b) \leftrightarrow e \notin (c, d)$. Second, we could not see how to do transfinite induction and recursion. Third, genuine non-sets make it easier to talk about the distinction between sets and conceptually non-set objects, e.g., to students. Fourth, we hope our approach might help a weak form of 'type checking', where a prover might more quickly solve or disprove subgoals, and if a user mistakenly requires a non-set to have a set member, this might be detected earlier and result in a more understandable failure message. Some further reasons are discussed in Sect. 1.

4   A Model of ZFP

We define within ZF a model for ZFP, i.e., an interpretation of the domain and predicate symbols of ZFP. A translation from a ZFP formula ψ to a ZF formula ψ^* is defined to interpret ZFP formulas in the model. Terms and formulas in this section belong to ZF except for the arguments of $(\,\cdot\,)^*$. All axioms of ZFP hold under this translation, which implies that if ZF is consistent, so is ZFP [4]. That each axiom's translation holds has been checked in Isabelle/ZF.

4.1   The Cumulative Hierarchy W

Like the Von Neumann universe $\mathbf{V}$ used as the domain of a model of ZF, our domain $\mathbf{W}$ is a set hierarchy indexed by ordinal numbers.

An *ordinal* is a *transitive* set that is totally ordered by $\in$, which we specify formally by $\mathsf{Ord}(x) := (\forall y \in x : y \subseteq x) \wedge (\forall y, z \in x : y = z \vee y \in z \vee z \in y)$. Let α and β range over ordinals. Let $0 := \emptyset$, $1 := 0^+$, $2 := 1^+$, and so on. Ordinal β is a *successor* ordinal iff $\beta = \alpha^+$ for some α. Ordinal β is a *limit* ordinal iff β is neither 0 nor a successor ordinal. Let λ range over limit ordinals. Let $(x < y) := (x \in y \wedge \mathsf{Ord}(y))$ and define related symbols (e.g., $\leq$) as usual.

Any model of ZFP must have some way of distinguishing between the objects in its domain representing ZFP sets, and those that represent ZFP pairs, i.e., ZFP needs a domain split into two disjoint subdomains. We model this in ZF using Kuratowski ordered pairs and cartesian products to tag all domain objects with 0 ('set') or 1 ('ordered pair').

Definition 4.1. *For ordinal α, define the set W_α via transfinite recursion thus:*

$$W_0 = \emptyset, \qquad W_{\beta^+} = (\{0\} \times \mathcal{P}(W_\beta)) \cup (\{1\} \times (W_\beta)^2), \qquad W_\lambda = \bigcup_{\beta \in \lambda} W_\beta$$

Starting from $\emptyset$, each successor tier W_{β^+} is built by taking the disjoint union of the power set and cartesian square of the previous tier. Each limit tier W_λ is the union of all preceding tiers. The use of disjoint union to build each successor tier W_{β^+} gives a set-theoretic universe split into two. Although our disjoint union uses Kuratowski pairs with 0 and 1 tags, we could use instead any two definable injective operators from a large enough class (e.g., the universe) to disjoint classes that raise rank by at most a constant.

Let $\mathbf{W}$ be the proper class such that $x \in \mathbf{W}$ iff $x \in W_\alpha$ for some α. We use a bold upright serif font to emphasize that $\mathbf{W}$ is not a ZF set.[6] By the transfinite recursion theorem, given x there is a definite description $\mathsf{W}(x)$ that evaluates to W_α when x evaluates to α.[7] We express X belonging to $\mathbf{W}$ as follows:

Definition 4.2. $\mathcal{H}(X) := (\exists y : \mathsf{Ord}(y) \wedge X \in \mathsf{W}(y))$.

---

[6] $\mathbf{W}$ is a mathematical object in some other set theories.

[7] A nested definite description is used that specifies the function f such that $f(\beta) = W_\beta$ for $\beta \leq \alpha$, i.e., f is an initial prefix of the hierarchy. Then $f(\alpha)$ is returned.

Let an *m-object* be any member of **W** (i.e., a ZF set x such that $\mathcal{H}(x)$ holds), an *m-set* be any m-object of the form $\langle 0, x \rangle$, and an *m-pair* be any m-object of the form $\langle 1, x \rangle$. The following result says every m-object x is either an m-set or an m-pair, and tells where in the hierarchy the contents of x are.

Lemma 4.3. *Suppose $\mathcal{H}(x)$, so that $x \in W_\alpha$. Then for some $\beta < \alpha$ either:*

$$x = \langle 0, x' \rangle \ \text{where } x' \subseteq W_\beta, \quad or \quad x = \langle 1, \langle a, b \rangle \rangle \ \text{where } a, b \in W_\beta.$$

It holds that **W** is a cumulative hierarchy:

Lemma 4.4. *If $\alpha \leq \beta$, then $W_\alpha \subseteq W_\beta$.*

4.2   Interpreting ZFP in ZF

As explained above, we interpret the sets and ordered pairs of ZFP as the members of **W**. Lemma 4.3 says any m-object is an ordered pair whose left projection is an integer which decides its 'type' and whose right projection is either a set or an ordered pair. We define our interpretations of ZFP's predicate symbols:

Definition 4.5. *Let $\widehat{\in}$, $\widehat{\pi}_1$, and $\widehat{\pi}_2$ be defined by these abbreviations:*

$$
\begin{aligned}
a \mathbin{\widehat{\in}} x &:= (\exists y : x = \langle 0, y \rangle \land a \in y) \\
a \mathbin{\widehat{\pi}_1} p &:= (\exists u, v : p = \langle 1, \langle u, v \rangle \rangle \land a = u) \\
a \mathbin{\widehat{\pi}_2} p &:= (\exists u, v : p = \langle 1, \langle u, v \rangle \rangle \land a = v)
\end{aligned}
$$

W is downward closed under these three relations. That is:

Lemma 4.6. *Suppose $\mathcal{H}(x)$, i.e., $x \in W_\alpha$ for some α. Suppose $a \mathbin{\widehat{\in}} x$, $a \mathbin{\widehat{\pi}_1} x$, or $a \mathbin{\widehat{\pi}_2} x$ for some a. Then $a \in W_\beta$ for some $\beta < \alpha$, and thus $\mathcal{H}(a)$.*

To interpret a ZFP formula φ in ZF, we must show the formula holds when quantification is restricted to the domain **W**, and the predicate symbols are replaced by the interpretations defined above.

Definition 4.7. *Let φ be a ZFP formula. Define φ^* recursively as follows:*

$$
\begin{aligned}
(X \in Y)^* &:= (X^*) \mathbin{\widehat{\in}} (Y^*) & (\varphi \to \psi)^* &:= (\varphi^*) \to (\psi^*) \\
(X \mathbin{\pi_1} Y)^* &:= (X^*) \mathbin{\widehat{\pi}_1} (Y^*) & (\neg \varphi)^* &:= \neg(\varphi^*) \\
(X \mathbin{\pi_2} Y)^* &:= (X^*) \mathbin{\widehat{\pi}_2} (Y^*) & (\forall x : \varphi)^* &:= (\forall x : \mathcal{H}(x) \to (\varphi^*)) \\
x^* &:= x & (\imath x : \varphi)^* &:= (\imath x : \mathcal{H}(x) \land (\varphi^*))
\end{aligned}
$$

Lemma 4.8. $(\exists x : \varphi)^* \leftrightarrow (\exists x : \mathcal{H}(x) \land (\varphi^*))$.

Because the translation $(\,\cdot\,)^*$ inserts quite a lot of extra structure, a ZFP user wanting to understand "the ZF formula corresponding to the ZFP formula ψ" might be tempted to instead translate ZFP's $\in$ directly to ZF's $\in$ and ZFP's π_1 and π_2 to the ZF abbreviations for π_1 and π_2 defined in Sect. 2.3. However, as discussed in Sect. 1.2, the user then would need to carefully prove that no problems arise from the coincidences where a ZFP set x and a ZFP primitive ordered pair p would be represented by the same ZF set y.

Observe that the ZFP abbreviations Set and Pair from Sect. 3.1 that act like unary predicates are interpreted in ZF as follows:

$$\mathsf{Pair}(x)^* := (\exists a : \mathcal{H}(a) \wedge a \, \widehat{\pi}_1 \, x) \qquad \mathsf{Set}(x)^* := \neg(\mathsf{Pair}(x)^*)$$

These predicates are clearly meaningful within the model because:

Lemma 4.9. *Suppose that* $\mathcal{H}(x)$*, then we have that:*

$$\mathsf{Pair}(x)^* \leftrightarrow (\exists a, b : x = \langle 1, \langle a, b \rangle \rangle) \qquad \mathsf{Set}(x)^* \leftrightarrow (\exists y : x = \langle 0, y \rangle)$$

Now we reach our main result, which implies ZFP is consistent if ZF is [4]:

Theorem 4.10. *For each ZFP axiom* φ*, the translation* φ^* *holds in ZF.*

The proof of this theorem simply observes the conjunction of a number of lemmas, each of which shows for a ZFP axiom ϕ that ϕ^* holds in ZF. Most of these lemmas are straightforward. Here we show a representative example:

Lemma 4.11. *The translation of ZFP's Power Set axiom holds in ZF.*

Proof. First, we find the translation using Definition 4.7 and Lemma 4.8:

$$\forall x : \mathcal{H}(x) \rightarrow (\mathsf{Set}(x)^* \rightarrow (\exists y : \mathcal{H}(y) \wedge \forall z : \mathcal{H}(z) \rightarrow (z \, \widehat{\in} \, y \leftrightarrow ((z \subseteq x)^*))))$$

Let x be such that $\mathcal{H}(x)$, and suppose $\mathsf{Set}(x)^*$. By Lemma 4.9, $x = \langle 0, x' \rangle$ for some set x'. Let $y = \langle 0, y' \rangle$ where $y' = \{0\} \times \mathcal{P}(x')$ be our candidate for the power set. We must show that y has the property $\forall z : \mathcal{H}(z) \rightarrow (z \, \widehat{\in} \, y \leftrightarrow (z \subseteq x)^*)$, and also that y is indeed a member of **W**. Fix z and assume $\mathcal{H}(z)$, then:

$$
\begin{aligned}
z \, \widehat{\in} \, y &\leftrightarrow z \in y' && \text{by def of } y \text{ and } \widehat{\in} \\
&\leftrightarrow z \in \{0\} \times \mathcal{P}(x') && \text{by def of } y' \\
&\leftrightarrow \exists z' : z = \langle 0, z' \rangle \wedge z' \subseteq x' && \text{by def of } \times \text{ and } \mathcal{P} \\
&\leftrightarrow \mathsf{Set}(z)^* \wedge (\forall a : a \, \widehat{\in} \, z \rightarrow a \, \widehat{\in} \, x) && \text{since } z = \langle 0, z' \rangle, z' \subseteq x' \\
&\leftrightarrow \mathsf{Set}(z)^* \wedge \mathsf{Set}(x)^* \wedge (\forall a : a \, \widehat{\in} \, z \rightarrow a \, \widehat{\in} \, x) && \text{since } \mathcal{H}(x), x = \langle 0, x' \rangle \\
&\leftrightarrow (z \subseteq x)^* && \text{because } \mathcal{H}(z)
\end{aligned}
$$

It now remains to show that $\mathcal{H}(y)$. From $\mathcal{H}(x)$, we have that $x \in W_\alpha$ for some ordinal α. By Lemma 4.4, $x \in W_{\alpha+}$, and by Lemma 4.3, $x' \subseteq W_\alpha$. Then:

$$
\begin{aligned}
x' \subseteq W_\alpha &\rightarrow \mathcal{P}(x') \subseteq \mathcal{P}(W_\alpha) \\
&\rightarrow \{0\} \times \mathcal{P}(x') \subseteq \{0\} \times \mathcal{P}(W_\alpha) \\
&\rightarrow y' \subseteq \{0\} \times \mathcal{P}(W_\alpha) && \text{by def of } y' \\
&\rightarrow y' \subseteq W_{\alpha+} && \text{because } \{0\} \times \mathcal{P}(W_\alpha) \subseteq W_{\alpha+} \\
&\rightarrow y \in W_{\alpha++} && \text{by def of } y = \langle 0, y' \rangle \\
&\rightarrow \mathcal{H}(y) && \text{by def of } \mathcal{H}
\end{aligned}
$$

$\square$

5   Conclusion

5.1   Summary of Contributions

Presenting ZF Set Theory Using Definite Descriptions. In Sect. 2, we give a formal presentation of ZF that accounts for the technical details, whilst also defining notation for widely used operations. Although correct formal definitions of this notation can be found in computer implementations of set theory, we have not seen definite descriptions used for this in published articles. Definite descriptions allow defining terms in a compact and readable way without needing to add FOL function symbols, extend the model, or otherwise appeal to the meta-level. We show precisely how Kuratowski pairs and their operations are defined and highlight issues arising from their set representations.

Axiomatizing ZFP. Motivated by issues with the set representation in pure ZF set theory of conceptually non-set objects, in Sect. 3 we introduce Zermelo-Fraenkel Set Theory with Ordered Pairs, which extends ZF with predicate symbols π_1 and π_2 and axioms to implement primitive non-set ordered pairs. ZFP is akin to some alternative set theories that use urelements as genuine non-set objects in the domain, with the difference that ZFP's urelements have meaningful internal structure endowed by the axiomatisation of π_1 and π_2. The design of ZFP is deliberately similar to that of ZF, so that we can better understand the relationship between the two theories. We axiomatize ZFP, and discuss how the axioms of ZF were modified to yield the axioms of ZFP. As a result, we gain a set theory with two types of individuals, both of which have a notion of 'container', which is unusual as urelements are usually structureless. The primitive ordered pairs of ZFP are unlike those typical of set theory, as they are free from any notion of representation.

Showing ZFP Consistent. In Sect. 4, we construct a transfinite hierarchy to be the domain of a model for ZFP and we define relations on this domain to be interpretations for $\in$, π_1, and π_2. We show that the resulting structure satisfies the axioms of ZFP, i.e., it is a model for ZFP. As a result, we show ZFP is consistent if ZF is.

5.2   Future Work

Model Theoretic Status of ZF and ZFP. Axiomatisations of both ZF and ZFP are given within this paper, and we are aware that the sets of ZFP behave in a similar fashion to those in ZF. We suggest employing model-theoretic techniques to give a more detailed formal account of the relationship between the formulas of both theories, as well as the models.

Implementing ZFP. Preliminary experiments have taken place in implementing ZFP as an object logic for Isabelle. Further work on this will allow comparing mathematics formalised in ZF and in ZFP, and thus allow comparing the expressivity, and automatability of both theories. Moreover, there is already a large library of mathematics formalised in Isabelle/ZF. Once the formal relationship between ZF and ZFP has been established, we will attempt to translate mathematics between both bases.

Towards Abstract Data Types in Set Theory. In this paper we identified a role performed by some sets in ZF, namely the role of being an ordered pair for some representation (e.g., Kuratowski), together with the FOL abbreviations for their relations. We axiomatised a new set theory in which this role can be performed by non-set objects, yet maintain the same existence conditions and abstract behaviour of this role. We will attempt to abstract and adapt this method, to yield set theories in which the members of mathematical structures can be genuine non-sets dedicated to their role. We believe such a framework could be helpful when using set theory to formalise mathematics.

References

1. Aczel, P.: Generalised set theory. In: Logic, Language and Computation. CSLI Lecture Notes, vol. 1, pp. 1–17 (1996)
2. Barwise, J.: Admissible Sets and Structures. Cambridge University Press, Cambridge (2017). Originally published by Springer in 1976
3. Ebbinghaus, H.-D.: Ernst Zermelo. Springer, Heidelberg (2007)
4. Enderton, H.B.: A Mathematical Introduction to Logic, 2nd edn. Elsevier, Amsterdam (2001)
5. Farmer, W.M.: Chiron: a multi-paradigm logic. Stud. Logic Gramm. Rhetor. **10**(23), 1–19 (2007)
6. Harrison, J.: Let's make set theory great again! (2018). http://aitp-conference.org/2018/slides/JH.pdf. Accessed 27 May 2020
7. Holmes, M.R.: Alternative axiomatic set theories. In: The Stanford Encyclopedia of Philosophy. Stanford University (2017)
8. Kanamori, A.: The empty set, the singleton, and the ordered pair. Bull. Symb. Logic **9**(3), 273–298 (2003)
9. Kubota, K.: Foundations of mathematics. Genealogy and overview (2018). https://owlofminerva.net/files/fom_2018.pdf. Accessed 27 May 2020
10. Megill, N., Wheeler, D.A.: Metamath: A Computer Language for Mathematical Proofs. LULU Press, Morrisville (2019)
11. Paulson, L.C.: Set theory for verification: I. From foundations to functions. J. Autom. Reason. **11**(3), 353–389 (1993)
12. Quinlan, D., Wells, J.B., Kamareddine, F.: BNF-style notation as it is actually used. In: Kaliszyk, C., Brady, E., Kohlhase, A., Sacerdoti Coen, C. (eds.) CICM 2019. LNCS (LNAI), vol. 11617, pp. 187–204. Springer, Cham (2019). https://doi.org/10.1007/978-3-030-23250-4_13
13. Wiedijk, F.: Is ZF a hack?: Comparing the complexity of some (formalist interpretations of) foundational systems for mathematics. J. Appl. Logic **4**(4), 622–645 (2006)

A Framework for Formal Dynamic Dependability Analysis Using HOL Theorem Proving

Yassmeen Elderhalli$^{(\boxtimes)}$, Osman Hasan, and Sofiène Tahar

Electrical and Computer Engineering, Concordia University, Montréal, Canada
{y_elderh,o_hasan,tahar}@ece.concordia.ca

Abstract. Dependability analysis is an essential step in the design process of safety-critical systems, where the causes of failure and some other metrics, such as reliability, should be identified at an early design stage. The dynamic failure characteristics of real-world systems are usually captured by various dynamic dependability models, such as continuous time Markov chains (CTMCs), dynamic fault trees (DFTs) and dynamic reliability block diagrams (DRBDs). In order to conduct the formal dependability analysis of systems that exhibit dynamic failure behaviors, these models need to be captured formally. In this paper, we describe recent developments towards this direction along with a roadmap on how to be able to develop a framework for formal reasoning support for DFTs, DRBDs and CTMCs in a higher-order-logic theorem prover.

Keywords: Dynamic dependability analysis · Dynamic fault trees · Dynamic reliability block diagrams · Continuous time Markov chains · HOL theorem proving

1 Introduction

Dependability is a general concept that encompasses many attributes, such as reliability, availability, security and safety [1]. Reliability is the ability of a system to provide a correct service within a given period of time [1] and it is quantified by evaluating the probability of delivering such service. On the other hand, availability is the probability of a system or component to provide its correct service at a given moment of time [1]. Many real-world systems exhibit sequential failures and dependencies among system components that cannot be captured using traditional dependability models, such as static fault trees (SFTs) and static reliability block diagrams (SRBDs). Therefore, dynamic dependability models are used to capture the dynamic failure behavior of these systems. These models include Continuous time Markov chains (CTMCs) [2], dynamic fault trees (DFTs) [3] and dynamic reliability block diagrams (DRBDs) [4].

Dynamic dependability analysis identifies the sequences of failure of system components and their effect on the overall system behavior. This helps devising

© Springer Nature Switzerland AG 2020
C. Benzmüller and B. Miller (Eds.): CICM 2020, LNAI 12236, pp. 105–122, 2020.
https://doi.org/10.1007/978-3-030-53518-6_7

solutions to enhance the overall system dependability. Therefore, this analysis process should be handled carefully in a sound environment to produce accurate results. Traditionally, dependability models are analyzed using paper-and-pencil based proof methods or using simulation. The former provides a flexible way to model and analyze systems, but it is prone to human errors. On the other hand, simulation provides an easy automated method to conduct the analysis, which justifies its common use in analyzing a wide range of applications. However, due to the high computational cost of simulation, only part of the space could be analyzed, and thus the results cannot be termed as accurate or complete.

Formal methods, such as model checking [5] and theorem proving [6], have been used for the analysis of dependability models, to overcome the inaccuracy limitations of the above-mentioned techniques. For example, the STORM model checker [7] has been successfully used in the safety analysis of a vehicle guidance system [8] using DFTs. Although probabilistic model checkers (PMCs) provide an automatic way to conduct the analysis of dependability models, the state space explosion problem often limits its scope especially when analyzing complex systems. Moreover, the reduction algorithms embedded in these tools are usually not formally verified, which questions the accuracy of the reduced models [9]. This becomes an issue when analyzing safety-critical systems, where the smallest error cannot be tolerated. More importantly, PMCs inherently assume the failures to be exponentially distributed for system components [10], and thus cannot capture, for example, their aging factor. Although higher-order logic (HOL) theorem proving has been used in the analysis of traditional (static) dependability models, such as SFTs [11] and SRBDs [12], these models cannot capture the dynamic aspects of real-world systems and thus cannot fulfill the objective of the projected work. However, using a theorem prover in the analysis allows having verified, within a sound environment, generic expressions of dependability that are independent of the distribution of system components. Thus, the results are not limited to exponential distributions as with PMCs.

In this paper, we describe an ongoing project for building a complete framework to formally analyze dynamic dependability models using HOL theorem proving. The project had started at the Hardware Verification Group of Concordia University in 2017 with a clear roadmap. In this regard, we formalized DFTs in the HOL4 theorem prover [13], which allows formally verifying generic expressions of the probability of failure of DFTs [14] and thus can be used to conduct formal dynamic dependability analysis. Furthermore, we proposed a novel algebra to analyze DRBDs with certain structures and verified their mathematical foundations using the HOL4 theorem prover [15]. On the other hand, a formalization for general CTMCs [16] is available in Isabelle/HOL [17]. However, this formalization has not been used in the context of dynamic dependability analysis. Therefore, we plan to develop a CTMC formalization to be used in this context. The present paper mainly summarizes our developed formalization and shares our plans for the development of a complete framework for the formal dependability analysis of real-world systems using a theorem prover.

The rest of the paper is structured as follows: Sect. 2 presents our proposed framework for the formal dynamic dependability analysis. Section 3 provides a brief description of our formalization of DFTs. In Sect. 4, we present DRBDs and our developed DRBD algebra. Section 5 presents the required mathematical foundations of the CTMC dependability analysis. We report the current status of the project and the remaining milestones in Sect. 6. Finally, Sect. 7 concludes the paper.

2   Proposed Framework

Figure 1 shows an overview of our proposed framework for formal dynamic dependability analysis. This framework provides verified generic expressions of dependability in the HOL4 theorem prover using DFTs, DRBDs and CTMCs. The analysis starts by having a system description with some dependability requirements, such as a certain expression of reliability. The dependability of this system can be modeled using a DFT, DRBD or CTMC model according to its description. For the case of the DFTs and DRBDs, we need, respectively, a library of formalized DFT gates and DRBD constructs besides their simplification theorems and verified probabilistic behavior. For the CTMC formal analysis, it is required to have both formal transient and steady state analyses. The formal DFT and DRBD models can be analyzed qualitatively or quantitatively. In the former, the sources of vulnerabilities of the system are verified by identifying the cut sets and cut sequences. In the latter, we prove generic failure and reliability expressions of DFT and DRBD based systems, respectively. It is worth mentioning that unlike PMC approaches, the formally verified generic expressions of DFT and DRBD are independent of the probability distributions of the system

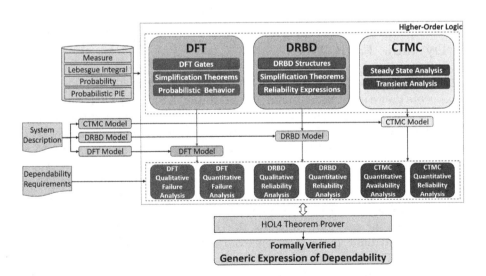

Fig. 1. Overview of the formal dependability analysis framework

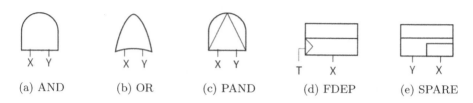

(a) AND	(b) OR	(c) PAND	(d) FDEP	(e) SPARE

Fig. 2. DFT gates

components. For CTMC based models, the proposed framework formally analyzes availability and reliability metrics by proving generic expressions of these dependability metrics that are independent of the failure rates of system components. We choose HOL4 in the development of the formalization of dynamic dependability models as this would facilitate using some of the available theories, such as the probabilistic PIE [18], Lebesgue integral [19] and probability [20].

Our ultimate goal in this project is to develop a tool that accepts the dependability model in either a graphical or simple textual format. Then, using a parser, the tool creates the HOL formal models of these formats that can be used in the formal analysis using a HOL theorem prover. The aim of this tool is to reduce the user interaction with the theorem proving environment, which would facilitate the usage of this framework by users who are not familiar with HOL theorem proving or the underlying mathematical foundations of the dependability models. This requires invoking several techniques, such as machine learning, to automatically (to a certain extent) verify the required expressions. Therefore, this proposed framework will allow conducting the dynamic dependability analysis of many real-world systems to provide generic expressions. We highlight the details of the proposed framework in the following sections including the current status of the formalization and provide some insights about the remaining steps.

3   Dynamic Fault Trees

Dynamic fault trees (DFTs) [3] model the failure dependencies among system components that cannot be captured using traditional SFTs. A DFT is a graphical representation of the sources of failure of a given system. The modeling starts by an undesired top event that represents the failure of a system or a subsystem. DFT inputs represent basic events that contribute to the occurrence (failure) of the top event. The relationships and dependencies among these basic events are modeled using DFT gates (Fig. 2). For example, the output event of the Priority-AND (PAND) gate occurs when both input events occur in sequence.

Fault tree analysis (FTA) can be generally carried out qualitatively and quantitatively [3]. In the *qualitative* analysis, the combinations and sequences of basic events that contribute to the occurrence of the top event (failure of the system) are identified. These combinations and sequences represent the cut sets and cut sequences [21], respectively. In the *quantitative* analysis, attributes, such as the mean-time-to-failure (MTTF) and the probability of failure, can be evaluated based on the failure distribution of the basic events and their relationships. Dynamic FTA has been commonly conducted using some sort of a DFT algebra (e.g., [22]) or by analyzing the corresponding CTMC of the given DFT [3]. In the former method, an algebra similar to the ordinary Boolean algebra is defined with some temporal operators and simplification properties that allow reducing the structure function of the top event. Based on this function, both the qualitative and quantitative analyses can be carried out, where the probability of failure of the DFT's top event can be expressed based on the failure distribution of the basic events. On the other hand, the given DFT can be converted into its equivalent CTMC, which can then be analyzed to find the probability of failure of the top event [3]. Complex systems can generate CTMCs with a large state space that can be handled by applying a modulerization approach, where the DFT is divided into static and dynamic parts. The static part can be analyzed using one of the conventional methods, such as binary decision diagrams (BDDs) [21]. The dynamic part can then be analyzed by converting it to its corresponding CTMC. This kind of modulerization is implemented in the Galileo tool [23].

The arithmetic foundations of the algebraic approach of [22] were not formally verified, which puts a question mark on the soundness of the reported results. In [24], we proposed to formalize this DFT algebra in higher-order logic theorem proving and developed an integrated methodology to conduct DFT's qualitative analysis using the HOL4 theorem prover and quantitative analysis using the STORM model checker. However, generic expressions of probability of failure cannot be obtained based on this methodology as a PMC is involved in the quantitative analysis. Moreover, our definitions in [24] could not cater for the DFT probabilistic analysis. Therefore, in [14,25], we improved our definitions of DFT gates to conduct both the DFT qualitative and quantitative analyses in the form of generic expressions in a theorem prover. Next, we provide the description of the DFT algebra and its formalization in order to have a better understanding of the first part of our proposed framework of Fig. 1.

3.1   DFT Operators and Simplification Properties

The DFT algebraic approach of [22] deals with the inputs of a DFT based on their time of failure. Therefore, all elements, operators and gates are defined based on this time of failure. It is assumed that the failure of a certain component causes the occurrence of its corresponding basic event. Moreover, it is also assumed that the components are non-repairable [22]. The algebraic approach defines two identity elements, which facilitate the simplification process of the structure function of a given DFT. These are the *ALWAYS* and *NEVER* elements. The *ALWAYS* element represents an event that always occurs, i.e., from time 0, while the *NEVER* element is an event that can never occur, i.e., the time of failure is $+\infty$. In order to capture the dynamic failure in DFTs, three temporal operators are introduced; *Before* ($\lhd$), *Simultaneous* (Δ), and *Inclusive Before* ($\unlhd$) [22]. The output of the before operator fails when the first input event occurs before the second. The output of the simultaneous operator fails when both input events happen at the same time. Finally, the output of the inclusive before operator fails when the first input occurs before or at the same time of the second input. We formally defined these elements and operators in HOL4 as extended-real functions of time [14]. The purpose of choosing extended-real numbers, which are real numbers besides $\pm\infty$, is to be able to model the NEVER event that returns $+\infty$ as its time of failure. Several simplification properties are introduced in the algebraic approach [22] to simplify the structure function of DFTs (the function of the top event). This reduced structure function can then be used in the probabilistic analysis. We verified over 80 simplification theorems [24] that vary from simple theorems to more complex ones. This enables having formally verified reduced cut sets and cut sequences, i.e., formal qualitative DFT analysis.

3.2   DFT Gates

DFTs use the ordinary FT gates, i.e., AND and OR gates, besides the dynamic gates (Fig. 2). AND ($\cdot$) and OR ($+$) are used in the algebraic approach as operators as well as FT gates. The output of the AND gate fails when both inputs fail. This means that the time of occurrence of the output event of the AND gate is the maximum time of occurrence of both input events. The output of the OR gate fails when at least one of the input events occurs. Therefore, the time of occurrence equals the minimum time of occurrence of its inputs. The Priority-AND (PAND) gate is similar to the AND gate, where the output fails when both inputs fail. However, the input events should occur in a certain sequence, conventionally, from left to right. The Functional DEPendency (FDEP) gate is used to model a situation when the failure of one system component triggers the failure of another. For the FDEP gate of Fig. 2, the occurrence of T triggers the occurrence of X. Finally, the spare gate models spare parts in systems, where the main part is replaced by the spare part after failure. In [14], we formally defined these gates as functions of time to enable the verification of their failure probabilistic expressions, as will be explained in the following section.

3.3   DFT Failure Analysis

In order to conduct the formal probabilistic failure analysis of DFTs, it is required first to formally verify the probability of failure of DFT gates. It is assumed that the basic events of DFT are independent. However, in case of the spare gate, the input events are not independent as the failure of the main part affects the failure behavior of the spare. In order to perform the failure analysis, we first formally define a DFT event that represents the set of time until which we are interested in finding the probability of failure [14].

In case of independent events, four expressions are used to determine the probability of failure of DFT gates [22].

$$Pr\{X \cdot Y\}(t) = F_X(t) \times F_Y(t) \tag{1a}$$

$$Pr\{X + Y\}(t) = F_X(t) + F_Y(t) - F_X(t) \times F_Y(t) \tag{1b}$$

$$Pr\{Y \cdot (X \lhd Y)\}(t) = \int_0^t f_Y(y)\, F_X(y)\, dy \tag{1c}$$

$$Pr\{X \lhd Y\}(t) = \int_0^t f_X(x)(1 - F_Y(x))\, dx \tag{1d}$$

where F_X and F_Y are the cumulative density functions of random variables X and Y, respectively, and f_X and f_Y are their probability density functions.

Equation (1a) represents the probability of the AND gate. In order to verify this equation, we first verified that the event of the output of the AND gate equals the intersection of the individual input events. Then, based on the independence of these events, the probability of their intersection equals the multiplication of their probabilities, i.e., their cumulative density functions [14]. Equation (1b) represents the probability of the OR gate. We verified this equation using the fact that the event of the OR gate equals the union of the individual input events. Equations (1c) and (1d) represent the probability of two inputs events occurring one after the other or one before the other, respectively. For the first case, it is required that both events occur in sequence. Whereas the second case requires that the first input event occurs before the second. So, it is not necessary that the second input event occurs. Using these expressions, the probability of the AND gate is expressed using Eq. (1a). The probabilities of failure of the OR and FDEP gates are expressed using Eq. (1b). Moreover, Eq. (1c) represents the probability of failure of the PAND gate for basic input events. Finally, Eq. (1d) represents the probability of failure of the before operator.

Similarly, the probability of failure of the spare gate can be expressed, but it requires dealing with conditional density functions as the time of failure of the main part affects the activation time of the spare part. This means that the input events are no longer independent. We verified these expressions in HOL4 by first defining a conditional density function and then proving the probability of failure of the spare gates [14]. In our verification process, we used the measure, Lebesgue integral, Lebesgue-Borel measure and the probability theories in order to verify a generic expression of failure of a given DFT. Based on this formalization, we conducted the formal dependability analysis of several safety-critical systems, such as a cardiac assist system [26] and a drive-by-wire system [27].

4   Dynamic Reliability Block Diagrams

A dynamic reliability block diagram (DRBD) models the paths of success in a given system. System components are represented as blocks that are connected in the traditional series, parallel, series-parallel and parallel-series structures.

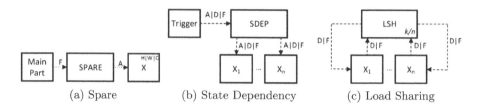

(a) Spare   (b) State Dependency   (c) Load Sharing

Fig. 3. Dynamic DRBD constructs

Additional constructs are used to model the dynamic dependencies among system blocks. The main dynamic constructs are: spare, state-dependencies and load sharing. The last two constructs enable modeling more realistic scenarios in system reliability that include the effect of activation/deactivation of one component on the rest of the components. This behavior cannot be captured using DFTs [28] as they can only capture the failure without considering the activation/deactivation effect.

Due to the dynamic nature of DRBDs, they can be analyzed by converting them into a state-space model, i.e., a Markov chain. Then, the resultant Markov chain can be analyzed using one of the traditional techniques, including analytical methods or simulation. Some tools, such as BlockSim [29], enable DRBD analysis by providing a graphical user interface to model DRBDs and conduct the analysis either analytically or using discrete event simulation. As mentioned previously, complex systems can generate Markov chains with a large number of states, which hinders the analysis process. Decomposition can be applied to divide the DRBD into a dynamic part that can be solved using Markov chains and a static part that can be analyzed using static RBD analysis techniques [30]. Although this decomposition would reduce the state space, such simulation based analysis cannot provide accurate and complete results.

The formal semantics of DRBDs were introduced in [31] using the Object-Z formalism [32]. Then, this DRBD is converted into a Colored Petri net (CPN), where it can be analyzed using existing Petri net tools. However, since the given DRBD is converted into a CPN, only state-based properties can be analyzed. In addition, generic expressions of reliability cannot be obtained, which represents our target in the proposed framework. HOL theorem proving has been only used for the analysis of traditional SRBDs [12], which cannot support the scope of the proposed framework, i.e., dynamic dependability. To the best of our knowledge, there is no support of DRBD analysis using a HOL theorem prover that can cater for the analysis of real-world systems that exhibit dynamic behavior. The main challenge towards this direction is the absence of a formal DRBD algebra that can provide similar analysis like DFTs. Therefore, we developed a novel algebra that allows conducting both the qualitative and quantitative analyses based on the structure function of DRBDs with spare constructs [15]. The formalization of this algebra in HOL facilitates the analysis using a theorem prover. Below, we provide an overview of DRBD constructs and structures.

4.1   DRBD Constructs and Structures

The main dynamic DRBD constructs are shown in Fig. 3 [33]. The *spare* construct is used to model spare parts in systems, similar to the DFT spare gate. The *state dependencies* are used to model the effect of activation(A)/deactivation(D)/failure(F) among system components. In Fig. 3(b), the A/D/F of the trigger will cause the state dependency controller (SDEP) to signal the A/D/F of components $X_1...X_n$. Finally, the *load sharing* (LSH) construct is used to model the effect of sharing a load on the overall system failure. For example, the LSH in Fig. 3 models a load that is shared among n components. It is required that at least k out of these n components to be working in order for the successful functionality of the overall system. Therefore, the D/F of some of these components may cause the D/F of the rest of the components.

Besides the dynamic DRBD constructs, system components are represented as blocks that can be connected in series, parallel, series-parallel and parallel-series fashion, as shown in Fig. 4 [34]. Each block in Fig. 4 represents either a simple system component or one of the DRBD dynamic constructs.

4.2   DRBD Algebra

We developed a DRBD algebra to perform both qualitative and quantitative analyses in the HOL theorem proving environment of a given DRBD. The developed algebra can model traditional DRBD structures, i.e., series and parallel, besides the spare construct by dealing with the time-to-failure functions. In the developed algebra, we defined DRBD operators, like the DFT algebra, to model the various relationships among system components. These operators are: 1) AND ($\cdot$) to model a situation where two system components are required to work for a successful system behavior (connected in series); 2) OR ($+$) to model system components that are connected in parallel; 3) After operator ($\triangleright$) which

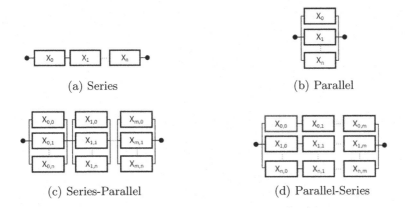

(a) Series

(b) Parallel

(c) Series-Parallel

(d) Parallel-Series

Fig. 4. DRBD structures

captures the situation where one system component is required to continue working after the failure of a second one; 4) Simultaneous operator (Δ) which is similar to the DFT simultaneous operator; and 5) Inclusive after ($\unrhd$) that combines the behavior of both the after and simultaneous operators. In [15] we provided mathematical expressions for these operators, and expressed the DRBD structures and spare construct based on their mathematical expressions.

4.3   DRBD Reliability Analysis

In our algebra, we assume that each system block is represented by a random variable, which is the time-to-failure function of this block. We also assume that the system components are non-repairable. Based on this time-to-failure function, the reliability of a single block is defined as [34]:

$$R_X(t) = Pr(X > t) = 1 - Pr(X \leq t) = 1 - F_X(t) \tag{2}$$

The DRBD blocks can be connected in several ways depending on the success paths of the modeled system. The definitions and reliability expressions of the structures of Fig. 4 are listed in Table 1 [34]. In the *series* structure, it is required that all blocks are working for the system to work. Therefore, the series structure can be modeled as the intersection of the individual block events, as listed in Table 1, where X_i represents the DRBD event of the ith block. This structure can be also modeled by ANDing the functions of these blocks. The reliability of this structure equals the multiplication of the reliability of the individual blocks. The *parallel* structure requires at least one of the blocks to be working for a successful system behavior. Hence, it is modeled as the union of the events of the individual blocks and it can be also modeled by ORing these functions. The *series-parallel* structure (Fig. 4(c)) represents a series structure of blocks each of which is a parallel structure. Therefore, it is modeled as the intersection of unions. The *parallel-series* structure (Fig. 4(d)), is a parallel structure of several series structures. It is modeled as the union of intersection of the individual block events. In [15], we formally verified these expressions besides the reliability of the spare construct. We plan to extend the DRBD algebra to model the remaining dynamic constructs, i.e., load sharing and state dependency. This requires modeling the deactivation state of system components and may include introducing new DRBD operators to capture such behavior.

Table 1. Mathematical and reliability expressions of DRBD structures

Structure	Mathematical expression	Reliability
Series	$\bigcap_{i=1}^{n} X_i$	$\prod_{i=1}^{n} R_{X_i}(t)$
Parallel	$\bigcup_{i=1}^{n} X_i$	$1 - \prod_{1=1}^{n}(1 - R_{X_i}(t))$
Series-parallel	$\bigcap_{i=1}^{m} \bigcup_{j=1}^{n} X_{(i,j)}$	$\prod_{i=1}^{m}(1 - \prod_{j=1}^{n}(1 - R_{X_{(i,j)}}(t)))$
Parallel-series	$\bigcup_{i=1}^{n} \bigcap_{j=1}^{m} X_{(i,j)}$	$1 - (\prod_{i=1}^{n}(1 - \prod_{j=1}^{m}(R_{X_{(i,j)}}(t))))$

5 Continuous Time Markov Chains

Continuous Time Markov Chains (CTMCs) are the most widely used stochastic processes in dynamic dependability analysis since they can capture the failure dependencies. A CTMC is a Markov process with discrete state space. The transition from one state to another can happen with a certain rate at any moment of time. Formal methods have been used in the analysis of CTMC based systems. For example, the PRISM model checker is utilized in [10] to model and analyze different case studies, such as dynamic voltage and molecular reactions. However, generic expressions cannot be obtained using such analysis. Utilizing the expressive nature of HOL, Markov chains are formalized in both HOL4 and Isabelle/HOL [17]. In [35], the formalization of discrete time Markov chains (DTMCs) is presented in HOL4 with some formalized attributes, such as steady state probabilities and stationary distribution. In [16], CTMCs are formally defined in Isabelle/HOL with the formalization of backward equations. Although Markov chains have been formalized in HOL, no work has been proposed yet regarding the dependability analysis of Markov chain based systems. Conducting the analysis of CTMCs to reason about dependability attributes, such as reliability and availability, would provide formally verified generic expressions of dependability, which is the scope of the third part of our proposed framework. In the sequel, we present some mathematical notations that are required for both CTMC transient and steady state analyses, which can be used for conducting the reliability and availability analyses of a given system.

5.1 CTMC Definition and Attributes

A stochastic process $\{X_t, t \in T\}$ is a collection of random variables indexed by $t \in T$ [36], where the time t can be continuous or discrete. The values that each random variable can take are called states and the set of these states is called the state space Ω. A Markov process is a stochastic process with the Markov property [35]. If the state space is finite or countably infinite, then the Markov process is called a *Markov Chain* (MC). The Markov property is defined as [2]:

$$Pr\big(X(t) = x|\ X(t_n) = x_n, X(t_{n-1}) = x_{n-1}, ..., X(t_0) = x_0\big) = \\ Pr\big(X(t) = x|\ X(t_n) = x_n\big) \tag{3}$$

If the transition can happen at any time, i.e., the time is continuous, then the MC is called a *Continuous Time Markov Chain* (CTMC). In the proposed framework, we are interested in CTMCs as they can capture the dynamic behavior at any instance of time. Once the process is in a certain state, i, the time it spends in this state is exponentially distributed with rate λ_i.

The probabilistic behavior of the CTMC is described by the initial state probability vector $\pi_k(t_0)$ [2], which is defined as $Pr\big(X(t_0 = k), k = 0, 1, 2, ...$ and the transition probabilities p_{ij} [2], where

$$p_{ij}(v, t) = Pr\big(X(t) = j \mid X(v) = i\big),\ 0 \le v \le t\ and\ i, j\ =\ 0, 1, 2, ... \tag{4}$$

The CTMC is *time non-homogeneous* if the transition probabilities are functions of time, while it is a *time homogeneous* CTMC if the transition probabilities depend on the time difference $(t - v)$ and not on the actual value of time [2].

$$p_{ij}(t) = Pr\big(X(t + v) = j \mid X(v) = i\big), \ 0 \leq v \tag{5}$$

Each CTMC has an embedded DTMC with a probability transition matrix **P**. The matrix entries are the one step probabilities from state i to state j. This matrix specifies the behavior of the embedded DTMC, however, it does not provide information about the transition rates. The Chapman-Kolmogorov equation [2] provides the probability of the transition from state i to state j in time period from v to t, where the system is taken to an intermediate state k during the time v to u, and from the intermediate state to state j during the time u to t. This equation can be described as [2]:

$$p_{ij}(v, t) = \sum_{k \in \Omega} p_{ik}(v, u) p_{kj}(u, t), \ \ 0 \leq v < u < t \tag{6}$$

The state probability or the unconditional probability of being in a certain state can be expressed using the total probability theorem as:

$$\pi_j(t) = \sum_{i \in \Omega} p_{ij}(v, t) \pi_i(v) \tag{7}$$

If we substitute v with 0, then, only the transition probabilities and the initial state probability vector are enough to describe the probabilistic behavior of the CTMC [2]. The state probability vector, $\pi(t)$, is a vector with an entry for each unconditional state probability. The sum of the entries in the state probability vector at any time is equal to 1, as the MC should be in a certain state.

$$\sum_{j \in \Omega} \pi_j(t) = 1 \tag{8}$$

The infinitesimal matrix (or the generator matrix), **G**, is a core element in the CTMC analysis process. It has all the information about the transition rates. The elements of the matrix **G** are defined by:

$$g_{ij} = \begin{cases} \lambda_{ij} & , i \neq j \\ -\lambda_i & , i = j \end{cases} \tag{9}$$

where λ_{ij} is the transition rate from state i to state j.

5.2 CTMC Dependability Analysis

A CTMC can be used to model the dependability of a certain system. For example, a state machine can start with an initial state, where all system components are working. Then, several states can be used to model the varying failure conditions of system components. Note that it is not necessary that the failure of a certain component in the system can lead to the failure of the whole system. So the failure of components in the system will cause the transition from one state in the CTMC to another. The transition rate depends on the failure rate of the component that failed. A fail state is used to model the fail state of the system. The CTMC quantitative analysis can be conducted using either the transient analysis or steady-state analysis depending on the dependability metric that we are interested in. These include the instantaneous availability, reliability and steady state availability, as will be described below:

Transient Analysis. The transition probabilities and the transition rates are related using Kolmogrov's forward or backward equations [2]. The backward Kolmogrov's equations are defined as:

$$p'_{ij}(t) = \sum_{k \neq i} \lambda_{ik} p_{ki}(t) - \lambda_i p_{ij}(t) \tag{10}$$

Equation 10 can be rewritten using the matrix form as:

$$\mathbf{P}'(t) = \mathbf{G}\mathbf{P}(t) \tag{11}$$

where $\mathbf{P}(t)$ is the matrix transition probability function. In a similar manner, the generator matrix can be used to find $\boldsymbol{\pi}(t)$ [2]:

$$\boldsymbol{\pi}'(t) = \boldsymbol{\pi}(t)\mathbf{G}(t) \tag{12}$$

Starting from a CTMC that models the failure behavior of a given system, we can find the probability of being available at a certain moment of time, i.e., instantaneous availability or the system reliability using this transient analysis. This is achieved by finding the probability of being in a fail or a working state.

Steady State Analysis. A stationary distribution is the vector of unconditional state probabilities that satisfies the following condition [36]:

$$\pi = \pi \mathbf{P}(t) \tag{13}$$

This means that if the CTMC starts with this initial stationary distribution, the unconditional state probabilities vector at any time will stay the same. The stationary distribution can be found by solving the following set of linear equations with the condition that $\sum_{j \in \Omega} \pi_j(t) = 1$ [36]:

$$\pi \mathbf{G} = 0 \tag{14}$$

Using this stationary distribution, we can find the overall probability of system availability by finding the probability of being in a working state. This means that we can find the fraction of time where the system is available during its life cycle, which represents the steady state availability.

6   Current Status and Future Milestones

The final objective of the proposed project is to develop a tool that can be used for the formal dynamic dependability analysis of DFT, DRBD and CTMC models. To achieve this goal, we had to extend the properties of the Lebesgue integral and probability theory in HOL4. This enabled us to verify several probabilistic expressions that are concerned with sequences of random variables. For example, we verified $Pr(X < Y)$, which is required to model the failure behavior of some DFT gates and the DRBD spare construct. Furthermore, we verified several properties for the independence of random variables and sets that are required for verifying the probability of a nested hierarchy of union and intersection of sets. These properties are useful in the analysis of complex DFT and DRBD models. We encountered several challenges during the formalization process including the lack of mathematical proofs in the literature that clearly identify the required steps or theorems that can be utilized to verify the required properties.

We used our formalization to formally model and verify the mathematical foundations of DFTs in the HOL4 theorem prover [14, 24, 25]. In particular, we modeled the DFT gates and operators and verified several simplification theorems. We illustrated the applicability of the proposed framework by conducting the formal analysis of a cardiac assist system and a drive-by-wire system. Furthermore, we proposed a roadmap [37] to use machine learning techniques to conduct the DFT analysis, which reduces the user interaction with the theorem proving environment. Tables 2 summarizes these accomplished tasks.

We developed a new algebra that allows the formal qualitative and quantitative analyses of DRBDs with spare constructs within a theorem proving environment [15]. We illustrated the usefulness and utilization of the proposed algebra in the formal DRBD based analysis of shuffle-exchange networks, which are used in multiprocessor systems, and a drive-by-wire system, as listed in Table 2.

The remaining tasks of this project can be divided into two main categories: 1) the development and formalization of the mathematical models; and 2) the development of the tool itself. For the first category, we need to extend the DRBD algebra to model the state dependency and load sharing constructs. This requires considering the deactivation process of system components instead of dealing only with the activation and failure. By modeling this behavior, we can consider, in the future, the repairing scenarios that are not currently supported in our DRBD algebra. Furthermore, we have to mathematically model CTMCs in HOL4. For this purpose, we need to extend the properties of conditional density and distribution functions. Modeling exponential distributions and formalizing their properties are also needed as the time spent in each CTMC state is exponentially distributed. Finally, we plan to conduct the dependability analysis using CTMCs including reliability and availability. We plan to utilize this formalization in the dependability analysis of real-world systems, such as solid state drives-RAID systems [38].

Regarding the second category, we plan to develop a parser that creates the HOL dependability models based on a textual or graphical input format. Furthermore, the end-user should be able to specify the type of analysis required (e.g., reliability or availability) and enter some requirements in the form of expressions. Thus, we have to develop a user friendly graphical user interface (GUI) to obtain these inputs. Then, we intend to invoke some machine learning (ML) algorithms that help in speeding up and automating the verification process. This includes classifying the useful theorems and choosing the proper tactics to be used in the verification of the input model. To achieve this step, we need to create training and test sets that can be used in developing the proper

Table 2. Roadmap

Task	Description	Duration
Accomplished tasks		
1	HOL Formalization of DFT algebra - Formal definitions of DFT gates and temporal operators [14] - Formalization of probabilistic behavior of dynamic gates [14, 25]	14 Months
2	DFT applications - Quantitative analysis of CAS [14] - DFT qualitative and quantitative analyses of CAS and DBW [25]	2 Months
3	New DRBD algebra [15]	2 Months
4	HOL formalization of DRBD algebra [15] - Formal definitions of DRBD structures and spare construct - Formalization of reliability expressions	9 Months
5	DRBD applications - Formal reliability analysis of DBW and SEN [15]	1 Month
Future plan		
6	More DRBD dynamic constructs - Formalization of state dependencies construct - Formalization of load sharing construct	6 Months
7	Formalization of CTMCs - Homogeneous - Non-homogeneous	9 Months
8	Formal CTMC analysis - Transient analysis - Steady state analysis	6 Months
9	Applications (Reliability of SSD RAID)	2 Months
10	Using machine learning to automate the analysis - Create training and test sets - Develop ML models	6 Months
11	Tool Development - Develop a GUI - Develop a parser - Program the core of the tool	3 Months
	Total time	60 Months

ML models. Finally, we have to program the core of the tool that connects the pieces of the framework together to enable the automatic dynamic dependability analysis. As the development of this tool is an incremental process, which can be improved with time, we plan to conduct some tutorials for end-users that are not familiar with HOL to train them and consider their feedback. This step is also important for verification and reliability engineers that are interested in enriching the underlying theories of the proposed framework. This helps in the sustainability of the proposed framework by engaging many users with different goals and backgrounds in the development of the framework and its tool. A summary of this roadmap is provided in Table 2.

7   Conclusions

In this paper, we proposed a comprehensive framework to conduct the formal dynamic dependability analysis using HOL theorem proving. We provided the details of the mathematical foundations of each part of the proposed framework. The main contributions of this work is the development of the proposed framework in the HOL4 theorem prover that includes the formalization of DFTs and CTMCs besides the development of the DRBD algebra. These formalized models allow the dependability analysis of many real-world system that exhibit dynamic behavior. We described the future milestones to complete the proposed project including the final tool that enables the (semi) automation of the analysis.

References

1. Avizienis, A., Laprie, J.C., Randell, B., Landwehr, C.: Basic concepts and taxonomy of dependable and secure computing. IEEE Trans. Dependable Secure Comput. 1(1), 11–33 (2004)
2. Trivedi, K.S.: Probability and Statistics with Reliability, Queuing and Computer Science Applications. Wiley, Hoboken (2002)
3. Stamatelatos, M., Vesely, W., Dugan, J., Fragola, J., Minarick, J., Railsback, J.: Fault Tree Handbook with Aerospace Applications. NASA Office of Safety and Mission Assurance (2002)
4. Distefano, S., Xing, L.: A new approach to modeling the system reliability: dynamic reliability block diagrams. In: Reliability and Maintainability Symposium, pp. 189–195. IEEE (2006)
5. Baier, C., Katoen, J.: Principles of Model Checking. MIT Press, Cambridge (2008)
6. Gordon, M.J., Melham, T.F.: Introduction to HOL: A Theorem Proving Environment for Higher-Order Logic. Cambridge University Press, Cambridge (1993)
7. Dehnert, C., Junges, S., Katoen, J.-P., Volk, M.: A storm is coming: a modern probabilistic model checker. In: Majumdar, R., Kunčak, V. (eds.) CAV 2017. LNCS, vol. 10427, pp. 592–600. Springer, Cham (2017). https://doi.org/10.1007/978-3-319-63390-9_31
8. Ghadhab, M., Junges, S., Katoen, J.-P., Kuntz, M., Volk, M.: Model-based safety analysis for vehicle guidance systems. In: Tonetta, S., Schoitsch, E., Bitsch, F. (eds.) SAFECOMP 2017. LNCS, vol. 10488, pp. 3–19. Springer, Cham (2017). https://doi.org/10.1007/978-3-319-66266-4_1

9. Elderhalli, Y., Volk, M., Hasan, O., Katoen, J.-P., Tahar, S.: Formal verification of rewriting rules for dynamic fault trees. In: Ölveczky, P.C., Salaün, G. (eds.) SEFM 2019. LNCS, vol. 11724, pp. 513–531. Springer, Cham (2019). https://doi.org/10.1007/978-3-030-30446-1_27

10. Kwiatkowska, M., Norman, G., Parker, D.: Quantitative analysis with the probabilistic model checker PRISM. Electron. Notes Theor. Comput. Sci. **153**(2), 5–31 (2006)

11. Ahmed, W., Hasan, O.: Formalization of fault trees in higher-order logic: a deep embedding approach. In: Fränzle, M., Kapur, D., Zhan, N. (eds.) SETTA 2016. LNCS, vol. 9984, pp. 264–279. Springer, Cham (2016). https://doi.org/10.1007/978-3-319-47677-3_17

12. Ahmed, W., Hasan, O., Tahar, S.: Formalization of reliability block diagrams in higher-order logic. J. Appl. Logic **18**, 19–41 (2016)

13. HOL4 (2020). https://hol-theorem-prover.org/

14. Elderhalli, Y., Ahmad, W., Hasan, O., Tahar, S.: Probabilistic analysis of dynamic fault trees using HOL theorem proving. J. Appl. Logics **6**, 467–509 (2019)

15. Elderhalli, Y., Hasan, O., Tahar, S.: A formally verified algebraic approach for dynamic reliability block diagrams. In: Ait-Ameur, Y., Qin, S. (eds.) ICFEM 2019. LNCS, vol. 11852, pp. 253–269. Springer, Cham (2019). https://doi.org/10.1007/978-3-030-32409-4_16

16. Hölzl, J.: Markov processes in Isabelle/HOL. In: ACM SIGPLAN Conference on Certified Programs and Proofs, pp. 100–111 (2017)

17. Isabelle (2020). https://isabelle.in.tum.de/

18. Ahmed, W., Hasan, O.: Towards formal fault tree analysis using theorem proving. In: Kerber, M., Carette, J., Kaliszyk, C., Rabe, F., Sorge, V. (eds.) CICM 2015. LNCS (LNAI), vol. 9150, pp. 39–54. Springer, Cham (2015). https://doi.org/10.1007/978-3-319-20615-8_3

19. Mhamdi, T., Hasan, O., Tahar, S.: On the formalization of the lebesgue integration theory in HOL. In: Kaufmann, M., Paulson, L.C. (eds.) ITP 2010. LNCS, vol. 6172, pp. 387–402. Springer, Heidelberg (2010). https://doi.org/10.1007/978-3-642-14052-5_27

20. Mhamdi, T., Hasan, O., Tahar, S.: Formalization of entropy measures in HOL. In: van Eekelen, M., Geuvers, H., Schmaltz, J., Wiedijk, F. (eds.) ITP 2011. LNCS, vol. 6898, pp. 233–248. Springer, Heidelberg (2011). https://doi.org/10.1007/978-3-642-22863-6_18

21. Ruijters, E., Stoelinga, M.: Fault tree analysis: a survey of the state-of-the-art in modeling. Anal. Tools Comput. Sci. Rev. **15–16**, 29–62 (2015)

22. Merle, G.: Algebraic modelling of dynamic fault trees, contribution to qualitative and quantitative analysis. Ph.D. thesis, ENS, France (2010)

23. Sullivan, K.J., Dugan, J.B., Coppit, D.: The galileo fault tree analysis tool. In: IEEE Symposium on Fault-Tolerant Computing, pp. 232–235 (1999)

24. Elderhalli, Y., Hasan, O., Ahmad, W., Tahar, S.: Formal dynamic fault trees analysis using an integration of theorem proving and model checking. In: Dutle, A., Muñoz, C., Narkawicz, A. (eds.) NFM 2018. LNCS, vol. 10811, pp. 139–156. Springer, Cham (2018). https://doi.org/10.1007/978-3-319-77935-5_10

25. Elderhalli, Y., Hasan, O., Tahar, S.: A methodology for the formal verification of dynamic fault trees using HOL theorem proving. IEEE Access **7**, 136176–136192 (2019)

26. Boudali, H., Crouzen, P., Stoelinga, M.: A rigorous, compositional, and extensible framework for dynamic fault tree analysis. IEEE Trans. Dependable Secure Comput. **7**, 128–143 (2010)

27. Altby, A., Majdandzic, D.: Design and implementation of a fault-tolerant drive-by-wire system. Master's thesis, Chalmers University of Technology, Sweden (2014)
28. Distefano, S., Puliafito, A.: Dynamic reliability block diagrams vs dynamic fault trees. In: Reliability and Maintainability Symposium, pp. 71–76. IEEE (2007)
29. BlockSim   (2020).   https://www.reliasoft.com/products/reliability-analysis/blocksim
30. Distefano, S.: System dependability and performances: techniques, methodologies and tools. Ph.D. thesis, University of Messina, Italy (2005)
31. Xu, H., Xing, L.: Formal semantics and verification of dynamic reliability block diagrams for system reliability modeling. In: International Conference on Software Engineering and Applications, pp. 155–162 (2007)
32. Smith, G.: The Object-Z Specification Language, vol. 1. Springer, Boston (2012). https://doi.org/10.1007/978-1-4615-5265-9
33. Xu, H., Xing, L., Robidoux, R.: Drbd: dynamic reliability block diagrams for system reliability modelling. Int. J. Comput. Appl. **31**(2), 132–141 (2009)
34. Hasan, O., Ahmed, W., Tahar, S., Hamdi, M.S.: Reliability block diagrams based analysis: a survey. In: International Conference of Numerical Analysis and Applied Mathematics, vol. 1648, p. 850129.1-4. AIP (2015)
35. Liu, L., Hasan, O., Tahar, S.: Formal reasoning about finite-state discrete-time Markov chains in HOL. J. Comput. Sci. Technol. **28**(2), 217–231 (2013)
36. Grimmett, G., Stirzaker, D., et al.: Probability and Random Processes. Oxford University Press, Oxford (2001)
37. Elderhalli, Y., Hasan, O., Tahar, S.: Using machine learning to minimize user intervention in theorem proving based dynamic fault tree analysis. In: Conference on Artificial Intelligence and Theorem Proving, pp. 36–37 (2019)
38. Li, Y., Lee, P.P.C., Lui, J.C.S.: Stochastic analysis on RAID reliability for solid-state drives. In: IEEE International Symposium on Reliable Distributed Systems, pp. 71–80 (2013)

Induction with Generalization in Superposition Reasoning

Márton Hajdú[1], Petra Hozzová[1], Laura Kovács[1,2(✉)], Johannes Schoisswohl[1,3], and Andrei Voronkov[3,4]

[1] TU Wien, Vienna, Austria
laura.kovacs@tuwien.ac.at
[2] Chalmers University of Technology, Gothenburg, Sweden
[3] University of Manchester, Manchester, UK
[4] EasyChair, Manchester, UK

Abstract. We describe an extension of automating induction in superposition-based reasoning by strengthening inductive properties and generalizing terms over which induction should be applied. We implemented our approach in the first-order theorem prover VAMPIRE and evaluated our work against state-of-the-art reasoners automating induction. We demonstrate the strength of our technique by showing that many interesting mathematical properties of natural numbers and lists can be proved automatically using this extension.

1 Introduction

Automating inductive reasoning opens up new possibilities for generating and proving inductive properties, for example properties with inductive data types [4,21] or inductive invariants in program analysis and verification [13,14]. Recent advances related to automating inductive reasoning, such as first-order reasoning with inductively defined data types [16], the AVATAR architecture [26], inductive strengthening of SMT properties [22], structural induction in superposition [10] and general induction rules within saturation [19], make it possible to re-consider the grand challenge of mechanizing mathematical induction [5]. In this paper, we contribute to these advances by *generalizing inductive reasoning within the saturation-based proof search* of first-order theorem provers using the superposition calculus.

It is common in inductive theorem proving, that given a formula/goal F, to try to prove a more general goal instead [5]. This makes no sense in saturation-based theorem proving, which is not based on a goal-subgoal architecture. As we aim to automate and generalize inductive reasoning within saturation-based proof search, *our work follows a different approach than the one used in inductive theorem provers*. Namely, our methodology in Sect. 4 picks up a formula F (not necessarily the goal) in the search space and *adds to the search space new induction axioms with generalization*, that is, instances of generalized induction schemata, aiming at proving both $\neg F$ and a more general formula than $\neg F$.

© Springer Nature Switzerland AG 2020
C. Benzmüller and B. Miller (Eds.): CICM 2020, LNAI 12236, pp. 123–137, 2020.
https://doi.org/10.1007/978-3-030-53518-6_8

In Sect. 3 we give a concrete example motivating our approach, illustrating the advantage of induction with generalization in saturation-based proof search. We then present our main contributions, as follows:

(1) We introduce a new inference rule for first-order superposition reasoning, called *induction with generalization* (Sect. 4). Our work extends [19] by proving properties with multiple occurrences of the same induction term and by instantiating induction axioms with logically stronger versions of the property being proved. Our approach is conceptually different from previous attempts to use induction with superposition [10,11,15], as we are not restricted to specific clause splitting algorithms and heuristics used in [10], nor are we limited to induction over term algebras with the subterm ordering in [11]. As a result, we stay within the standard saturation framework and do not have to introduce constraint clauses, additional predicates or change the notion of redundancy as in [11].

(2) We implemented our work in the VAMPIRE theorem prover [17] and compared it to state-of-the-art reasoners automating induction, including ACL2 [5], CVC4 [2], IMANDRA [18], ZENO [24] and ZIPPERPOSITION [10] (Sect. 5). We also provide a set of handcrafted mathematical problems over natural numbers and lists. We show that induction with generalization in VAMPIRE can solve problems that existing systems, including VAMPIRE without this rule, cannot.

(3) We provide a new digital dataset consisting of over 3,300 inductive benchmarks, for which generalized applications of induction is needed (Sect. 5). Our dataset is formalized within the SMT-LIB format using data types [3] and available at: https://github.com/vprover/inductive_benchmarks.

2 Preliminaries

We assume familiarity with multi-sorted first-order logic and saturation-based superposition reasoning. For details, we refer to [17]. Throughout this paper we denote fresh Skolem constants by σ, variables by x, y, z and terms by t, all possibly with indices. We denote the equality predicate by $=$ and consider $=$ as part of the language. Further, we write $t_1 \neq t_2$ for the formula $\neg(t_1 = t_2)$.

Given a set of formulas (including a negated conjecture), superposition-based theorem provers run saturation algorithms on a set of clauses corresponding to the clausal normal form (CNF) of the input set of formulas. We denote literals by L and clauses by C, all possibly with indices. We use $\square$ to denote the empty clause. In [16] we showed how superposition-based provers can be extended with reasoning about the theory for finite term algebras.

We will denote term algebras corresponding to natural numbers by $\mathbb{N}$ and lists of natural numbers by $\mathbb{L}$. We refer to the elements of the signature of the term algebras as *constructors*. We will use the same notations $\mathbb{N}$ and $\mathbb{L}$ for these term algebras extended by additional function and predicate symbols shown in Fig. 1.

	Natural numbers $\mathbb{N}$	Natural lists $\mathbb{L}$
Constructors	$0 : \mathbb{N}$ $s : \mathbb{N} \to \mathbb{N}$	$\mathtt{nil} : \mathbb{L}$ $\mathtt{cons} : \mathbb{N} \times \mathbb{L} \to \mathbb{L}$
Symbols	$+ : \mathbb{N} \times \mathbb{N} \to \mathbb{N}$ $\leq : \mathbb{N} \times \mathbb{N} \to \text{bool}$	$+\!\!+ : \mathbb{L} \times \mathbb{L} \to \mathbb{L}$ $\mathtt{prefix} : \mathbb{L} \times \mathbb{L} \to \text{bool}$
Axioms	$\forall y.(0 + y = y)$ $\forall x, y.(s(x) + y = s(x + y))$ $\forall x.0 \leq x$ $\forall x.\neg s(x) \leq 0$ $\forall x, y.\big(s(x) \leq s(y)$ $\qquad \leftrightarrow x \leq y\big)$	$\forall l.(\mathtt{nil} +\!\!+ l = l)$ $\forall x, l, k.(\mathtt{cons}(x, l) +\!\!+ k = \mathtt{cons}(x, l +\!\!+ k))$ $\forall l.\mathtt{prefix}(\mathtt{nil}, l)$ $\forall x, l.\neg\mathtt{prefix}(\mathtt{cons}(x, l), \mathtt{nil})$ $\forall x, l, y, k.\big(\mathtt{prefix}(\mathtt{cons}(x, l), \mathtt{cons}(y, k))$ $\qquad \leftrightarrow (x = y \land \mathtt{prefix}(l, k))\big)$

Fig. 1. Term algebras of $\mathbb{N}$ and $\mathbb{L}$, together with additional symbols and axioms.

Specifically, we will deal with $+$ and $\leq$ for $\mathbb{N}$ having their standard meaning and $+\!\!+$ and $\mathtt{prefix}$ for $\mathbb{L}$, denoting the list concatenation and the prefix relation, respectively. These additional symbols are axiomatized by first-order formulas corresponding to their recursive definitions, shown in Fig. 1.

While we use $\mathbb{N}$ and $\mathbb{L}$ for illustration, we however note that our approach can be used for proving properties over any other theories with various forms of induction.

Theorem proving of first-order properties of inductively defined data types needs to handle the domain closure, injectivity, distinctness and acyclicity axioms of term algebras – a detailed definition of these axioms can be found in [16,23]. The challenge we address in [16] is how to automate proving term algebras properties given the fact that the acyclicity axiom is not finitely axiomatizable.

Throughout this paper, we will be using the structural induction axiom and rule for $\mathbb{N}$, introduced in [19], for illustrating our approach. Given a literal $\neg L[t]$, where t is chosen as an induction term, a structural induction axiom for $\mathbb{N}$ is:

$$\big(L[0] \land \forall x.(L[x] \to L[s(x)])\big) \to \forall y.(L[y]). \tag{1}$$

Informally, the axiom expresses that if the base case holds, and if the induction step holds, then the literal holds for all possible values. The structural induction rule for $\mathbb{N}$, given a clause $\neg L[t] \lor C$, adds a clausified form of this axiom to the search space:

$$\frac{\neg L[t] \lor C}{(\neg L[0] \lor L[\sigma] \lor L[y]) \land (\neg L[0] \lor \neg L[s(\sigma)] \lor L[y])}. \tag{2}$$

After using the rule, the $L[y]$ in both resulting clauses can be resolved against the $\neg L[t]$ in the premise clause.

3   Motivating Example

Let us now motivate our approach to induction with generalization, by considering the following formula expressing the associativity of addition over $\mathbb{N}$:

$$\forall x, y, z.(x + (y + z) = (x + y) + z), \qquad \text{with } x, y, z \in \mathbb{N}. \tag{3}$$

$(C_1)\ \sigma_1 + (\sigma_2 + \sigma_3) \neq (\sigma_1 + \sigma_2) + \sigma_3$ [input]
$(C_2)\ 0 + (\sigma_2 + \sigma_3) \neq (0 + \sigma_2) + \sigma_3 \vee \sigma + (\sigma_2 + \sigma_3) = (\sigma + \sigma_2) + \sigma_3$ [induct. C_1]
$(C_3)\ 0 + (\sigma_2 + \sigma_3) \neq (0 + \sigma_2) + \sigma_3 \vee s(\sigma) + (\sigma_2 + \sigma_3) \neq (s(\sigma) + \sigma_2) + \sigma_3$ [induct. C_1]
$(C_4)\ 0 + (\sigma_2 + \sigma_3) \neq (0 + \sigma_2) + \sigma_3 \vee s(\sigma + (\sigma_2 + \sigma_3)) \neq s((\sigma + \sigma_2) + \sigma_3)$ [C_3 + axiom]
$(C_5)\ 0 + (\sigma_2 + \sigma_3) \neq (0 + \sigma_2) + \sigma_3 \vee \sigma + (\sigma_2 + \sigma_3) \neq (\sigma + \sigma_2) + \sigma_3$ [injective C_4]
$(C_6)\ 0 + (\sigma_2 + \sigma_3) \neq (0 + \sigma_2) + \sigma_3$ [res. C_2, C_5]
$(C_7)\ \sigma_2 + \sigma_3 \neq \sigma_2 + \sigma_3$ [C_6 + axiom]
$(C_8)\ \square$ [trivial ineq. C_7]

Fig. 2. Proof of associativity of $+$ in a saturation-based theorem prover with induction

The induction approach introduced in [19] is able to prove this problem. The main steps of such a proof are shown in Fig. 2 and discussed next. First, the negation of formula (3) is skolemized, yielding the (unit) clause C_1 of Fig. 2. As already mentioned, the σ_i denote fresh Skolem constants introduced during clausification. Next, the structural induction axiom (1) is instantiated so that its conclusion can resolve against C_1 using the constant σ_1 as the induction term, resulting in the formula:

$$\begin{aligned}
&\left(0 + (\sigma_2 + \sigma_3) = (0 + \sigma_2) + \sigma_3 \wedge \right. \\
&\left. \forall x.(x + (\sigma_2 + \sigma_3) = (x + \sigma_2) + \sigma_3 \rightarrow s(x) + (\sigma_2 + \sigma_3) = (s(x) + \sigma_2) + \sigma_3)\right) \\
&\rightarrow \forall y.(y + (\sigma_2 + \sigma_3) = (y + \sigma_2) + \sigma_3).
\end{aligned} \tag{4}$$

Then, the CNF of the induction axiom (4) is added to the search space using the following instance of the structural induction rule (2):

$$\frac{\sigma_1 + (\sigma_2 + \sigma_3) \neq (\sigma_1 + \sigma_2) + \sigma_3}{\substack{(0 + (\sigma_2 + \sigma_3) \neq (0 + \sigma_2) + \sigma_3 \vee \sigma + (\sigma_2 + \sigma_3) = (\sigma + \sigma_2) + \sigma_3 \vee \\ y + (\sigma_2 + \sigma_3) = (y + \sigma_2) + \sigma_3}} . \tag{5}$$

$$\wedge$$

$$(0 + (\sigma_2 + \sigma_3) \neq (0 + \sigma_2) + \sigma_3 \vee s(\sigma) + (\sigma_2 + \sigma_3) \neq (s(\sigma) + \sigma_2) + \sigma_3 \vee$$
$$y + (\sigma_2 + \sigma_3) = (y + \sigma_2) + \sigma_3$$

The clauses from the inference conclusion are resolved against C_1, yielding clauses C_2, C_3 of Fig. 2. Clause C_4 originates by repeated demodulation into C_3 using the second axiom of Fig. 1 over $\mathbb{N}$. Further, C_5 is derived from C_4 by using the injectivity property of term algebras and C_6 is a resolvent of C_2 and C_5. Clause C_7 is then derived by repeated demodulation into C_6, using the first axiom of Fig. 1 over $\mathbb{N}$. By removing the trivial inequality from C_7, we finally derive the empty clause C_8.

Consider now the following instance of the associativity property (3):

$$\forall x.(x + (x + x) = (x + x) + x). \tag{6}$$

While (6) is an instance of (3), we cannot prove it using the same approach. Let us explain why this is the case. By instantiating the induction axiom (1) using (6), we get:

$$\big(0 + (0 + 0) = (0 + 0) + 0 \wedge$$
$$\forall x.(x + (x + x) = (x + x) + x \rightarrow s(x) + (s(x) + s(x)) = (s(x) + s(x)) + s(x))\big) \tag{7}$$
$$\rightarrow \forall y.(y + (y + y) = (y + y) + y).$$

After resolving this axiom with the skolemized negation of (6), we get the following two clauses[1]:

$$0 + (0 + 0) \neq (0 + 0) + 0 \vee \sigma + (\sigma + \sigma) = (\sigma + \sigma) + \sigma \tag{8}$$
$$0 + (0 + 0) \neq (0 + 0) + 0 \vee s(\sigma) + (s(\sigma) + s(\sigma)) \neq (s(\sigma) + s(\sigma)) + s(\sigma) \tag{9}$$

While the first literals of (8) and (9) are easily resolved using axioms of $+$, not much can be done with the latter literals. We can only apply repeated demodulations over the second literal of (9) using axioms of $+$ and the injectivity property of term algebras, yielding $\sigma + s(\sigma + s(\sigma)) \neq (\sigma + s(\sigma)) + s(\sigma)$. No further inference over this formula can be applied, in particular it cannot be resolved against the second literal of (8). Hence, the approach of [19] fails proving (6).

The existing approaches to induction also suffer from the same problem. For example [2,5,10,18,24], can prove property (3) but fail to prove its weaker instance (6). The common recipe in inductive theorem proving [5] is to try to prove (3) in addition to trying to prove (6).

Interestingly, in saturation-based theorem proving we can do better. If we follow the common recipe, we would add a generalized goal and then an induction axiom for it. Instead, we only add the induction axiom instance corresponding to the generalized goal without adding the extra goal, which results in a smaller number of clauses. More precisely, in addition to the instance of the induction schema corresponding to (6), we also add instance (4) corresponding to (3). We call this new inference rule *induction with generalization*.

4   Induction with Generalization

Following [19], we consider an *induction axiom* to be any valid formula of the form $premise \rightarrow \forall y.(L[y])$, in the underlying theory, such as the theory of term algebras. An example of an induction axiom is the structural induction axiom (4). An *induction schema* is a collection of induction axioms. Each induction schema we consider is the set of first-order instances of some valid higher-order formula. The work [19] introduces a rule of induction where a ground literal $\neg L[t]$ appearing in the proof search triggers addition of the corresponding induction axioms $premise \rightarrow \forall y.(L[y])$ to the search space:

$$\frac{\neg L[t] \vee C}{\mathrm{CNF}(premise \rightarrow \forall y.(L[y]))}(\texttt{induction}), \tag{10}$$

---

[1] These clauses are instances of C_2 and C_3 from Fig. 2.

where $L[y]$ is obtained from $L[t]$ by replacing *all* occurrences of t by y. An example of an instance of the induction rule is (5).

While addition of a large number of such formulas may seem to blow up the search space, in practice VAMPIRE handles such addition with little overhead, resulting in finding proofs containing nearly 150 induction inferences [19]. The reason why the overhead of adding structural induction axioms is small is explained in [20]: the added clauses only contain one variable (the y in $L[y]$), and the clauses containing this literal are immediately subsumed by a ground clause. The net result is adding a small number of ground clauses, which are especially easy to handle in the AVATAR architecture implemented in VAMPIRE.

Induction with Generalization. In a nutshell, given a goal, we add an induction axiom corresponding to a more general one. The rule can be formulated in the same way as (10), yet with a different conclusion:

$$\frac{\neg L[t] \vee C}{\mathrm{CNF}(premise' \to \forall y.(L'[y]))}(\texttt{IndGen}), \tag{11}$$

where $L'[y]$ is obtained from $L[t]$ by replacing *some* occurrences of t by y, and *premise'* is the premise corresponding to $L'[y]$. Both induction rules are obviously sound because their conclusions are constructed such that they are valid in the underlying theory.

To implement `IndGen`, if a clause selected for inferences contains a ground literal $\neg L[t]$ having more than one occurrence of t, we should select a non-empty subset of occurrences of t in $L[t]$, select an induction axiom corresponding to this subset, and then apply the rule.

Motivating Example, Continued. Suppose that t is σ_1 and $\neg L[t]$ is $\sigma_1 + (\sigma_1 + \sigma_1) \neq (\sigma_1 + \sigma_1) + \sigma_1$, which is obtained by negating and skolemizing (6). Then by applying `IndGen` we can add the following induction axiom:

$$\begin{aligned}
&\big(0 + (\sigma_1 + \sigma_1) = (0 + \sigma_1) + \sigma_1 \wedge \\
&\forall x.(x + (\sigma_1 + \sigma_1) = (x + \sigma_1) + \sigma_1 \to s(x) + (\sigma_1 + \sigma_1) = (s(x) + \sigma_1) + \sigma_1)) \\
&\to \forall y.(y + (\sigma_1 + \sigma_1) = (y + \sigma_1) + \sigma_1),
\end{aligned} \tag{12}$$

which is different from (7). When we add this formula, we can derive the empty clause in the same way as in Fig. 2.

Saturation with Induction with Generalization. The main questions to answer when applying induction with generalization is which occurrences of the induction term in the induction literal we should choose.

Generally, if the subterm t occurs n times in the premise, there are $2^n - 1$ ways of applying the rule, all potentially resulting in *formulas not implying each other*. Thus, an obvious heuristic to use *all* non-empty subsets may result in too many formulas. For example, $\sigma_1 + (\sigma_1 + \sigma_1) \neq (\sigma_1 + \sigma_1) + \sigma_1$ would result in adding 63 induction formulas.

Another simple heuristic is to restrict the number of occurrences selected as induction term to a fixed number. This strategy reduces the number of applications of induction at the cost of losing proofs that would need subsets of cardinality larger than the limit. Finding possible heuristics for selecting specific subsets for common cases of literals can be subject of future work, especially interesting in proof assistants in mathematics.

Note that some of the conclusions of (11) can, in turn, have many children obtained by induction with generalization. Our experiments in Sect. 5 show that, even when we generate all possible children, VAMPIRE can still solve large examples with more than 10 occurrences of the same induction variable, again thanks to the effect that, for each application of induction, only a small number of ground clauses turn out to be added to the search space.

We therefore believe that our work can potentially be also useful for larger examples, and even in cases when the inductive property to be proved is embedded in a larger context.

5   Experiments

Implementation. We implemented induction with generalization in VAMPIRE, with two new options:

- boolean-valued option `indgen`, which turns on/off the application of induction with generalization, with the default value being off, and
- integer-valued option `indgenss`, which sets the maximum size of the subset of occurrences used for induction, with the default value 3. This option is ignored if `indgen` is off.

Our implementation of induction with generalization is available at: https://github.com/vprover/vampire.
In experiments described here, if `indgen` is off, VAMPIRE performs induction on all occurrences of a term in a literal as in [19]. In this section

- VAMPIRE refers to the (default) version of VAMPIRE with induction rule (10) (i.e., the option `-ind struct`)
- VAMPIRE* additionally uses the `IndGen` rule of induction with generalization (11) (i.e., the options `-ind struct -indgen on`).
- VAMPIRE** uses the same options as VAMPIRE* plus the option `-indoct on`, which applies induction to arbitrary ground terms, not just to constants as in VAMPIRE or in VAMPIRE*.

SMT-LIB Experiments. We evaluated our work using the UFDT and UFDTLIA problem sets from SMT-LIB [3], yielding all together 4854 problems. Many of these problems come from program analysis and verification and contain large numbers of axioms, so they are different from standard mathematical examples used in many other papers on automation of induction. Given the nature of the benchmarks, we were interested in two questions:

1. What is the overhead incurred by using induction with generalization in large search spaces, especially when it is not used in proofs? If the new rule is prohibitively expensive, this means it could probably only be used in smaller examples used in interactive theorem proving.

2. Is the new rule useful at all for this kind of benchmarks? While the new rule can be used in principle, should it (or can it) be used in program analysis and verification?

Our results show that *the overhead is relatively small* but we could not solve problems not solvable without the use of the new rule.

Induction (10) in VAMPIRE was already evaluated in [19] against other solvers on these examples. Hence, we only compare how VAMPIRE*/VAMPIRE** performs against VAMPIRE, using both the default and the portfolio modes. (In the default mode, VAMPIRE/VAMPIRE*/VAMPIRE** uses default values for all parameters except the ones specified by the user; in the portfolio mode, VAMPIRE/VAMPIRE*/VAMPIRE** sequentially tries different configurations for parameters not specified by the user.) Together, we ran 18 instances: VAMPIRE, VAMPIRE* with `indgenss` set to 2, 3, 4 and unlimited, and VAMPIRE** with the same four variants of `indgenss`; each of them in both default and portfolio mode. We ran our experiments on the StarExec cluster [25].

The best VAMPIRE*/VAMPIRE** solved 5 problems in the portfolio mode and 1 problem in the default mode not solved by VAMPIRE. However, the proofs found by them did not use induction with generalization. This is a common problem in experiments with saturation theorem proving: new rules change the direction of the proof search and may result in new simplifications that also drastically affect the search space. As a result, new proofs may be found, yet these proofs do not actually use the new rule. There were no problems solved by VAMPIRE that were not solved by any VAMPIRE*/VAMPIRE**.

The maximum number of `IndGen` applications in proofs was 3 and the maximum depth of induction was 4. VAMPIRE*/VAMPIRE** used generalized induction in proofs of 10 problems. However, these problems are also solvable by VAMPIRE (without generalized induction). Thus, we conclude that SMT-LIB problems (probably as well as other typical program analysis and verification benchmarks) typically do not gain from using generalization.

Experiments with Mathematical Problems. We handcrafted a number of natural problems over natural numbers and lists and tested the new rule on these problems. Our benchmarks are available at: https://github.com/vprover/inductive_benchmarks.

Table 1 lists 16 of such examples using the functions defined in Fig. 1. Some examples were taken from or inspired by the TIP benchmark library [9]: e.g., the seventh benchmark in Table 1 is adapted from the TIP library and the second problem is inspired by a symmetric problem from the TIP library, $\forall x.(s(x)+x = s(x+x))$. While they are handcrafted, we believe they are representative since no attempt was done to exclude problems not solvable by VAMPIRE using induction with generalization.

We evaluated and compared several state-of-the-art reasoners supporting standard input formats and, due to the nature of our work, either superposition-based approaches or approaches to generalization. It was not easy to make these experiments since provers use different input syntaxes (see Table 2). As a result, we also had to design translations of our benchmarks.

Table 1. Experiments with 16 handcrafted benchmarks. "✓" denotes success, "–" denotes failure.

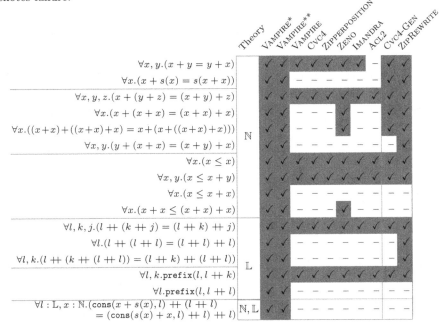

Except for IMANDRA (which is a cloud-based service), we ran our experiments on a 2,9 GHz Quad-Core Intel Core i7 machine. We ran each solver as a single-threaded process with a 5 s time limit. Our results are summarized in Table 1, where CVC4-GEN refers to the solver CVC4 with the automatic lemma discovery enabled. ZIPREWRITE refers to ZIPPERPOSITION with function and predicate definitions encoded as rewrite rules instead of ordinary logical formulas, in order to trigger its generalization heuristics [10]. Configurations used for running all solvers are listed in Table 2.

Table 1 shows that VAMPIRE*/VAMPIRE** (with `indgenss=3`) outperforms all solvers, including VAMPIRE itself. When considering solvers without fine-tuned heuristics, such as in ZIPREWRITE and CVC4-GEN, VAMPIRE** solves many more problems. Interestingly, ZIPREWRITE heuristics work well with addition and list concatenation, but not with orders. Further, CVC4-GEN heuristics prove associativity of addition, but not the list counterpart for concatenation. We believe our experiments show the potential of using induction with generalization as a new inference rule since it outperforms heuristic-driven approaches with no special heuristics or fine-tuning added to VAMPIRE.

Experiments with Problems Requiring Associativity and Commutativity. The $(x + x) + x = x + (x + x)$ is a special case of a family of problems over natural numbers. The problems can be formulated as follows.

Let t_1 and t_2 be two terms built using variables, $+$ and the successor function. Then the equality $t_1 = t_2$ is valid over natural numbers if and only if they have the same number of occurrences of the successor function and each variable of *this equality has the same number of occurrences in t_1 and t_2.* For example, the following equality is valid over natural numbers:

$$s(x + (x + s(y + z))) + s(z) = (z + s(x)) + (x + s(s((z + y)))).$$

To prove such problems over $\mathbb{N}$, one needs both induction and generalization. Without the successor function, they can be easily proved using associativity and commutativity of $+$, but associativity and commutativity are not included in the axioms of $\mathbb{N}$. When the terms are large, the problems become highly challenging.

Table 2. Configurations and input format of solvers for the mathematical problems.

Solver	Configuration	Input format
VAMPIRE	`-ind struct`	SMT-LIB
VAMPIRE*	`-ind struct -indgen on`	SMT-LIB
VAMPIRE**	`-ind struct -indgen on -indoct on`	SMT-LIB
CVC4	`--quant-ind`	SMT-LIB
CVC4-GEN	`--quant-ind --conjecture-gen`	SMT-LIB
ZIPPERPOSITION	default mode	`.zf` (native input format)
ZIPREWRITE	default mode	`.zf` with definitions as rewrite rules
ZENO	default mode	functional program encoding
IMANDRA	default mode	functional program encoding
ACL2	default mode	functional program encoding

We generated a set of instances of these problems (with and without the successor function, and also other functions and predicates) by increasing term sizes. We also generated similar problems for lists using concatenation and reverse functions, and prefix predicate. Some of the terms were, e.g., variations of (6) with 20 occurrences of x. Our entire dataset, containing over 3,300 examples, is available at the previously mentioned URL.

We were again interested in evaluating and comparing various reasoners and approaches on these problems. The interesting feature of these problems is that they are natural yet we can generate problems of almost arbitrary complexity.

We evaluated and compared VAMPIRE*, VAMPIRE**, CVC4-GEN, ZENO and ZIPREWRITE, that is the best performing solvers on inductive reasoning with generalization according to Table 1, using the same experimental setting as already described for Table 1. Table 3 lists a partial summary of our experiments, displaying results for 2,007 large instances of four simple properties with one variable, corresponding to the fourth, ninth, twelfth and fifteenth problem from Table 1. (Due to space constraints, we chose these problems as a representative subset of our large benchmarks, since the solvers' performance was very similar for the whole benchmark set.)

In Table 3, we use the following notation. By $nx = nx$ we denote formulas of the form $x \circ ... \circ x = x \circ ... \circ x$ with n occurrences of x on both sides of the equality, and parentheses on various places in the expressions, with $\circ$ being $+$, or

++ for the datatypes $\mathbb{N}$ and $\mathbb{L}$, respectively. By $mx \leq nx$ and $\texttt{prefix}(mx, nx)$ we denote formulas of the form $x+...+x \leq x+...+x$ and $\texttt{prefix}(x \mathbin{++} ... \mathbin{++} x, x \mathbin{++} ... \mathbin{++} x)$, respectively, with m occurrences of x on the left and n occurrences of x on the right hand side of the $\leq$ or $\texttt{prefix}$ predicates, and with parentheses on various places in the expressions. Result $N\%(M)$ means that the solver solved M of the problems from this category, which corresponds to $N\%$.

From Table 3, we conclude that VAMPIRE** scales better than CVC4-GEN on a large majority of benchmarks, and scales comparably to ZENO. While ZIPREWRITE can solve more problems than VAMPIRE**, VAMPIRE** is more consistent in solving at least some problems from each category. ZIPREWRITE can solve many problems thanks to treatment of equalities as rewrite rules. We are planning to add an option of using recursive definitions as rewrite rules in VAMPIRE in the future too.

6 Related Work

Research into automating induction has a long history with a number of techniques developed, including for example approaches based on semi-automatic inductive theorem proving [5,7,8,18], specialized rewriting procedures [12], SMT reasoning [22] and superposition reasoning [10,11,15,19].

Previous works on automating induction mainly focus on inductive theorem proving [7,8,24]: deciding when induction should be applied and what induction axiom should be used. Further restrictions are made on the logical expressiveness, for example induction only over universal properties [5,24] and without uninterpreted symbols [18], or only over term algebras [11,15]. Inductive proofs usually rely on auxiliary lemmas to help proving an inductive property. In [8] heuristics for finding such lemmas are introduced, for example by randomly generating equational formulas over random inputs and using these formulas if they hold reasonably often. The use of [8] is therefore limited to the underlining heuristics. Other approaches to automating induction circumvent the need for auxiliary lemmas by using uncommon cut-free proof systems for inductive reasoning, such as a restricted ω-rule [1], or cyclic reasoning [6].

The work presented in this paper automates induction by integrating it directly in superposition-based proof search, without relying on rewrite rules and external heuristics for generating auxiliary inductive lemmas/subgoals as in [5,7,8,18,24]. Our new inference rule $\texttt{IndGen}$ for induction with generalization adds new formulas to the search space and can replace lemma discovery heuristics used in [7,8,22]. Our work also extends [19] by using and instantiating induction axioms with logically stronger versions of the property being proved. Unlike [10], our methods do not necessarily depend on AVATAR [26], can be used with any (inductive) data type and target induction rules different than structural induction. Contrarily to [11], we are not limited to induction over term algebras with the subterm ordering and we stay in a standard saturation framework. Moreover, compared to [5,7,8,22], one of the main advantages of our approach is that it does not use a goal-subgoal architecture and can, as a result, combine superposition-based equational reasoning with inductive reasoning.

Table 3. Experiments on 2,007 arithmetical problems.

	Theory	Vampire*	Vampire**	Cvc4-Gen	Zeno	ZipRewrite
$3x = 3x$	N	100% (1)	100% (1)	100% (1)	100% (1)	100% (1)
$4x = 4x$		90% (9)	100% (10)	100% (10)	20% (2)	100% (10)
$5x = 5x$		30% (15)	50% (25)	100% (50)	12% (6)	100% (50)
$6x = 6x$		8% (4)	18% (9)	100% (50)	22% (11)	100% (50)
$7x = 7x$		–	10% (5)	100% (50)	2% (1)	100% (50)
$8x = 8x$		–	2% (1)	100% (50)	4% (2)	100% (50)
$9x = 9x$		–	2% (1)	100% (50)	8% (4)	84% (42)
$10x = 10x$		–	–	100% (50)	8% (4)	90% (45)
$3x = 3x$	L	100% (1)	100% (1)	–	–	100% (1)
$4x = 4x$		70% (7)	90% (9)	–	–	100% (10)
$5x = 5x$		46% (23)	48% (24)	–	–	100% (50)
$6x = 6x$		6% (3)	26% (13)	–	6% (3)	100% (50)
$7x = 7x$		2% (1)	6% (3)	–	–	100% (50)
$8x = 8x$		–	–	–	–	90% (45)
$9x = 9x$		–	–	–	–	88% (44)
$10x = 10x$		–	–	–	–	68% (34)
$3x \leq 3x$	N	100% (2)	100% (2)	100% (2)	100% (2)	100% (2)
$4x \leq 4x$		–	15% (3)	100% (20)	20% (4)	100% (20)
$5x \leq 5x$		–	4% (2)	100% (50)	12% (6)	100% (50)
$1x \leq 2x$		100% (1)	100% (1)	–	–	–
$2x \leq 3x$		50% (1)	50% (1)	–	100% (2)	–
$3x \leq 4x$		–	30% (3)	–	40% (4)	–
$4x \leq 5x$		–	8% (4)	–	16% (8)	–
$5x \leq 6x$		–	6% (3)	–	10% (5)	–
$1x \leq 3x$		100% (2)	100% (2)	–	100% (2)	100% (2)
$2x \leq 4x$		–	40% (2)	–	40% (2)	100% (5)
$3x \leq 5x$		–	14% (4)	–	28% (8)	100% (28)
$4x \leq 6x$		–	10% (5)	–	18% (9)	100% (50)
$5x \leq 7x$		–	4% (2)	–	18% (9)	100% (50)
$1x \leq 4x$		100% (5)	100% (5)	–	80% (4)	100% (5)
$2x \leq 5x$		–	35% (5)	–	42% (6)	100% (14)
$3x \leq 6x$		–	18% (9)	–	38% (19)	100% (50)
$4x \leq 7x$		–	6% (3)	–	16% (8)	100% (50)
$5x \leq 8x$		–	–	–	6% (3)	100% (50)
$1x \leq 5x$		100% (14)	100% (14)	–	85% (12)	100% (14)
$2x \leq 6x$		–	33% (14)	–	26% (11)	100% (42)
$3x \leq 7x$		–	14% (7)	–	32% (16)	100% (50)
$4x \leq 8x$		–	4% (2)	–	18% (9)	100% (50)
$5x \leq 9x$		–	–	–	14% (7)	100% (50)
$\texttt{prefix}(3x, 3x)$		100% (2)	50% (1)	–	–	100% (2)
$\texttt{prefix}(4x, 4x)$		–	25% (5)	–	–	100% (20)
$\texttt{prefix}(5x, 5x)$		–	2% (1)	–	4% (2)	100% (50)
$\texttt{prefix}(1x, 2x)$		100% (1)	100% (1)	–	–	–
$\texttt{prefix}(2x, 3x)$		–	50% (1)	–	50% (1)	–
$\texttt{prefix}(3x, 4x)$		–	20% (2)	–	20% (2)	–
$\texttt{prefix}(4x, 5x)$		–	8% (4)	–	8% (4)	–
$\texttt{prefix}(5x, 6x)$		–	–	–	–	–
$\texttt{prefix}(1x, 3x)$		100% (2)	100% (2)	–	50% (1)	100% (2)
$\texttt{prefix}(2x, 4x)$		20% (1)	40% (2)	–	20% (1)	100% (5)
$\texttt{prefix}(3x, 5x)$		–	14% (4)	–	14% (4)	100% (28)
$\texttt{prefix}(4x, 6x)$	L	–	6% (3)	–	8% (4)	100% (50)
$\texttt{prefix}(5x, 7x)$		–	2% (1)	–	2% (1)	100% (50)
$\texttt{prefix}(1x, 4x)$		100% (5)	100% (5)	–	40% (2)	100% (5)
$\texttt{prefix}(2x, 5x)$		–	35% (5)	–	21% (3)	100% (14)
$\texttt{prefix}(3x, 6x)$		–	14% (7)	–	12% (6)	100% (50)
$\texttt{prefix}(4x, 7x)$		–	4% (2)	–	4% (2)	100% (50)
$\texttt{prefix}(5x, 8x)$		–	–	–	4% (2)	100% (50)
$\texttt{prefix}(1x, 5x)$		100% (14)	100% (14)	–	42% (6)	100% (14)
$\texttt{prefix}(2x, 6x)$		–	33% (14)	–	21% (9)	100% (42)
$\texttt{prefix}(3x, 7x)$		–	16% (8)	–	16% (8)	100% (50)
$\texttt{prefix}(4x, 8x)$		–	10% (5)	–	12% (6)	100% (50)
$\texttt{prefix}(5x, 9x)$		–	–	–	–	100% (50)

Normally, generalization in theorem proving means that given a goal F, we try to prove a more general goal. In logic, a statement F' is more general than F if F' implies F. Thus, by proving F' we also prove F. One way to generalize is to replace one or more occurrences of a subterm by a fresh variable, using the fact that $\forall x.(F[x])$ implies $F[t]$. This is essentially the idea behind approaches to generalization in all systems we compared with. While our approach is superficially similar, it does something *fundamentally different*. Instead of (or in addition to) adding an instance I of the induction schema that can be used to prove $F[t]$, we add an instance I' that can be used to prove $\forall x.(F[x])$. An interesting observation is that, in general, neither I implies I', nor I' implies I, so neither of I and I' is more general.

The *second fundamental difference* is that, because induction in VAMPIRE is not based on a goal-subgoal architecture, we can add both induction formulas I and I' at the same time. While this may seem inefficient, for some induction schemata, including structural induction, the overhead is very small (as also confirmed by our experiments).

7   Conclusions

We introduced a new rule for induction with generalization in saturation-based reasoning based on adding induction axioms for proving generalizations of the goals appearing during proof-search. Our experiments show that we solve many problems that other existing systems cannot solve. Future work includes designing heuristics to guide proof search, using rewriting approaches, and performing other kinds of generalization and induction.

Acknowledgments. We thank Giles Reger for discussions related to the work. We acknowledge funding supporting this work, in particular the ERC starting grant 2014 SYMCAR 639270, the EPSRC grant EP/P03408X/1, the ERC proof of concept grant 2018 SYMELS 842066, the Wallenberg Academy fellowship 2014 TheProSE, the Austrian FWF research project W1255-N23, and the Hungarian-Austrian project 101öu8.

References

1. Baker, S., Ireland, A., Smaill, A.: On the use of the constructive omega-rule within automated deduction. In: Voronkov, A. (ed.) LPAR 1992. LNCS, vol. 624, pp. 214–225. Springer, Heidelberg (1992). https://doi.org/10.1007/BFb0013063
2. Barrett, C., et al.: CVC4. In: Gopalakrishnan, G., Qadeer, S. (eds.) CAV 2011. LNCS, vol. 6806, pp. 171–177. Springer, Heidelberg (2011). https://doi.org/10.1007/978-3-642-22110-1_14
3. Barrett, C., Fontaine, P., Tinelli, C.: The Satisfiability Modulo Theories Library (SMT-LIB) (2016). www.SMT-LIB.org
4. Blanchette, J.C., Peltier, N., Robillard, S.: Superposition with datatypes and codatatypes. In: Galmiche, D., Schulz, S., Sebastiani, R. (eds.) IJCAR 2018. LNCS (LNAI), vol. 10900, pp. 370–387. Springer, Cham (2018). https://doi.org/10.1007/978-3-319-94205-6_25

5. Boyer, R.S., Moore, J.S.: A Computational Logic Handbook, Perspectives incomputing, vol. 23. Academic Press, Cambridge (1979)
6. Brotherston, J., Simpson, A.: Sequent calculi for induction and infinite descent. J. Log. Comput. **21**(6), 1177–1216 (2011)
7. Bundy, A., Stevens, A., van Harmelen, F., Ireland, A., Smaill, A.: Rippling: a heuristic for guiding inductive proofs. Artif. Intell. **62**(2), 185–253 (1993)
8. Claessen, K., Johansson, M., Rosén, D., Smallbone, N.: HipSpec: automating inductive proofs of program properties. In: Proceedings of the ATx/WInG, pp. 16–25 (2012)
9. Claessen, K., Johansson, M., Rosén, D., Smallbone, N.: TIP: tons of inductive problems. In: Kerber, M., Carette, J., Kaliszyk, C., Rabe, F., Sorge, V. (eds.) CICM 2015. LNCS (LNAI), vol. 9150, pp. 333–337. Springer, Cham (2015). https://doi.org/10.1007/978-3-319-20615-8_23
10. Cruanes, S.: Superposition with structural induction. In: Dixon, C., Finger, M. (eds.) FroCoS 2017. LNCS (LNAI), vol. 10483, pp. 172–188. Springer, Cham (2017). https://doi.org/10.1007/978-3-319-66167-4_10
11. Echenim, M., Peltier, N.: Combining induction and saturation-based theorem proving. J. Autom. Reason. **64**(2), 253–294 (2019). https://doi.org/10.1007/s10817-019-09519-x
12. Falke, S., Kapur, D.: Rewriting induction + linear arithmetic = decision procedure. In: Gramlich, B., Miller, D., Sattler, U. (eds.) IJCAR 2012. LNCS (LNAI), vol. 7364, pp. 241–255. Springer, Heidelberg (2012). https://doi.org/10.1007/978-3-642-31365-3_20
13. Gleiss, B., Kovács, L., Robillard, S.: Loop analysis by quantification over iterations. In: Proceedings of the LPAR, pp. 381–399 (2018)
14. Gurfinkel, A., Shoham, S., Vizel, Y.: Quantifiers on demand. In: Lahiri, S.K., Wang, C. (eds.) ATVA 2018. LNCS, vol. 11138, pp. 248–266. Springer, Cham (2018). https://doi.org/10.1007/978-3-030-01090-4_15
15. Kersani, A., Peltier, N.: Combining superposition and induction: a practical realization. In: Fontaine, P., Ringeissen, C., Schmidt, R.A. (eds.) FroCoS 2013. LNCS (LNAI), vol. 8152, pp. 7–22. Springer, Heidelberg (2013). https://doi.org/10.1007/978-3-642-40885-4_2
16. Kovács, L., Robillard, S., Voronkov, A.: Coming to terms with quantified reasoning. In: Proceedings of POPL, pp. 260–270 (2017)
17. Kovács, L., Voronkov, A.: First-order theorem proving and VAMPIRE. In: Sharygina, N., Veith, H. (eds.) CAV 2013. LNCS, vol. 8044, pp. 1–35. Springer, Heidelberg (2013). https://doi.org/10.1007/978-3-642-39799-8_1
18. Passmore, G., et al.: The Imandra automated reasoning system. In: Proceedings of the IJCAR (2020, to appear)
19. Reger, G., Voronkov, A.: Induction in saturation-based proof search. In: Fontaine, P. (ed.) CADE 2019. LNCS (LNAI), vol. 11716, pp. 477–494. Springer, Cham (2019). https://doi.org/10.1007/978-3-030-29436-6_28
20. Reger, G., Voronkov, A.: Induction in Saturation-Based Proof Search. EasyChair Smart Slide (2020). https://easychair.org/smart-slide/slide/hXmP
21. Reynolds, A., Blanchette, J.C.: A decision procedure for (Co)datatypes in SMT solvers. In: Felty, A.P., Middeldorp, A. (eds.) CADE 2015. LNCS (LNAI), vol. 9195, pp. 197–213. Springer, Cham (2015). https://doi.org/10.1007/978-3-319-21401-6_13
22. Reynolds, A., Kuncak, V.: Induction for SMT solvers. In: D'Souza, D., Lal, A., Larsen, K.G. (eds.) VMCAI 2015. LNCS, vol. 8931, pp. 80–98. Springer, Heidelberg (2015). https://doi.org/10.1007/978-3-662-46081-8_5

23. Rybina, T., Voronkov, A.: A decision procedure for term algebras with queues. ACM Trans. Comput. Log. **2**(2), 155–181 (2001)

24. Sonnex, W., Drossopoulou, S., Eisenbach, S.: Zeno: an automated prover for properties of recursive data structures. In: Flanagan, C., König, B. (eds.) TACAS 2012. LNCS, vol. 7214, pp. 407–421. Springer, Heidelberg (2012). https://doi.org/10.1007/978-3-642-28756-5_28

25. Stump, A., Sutcliffe, G., Tinelli, C.: StarExec: a cross-community infrastructure for logic solving. In: Demri, S., Kapur, D., Weidenbach, C. (eds.) IJCAR 2014. LNCS (LNAI), vol. 8562, pp. 367–373. Springer, Cham (2014). https://doi.org/10.1007/978-3-319-08587-6_28

26. Voronkov, A.: AVATAR: the architecture for first-order theorem provers. In: Biere, A., Bloem, R. (eds.) CAV 2014. LNCS, vol. 8559, pp. 696–710. Springer, Cham (2014). https://doi.org/10.1007/978-3-319-08867-9_46

A Survey of Languages for Formalizing Mathematics

Cezary Kaliszyk[1] and Florian Rabe[2(✉)]

[1] University of Innsbruck, Innsbruck, Austria
[2] University Erlangen-Nürnberg, Erlangen, Germany
florian.rabe@fau.de

Abstract. In order to work with mathematical content in computer systems, it is necessary to represent it in formal languages. Ideally, these are supported by tools that verify the correctness of the content, allow computing with it, and produce human-readable documents. These goals are challenging to combine and state-of-the-art tools typically have to make difficult compromises.

In this paper we discuss languages that have been created for this purpose, including logical languages of proof assistants and other formal systems, semi-formal languages, intermediate languages for exchanging mathematical knowledge, and language frameworks that allow building customized languages.

We evaluate their advantages based on our experience in designing and applying languages and tools for formalizing mathematics. We reach the conclusion that no existing language is truly good enough yet and derive ideas for possible future improvements.

1 Introduction

Today's formal systems can verify advanced theorems in mathematics [Hal14], such as the Kepler conjecture [Hal12] or the Feit–Thompson theorem [GAA+13], as well as certify important computer systems, such as the CompCert C compiler [Ler09] and the seL4 microkernel [KAE+14]. All these systems and projects use advanced logical languages that are computer-understandable but hard for humans to write and read.

Computer science commonly defines and implements such *formal* languages for mathematical content that define syntax and semantics and offer strong automation support. However, non-trivial and expensive transformation steps are needed to formalize human-near *natural* language texts in them.

This is in contrast to standard approaches to writing mathematics or specifying computer systems, which use *natural* language with interspersed syntactically unrestricted formulas, e.g., as written in LaTeX. While interpreting this natural language is very difficult for computers (arguably AI-complete), it is extremely

C. Kaliszyk—Supported by ERC starting grant no. 714034 *SMART*.
F. Rabe—Supported by DFG grant RA-1872/3-1 OAF and EU grant Horizon 2020 ERI 676541 OpenDreamKit.

C. Benzmüller and B. Miller (Eds.): CICM 2020, LNAI 12236, pp. 138–156, 2020.
https://doi.org/10.1007/978-3-030-53518-6_9

effective for humans in a way that formal languages have so far not been able to capture. In fact, in 2007, Wiedijk claimed [Wie07], citing four representative statements, that no existing formal system was sufficient to naturally express basic mathematical content. Despite the progress made since then, his critique still applies.

We give an introduction to the objectives and main approaches in Sect. 2. Then Sects. 3 and 4 describe the main approaches: formal system and intermediate languages in more detail. Sections 5 and 6 describe closely related orthogonal aspects: language frameworks and interchange libraries. We evaluate our findings and conclude in Sect. 7.

2 Overview

2.1 Objectives

Thus, a big picture goal of the field is a tighter integration of (i) natural language mathematical content such as textbooks or software specifications, and (ii) formalization of such content in logics and theorem proving systems. We can identify the following overarching objectives:

A Universal Formal Language for Mathematical Content that Supports Complex Structuring Mechanisms. We want a language that combines the universality of natural mathematical languages with the automation support of formal logics and programming languages. It should be closer to mathematics than these formal languages in regards to abstract syntax, notations, and type system. This is critical not only for generality but also to appeal to mathematicians at all because, as Wiedijk observes, most mathematicians do not like to read (or write) code [Wie07]. On the other hand, it should be fully formal including automation support for type, module, and proof systems of formal languages that have proved critical for large scale applications.

A Comprehensive Standard Library of Mathematical Concepts. The language must allow for building a standard library of mathematical concepts. In order to allow for semantics-aware machine support, it should be more formal than existing informal libraries such as induced by Wikipedia or PlanetMath by including formal types, notations, and properties. On the other hand, in order to achieve generality and support interoperability, it should not be committed to a particular logic like all the major formal libraries are. This combination of advantages would allow it to serve as a *standard* library, i.e., a central community resource to be used, e.g., to cross-link between existing libraries in a star-shaped network or to provide a basis for projects like FAbstracts [Hal17].

Practical Workflows that Integrate Natural and Formal Languages. Such a language and standard library would enable substantially better tool support for working researchers in mathematical sciences: Being structurally similar to both natural and formal languages, they could serve as an interface language for tools of either kind. This would allow enriching existing workflows such as LaTeX-based authoring or proof-assistant–based verification. For example, researchers could easily formalize conjectures and their proof outlines in a general language as a first and cheap formalization step, before or instead of a full verification of the proof. This would avoid hindering practicians as today's all-or-nothing approach of formalization in proof assistants tends to do [KR16]. It is critical for success here to retain existing workflows instead of trying to develop a single be-all-end-all tool that no one would adopt. Therefore, any major project in this direction must aim at developing concrete improvements to the current ecosystem.

2.2   Approaches

The most successful formal languages for mathematical content have been developed in the areas of formal logic where they occur most prominently as the input languages of proof assistants as well as in computer algebra where they occur as programming languages fitted to mathematical algorithms. These combine formal foundations with complex structuring mechanisms, especially type, module, proof, and computation systems, which have proved critical to achieve efficient large scale tool support. Importantly, these fix not only the syntax but also the semantics of, e.g., proofs and computations On the contrary, in natural language, these are not spelled out at all, let alone explicated as a primitive feature—instead, they are emergent features driven by conventions and flexibly adaptable to different contexts. Consequently, formalization is usually a non-structure-preserving transformation that is often prohibitively expensive and creates an entry barrier for casual users. For example, the mathematician Kevin Buzzard admonishes computer scientists to build more human-near languages "so users can at least read sentences they understand and try to learn to write these sentences".

Between the extremes of natural and formal languages, a variety of *intermediate* languages make different trade-offs aiming at combining the universal applicability of natural language with the advantages of formal semantics. A central observation is that

– existing intermediate languages apply only the formal syntax and (to varying degrees) semantics of formal languages but not their complex structuring mechanisms, and
– this limitation is not necessarily an inherent feature of the approach but rather a frontier of research.

The following table summarizes the resulting trichotomy and shows how each kind of language satisfies only two out of three essential requirements:

Language properties	Natural	Intermediate	Formal
Formal syntax and semantics	–	+	+
Complex structuring	+	–	+
Universal applicability	+	+	–

In the subsequent sections, we discuss the state of the art for these languages in more detail.

3   Formal Languages

Formal languages use a wide variety of foundations and complex structuring mechanisms. This unfortunately means that it is rare for two tools to be compatible with each other. Additionally, all are quite removed from natural language. In the sequel, we discuss the most important complex structuring features.

3.1   Type Systems

Many formal systems use what we call *hard* type systems, which assign a unique type to each object and are thus easiest to automate. Systems derived from Martin-Löf type theory [ML74] or the calculus of constructions [CH88] usually use the proofs-as-programs correspondence (Curry-Howard [CF58,How80]) that represents mathematical properties as types and proofs as data. These include Agda [Nor05], Coq [Coq15], Lean [dKA+15], Matita [ASTZ06] as well as Nuprl [CAB+86]. Systems derived from Church's higher-order logic [Chu40] usually use the LCF architecture [Mil72] that uses an abstract type of proved theorems. These include HOL4 [HOL], ProofPower [Art], Isabelle [NPW02], and HOL Light [Har96].

Hard type systems are at odds with natural language as the unique-type property precludes representing mathematical sets and subsets as types and subtypes. In particular, the lack of expressive subtyping in hard type systems is fundamentally at odds with every day mathematics, where sets and subsets are used throughout: hard type system precludes a direct representation of sets as types because they cannot represent the rich (even undecidable) subset relation using subtyping.

Multiple systems have explored compromises. We speak of *semi-soft* type systems if a hard type system is extended with variants of subtyping. For example, PVS [ORS92] uses predicate subtypes, Lean [dKA+15] and Nurpl [CAB+86] support predicate subtypes and quotient types, and IMPS uses [FGT93] refinement types.

Both hard and semi-soft type systems force users to choose between representing information using the type system (e.g., $\forall x : \mathbb{N}.P(x)$) or the logical system (e.g., $\forall x.x \in \mathbb{N} \Rightarrow P(x)$). Problematically, this choice usually has far-reaching consequences, e.g., the type system may be decidable but the logic system undecidable. But from the perspective of mathematics this distinction is artificial, and the fact that the two resulting representations may be entirely incompatible down the road is very awkward.

These problems are avoided in *untyped* languages. ACL2 [KMM00] is a first-order logic on top of the untyped λ-calculus of Lisp that strongly emphasizes computation. Untyped set theory is used in Isabelle/ZF [PC93], Metamath [Meg07], and the B method [Abr96]. Untyped languages are also common in virtually all computer algebra systems, such as Mathematica [Wol12] or Sage-Math [S+13].

We speak of *soft type systems* if unary predicates on the untyped objects mimic types and the type system is an emergent feature of the logical system. These are used most prominently in Mizar [TB85] among proof assistants and GAP [Lin07] among computer algebra systems. Both use the types-as-predicates approach, where the semantics of a type is given by a unary predicate ranging over untyped objects. Both allow declaring functions and dependent types (i.e., predicates $n + 1$ arguments that return a unary predicate after fixing the first n arguments) that have type constraints on the arguments. Soft type systems are generally hardest to automate because type-checking is reduced to undecidable theorem proving. Here Mizar leverages theorem proving: the type checker is guided by user-stated typing rules (called registrations), which are specially marked theorems about typing properties. GAP leverages computation: the typing predicates must be computable properties, which are computed and cached at run-time for every object.

Thus, soft type systems are heuristic, which makes implementations more difficult for the developer and their behavior less predictable for the user. But they are the most human-friendly. A combination of hard and soft type systems, where advanced hard type systems are emergent features built systematically on top of a soft one, could potentially model mathematical content best but has so far received much less systematic attention than the above approaches. But as theorem proving technology becomes more routine, they become more and more attractive.

An example soft type system has been recently developed on top of a hard-typed Isabelle for the Isabelle/Mizar object logic [KP19a], which expresses the largest softly typed proof library in a logical framework. As part of this research, the type system of Mizar has been formalized including its intersection type constructions, various ways to express set-theoretic structures, and declarative proof translations [KP19b] have been investigated. Furthermore, a common foundation for proofs that allows practically combining results between HOL and set theory has been developed [BKP19].

3.2   Module Systems

A key use of modules is to represent structures (also called records or theories); here the abstract definition (e.g., "group") is represented as a module, and concrete models (e.g., individual groups) are represented as instances of the module. The used module systems vary widely but roughly fall into the following groups.

Firstly, ML-inspired *external* module systems use a two-layer language where the module language is external to the logical language. These allow for inheritance, refinement, and instantiation (e.g., Coq modules, Isabelle locales, PVS theories, SageMath categories, Axiom categories) as well as more advanced structuring such as parametric modules (e.g., PVS), module expressions (e.g., Isabelle locales, Axiom joins), or morphisms between modules (Isabelle, IMPS). Hard module systems differ greatly from natural language where no two-layer language is fixed.

Secondly, *internal* module systems use record types to mimic modular structure inside the type system. This is possible in all systems that support record types (e.g., Agda, Coq, Isabelle, Lean, PVS); Mizar's structures behave similarly. Soft modules are more flexible and thus similar to natural language, but the lack of a concise module system makes modular reasoning like inheritance and refinement more difficult. For example, soft module systems must manually employ extra-logical conventions (e.g., [GGMR09]), and combining modules built with different conventions quickly becomes impractical. This is even worse in the common case where both hard and soft module systems are present in parallel (we have initiated work in this direction in [MRK18]).

Both of the above can be seen as *hard* module systems in the sense that a module encapsulates a fixed set of declarations that induce selectors that can be applied to the module's instances. A third group, which we call *soft* module systems is somewhat hypothetical as it is used much less widely. Here, in analogy to soft tying, modules are treated as unary predicates that range over objects. Inheritance then becomes a special case of implication. This idea is used in the GAP module system, whose soft types (called properties) and soft modules (called categories) are treated very similarly: they are jointly filters, and the run-time system tracks which object satisfies which filters. The main difference between them is that categories can have constructors and thus allow for filters that are satisfied by construction.

Finally, since module systems have mostly been designed as extensions of existing logical languages, both hard and soft module systems fail to capture a number of essential features of natural mathematical language: the identification of isomorphic instances of the same module; the seamless extension of operations across substructures and quotient structures (e.g., $+$ is first defined on $\mathbb{N}$, then extended to $\mathbb{Z}$); the flexibility of presence and order of fields in a structure (e.g., $(\mathbb{Z}, +, *)$ and $(\mathbb{Z}, +, 0, -, *, 1)$ should be the same ring); the context-sensitive meaning of structures (e.g., $\mathbb{Z}$ should be a ring or a total order, depending on the context); and in many systems also the implicit application of forgetful functors (e.g., a group is not automatically also a monoid).

3.3 Proof Systems

Formal languages shine when using logics implemented in proof assistants to find and check proofs automatically. *Tactic-based* proof systems (e.g., HOL Light) are optimized for efficiency of proof checking but have an imperative flavor that is very different from natural mathematical language. *Declarative* proof systems (e.g. Mizar, Isabelle/Isar) were designed to be closer to natural language.

While many current tools support declarative proofs using quite similar languages, all of these are intertwined with the respective logic and therefore not immediately reusable as a universally applicable declarative proof language. In particular, the expressivity of these languages is limited by the strength of the underlying logic, i.e., they can only express the kind of proof steps that can be potentially verified by the tool. Declarative proof languages are conceptually close to natural mathematics but technically tied to specific logics. We discuss logical languages in more detail in Sect. 5.

In computer algebra systems no formal logics are implied and automated reasoning is restricted to computable properties. Additionally, these systems can capture logical properties by user declaration: for example, most systems' libraries distinguish between groups and commutative groups and allow users to construct a group as commutative even if that property is not proved.

3.4   Computation Systems

The second major application of formal languages stems from computer algebra systems, which use mathematics-customized variants of general purpose programming languages for efficient computation.

Even though mathematics uses mostly pure functions, most systems are based on Turing-complete imperative programming, mostly to reuse existing user knowledge and fast implementations. It is common to use the same language for pure mathematical algorithms and interspersed imperative meta-operations like I/O, logging, memoization, or calling external tools (in particular in SageMath).

Proof assistants take a much more restricted approach to integrate pure computations with a logic. Three main approaches exist. Firstly, normalization in the type theory, in particular β-reduction is a primitive form of computation. It becomes much stronger when combined with (co)inductive types and recursion, and these are primitive features in most complex type theories like Coq. Systems then usually include heuristic termination criteria to check the soundness of the functions, which leads to a trade-off between logical and Turing-completeness. Secondly, certain theorems such as Horn formulas about equality can be interpreted as conditional rewrite rules. Typically, systems require the user to choose which theorems to use and then exhaustively rewrite expressions with them. This is much slower but allows for a much simpler language as computation is relegated to the meta-level. This is the main method used in systems without primitive (co)inductive types such as Isabelle. Thirdly, computation can be supplied by external tools or special kernel modules. This computation can be a part of the, consequently rather big, trusted code base, such as in PVS decision procedures, the usage of SAT solvers is Mizar [Nau14]. This is also the case in Theorema: As the proof assistant is written in the Mathematica computer algebra system, it is in principle possible to use most Mathematica's algorithms inside Theorema [Win14]. In some cases, a trade-off is possible where computations are run externally and their results are efficiently verified by the prover.

4   Intermediate Languages

Intermediate languages try to capture the advantages of natural languages in a formal language. There is a rather diverse set of such approaches, which we

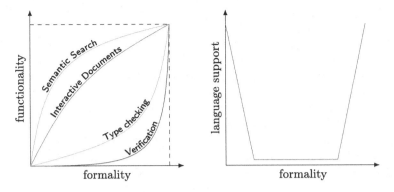

Fig. 1. Functionality for intermediate languages (left) market gap for stepwise formalization support (right)

describe in groups below. However, we can identify some general effects that motivate the design of many intermediate languages.

Firstly, an intermediate language can already provide sufficient automation support for some tasks. Thus, it can serve as a more natural and easier-to-use target language for (partial) formalization if the task at hand is supported. For example, search, interactive documents, or dependency management can be realized well in some intermediate languages and even benefit from structural similarity to the human-near natural language formulation. The main counter-examples are verification and computation, which requires a lot more formalization. This is indicated in Fig. 1 (left).

Secondly, an intermediate language can serve as an interface between human-near natural language and a verification- or computation-oriented formal language. This enables stepwise formalization and thus a smoother transition from the informal to the formal realm. It may also allow for a separation of concerns where a domain experts transform content from informal to intermediate in a first step and a formalization transforms from intermediate to formal in a second step. The relative lack of highly successful approaches in this style is indicated in Fig. 1 (right).

Thirdly, the intermediate representation is often not or only barely committed to a particular formal language (e.g., a particular type system, module system, proof system or computation system). During stepwise formalization, this means that the first step only needs to be done once and can then be reused for different second steps targeting different formal languages. Expanding on this, we see that an intermediate language can provide an interoperability layer between formal languages. That can help with the notorious lack of interoperability between formal systems (see also Sect. 6).

4.1   Controlled Natural Language

These approaches combine formal grammars for fragments of natural language with formal languages for formulas. Their goal is to make the surface syntax of a formal language as close to traditional mathematics as possible while retaining a formal grammar that allows for automated parsing. While the languages often look similar to some semi-formal languages discussed below, we classify them differently because they use a formal logic-near language in their kernel.

This method is applied in MathLang [KW08, KWZB14], MathNat [Hum12], in [KN12] within the FMathL project, and Naproche [CFK+09]. Mizar [TB85] is a logical language whose surface syntax has been carefully designed to look like a small fragment of natural language and thus looks similar to controlled natural language systems without being one.

These systems vary in how the semantics of the language is defined and how much implementation support is provided. Both MathLang and Naproche use, effectively, a soft type system on top of set theory to define the semantics. MathLang allows for translating content into proof assistants (Isabelle, Coq) for users to finish and check proofs, and Naproche uses automated first-order theorem provers to discharge proof obligations automatically.

Contrary to the verification/computation-oriented formal languages, where large libraries of formal content (up to $\sim 10^5$ theorems in the biggest systems) are developed and shared in vibrant communities, none of the controlled natural language systems provides a substantial library. This is a hen-egg problem since large libraries often result from the practical necessities caused by verification and computation. A critical limiting factor of existing controlled natural languages is the lack of scalable automation support and large libraries.

4.2   Semi-formal Languages

These approaches aim at combining unrestricted natural mathematical language and formal language in the same document. Contrary to the controlled natural language approaches discussed above, the interpretation of the natural language parts remains AI-complete.

Flexiformal systems use informal and formal language as alternatives, i.e., content may be written informally or formally. Thus, not all mathematical content is formalized, and all tool support must degrade gracefully when informal and thus uninterpretable content is encountered. The sTeX system [Koh08] is a LaTeX package for annotating informal mathematical texts with its formal meaning, which then allows for writing (parts of) formulas in formal logical syntax. In addition to pdf, sTeX documents can be processed into OMDoc documents [Koh06], which makes them available for further machine processing. sTeX provides no type system and only a very simple hard module system. It has been used by the developer to write his introductory computer science lecture notes.

Literate programming [Knu84] and approaches inspired by it allow for natural and formal language to appear in parallel. Here, content is described twice: the formal version defines the semantics, and the informal version provides documentation. Contrary to the other approaches mentioned here, this is not a third language in between formal and natural, but a combination of the two. Several formal systems provide mature support for writing content in literate programming style such as Agda, Isabelle (see [Wen11]), and Axiom.

Discourse representation languages [KR93] perform an analysis of the language used in written mathematics and design a fixed set of disambiguation conventions. Ganesalingam [Gan13] proposes a system of types that together with a parsing procedure and the set of disambiguation conventions could be used to parse non-foundational mathematics. Apart from the foundational issues, the approach also has a problem with adaptivity of mathematical texts.

4.3   Interchange Languages

These approaches apply the general principles of formal languages while avoiding a commitment to a particular logic or implementation. A major goal is system interoperability.

Standardized representation languages have been developed in the area of knowledge management such as OPENMATH [BCC+04], content MATHML [ABC+10], and OMDOC [Koh06]. These prioritize standardizing the syntax using standard machine-friendly representation formats such as XML (where the formal structure of objects is explicit). They do not specify user-friendly surface syntaxes (where the formal structure would have to be inferred through complex parsing and disambiguation) or rigorous semantics. This allows their use as interchange languages (e.g., in the SCIEnce [HR09] and OpenDreamKit [DIK+16] EU projects), as a basis for integrating mathematics with the semantic web (e.g., in the MONET and HELM/MoWGLI FP6 projects), or as markup languages for web browsers (e.g., by the integration of MathML into HTML5).

A different trade-off is made in **interchange languages** mostly developed for theorem provers. They are restricted to small families of logical languages used in theorem provers. Thus, they are more widely applicable than individual logical languages but less widely than the truly universal standard representation languages. The TPTP [Sut09] family of languages has played a major role in the community: it serves the role of a common language for automated theorem prover inputs and outputs. TPTP was originally restricted to first-order logics, and a few extensions exist [BRS08, SSCB12], which co-evolve with the available theorem provers, thus offering the possibility of problem exchange also between formal proof systems. OpenTheory [Hur09] is restricted to the HOL-based proof assistants. It offers some support for abstracting from the systems' idiosyncrasies in order to increase portability, and some HOL theories have been manually refactored to make use of this abstraction. The ISO-standardized Common Logic [edi07] has a broader ambition, aiming at interchanging between any knowledge-based systems. But its applicability to mathematics is limited by its focus on first-order logic and a lack of integration with mathematical software.

Overall, interchange languages focus mostly on a universal formal *syntax* while sacrificing a universal semantics or restrict attention to small families of languages. Neither provides strong support for type/module/proof/computation systems that would be critical to capture the complexity of large scale formal libraries. A partial exception is the second author's MMT system, which combines aspects of standard languages [DIK+16,KMP+17] and prover interchange languages [BRS08,HR15,KRS16] with hard type and module systems [RK13]. The OAF project [KR16,KR20] used MMT to represent large libraries of proof assistants in a standard representation language, including those of Mizar in [IKR11], HOL Light in [KR14], PVS in [KMOR17] (including the NASA library), Coq in [MRS19] (including all available libraries), and Isabelle in [KRW20] (including the Archive of Formal Proofs).

5   Language Frameworks

Language frameworks are formal languages in which the syntax and semantics of other languages can be represented. They are superficially related to parser frameworks but much stronger because they (i) allow specifying not only the syntax but also the semantics of a language, (ii) often offer strong support for context-sensitivity, which is critical in mathematics.

Logical frameworks are language frameworks for building formal language. Examples are Isabelle [Pau94], Dedukti [BCH12], λProlog [MN86], or the LF [HHP93] family including Twelf [PS99] and others. Frameworks also exist for building controlled natural languages such as GF [Ran11].

Contrary to the approaches discussed above, these frameworks do not in themselves provide languages for formalizing mathematics. But they are worth discussing in this context for two reasons: Firstly, they allow the rapid prototyping of implementations, which speeds up the feedback loop between language design and applications. Thus, users can experiment with new languages and conduct large case studies in parallel. Secondly, they allow developing scalable applications language-independently such that they are immediately applicable for any language defined in the framework. That is important because evaluating formal languages often requires building (or trying to build) *large* libraries in them. Such applications include at least parsing and type-checking but can also include meta-reasoning (e.g., Twelf), interactive theorem proving (e.g., Isabelle), or language translation (e.g., GF).

Despite many successes in representing logical languages in logical frameworks (e.g., [CHK+11,KR14,KMOR17,MRS19]), current frameworks cover only unrealistically simple languages compared to the needs for mathematically structured content and do not have good support for, e.g., soft type systems and soft module systems and practical proof systems. Thus, even the representation of the already insufficient languages discussed above is often very difficult or not possible.

Therefore, more flexible logical frameworks were developed recently. Both ELPI [DGST15] and MMT [Rab17,Rab18] allow users to flexibly change critical algorithms whenever a concrete language definition needs it. That makes them more promising for representing languages designed for mathematical content (and can even allow sharing some functionality across incompatible foundations).

MMT [Rab13, RK13] is a logic-independent representation and management system for formal logical content that uses logical frameworks to provide a rigorous semantics for OMDOC and OPENMATH. It manages all aspects of language design in a coherent framework including language definition, rapid prototyping of tools, and library development. Fully parametric in the choice of formal system, it maximizes the reuse of concepts, formalizations, and tool support. It subsumes in particular logical frameworks such as the LF family [MR19]. The LATIN project [CHK+11] used an MMT precursor language based on the Twelf module system [RS09] to build a library of common logics of symbolic software systems and proof checkers. It contains close to 1000 modules (theories and morphisms between them), which can be imported into MMT.

[KRSS20] makes the first steps towards combining the advantages of MMT and ELPI. [KS19] uses MMT to extend LF-like logical frameworks with the natural language framework GF.

6 Interchange Libraries

The quest for the best formal language for mathematics is likely to never-ending. Therefore, it is important to investigate how to combine the existing libraries of formalized content. Due to major incompatibilities between the various formal systems, this is an extremely difficult problem, and it would go beyond the scope of this paper to discuss approaches in detail. But we want to mention the idea of interchange libraries because we consider it to be one of the most promising ideas.

An interchange library I is a formalization of mathematics written in an intermediate language with the goal of serving as an interoperability layer between formal systems. The main idea is that all translations from source system S to target system T are split into two steps $S \to I$ and $I \to T$.

Both steps have characteristic difficulties. The step $S \to I$ is usually a partial translation because every formal systems uses idiosyncratic features that cannot be represented in I and optimizations for verification/computation that need not be represented in I. The step $I \to T$ tends to be easier, but there is a tricky trade-off in the design of I: the less I commits to a particular formal system, the more systems T can be handled but the more difficult the individual translations $I \to T$ become. In practice, a further major logistic problem is that I and the translations via it needs to be built and maintained, which is even harder to organize and fund than for the systems S and T themselves.

The standard content dictionaries written in OpenMath [BCC+04] were the first concerted effort to build an interchange library. 214 dictionaries (including contributed ones) declaring 1578 symbols are maintained by the OpenMath Society. These focus on declaring names for mathematical symbols and describing their semantics verbally and with formal axioms. However, the approach was not widely adopted as little tool support existed for OpenMath itself and for OpenMath-based interoperability. Individual formal systems were also less able to export/import their objects at all.

Recently, the idea was picked up again in the OpenDreamKit project. It uses MMT (whose language of theories and expressions essentially subsumes Open-Math CDs and objects) to write a formal interchange library (dubbed MitM for Math-in-the-middle) [DIK+16]. MitM is more formal than the OpenMath CDs, in particular employing a hard type and module system. It was used as an inter-operability layer for computer algebra systems [KMP+17] and mathematical databases [WKR17,BKR19].

A complementary approach is SMGloM [GIJ+16], a multi-lingual glossary of mathematical concepts. It retains the untyped natural of OpenMath CDs but uses sTeX to obtain tool support for writing the library.

SMGloM and MitM serve similar purposes with different methods that recall the distinctions described in Sect. 2: SMGloM uses mostly natural language, and MitM uses formal language with hard type and module system. The short-comings of these efforts seem to indicate that soft types and modules may be the best trade-off for building an interchange library.

In order to streamline the process of building the translations $S \to I$ and $I \to T$, the concept of *alignments* was developed [KKMR16]. An alignment between two symbols c and c' in different libraries captures that translations should try to translate objects with c to objects with head d. Both exact manual efforts [MRLR17] and machine learning–based heuristic approaches were used to find alignments across formal libraries. The latter includes alignment from six proof assistants [GK19], showing that such alignments allow both conjecturing and more powerful automation [GK15]. The same approach has been used to obtain alignments between informal and formal libraries, which can be used to automatically formalize parts of mathematical texts, both statistically [KUV17] and using deep learning techniques [WKU18]. Similarly, [GC14] automatically obtains alignments between informal libraries.

7 Conclusion

We have presented a survey of languages for formalizing mathematics. The various languages have been designed and implemented for different purposes and have different features, and their many distinguishing features give them char-acteristic advantages and disadvantages. Natural language that mathematicians are used to lacks formal semantics (and in many cases even formal syntax). But fully formal languages are still very far from natural language. And existing intermediate languages lack complex structuring features and large libraries and scalable tools that would make them directly usable for formalization.

We expect that future research in the domain must continue to experiment with language development aiming at the formal representation of syntax and semantics while preserving natural readability and extensibility and large-scale structuring features. The use of language frameworks will be helpful to rapidly experiment with these novel ideas. We see a lot of potential in the development of a new intermediate language along those lines that could enable partial and stepwise formalization as well as provide an interoperability layer for formal languages. Concretely, we expect this future language to feature at least a combination of soft type and module systems with rigorous development of their hard analogues as emergent features.

References

[ABC+10] Ausbrooks, R., et al.: Mathematical Markup Language (MathML) Version 3.0. Technical report, World Wide Web Consortium (2010). http://www.w3.org/TR/MathML3

[Abr96] Abrial, J.: The B-Book: Assigning Programs to Meanings. Cambridge University Press, Cambridge (1996)

[Art] Arthan, R.: ProofPower. http://www.lemma-one.com/ProofPower/

[ASTZ06] Asperti, A., Coen, C.S., Tassi, E., Zacchiroli, S.: Crafting a proof assistant. In: Altenkirch, T., McBride, C. (eds.) TYPES 2006. LNCS, vol. 4502, pp. 18–32. Springer, Heidelberg (2007). https://doi.org/10.1007/978-3-540-74464-1_2

[BCC+04] Buswell, S., Caprotti, O., Carlisle, D., Dewar, M., Gaetano, M., Kohlhase, M.: The Open Math Standard, Version 2.0. Technical report, The Open Math Society (2004). http://www.openmath.org/standard/om20

[BCH12] Boespflug, M., Carbonneaux, Q., Hermant, O.: The $\lambda\Pi$-calculus modulo as a universal proof language. In: Pichardie, D., Weber, T. (eds.) Proceedings of PxTP2012: Proof Exchange for Theorem Proving, pp. 28–43 (2012)

[BKP19] Brown, C., Kaliszyk, C., Pąk, K.: Higher-order Tarski Grothendieck as a foundation for formal proof. In: Harrison, J., O'Leary, J., Tolmach, A. (eds.) Interactive Theorem Proving. LIPIcs, vol. 141, pp. 9:1–9:16 (2019)

[BKR19] Berčič, K., Kohlhase, M., Rabe, F.: Towards a unified mathematical data infrastructure: database and interface generation. In: Kaliszyk, C., Brady, E., Kohlhase, A., Sacerdoti Coen, C. (eds.) CICM 2019. LNCS (LNAI), vol. 11617, pp. 28–43. Springer, Cham (2019). https://doi.org/10.1007/978-3-030-23250-4_3

[BRS08] Benzmüller, C., Rabe, F., Sutcliffe, G.: THF0 – the core of the TPTP language for higher-order logic. In: Armando, A., Baumgartner, P., Dowek, G. (eds.) IJCAR 2008. LNCS (LNAI), vol. 5195, pp. 491–506. Springer, Heidelberg (2008). https://doi.org/10.1007/978-3-540-71070-7_41

[CAB+86] Constable, R., et al.: Implementing Mathematics with the Nuprl Development System. Prentice-Hall, Upper Saddle River (1986)

[CF58] Curry, H., Feys, R.: Combinatory Logic. North-Holland, Amsterdam (1958)

[CFK+09] Cramer, M., Fisseni, B., Koepke, P., Kühlwein, D., Schröder, B., Veldman, J.: The Naproche project controlled natural language proof checking of mathematical texts. In: Fuchs, N.E. (ed.) CNL 2009. LNCS (LNAI), vol. 5972, pp. 170–186. Springer, Heidelberg (2010). https://doi.org/10.1007/978-3-642-14418-9_11

[CH88] Coquand, T., Huet, G.: The calculus of constructions. Inf. Comput. **76**(2/3), 95–120 (1988)

[CHK+11] Codescu, M., Horozal, F., Kohlhase, M., Mossakowski, T., Rabe, F.: Project abstract: logic atlas and integrator (LATIN). In: Davenport, J.H., Farmer, W.M., Urban, J., Rabe, F. (eds.) CICM 2011. LNCS (LNAI), vol. 6824, pp. 289–291. Springer, Heidelberg (2011). https://doi.org/10.1007/978-3-642-22673-1_24

[Chu40] Church, A.: A formulation of the simple theory of types. J. Symb. Log. **5**(1), 56–68 (1940)

[Coq15] Coq Development Team: The Coq proof assistant: reference manual. Technical report, INRIA (2015)

[DGST15] Dunchev, C., Guidi, F., Sacerdoti Coen, C., Tassi, E.: ELPI: fast, embeddable, λprolog interpreter. In: Davis, M., Fehnker, A., McIver, A., Voronkov, A. (eds.) LPAR 2015. LNCS, vol. 9450, pp. 460–468. Springer, Heidelberg (2015). https://doi.org/10.1007/978-3-662-48899-7_32

[DIK+16] Dehaye, P.-O., et al.: Interoperability in the OpenDreamKit project: the math-in-the-middle approach. In: Kohlhase, M., Johansson, M., Miller, B., de de Moura, L., Tompa, F. (eds.) CICM 2016. LNCS (LNAI), vol. 9791, pp. 117–131. Springer, Cham (2016). https://doi.org/10.1007/978-3-319-42547-4_9

[dKA+15] de Moura, L., Kong, S., Avigad, J., van Doorn, F., von Raumer, J.: The lean theorem prover (system description). In: Felty, A.P., Middeldorp, A. (eds.) CADE 2015. LNCS (LNAI), vol. 9195, pp. 378–388. Springer, Cham (2015). https://doi.org/10.1007/978-3-319-21401-6_26

[edi07] Common Logic editors: Common Logic (CL) – A framework for a family of logic-based languages. Technical Report 24707, ISO/IEC (2007)

[FGT93] Farmer, W., Guttman, J., Thayer, F.: IMPS: an interactive mathematical proof system. J. Autom. Reason. **11**(2), 213–248 (1993)

[GAA+13] Gonthier, G., et al.: A machine-checked proof of the odd order theorem. In: Blazy, S., Paulin-Mohring, C., Pichardie, D. (eds.) ITP 2013. LNCS, vol. 7998, pp. 163–179. Springer, Heidelberg (2013). https://doi.org/10.1007/978-3-642-39634-2_14

[Gan13] Ganesalingam, M.: The language of mathematics. In: Ganesalingam, M. (ed.) The Language of Mathematics. LNCS, vol. 7805, pp. 17–38. Springer, Heidelberg (2013). https://doi.org/10.1007/978-3-642-37012-0_2

[GC14] Ginev, D., Corneli, J.: NNexus reloaded. In: Watt, S.M., Davenport, J.H., Sexton, A.P., Sojka, P., Urban, J. (eds.) CICM 2014. LNCS (LNAI), vol. 8543, pp. 423–426. Springer, Cham (2014). https://doi.org/10.1007/978-3-319-08434-3_31

[GGMR09] Garillot, F., Gonthier, G., Mahboubi, A., Rideau, L.: Packaging mathematical structures. In: Berghofer, S., Nipkow, T., Urban, C., Wenzel, M. (eds.) TPHOLs 2009. LNCS, vol. 5674, pp. 327–342. Springer, Heidelberg (2009). https://doi.org/10.1007/978-3-642-03359-9_23

[GIJ+16] Ginev, D., et al.: The SMGloM project and system: towards a terminology and ontology for mathematics. In: Greuel, G.-M., Koch, T., Paule, P., Sommese, A. (eds.) ICMS 2016. LNCS, vol. 9725, pp. 451–457. Springer, Cham (2016). https://doi.org/10.1007/978-3-319-42432-3_58

[GK15] Gauthier, T., Kaliszyk, C.: Sharing HOL4 and HOL light proof knowledge. In: Davis, M., Fehnker, A., McIver, A., Voronkov, A. (eds.) LPAR 2015. LNCS, vol. 9450, pp. 372–386. Springer, Heidelberg (2015). https://doi.org/10.1007/978-3-662-48899-7_26

[GK19] Gauthier, T., Kaliszyk, C.: Aligning concepts across proof assistant libraries. J. Symb. Comput. **90**, 89–123 (2019)

[Hal12] Hales, T.: Dense Sphere Packings: A Blueprint for Formal Proofs. London Mathematical Society Lecture Note Series, vol. 400. Cambridge University Press (2012)

[Hal14] Hales, T.: Developments in formal proofs. Séminaire Bourbaki, 1086, 2013–2014. arxiv.org/abs/1408.6474

[Hal17] Hales, T.: The formal abstracts project (2017). https://formalabstracts. github.io/

[Har96] Harrison, J.: HOL light: a tutorial introduction. In: Srivas, M., Camilleri, A. (eds.) FMCAD 1996. LNCS, vol. 1166, pp. 265–269. Springer, Heidelberg (1996). https://doi.org/10.1007/BFb0031814

[HHP93] Harper, R., Honsell, F., Plotkin, G.: A framework for defining logics. J. Assoc. Comput. Mach. **40**(1), 143–184 (1993)

[HOL] HOL4 development team. https://hol-theorem-prover.org/

[How80] Howard, W.: The formulas-as-types notion of construction. In: To, H.B. (ed.) Curry: Essays on Combinatory Logic, Lambda-Calculus and Formalism, pp. 479–490. Academic Press, Cambridge (1980)

[HR09] Horn, P., Roozemond, D.: OpenMath in SCIEnce: SCSCP and POPCORN. In: Carette, J., Dixon, L., Coen, C.S., Watt, S.M. (eds.) CICM 2009. LNCS (LNAI), vol. 5625, pp. 474–479. Springer, Heidelberg (2009). https://doi.org/10.1007/978-3-642-02614-0_38

[HR15] Horozal, F., Rabe, F.: Formal logic definitions for interchange languages. In: Kerber, M., Carette, J., Kaliszyk, C., Rabe, F., Sorge, V. (eds.) CICM 2015. LNCS (LNAI), vol. 9150, pp. 171–186. Springer, Cham (2015). https://doi.org/10.1007/978-3-319-20615-8_11

[Hum12] Humayoun, M.: Developing system MathNat for automatic formalization of mathematical texts. Ph.D. thesis, Université de Grenoble (2012)

[Hur09] Hurd, J.: OpenTheory: package management for higher order logic theories. In: Dos Reis, G., Théry, L. (eds.) Programming Languages for Mechanized Mathematics Systems, pp. 31–37. ACM (2009)

[IKR11] Iancu, M., Kohlhase, M., Rabe, F.: Translating the Mizar Mathematical Library into OMDoc format. Technical Report KWARC Report-01/11, Jacobs University Bremen (2011)

[KAE+14] Klein, G., et al.: Comprehensive formal verification of an OS microkernel. ACM Trans. Comput. Syst. **32**(1), 2 (2014)

[KKMR16] Kaliszyk, C., Kohlhase, M., Müller, D., Rabe, F.: A standard for aligning mathematical concepts. In: Kohlhase, A., et al. (eds.) Work in Progress at CICM 2016, pp. 229–244. CEUR-WS.org (2016)

[KMM00] Kaufmann, M., Manolios, P., Moore, J.: Computer-Aided Reasoning: An Approach. Kluwer Academic Publishers, Boston (2000)

[KMOR17] Kohlhase, M., Müller, D., Owre, S., Rabe, F.: Making PVS accessible to generic services by interpretation in a universal format. In: Ayala-Rincón, M., Muñoz, C.A. (eds.) ITP 2017. LNCS, vol. 10499, pp. 319–335. Springer, Cham (2017). https://doi.org/10.1007/978-3-319-66107-0_21

[KMP+17] Kohlhase, M., et al.: Knowledge-based interoperability for mathematical software systems. In: Blömer, J., Kotsireas, I.S., Kutsia, T., Simos, D.E. (eds.) MACIS 2017. LNCS, vol. 10693, pp. 195–210. Springer, Cham (2017). https://doi.org/10.1007/978-3-319-72453-9_14

[KN12] Kofler, K., Neumaier, A.: DynGenPar – a dynamic generalized parser for common mathematical language. In: Jeuring, J., et al. (eds.) CICM 2012. LNCS (LNAI), vol. 7362, pp. 386–401. Springer, Heidelberg (2012). https://doi.org/10.1007/978-3-642-31374-5_26

[Knu84] Knuth, D.: Literate programming. Comput. J. **27**(2), 97–111 (1984)

[Koh06] Kohlhase, M.: OMDoc – An Open Markup Format for Mathematical Documents [version 1.2]. LNCS (LNAI), vol. 4180. Springer, Heidelberg (2006). https://doi.org/10.1007/11826095

[Koh08] Kohlhase, M.: Using LaTeX as a semantic markup format. Math. Comput. Sci. **2**(2), 279–304 (2008)

[KP19a] Kaliszyk, C., Pąk, K.: Semantics of Mizar as an Isabelle object logic. J. Autom. Reason. **63**(3), 557–595 (2019)

[KP19b] Kaliszyk, C., Pąk, K.: Declarative proof translation (short paper). In: Harrison, J., O'Leary, J., Tolmach, A. (eds.) 10th International Conference on Interactive Theorem Proving (ITP 2019). LIPIcs, vol. 141, pp. 35:1–35:7 (2019)

[KR93] Kamp, H., Reyle, U.: From Discourse to Logic. Introduction to Modeltheoretic Semantics of Natural Language, Formal Logic and Discourse Representation Theory, Studies in Linguistics and Philosophy, vol. 42. Springer, Heidelberg (1993). https://doi.org/10.1007/978-94-017-1616-1

[KR14] Kaliszyk, C., Rabe, F.: Towards knowledge management for HOL light. In: Watt, S.M., Davenport, J.H., Sexton, A.P., Sojka, P., Urban, J. (eds.) CICM 2014. LNCS (LNAI), vol. 8543, pp. 357–372. Springer, Cham (2014). https://doi.org/10.1007/978-3-319-08434-3_26

[KR16] Kohlhase, M., Rabe, F.: QED reloaded: towards a pluralistic formal library of mathematical knowledge. J. Form. Reason. **9**(1), 201–234 (2016)

[KR20] Kohlhase, M., Rabe, F.: Experiences from Exporting Major Proof Assistant Libraries (2020). https://kwarc.info/people/frabe/Research/KR_oafexp_20.pdf

[KRS16] Kaliszyk, C., Rabe, F., Sutcliffe, G.: TH1: the TPTP typed higher-order form with rank-1 polymorphism. In: Fontaine, P., Schulz, S., Urban, J. (eds.) Workshop on Practical Aspects of Automated Reasoning, pp. 41–55 (2016)

[KRSS20] Kohlhase, M., Rabe, F., Sacerdoti Coen, C., Schaefer, J.: Logic-independent proof search in logical frameworks (short paper). In: Peltier, N., Sofronie-Stokkermans, V. (ed.) Automated Reasoning, vol. 12166, pp. 395–401. Springer (2020)

[KRW20] Kohlhase, M., Rabe, F., Wenzel, M.: Making Isabelle Content Accessible in Knowledge in Representation Formats (2020). https://kwarc.info/people/frabe/Research/KRW_isabelle_19.pdf

[KS19] Kohlhase, M., Schaefer, J.: GF + MMT = GLF - from language to semantics through LF. In: Miller, D., Scagnetto, I. (eds.) Logical Frameworks and Meta-Languages: Theory and Practice, pp. 24–39. Open Publishing Association (2019)

[KUV17] Kaliszyk, C., Urban, J., Vyskočil, J.: Automating formalization by statistical and semantic parsing of mathematics. In: Ayala-Rincón, M., Muñoz, C.A. (eds.) ITP 2017. LNCS, vol. 10499, pp. 12–27. Springer, Cham (2017). https://doi.org/10.1007/978-3-319-66107-0_2

[KW08] Kamareddine, F., Wells, J.: Computerizing mathematical text with MathLang. In: Ayala-Rincón, M., Haeusler, E. (eds.) Logical and Semantic Frameworks, with Applications, pp. 5–30. ENTCS (2008)

[KWZB14] Kamareddine, F., Wells, J., Zengler, C., Barendregt, H.: Computerising mathematical text. In: Siekmann, J. (ed.) Computational Logic. Elsevier (2014)

[Ler09] Leroy, X.: Formal verification of a realistic compiler. Commun. ACM **52**(7), 107–115 (2009)

[Lin07] Linton, S.: GAP: groups, algorithms, programming. ACM Commun. Comput. Algebr. **41**(3), 108–109 (2007)

[Meg07] Megill, N.: Metamath: A Computer Language for Pure Mathematics. Lulu Press, Morrisville (2007)

[Mil72] Milner, R.: Logic for computable functions: descriptions of a machine implementation. ACM SIGPLAN Not. **7**, 1–6 (1972)

[ML74] Martin-Löf, P.: An intuitionistic theory of types: predicative part. In: Proceedings of the '73 Logic Colloquium, pp. 73–118. North-Holland (1974)

[MN86] Miller, D.A., Nadathur, G.: Higher-order logic programming. In: Shapiro, E. (ed.) ICLP 1986. LNCS, vol. 225, pp. 448–462. Springer, Heidelberg (1986). https://doi.org/10.1007/3-540-16492-8_94

[MR19] Müller, D., Rabe, F.: Rapid prototyping formal systems in MMT: case studies. In: Miller, D., Scagnetto, I. (eds.) Logical Frameworks and Meta-languages: Theory and Practice, pp. 40–54 (2019)

[MRK18] Müller, D., Rabe, F., Kohlhase, M.: Theories as types. In: Galmiche, D., Schulz, S., Sebastiani, R. (eds.) IJCAR 2018. LNCS (LNAI), vol. 10900, pp. 575–590. Springer, Cham (2018). https://doi.org/10.1007/978-3-319-94205-6_38

[MRLR17] Müller, D., Rothgang, C., Liu, Y., Rabe, F.: Alignment-based translations across formal systems using interface theories. In: Dubois, C., Woltzenlogel Paleo, B. (eds.) Proof eXchange for Theorem Proving, pp. 77–93. Open Publishing Association (2017)

[MRS19] Müller, D., Rabe, F., Sacerdoti Coen, C.: The Coq library as a theory graph. In: Kaliszyk, C., Brady, E., Kohlhase, A., Sacerdoti Coen, C. (eds.) CICM 2019. LNCS (LNAI), vol. 11617, pp. 171–186. Springer, Cham (2019). https://doi.org/10.1007/978-3-030-23250-4_12

[Nau14] Naumowicz, A.: SAT-enhanced MIZAR proof checking. In: Watt, S.M., Davenport, J.H., Sexton, A.P., Sojka, P., Urban, J. (eds.) CICM 2014. LNCS (LNAI), vol. 8543, pp. 449–452. Springer, Cham (2014). https://doi.org/10.1007/978-3-319-08434-3_37

[Nor05] Norell, U.: The Agda WiKi (2005). http://wiki.portal.chalmers.se/agda

[NPW02] Nipkow, T., Wenzel, M., Paulson, L.C. (eds.): Isabelle/HOL—A Proof Assistant for Higher-Order Logic. LNCS, vol. 2283. Springer, Heidelberg (2002). https://doi.org/10.1007/3-540-45949-9

[ORS92] Owre, S., Rushby, J.M., Shankar, N.: PVS: a prototype verification system. In: Kapur, D. (ed.) CADE 1992. LNCS, vol. 607, pp. 748–752. Springer, Heidelberg (1992). https://doi.org/10.1007/3-540-55602-8_217

[Pau94] Paulson, L.: Isabelle: A Generic Theorem Prover. LNCS, vol. 828. Springer, Heidelberg (1994). https://doi.org/10.1007/BFb0030541

[PC93] Paulson, L., Coen, M.: Zermelo-Fraenkel Set Theory. Isabelle distribution, ZF/ZF.thy (1993)

[PS99] Pfenning, F., Schürmann, C.: System description: Twelf - a meta-logical framework for deductive systems. In: Ganzinger, H. (ed.) Automated Deduction, pp. 202–206 (1999)

[Rab13] Rabe, F.: A logical framework combining model and proof theory. Math. Struct. Comput. Sci. **23**(5), 945–1001 (2013)

[Rab17] Rabe, F.: How to identify, translate, and combine logics? J. Log. Comput. **27**(6), 1753–1798 (2017)

[Rab18] Rabe, F.: A Modular type reconstruction algorithm. ACM Trans. Comput. Log. **19**(4), 1–43 (2018)

[Ran11] Ranta, A.: Grammatical Framework: Programming with Multilingual Grammars. CSLI Publications, Stanford (2011)

[RK13]   Rabe, F., Kohlhase, M.: A scalable module system. Inf. Comput. **230**(1), 1–54 (2013)

[RS09]   Rabe, F., Schürmann, C.: A practical module system for LF. In: Cheney, J., Felty, A. (eds.) Proceedings of the Workshop on Logical Frameworks: Meta-Theory and Practice (LFMTP), pp. 40–48. ACM Press (2009)

[S+13]   Stein, W., et al.: Sage Mathematics Software. The Sage Development Team (2013). http://www.sagemath.org

[SSCB12] Sutcliffe, G., Schulz, S., Claessen, K., Baumgartner, P.: The TPTP typed first-order form with arithmetic. In: Bjørner, N., Voronkov, A. (eds.) LPAR 2012. LNCS, vol. 7180, pp. 406–419. Springer, Heidelberg (2012). https://doi.org/10.1007/978-3-642-28717-6_32

[Sut09] Sutcliffe, G.: The TPTP problem library and associated infrastructure: the FOF and CNF Parts, v3.5.0. J. Autom. Reason. **43**(4), 337–362 (2009)

[TB85]   Trybulec, A., Blair, H.: Computer assisted reasoning with MIZAR. In: Joshi, A. (eds.) Proceedings of the 9th International Joint Conference on Artificial Intelligence, pp. 26–28. Morgan Kaufmann (1985)

[Wen11] Wenzel, M.: Isabelle as document-oriented proof assistant. In: Davenport, J.H., Farmer, W.M., Urban, J., Rabe, F. (eds.) CICM 2011. LNCS (LNAI), vol. 6824, pp. 244–259. Springer, Heidelberg (2011). https://doi.org/10.1007/978-3-642-22673-1_17

[Wie07] Wiedijk, F.: The QED manifesto revisited. In: From Insight to Proof, Festschrift in Honour of Andrzej Trybulec, pp. 121–133 (2007)

[Win14] Windsteiger, W.: Theorema 2.0: a system for mathematical theory exploration. In: Hong, H., Yap, C. (eds.) ICMS 2014. LNCS, vol. 8592, pp. 49–52. Springer, Heidelberg (2014). https://doi.org/10.1007/978-3-662-44199-2_9

[WKR17] Wiesing, T., Kohlhase, M., Rabe, F.: Virtual theories – a uniform interface to mathematical knowledge bases. In: Blömer, J., Kotsireas, I.S., Kutsia, T., Simos, D.E. (eds.) MACIS 2017. LNCS, vol. 10693, pp. 243–257. Springer, Cham (2017). https://doi.org/10.1007/978-3-319-72453-9_17

[WKU18] Wang, Q., Kaliszyk, C., Urban, J.: First experiments with neural translation of informal to formal mathematics. In: Rabe, F., Farmer, W.M., Passmore, G.O., Youssef, A. (eds.) CICM 2018. LNCS (LNAI), vol. 11006, pp. 255–270. Springer, Cham (2018). https://doi.org/10.1007/978-3-319-96812-4_22

[Wol12] Wolfram. Mathematica (2012)

OntoMath^{Edu}: A Linguistically Grounded Educational Mathematical Ontology

Alexander Kirillovich[1,2]($\boxtimes$) , Olga Nevzorova[1] , Marina Falileeva[1] ,
Evgeny Lipachev[1] , and Liliana Shakirova[1]

[1] Kazan Federal University, Kazan, Russia
[2] Joint Supercomputer Center of the Russian Academy of Sciences, Kazan, Russia
alik.kirillovich@gmail.com, onevzoro@gmail.com, mmwwff@yandex.ru,
elipachev@gmail.com, liliana008@mail.ru

Abstract. We present the first release of OntoMath^{Edu}, a new educational mathematical ontology. The ontology is intended to be used as a Linked Open Data hub for mathematical education, a linguistic resource for intelligent mathematical language processing and an end-user reference educational database. The ontology is organized in three layers: a foundational ontology layer, a domain ontology layer and a linguistic layer. The domain ontology layer contains language-independent concepts, covering secondary school mathematics curriculum. The linguistic layer provides linguistic grounding for these concepts, and the foundation ontology layer provides them with meta-ontological an-notations. The concepts are organized in two main hierarchies: the hierarchy of objects and the hierarchy of reified relationships. For our knowledge, OntoMath^{Edu} is the first Linked Open Data mathematical ontology, that respects ontological distinctions provided by a foundational ontology; represents mathematical relationships as first-oder entities; and provides strong linguistic grounding for the represented mathematical concepts.

Keywords: Ontology · Mathematics education · Linked Open Data · Natural language processing · Mathematical knowledge management · OntoMath^{Edu}

1 Introduction

We present the first release of OntoMath^{Edu}, a new educational mathematical ontology. This ontology is intended to be:

- A Linked Open Data hub for mathematical education. In this respect, the ontology lies at the intersection of two long-established trends of using LOD for educational purposes [1–4] and for mathematical knowledge management [5,6].
- A linguistic resource for common mathematical language processing. In this respect, the ontology can complement mathematical linguistic resources, such as SMGloM [7,8], and serve as an interface between raw natural language texts and mathematical knowledge management applications.

© Springer Nature Switzerland AG 2020
C. Benzmüller and B. Miller (Eds.): CICM 2020, LNAI 12236, pp. 157–172, 2020.
https://doi.org/10.1007/978-3-030-53518-6_10

– An end-user reference educational database, and play the same role in secondary school math, that PlanetMath or MathWorld play in professional mathematics.

This ontology is a central component of the digital educational platform under development, which is intended for solving such tasks as: (1) automatic questions generation; (2) automatic recommendation of educational materials according to an individual study plan; (3) semantic annotation of educational materials.

In the development of OntoMath^{Edu} we would rely on our experience of the development of OntoMath^{PRO} (http://ontomathpro.org/) [9], an ontology of professional mathematics. This ontology underlies a semantic publishing platform [10,11], that takes as an input a collection of mathematical papers in LaTeX format and builds their ontology-based Linked Open Data representation. The semantic publishing platform, in turn, is a central component of OntoMath digital ecosystem [12,13], an ecosystem of ontologies, text analytics tools, and applications for mathematical knowledge management, including semantic search for mathematical formulas [14] and a recommender system for mathematical papers [15].

Despite the fact that OntoMath^{PRO} has proved to be effective in several educational applications, such as assessment of the competence of students [9] and recommendation of educational materials in Virtual Learning Communities [16–19], its focus on professional mathematics rather than on education prevents it to be a strong foundation for the digital educational platform. The main differences between OntoMath^{PRO} and a required educational ontology are the following:

– *Conceptualization.* OntoMath^{PRO} ontology specifies a conceptualization of professional mathematics, whilst the required educational ontology must specify a conceptualization of school mathematics. These conceptualizations are noticeably different, for example, in school conceptualization, *Number* is a primitive notion, while in professional conceptualization it is defined as a subclass of *Set*.
– *Selection of concepts.* The required educational ontology must contain concepts from a school mathematics curriculum.
– *Terminology.* Concepts of OntoMath^{PRO} ontology are denoted by professional terms, whilst concepts of the required educational ontology must be denoted by school math terms. There isn't so much difference between professional and educational terminology in English, but this difference is more salient in such languages as Russian or Tatar. For example, the term 'mnogochlen' (the native word for 'polynom') should be used instead of the professional term 'polinom' (the Greek loan word with the same meaning) in educational environment.
– *Prerequisite relations.* In the required educational ontology, logical relations between concepts must be complemented with prerequisite ones. The concept A is called a prerequisite for the concept B, if a learner must study the concept A before approaching the concept B. For example, comprehension of

the *Addition* concept is required to grasp the concept of *Multiplication*, and, more interesting, to grasp the very concept of *Function*, even though, from the logical point of view the later concept is more fundamental and is used in the definitions of the first two.

– *Points of view.* In addition to universal statements, the required educational ontology must contain statements relativized to particular points of view, such as different educational levels. For example, a concept can be defined differently on different educational stages; and a statement can be considered as an axiom according to one axiomatization, and as a theorem according to another.

Concerning to common mathematical language processing, OntoMath^{PRO} is suitable for extraction of separate mathematical objects, but not for extraction facts about them. The same fact can be linguistically manifested in many different ways. For example, the incidence relation between point a and line l can be represented by a transitive verb ("*l* contains *a*"), a verb with a preposition ("*a* lies on *l*"), an adjective with a preposition ("*a* is incident with *l*") and an adjective with a collective subject ("*a* and *l* are incident") [20]. So, the required ontology should define concepts for representing mathematical facts as well as mappings to their natural language manifestations.

With regard to the foregoing, we have lunched a project for developing a new educational ontology OntoMath^{Edu}. The project was presented at the work-in-progress track of CICM 2019 *cicm2019* and was recommended by PC to be re-submitted to the main track after the release of the first stable version. In this paper, we describe the overall project as well as the first release, consisting in the domain ontology layer for Euclidean plane geometry domain.

2   Ontology Structure

According to the project, OntoMath^{Edu} ontology is organized in three layers:

1. **Foundational ontology layer**, where a chosen foundational ontology is UFO [22].
2. **Domain ontology layer**, which contains language-independent math concepts from the secondary school mathematics curriculum. The concepts are grouped into several modules, including the general concepts module and modules for disciplines of mathematics, e.g. Arithmetic, Algebra and Plane Geometry. The concepts will be interlinked with external LOD resources, such as DBpedia [23], ScienceWISE [24] and OntoMath^{PRO}. Additionally, relaying on the MMT URIs scheme [25], the concepts can be aligned with MitM ontology [26], and through it with the concepts of several computer algebra systems.
3. **Linguistic layer**, containing multilingual lexicons, that provide linguistic grounding of the concepts from the domain ontology layer. The lexicons will be interlinked with the external lexical resources from the Linguistic Linked Open Data (LLOD) cloud [27,28], first of all in English [29,30], Russian [31] and Tatar [32] (Fig. 1).

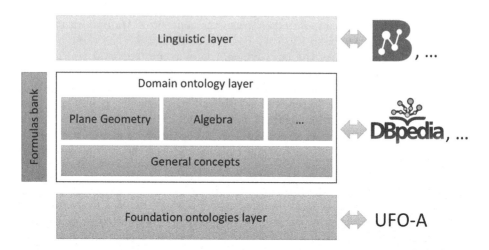

Fig. 1. OntoMath^{PRO} ontology structure.

3 Domain Ontology Layer

The domain ontology layer of OntoMath^{Edu} is being developed according to the following modelling principles:

1. Common mathematical language conceptualization. OntoMathEdu reflects the conceptualization of the Common mathematical language (CML) [33], not that of the language of fully formalized mathematics. These conceptualizations are very different. For example, according to the fully formalized mathematics conceptualization, the *Set* concept subsumes the *Vector* concept, but in the CML conceptualization *Vector* is represented by *Set*, and is not subsumed by it. More important, in contrast to the fully formalized mathematics conceptualization, according to the CML conceptualization, mathematical objects are neither necessary nor timeless, and the domain of discourse can expand in a process of problem-solving.
2. Strict adherence to ontological distinctions provided by the foundational ontology. For example, we explicitly mark concepts as Kinds or Roles.
3. Reification of domain relations. Mathematical relations are represented as concepts, not as object properties. Thus, the mathematical relationships between concepts are first-order entities, and can be a subject of a statement.
4. Multilinguality. Concepts of ontology contains labels in English, Russian and Tatar.
5. Educational literature warrant. The ontology contains only those concepts, that are represented in actual education literature.

Current version of OntoMath^{Edu} contains 823 concepts from the secondary school Euclidean plane geometry curriculum (5th–9th grades), manually developed by experts relying on mathematical textbooks. The description of a concept contains its name in English, Russian and Tatar, axioms, relations with other concepts, and links to external resources of the LOD cloud and educational reference databases.

The concepts are organized in two main hierarchies: the hierarchy of objects and the hierarchy of reified relationships.

3.1   Hierarchy of Objects

The top level of the hierarchy of objects consists of the following classes:

1. *Plane Figure*, with subclasses such as *Line, Polygon, Ellipse, Angle, Median of a Triangle* or *Circumscribed Circle*.
2. *Plane Geometry Statement*, with subclasses such as *Axiom of construction of a circle with a given center and radius* or *Pythagorean Theorem*.
3. *Plane Geometry Problem* with subclasses such as *Problem of straightedge and compass construction* or *Heron's problem*.
4. *Plane Geometry Method* with subclasses such as *Constructing an additional line for solving plane geometry problem*.
5. *Unit of Measurement*, with subclasses such as *Centimeter, Radian*, or *Square meter*.
6. *Measurement and Construction Tool*, with subclasses such as *Protractor, Astrolabe, T-square, Sliding T bevel*, or *Marking gauge*.

A fragment of the hierarchy of objects is represented at the Fig. 2.

There are two meta-ontological types of the concepts: kinds and roles.

A kind is a concept that is rigid and ontologically independent [22,34]. So, for example, the *Triangle* concept is a kind, because any triangle is always a triangle, regardless of its relationship with other figures.

A role is a concept that is anti-rigid and ontologically dependent [22,34]. An object can be an instance of a role class only by virtue of its relationship with another object. So, for example, the *Median* concept is a role, since any line segment is a median not by itself, but only in relation to a certain triangle. Any role concept is a subclass of some kind concept. For example, the *Median* role concept is a subclass of *Line* segment kind concept.

Figure 3 represents the *Median* role concept and one of its instances, namely median *AO*, related to triangle *ABC*.

3.2   Hierarchy of Reified Relationships

Relations between concepts are represented in ontology in a reified form, i.e. as concepts, not as object properties (such representation fits the standard ontological pattern for representing N-ary relation with no distinguished participant [35], but is applied to binary relations too). Thus, the relationships between concepts are first-order entities, and can be a subject of a statement.

The top level of the hierarchy of reified relationships consists of the following classes:

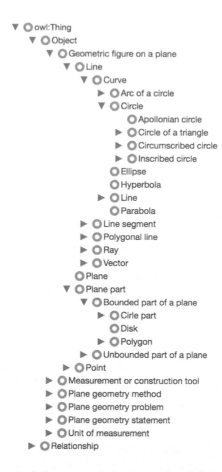

Fig. 2. A fragment of the hierarchy of objects.

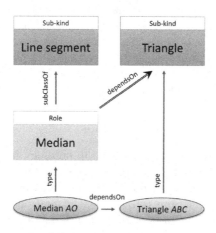

Fig. 3. A role example.

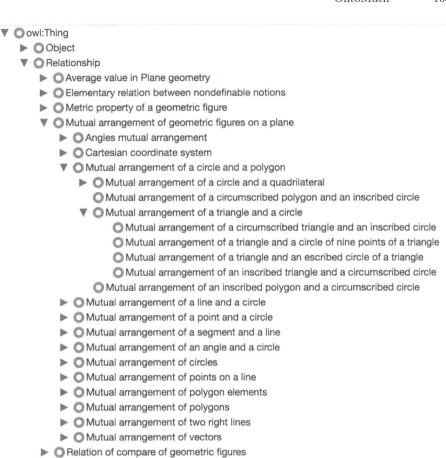

Fig. 4. A fragment of the hierarchy of reified relationships.

1. *Mutual arrangement of geometric figures on a plane*, with subclasses such as *Inscribed polygon* or *Triangle with vertices at Euler points*.
2. *Comparison relation between plane figures*, with subclasses such as *Congruent Triangles* or *Similar Polygons*.
3. *Plane Transformation*, with subclasses such as *Translation* or *Axial Symmetry*.
4. *Metric property of a plane figure*, with subclasses such as *Length of a circle*, *Tangent of acute angle in right triangle*, or *Eccentricity of an ellipse*.

A fragment of this hierarchy is represented at the Fig. 4.

Reified relationships are linked to their participants by has argument object properties and their subproperties.

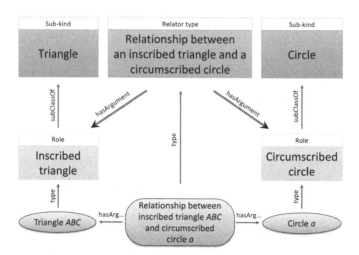

Fig. 5. An example of a reified relationship, and its instance corresponding to the "Triangle *ABC* is inscribed in circle *a*" statement.

Figure 5 shows one of the relations, represented by the *Relationship between an inscribed triangle and a circumscribed circle concept*. This relation is linked to its participants, represented by *Inscribed triangle* and *Circumscribed circle* role concepts. These roles, in turn, are defined as subclasses of the *Triangle* and the *Circle* kind concepts respectively. The bottom of the figure depicts an instance of this relation, namely the *Relationship between inscribed triangle ABC and circumscribed circle a*, that binds triangle *ABC* and circle *a*.

This relationship is a representation of natural language statement "Triangle *ABC* is inscribed in circle *a*". The mappings between ontology concepts and corresponding natural language statements are defined at the linguistic level of the ontology.

3.3   Network of Points of View

Points of view are represented using the "Descriptions and Situations" design pattern, and are based on the top-level ontology DOLCE + DnS Ultralite [36–38]. The network of points of view is under development now and is not included in the first release of the ontology.

3.4   Object and Annotation Properties

The ontology defines the following relations, represented by the object and annotation properties as well as their subproperties:

1. *Has argument* relation, that binds a reified relationship and its participants.
2. Relation of *Ontological dependence* that binds a role concept to its dependee concept.

3. *Has part* relation. For example, any *Vertex of a Triangle* is a part of a *Triangle*.

4. *Aboutness* relation that holds between a *Statement* and the subject matter of this statement. For example, *Heron's formula* is related to the *Area of a polygon* concept.

5. *Prerequisite relation.* The concept A is called a prerequisite for the concept B, if a learner must study the concept A before approaching the concept B. In the first release of the ontology, these relations are introduced only indirectly in coarse-grained manner by arrangement of the concepts by successive educational levels.

6. *Belongs to educational level*, that binds a concept and an educational level (such as an age of leaning) at which the concept is firstly introduced.

7. *External resource*, that interlinks a concept and an external Linked Open Data or reference educational resource describing this concept.

3.5   External Links

Currently, OntoMath^{Edu} ontology has been interlinked with the following external resources:

DBpedia. The mapping was constructed semi-automatically on the base of the method proposed in [41] and then manually verified. This mapping contains 154 connections, expressed by the skos:closeMatch properties.

External Reference Educational Resources. The mapping was constructed manually and contains 71 connections, expressed by the ome:eduRef annotation properties and its subproperties.

4   Linguistic Layer

The linguistic layer contains multilingual lexicons, that provide linguistic grounding of the concepts from the domain ontology layer.

Currently we are developing Russian and English lexicons and are going to develop the lexicon for Tatar.

A lexicon consists in:

– Lexical entries, denoting mathematical concepts. Examples of lexical entries are "triangle", "right triangle", "side of a polygon", "Riemann integral of f over x from a to b", "to intersect", "to touch", etc.
– Forms of lexical entries (in different numbers, cases, tenses, etc).
– Syntactic trees of multi-word lexical entries.
– Syntactic frames of lexical entries. A syntactic frame represents the syntactic behavior of a predicate, defining the set of syntactic arguments this predicate requires and their mappings to ontological entities. For example, a syntactic frame of the "to touch" verb determines that in "X touches Y at Z" phrase, subject X represents a tangent line to a curve, direct object Y represents the curve, and prepositional adjunct Z represents the point of tangency.

```
@prefix : <http://ontomathpro.org/ontomathedu/lexicons/>.
@prefix ome: <http://ontomathpro.org/ontomathedu#>.
@prefix ontolex: <http://www.w3.org/ns/lemon/ontolex#>.
@prefix synsem: <http://www.w3.org/ns/lemon/synsem#>.
@prefix lexinfo: <http://www.lexinfo.net/ontology/2.0/lexinfo#>.

#The "to touch" verb
:EN-v-touch
  a ontolex:LexicalEntry;
  lexinfo:partOfSpeech lexinfo:verb;
  ontolex:canonicalForm :EN-v-touch-form0;
  synsem:synBehavior :EN-v-touch-frame1;
  ontolex:sense :EN-v-touch-sense1.

#The canonical form of this verb
:EN-v-touch-form0
  a ontolex:Form;
  ontolex:writtenRep "touch"@en.

#A syntactic frame "X touches Y at Z"
:EN-v-touch-frame1
  a lexinfo:TransitivePPFrame;

  lexinfo:subject :EN-v-touch-frame1-subj;
  lexinfo:directObject :EN-v-touch-frame1-obj;
  lexinfo:prepositionalArg :EN-v-touch-frame1-pp_at.

#The subject of the verb
:EN-v-touch-frame1-subj
  a lexinfo:Subject.

#The direct object of the verb
:EN-v-touch-frame1-obj
  a lexinfo:DirectObject.

#A prepositional adjunct of the verb
:EN-v-touch-frame1-pp_at
  a lexinfo:PrepositionalAdjunct;
  synsem:marker :EN-prep-at;
  synsem:optional "true"^^xsd:boolean.

#A lexical sense, expressing the mapping
#of the verb to the ontology
:EN-v-touch-sense1
  a ontolex:LexicalSense, synsem:OntoMap;
  synsem:ontoMapping :EN-v-touch-sense1;
```

Fig. 6. "To touch" lexical entry

```
ontolex:reference
  ome:Relationship_between_a_tangent_line_and_a_curve;
synsem:submap
  [
  a synsem:OntoMap;
  ontolex:reference
    ome:Relationship_between_a_tangent_line_and_a_curve;
  synsem:isA _:Relationship1
  ],
  [
  a synsem:OntoMap;
  ontolex:reference ome:tangent_line;
  synsem:subjOfProp _:Relationship1;
  synsem:objOfProp :EN-v-touch-frame1-subj
  ],
  [
  a synsem:OntoMap;
  ontolex:reference ome:curve;
  synsem:subjOfProp _:Relationship1;
  synsem:objOfProp :EN-v-touch-frame1-obj
  ],
  [
  a synsem:OntoMap;
  ontolex:reference ome:tangent_point;
  synsem:subjOfProp _:Relationship1;
  synsem:objOfProp :EN-v-touch-frame1-pp_at
  ],
  [
  a synsem:OntoMap;
  ontolex:reference ome:Tangent_line;
  synsem:isA :EN-v-touch-frame1-subj
  ],
  [
  a synsem:OntoMap;
  ontolex:reference ome:Tangent_point;
  synsem:isA :EN-v-touch-frame1-pp_at
  ].
```

Fig. 6. (*continued*)

The lexicons are expressed in terms of Lemon [43,44], LexInfo, OLiA [45] and PreMOn [46] ontologies.

Figure 6 represents an example of the "to touch" verb, its canonical form, syntactic frame and lexical sense. The syntactic frame defines three arguments of this verb: a subject, a direct object and an optional prepositional adjunct, marked by the "at" preposition. The lexical sense defines a mapping of the verb and its syntactic arguments to the corresponding ontological concepts. According to the mapping, the verb denotes the reified relationship between a tangent line and a curve, while the syntactic arguments express the participants of this relationship: the subject expresses a tangent line to a curve, the direct object expresses the curve, and the prepositional adjunct expresses the tangent point.

5   Conclusions

In this paper, we present the first release of OntoMath^{Edu}, a new educational mathematical ontology.

While there are many educational ontologies on the one hand, and several mathematical ontologies on the other, to our knowledge, OntoMath^{Edu} is the first general-purpose educational mathematical ontology. Additionally, it is the first Linked Open Data mathematical ontology, intended to: (1) respect ontological distinctions provided by a foundational ontology; (2) represent mathematical relationships as first-order entities; and (3) provide strong linguistic grounding for the represented mathematical concepts.

Currently, our first priority is to release the linguistic layer of the ontology that is still under development and hasn't been published yet. After that, we will extend the ontology to other fields of secondary school mathematics curriculum, such as Arithmetic, Algebra and Trigonometry.

Finally, we are going to apply the modeling principles, drafted on this project, in the development of the new revised version of the ontology of professional mathematics OntoMath^{PRO}.

Acknowledgements. The first part of the work, the development of the domain ontology layer, was partially funded by RFBR, projects # 19-29-14084. The second part of the work, the development of the linguistic layer, was funded by Russian Science Foundation according to the research project no. 19-71-10056.

References

1. Pereira, C.K., Matsui Siqueira, S.W., Nunes, B.P., Dietze, S.: Linked data in education: a survey and a synthesis of actual research and future challenges. IEEE Trans. Learn. Technol. **11**(3), 400–412 (2018). https://doi.org/10.1109/TLT.2017. 2787659
2. d'Aquin, M.: On the use of linked open data in education: current and future practices. In: Mouromtsev, D., d'Aquin, M. (eds.) Open Data for Education. LNCS, vol. 9500, pp. 3–15. Springer, Cham (2016). https://doi.org/10.1007/978-3-319-30493-9_1
3. Taibi, D., Fulantelli, G., Dietze, S., Fetahu, B.: Educational linked data on the web - exploring and analysing the scope and coverage. In: Mouromtsev, D., d'Aquin, M. (eds.) Open Data for Education. LNCS, vol. 9500, pp. 16–37. Springer, Cham (2016). https://doi.org/10.1007/978-3-319-30493-9_2

4. Nahhas, S., Bamasag, O., Khemakhem, M., Bajnaid, N.: Added values of linked data in education: a survey and roadmap. Computers **7**(3) (2018). https://doi.org/10.3390/computers7030045

5. Lange, C.: Ontologies and languages for representing mathematical knowledge on the Semantic Web. Semant. Web **4**(2), 119–158 (2013). https://doi.org/10.3233/SW-2012-0059

6. Elizarov, A.M., Kirillovich, A.V., Lipachev, E.K., Nevzorova, O.A., Solovyev, V.D., Zhiltsov, N.G.: Mathematical knowledge representation: semantic models and formalisms. Lobachevskii J. Math. **35**(4), 348–354 (2014). https://doi.org/10.1134/S1995080214040143

7. Ginev, D., et al.: The SMGloM project and system: towards a terminology and ontology for mathematics. In: Greuel, G.-M., Koch, T., Paule, P., Sommese, A. (eds.) ICMS 2016. LNCS, vol. 9725, pp. 451–457. Springer, Cham (2016). https://doi.org/10.1007/978-3-319-42432-3_58

8. Kohlhase, M.: A data model and encoding for a semantic, multilingual terminology of mathematics. In: Watt, S.M., Davenport, J.H., Sexton, A.P., Sojka, P., Urban, J. (eds.) CICM 2014. LNCS (LNAI), vol. 8543, pp. 169–183. Springer, Cham (2014). https://doi.org/10.1007/978-3-319-08434-3_13

9. Nevzorova, O.A., Zhiltsov, N., Kirillovich, A., Lipachev, E.: *OntoMath* ^{PRO} ontology: a linked data hub for mathematics. In: Klinov, P., Mouromtsev, D. (eds.) KESW 2014. CCIS, vol. 468, pp. 105–119. Springer, Cham (2014). https://doi.org/10.1007/978-3-319-11716-4_9

10. Nevzorova, O., et al.: Bringing math to LOD: a semantic publishing platform prototype for scientific collections in mathematics. In: Alani, H., et al. (eds.) ISWC 2013. LNCS, vol. 8218, pp. 379–394. Springer, Heidelberg (2013). https://doi.org/10.1007/978-3-642-41335-3_24

11. Elizarov, A.M., Lipachev, E.K., Nevzorova, O.A., Solov'ev, V.D.: Methods and means for semantic structuring of electronic mathematical documents. Dokl. Math. **90**(1), 521–524 (2014). https://doi.org/10.1134/S1064562414050275

12. Elizarov, A., Kirillovich, A., Lipachev, E., Nevzorova, O.: Digital ecosystem OntoMath: mathematical knowledge analytics and management. In: Kalinichenko, L., Kuznetsov, S.O., Manolopoulos, Y. (eds.) DAMDID/RCDL 2016. CCIS, vol. 706, pp. 33–46. Springer, Cham (2017). https://doi.org/10.1007/978-3-319-57135-5_3

13. Elizarov, A.M., Zhiltsov, N.G., Kirillovich, A.V., Lipachev, E.K., Nevzorova, O.A., Solovyev, V.D.: The OntoMath ecosystem: ontologies and applications for math knowledge management. In: Semantic Representation of Mathematical Knowledge Workshop, 5 February 2016. http://www.fields.utoronto.ca/video-archive/2016/02/2053-14698

14. Elizarov, A., Kirillovich, A., Lipachev, E., and Nevzorova, O.: Semantic formula search in digital mathematical libraries. In: Proceedings of the 2nd Russia and Pacific Conference on Computer Technology and Applications (RPC 2017), pp. 39–43. IEEE (2017). https://doi.org/10.1109/RPC.2017.8168063

15. Elizarov, A.M., Zhizhchenko, A.B., Zhil'tsov, N.G., Kirillovich, A.V., Lipachev, E.K.: Mathematical knowledge ontologies and recommender systems for collections of documents in physics and mathematics. Dokl. Math. **93**(2), 231–233 (2016). https://doi.org/10.1134/S1064562416020174

16. Barana, A., Di Caro, L., Fioravera, M., Marchisio, M., Rabellino, S.: Ontology development for competence assessment in virtual communities of practice. In: Penstein Rosé, C., et al. (eds.) AIED 2018, Part II. LNCS (LNAI), vol. 10948, pp. 94–98. Springer, Cham (2018). https://doi.org/10.1007/978-3-319-93846-2_18

17. Barana, A., Di Caro, L., Fioravera, M., Floris, F., Marchisio, M., Rabellino, S.: Sharing system of learning resources for adaptive strategies of scholastic remedial intervention. In: Proceedings of the 4th International Conference on Higher Education Advances (HEAd 2018), pp. 1495–1503. Editorial Universitat Politècnica de València (2018). https://doi.org/10.4995/HEAd18.2018.8232

18. Marchisio, M., Di Caro, L., Fioravera, M., Rabellino, S.: Towards adaptive systems for automatic formative assessment in virtual learning communities. In: Sorel Reisman, et al. (eds.) Proceedings of the 42nd IEEE Annual Computer Software and Applications Conference (COMPSAC 2018), pp. 1000–1005. IEEE (2018). https://doi.org/10.1109/COMPSAC.2018.00176

19. Barana, A., Di Caro, L., Fioravera, M., Floris, F., Marchisio, M., Rabellino, S.: Developing competence assessment systems in e-learning communities. In: Volun-geviciene, A., Szücs, A. (eds.) Proceedings of the European Distance and E-Learning Network 2018 Annual Conference: Exploring the Micro, Meso and Macro (EDEN 2018), pp. 879–888. EDEN (2018)

20. Kirillovich, A., Nevzorova, O., Falileeva, M., Lipachev, E., Shakirova, L.: OntoMathEdu: towards an educational mathematical ontology. In: Kaliszyk, C., et al. (eds.) Workshop Papers at 12th Conference on Intelligent Computer Mathematics (CICM-WS 2019). CEUR Workshop Proceedings (2019, forthcoming)

21. Ranta, A.: Syntactic categories in the language of mathematics. In: Dybjer, P., Nordström, B., Smith, J. (eds.) TYPES 1994. LNCS, vol. 996, pp. 162–182. Springer, Heidelberg (1995). https://doi.org/10.1007/3-540-60579-7_9

22. Guizzardi, G.: Ontological Foundations for Structural Conceptual Models. CTIT, Enschede (2005)

23. Lehmann, J., et al.: DBpedia: a large-scale, multilingual knowledge base extracted from Wikipedia. Semant. Web J. **6**(2), 167–195 (2015). https://doi.org/10.3233/SW-140134

24. Astafiev, A., Prokofyev, R., Guéret, C., Boyarsky, A., Ruchayskiy, O.: Science-WISE: a web-based interactive semantic platform for paper annotation and ontology editing. In: Simperl, E., et al. (eds.) ESWC 2012. LNCS, vol. 7540, pp. 392–396. Springer, Heidelberg (2015). https://doi.org/10.1007/978-3-662-46641-4_33

25. Müller, D., Gauthier, T., Kaliszyk, C., Kohlhase, M., Rabe, F.: Classification of alignments between concepts of formal mathematical systems. In: Geuvers, H., England, M., Hasan, O., Rabe, F., Teschke, O. (eds.) CICM 2017. LNCS (LNAI), vol. 10383, pp. 83–98. Springer, Cham (2017). https://doi.org/10.1007/978-3-319-62075-6_7

26. Dehaye, P.-O., et al.: Interoperability in the OpenDreamKit project: the math-in-the-middle approach. In: Kohlhase, M., Johansson, M., Miller, B., de de Moura, L., Tompa, F. (eds.) CICM 2016. LNCS (LNAI), vol. 9791, pp. 117–131. Springer, Cham (2016). https://doi.org/10.1007/978-3-319-42547-4_9

27. McCrae, J.P., et al.: The open linguistics working group: developing the linguistic linked open data cloud. In: Calzolari N., et al. (eds.) Proceedings of the 10th International Conference on Language Resources and Evaluation (LREC 2016), pp. 2435–2441. ELRA (2016)

28. Cimiano, P., Chiarcos, C., McCrae, J.P., Gracia, J.: Linguistic linked open data cloud. Linguistic Linked Data, pp. 29–41. Springer, Cham (2020). https://doi.org/10.1007/978-3-030-30225-2_3

29. McCrae, J.P., Fellbaum, C., Cimiano, P.: Publishing and linking WordNet using lemon and RDF. In: Chiarcos, C., et al. (eds.) Proceedings of the 3rd Workshop on Linked Data in Linguistics (LDL-2014), pp. 13–16. ELRA (2014)

30. Ehrmann, M., Cecconi, F., Vannella, D., McCrae, J., Cimiano, P., Navigli, R.: Representing multilingual data as linked data: the case of BabelNet 2.0. In: Calzolari N., et al. (eds.) Proceedings of the 9th International Conference on Language Resources and Evaluation (LREC 2014), pp. 401–408. ELRA (2014)
31. Kirillovich, A., Nevzorova, O., Gimadiev, E., Loukachevitch, N.: RuThes Cloud: towards a multilevel linguistic linked open data resource for Russian. In: Różewski, P., Lange, C. (eds.) KESW 2017. CCIS, vol. 786, pp. 38–52. Springer, Cham (2017). https://doi.org/10.1007/978-3-319-69548-8_4
32. Galieva, A., Kirillovich, A., Khakimov, B., Loukachevitch, N., Nevzorova, O., Suleymanov, D.: Toward domain-specific Russian-tatar thesaurus construction. In: Proceedings of the International Conference IMS-2017, pp. 120–124. ACM (2017). https://doi.org/10.1145/3143699.3143716
33. Ganesalingam, M.: The Language of Mathematics, vol. 7805. Springer, Heidelberg (2013). https://doi.org/10.1007/978-3-642-37012-0
34. Guarino, N., Welty, C.A.: A formal ontology of properties. In: Dieng, R., Corby, O. (eds.) EKAW 2000. LNCS (LNAI), vol. 1937, pp. 97–112. Springer, Heidelberg (2000). https://doi.org/10.1007/3-540-39967-4_8
35. Noy, N., Rector, A.: Defining N-ary Relations on the Semantic Web. W3C Working Group Note, 12 April 2006. https://www.w3.org/TR/swbp-n-aryRelations/
36. Borgo, S., Masolo, C.: Ontological foundations of DOLCE. In: Poli, R., Healy, M., Kameas, A. (eds.) Theory and Applications of Ontology: Computer Applications, pp. 279–295. Springer, Dordrecht (2010). https://doi.org/10.1007/978-90-481-8847-5_13
37. Borgo, S., Masolo, C.: Foundational choices in DOLCE. In: Staab, S., Studer, R. (eds.) Handbook on Ontologies. IHIS, pp. 361–381. Springer, Heidelberg (2009). https://doi.org/10.1007/978-3-540-92673-3_16
38. Gangemi, A., Mika, P.: Understanding the semantic web through descriptions and situations. In: Meersman, R., Tari, Z., Schmidt, D.C. (eds.) OTM 2003. LNCS, vol. 2888, pp. 689–706. Springer, Heidelberg (2003). https://doi.org/10.1007/978-3-540-39964-3_44
39. Brasileiro, F., Almeida, J.P.A., Carvalho, V.A., Guizzardi, G.: Expressive multi-level modeling for the semantic web. In: Groth, P., et al. (eds.) ISWC 2016, Part I. LNCS, vol. 9981, pp. 53–69. Springer, Cham (2016). https://doi.org/10.1007/978-3-319-46523-4_4
40. Carvalho, V.A., Almeida, J.P.A., Fonseca, C.M., Guizzardi, G.: Multi-level ontology-based conceptual modeling. In: Data & Knowledge Engineering, vol. 109, pp. 3–24, May 2017. https://doi.org/10.1016/j.datak.2017.03.002
41. Kirillovich, A., Nevzorova, O.: Ontological analysis of the Wikipedia category system. In: Aveiro, D., et al. (eds.) Proceedings of the 10th International Joint Conference on Knowledge Discovery, Knowledge Engineering and Knowledge Management (IC3K 2018), Seville, Spain, 18–20 September 2018. KEOD, vol. 2, pp. 358–366. SCITEPRESS (2018)
42. Guarino, N., Welty, C.A.: An overview of OntoClean. In: Staab, S., Studer, R. (eds.) Handbook on Ontologies. IHIS, pp. 201–220. Springer, Heidelberg (2009). https://doi.org/10.1007/978-3-540-92673-3_9
43. Cimiano, P., McCrae, J.P., Buitelaar, P.: Lexicon model for ontologies. Final Community Group Report, 10 May 2016. https://www.w3.org/2016/05/ontolex/
44. McCrae, J.P., Bosque-Gil, J., Gracia, J., Buitelaar, P., Cimiano, P.: The OntoLex-Lemon model: development and applications. In: Kosem I., et al. (eds.) Proceedings of the 5th biennial conference on Electronic Lexicography (eLex 2017), pp. 587–597. Lexical Computing CZ (2017)

45. Chiarcos, C.: OLiA - ontologies of linguistic annotation. Semant. Web **6**(4), 379–386 (2015). https://doi.org/10.3233/SW-140167
46. Rospocher, M., Corcoglioniti, F., Palmero Aprosio, A.: PreMOn: LODifing linguistic predicate models. Lang. Resour. Eval. **53**(3), 499–524 (2018). https://doi.org/10.1007/s10579-018-9437-8

FrameIT: Detangling Knowledge Management from Game Design in Serious Games

Michael Kohlhase[ID], Benjamin Bösl, Richard Marcus[✉][ID], Dennis Müller[ID], Denis Rochau, Navid Roux[ID], John Schihada, and Marc Stamminger

Computer Science, FAU Erlangen-Nürnberg, Erlangen, Germany
richard.marcus@fau.de

Abstract. Serious games are an attempt to leverage the inherent motivation in game-like scenarios for an educational application and to transpose the learning goals into real-world applications. Unfortunately, serious games are also very costly to develop and deploy. For very abstract domains like mathematics, already the representation of the knowledge involved becomes a problem.

We propose the **FrameIT Method** that uses OMDoc/Mmt theory graphs to represent and track the underlying knowledge in serious games. In this paper we report on an implementation and experiment that tests the method. We obtain a simple serious game by representing a "word problem" in OMDoc/Mmt and connecting the Mmt API with a state-of-the-art game engine.

1 Introduction

Serious games could be a solution to the often-diagnosed problem that traditional education via personal instruction and educational documents has serious scalability, subject specificity, and motivation limitations. A serious game is *"a mental contest, played with a computer in accordance with specific rules, that uses entertainment to further government or corporate training, education, health, public policy, and strategic communication objectives"* [Zyd05]. Beyond educational games for students, the term "Serious Game" is used for games that help to acquire skills in general. This includes training professionals of basically all industry sectors.

Serious games have the power to effectively supplement technical documents and online courses and thereby allow students to learn how to apply their knowledge to real world scenarios. Moreover, serious games very elegantly solve the motivation problem many people experience when studying technical subjects. Through gamification [Det+11] a serious game can be very entertaining while at the same time providing educational value to the user.

Unfortunately, serious games for complex subjects like science, technology, engineering, and mathematics (STEM) are currently very complex, domain-specific, and expensive even though their motivational effects could be disruptive

© Springer Nature Switzerland AG 2020
C. Benzmüller and B. Miller (Eds.): CICM 2020, LNAI 12236, pp. 173–189, 2020.
https://doi.org/10.1007/978-3-030-53518-6_11

right in these areas. Even more seriously, developers of such games need to combine the skill sets of game development, pedagogy, and domain expertise, a rare combination indeed.

To alleviate this, we propose the **Frame IT Method**, which – instead of using ad-hoc methods for dealing with the underlying STEM domain knowledge in the game – uses established mathematical knowledge management (MKM) techniques and implementations. It loosely couples a game engine for interacting with virtual worlds with the MMT system, which performs knowledge representation and management services, thus detangling the domain knowledge integration from the game development process. The main mechanism involved is the maintenance of a mapping between objects of the virtual world and their properties ("facts"), which are formally represented in OMDoc/MMT. On this basis, learning objects in the form of represented theorem statements can *i)* be visualized in the game world ("scrolls") for the player to understand, *ii)* be instantiated by the player by assigning a game object to every required assumption, and *iii)* can, together with their instantiations, be represented in MMT as OMDoc/MMT views. The latter enables validity checking and computation of results which can then be transferred back into the game world bringing things full circle.

The Frame IT Method is supposed to increase a player's understanding of formulae by making them apply such abstract formulae in concrete settings happening within a game world. To fulfill a formula's assumptions, the player has to perform a combination of selecting, moving, and generating game objects. With the help of OMDoc/MMT in the background and back-and-forth synchronization, concrete outcomes of formula applications can immediately be visualized for the user in the game world, too.

The Tree Example. At this point, we would like to introduce a running example of an in-game word problem for a serious game. We use this problem in our serious game prototype as well throughout this document to progressively explain the Frame IT Method.

Concretely, the player is presented a tree in a forested 3D world and is asked to determine its height using a limited set of **gadgets**; each of those providing **facts** about the world, e.g. acquirable angles and lengths from the player's perspective (cf. Fig. 1). The intended solution is to frame this problem in the language of trigonometry as finding the length of the

Word Problem	Game Problem
How can you measure the height of a tree you cannot climb, when you only have a laser angle finder and a tape measure at hand?	

Fig. 1. Example problem

opposite side given an angle and the adjacent side. Other solutions are also possible, e.g. choosing an isosceles 45°-45°-90° triangle, for which both legs of the triangle then have the same length.

Didactically, the game world is rigged so that the gadgets produce only facts acquirable from the player's perspective. For instance, they cannot climb the tree, and hence the provided measuring tape gadget disallows measuring the tree's height. Instead, the user is expected to use **scrolls**[1] to discover new facts about the world in alternative ways. In the problem at hand, such a scroll on trigonometry could provide the length of the opposite side of a right-angled triangle given an angle and the length of an adjacent side – both of which are acquirable from the player's perspective.

Contribution. In this paper, we present the Frame IT Method as a new approach to knowledge management in serious games and an implementation of this, the UFrame IT system. We have implemented all system components and developed APIs that allow an integration of the MMT system with Unity, a state-of-the-art game engine. With the new framework, building a serious game should be a matter of formalizing the background knowledge in OMDOC/MMT and providing the necessary gadgets and scrolls. We confirm this hypothesis by instantiating UFrame IT into a very simple serious game: FrameWorld-1. The project is available on GitHub, we provide a demo video and a playable prototype; all of these can be found at https://uframeit.github.io/.

Related Work. We limit ourselves to describing how our primary contribution, the Frame IT Method, fits into the spectrum of existing methods of knowledge management in (educational) games and tools. The concerns of knowledge management and actual game realization in source code can be completely intermingled. This is especially the case in games that are built from the ground up. Going noticeably further, we can find games employing dedicated physics engines and frameworks for handling user objects. One noteworthy library of such small-scale yet modular games for STEM education are the PhET Interactive Simulations [PhET]. Continuing on the spectrum, we can identify domain-specific languages being increasingly used. A well-known example of this is GeoGebra [GG], a graphics calculator employing a dedicated computer algebra system. The concept of explicit knowledge integration can also be found in state-of-the-art game engines. There, various forms of dataflow programming are used, for instance, to construct graphs to specify shader materials, visual effects, animation transitions, and even gameplay interactions. Finally, instead of DSLs we can also use a dedicated MKM system (our approach), which gives us the most flexibility in knowledge formalization.

Overview. In the next section, we mainly recap previous work on OMDOC/MMT. We then continue describing our approach in a progressive, threefold way.

---

[1] The name "scroll" is meant to evoke the fact that the knowledge contained in it is a valuable commodity in the game.

In Sect. 3, we first describe the FrameIT Method from a purely conceptional viewpoint. Then, instantiating that concept, we present and discuss our implemented framework UFrameIT in Sect. 4. Finally, in Sect. 5 we show our realization of the running example within UFrameIT. In Sect. 6, we give a short conceptual evaluation of the FrameIT Method and conclude the paper in Sect. 7.

Acknowledgements. The development of the FrameIT Method has profited from discussions in the KWARC group, in particular from contributions by Mihnea Iancu and Andrea Kohlhase. The implementation reported on in this paper completely re-implements [RKM16] and extends it significantly.

2   Preliminaries

For the concept and implementation of the FrameIT Method, we require an MKM system capable of storing, relating, and combining knowledge items in a structured knowledge graph. To the best of our knowledge, besides the MMT system, the only other systems supporting this sufficiently are Hets [MML07] and Specware [SPEC].

2.1   Learning Object Graphs as OMDoc/MMT Theories

In this work, we choose the OMDoc/MMT language [RK13] as a fitting theoretical framework together with its reference implementation in the MMT system [Rab13], which is a general foundation- and logic-independent framework for creating formal systems [MR19]. Below, we briefly recap the language in a way suited for our applications in this paper. Nonetheless, our methods are agnostic on the specific choice of an MKM system as long as it supports the features elaborated on below in some way. Indeed, we reflect the loose coupling of our approach in the structure of this paper by having Sect. 3 detailing the FrameIT Method without assumption of any implementation details.

Storing. OMDoc/MMT organizes knowledge into theories and relates theories via views. A **theory** is essentially a list of typed constant declarations of the form $c \colon E \ [= e] \ [\# \ N]$. Here, c is the (theory-local) identifier, the well-typed expressions E and e the type and definiens, and N some notation. Expressions are well-formed terms over all previous declarations in scope. By leveraging a suitable foundation and logic as well as the Curry-Howard correspondence, we can represent a wide range of formal knowledge including type, function, and predicate symbols, axioms, theorems, judgements, and inference rules. Moreover, for structuring purposes, theories can include (import) knowledge of other theories. Since inclusions are a special case of views, we suggestively write $S \hookrightarrow T$ for a theory S being included in a theory T.

Relating. In general, two theories S and T can be related by a **view** $v \colon S \rightsquigarrow T$, which is a well-typed map mapping every declaration in S to a T-expression. Views can be thought of as refinements from some abstract theory S to a more concrete theory T. For instance, in our running example we could represent a theory of triangles in S, a concrete game world set up by the player in T, and utilize a view $S \rightsquigarrow T$ to understand the tree and the shadow cast by it as forming a triangle. In particular, as a result of well-typedness we get *truth preservation* as a metatheorem: under a view, the images of axioms/theorems and proofs in the domain theory are again theorems and proofs in the codomain theory. In the context of our example, this enables instantiating abstract theorems, such as trigonometric identities, in the concrete world, e.g. to compute the tree's height by only knowing the shadow's (projected) width and the enclosed angle.

A **theory graph** is a multigraph emerging from a collection of theories and views together. We will use theory graphs as **learning object graphs** in the Frame IT context. They form the fundamental basis for the Frame IT Method as they allow us to relate different learning objects with each other in a machine understandable and logical way.

Combining. The final feature we require from an MKM system for our purposes is to *combine* knowledge. In the OMDoc/MMT language, we can phrase this as computing pushouts in the category of theories and views. In this category, pushouts along inclusions always exist; see Fig. 2 for the general scheme. Intuitively, the pushout P is formed as the union of S and T such that they exactly share R. In the Frame IT Method, we make extensive use of pushouts as a way

Fig. 2. Pushout

to translate abstract conclusions in T into the context of a concrete situation in S. This is legitimized by first constructing the upper view v in Fig. 2, which serves to *frame* parts of S as the abstract preconditions stored in R; hence the name Frame IT.

2.2   Unity: A Multi-platform Game Engine

Since our goal is the development of a knowledge-based engine for serious math games, we encounter the need for a correspondent graphics engine twice: once, to create a system that can interoperate with the MKM system and, once, to actually implement a game prototype using this framework. To cope with this, we use the Unity game engine [Uni]. As an industry standard with a big community – providing materials, assets and tutorials – it meets all our requirements. While it is easy to learn the basics, it is yet a powerful and flexible tool, supporting deployment to basically every platform, including VR and AR devices. It greatly reduces the amount of effort to create virtual worlds by largely taking care of rendering as part of its huge API to implement game interactions and interfaces. In particular, it also offers an interface for communicating with a *RESTful* API, which we exploit in our implementation to interact with the MMT system.

3   The FrameIT Method

We propose that – at least for the domain of mathematical knowledge – serious games be implemented with a dedicated MKM system in the background leveraged for storing, relating, and combining knowledge. In our concept, we exploit features provided by the MKM system and expose them to the player by means of appropriate user interfaces such that players can easily explore, play, compute, and verify solutions to in-game puzzles. From the many conceivable kinds of applications, in this work we focus on the task of **framing puzzles**. Such puzzles challenge the user to frame concrete tasks in the 3D game world, such as measuring a tree's height, as abstract problems, such as finding an opposite's length in trigonometry.

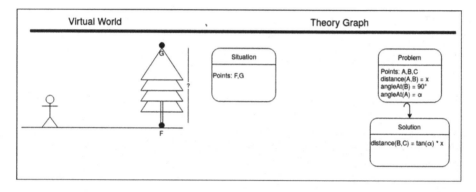

Fig. 3. The FrameIT Method as a process – initializiation

3.1   Exemplary Playflow

The main contribution of the FrameIT Method is the division of labor between game engine and MKM system, which offers several advantages regarding development workflows and knowledge management. To get a better intuition of the method, we will go through the process of solving our tree example step-by-step showing what goes on in both subsystems (on the left and right of the Figs. 3 and 5 to 7). This also allows us to introduce the pertinent concepts by way of our running example.

Initially in the game, the user is presented our word problem together with some initial "background knowledge" they are allowed to apply throughout solving the puzzle (cf. Fig. 3). This background knowledge encompasses *facts* and *scrolls*: **Facts** are typed and arbitrarily complex knowledge items. For example, labelled 3D points marked in the world, such as $A := (1, 0, 0)$, can be facts. They can originate from multiple sources including level-dependent background knowledge and in-game exploration by the player themself. In our example, the user initially gets two point facts (namely F and G) marking the tree's endpoints. As is the case with all facts, they are kept synchronized with the knowledge side, which we can observe in Fig. 3 as declarations in the **situation theory**. This theory is a designated, possibly level-dependent theory encompassing the world knowledge provided or gained so far.

Scrolls complement the concept of facts via a mechanism to obtain new facts from existing ones – much like mathematical theorems. The game provides the user with the OppositeLen scroll (see Fig. 4), which operationalizes the mathematical theorem the game wants to teach. Namely, it requires three point facts a, b, c, the angle $\angle cab$, and the knowledge of $\angle abc = 90°$ as input and in return provides an identity about $|\overline{bc}|$.

This way, we see that scrolls can serve us as **learning objects** in serious games. On the knowledge side, we can represent them as **Problem/Solution theory pairs** (cf. Fig. 5), where the problem theory encapsulates the scroll's universal variables and preconditions, and the solution theory contains the desired assertions (results) in context of the former. In the process below, we will see that theorem application then becomes pushout computation in our sense.

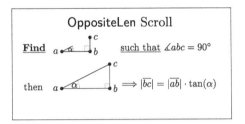

Fig. 4. The OppositeLen scroll

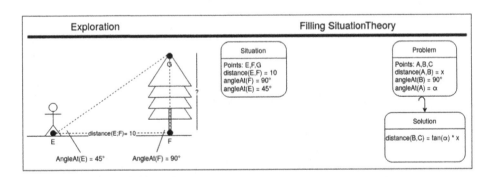

Fig. 5. The Frame IT Method as a process – step 2

In the second step, the user explores the virtual world and experiments with the given facts and scrolls. In some serious games, this happens off-band by the player with pen and paper. By contrast, the Frame IT Method actively encourages in-game exploration and even requires it to solve puzzles. World exploration can involve marking new points and lines within the world, possibly guided by scrolls like the OppositeLen scroll our player has been presented. Concretely, we imagine they use the **pointer gadget** in the game UI to mark a point E on the ground and the **line gadget** to mark a triangle through E and the tree's endpoints.

Moreover, they measure $\angle GEF = 45°$ and $\angle EFG = 90°$ using some protractor gadget. On the side of the MKM system in Fig. 5, we see that the collected facts are communicated to the MKM system as soon as they are created: the situation theory grows.

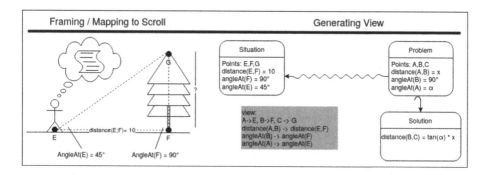

Fig. 6. The Frame IT Method as a process – step 3

In the third step, the player **frames** the in-game word problem in terms of the OppositeLen scroll by mapping every scroll input to a game world object. Here, the inputs for the point facts a, b, c, the enclosed angle $\angle cab$, and the right angle $\angle abc$ are mapped to the facts E, F, G, $\angle GEF = 45°$, and $\angle EFG = 90°$, respectively. This assignment is communicated to the MKM system which establishes that it constitutes a view – we call it the **application view** (cf. Fig. 6). Critically for our serious game use case, it establishes the precondition that $\triangle abc$ is a right-angled triangle which justifies the application of the OppositeLen scroll. If the player frames the game problem with an assignment that does *not* lead to a view – e.g. if the ground the tree stands on is sloped and thus the angle $\angle EFG$ is different from 90° – the MKM system will reject the framing and can pinpoint exactly where the error lies.

In the final step (cf. Fig. 7), the MKM system computes the pushout of the application view over the inclusion of the problem into the solution theory. Moreover, it simplifies terms, computes values, and reports to the game engine that the user has solved the puzzle. Concretely, success was determined by checking whether the fact $|\overline{FG}|$ simplifies to a numeric value in context of the pushout theory. This formal notion corresponds to the intuitive puzzle objective of finding that length.

Having solved the puzzle, the player can now proceed to choose a new puzzle to play. Importantly, the knowledge gained so far is *not* thrown away, but kept for future use by the player. For example, in subsequent puzzles the player can use the tree's height as input for other scrolls. This effect is easily achieved by updating the pointer to the situation theory to the computed pushout theory in the course of the last step.

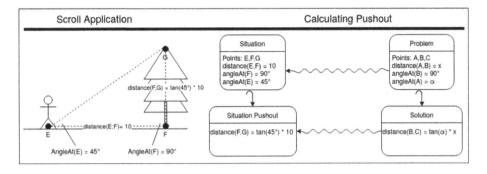

Fig. 7. The Frame IT Method as a process – step 4

Playing in Practice. Note that we presented an idealistic chronological order for simplicity only. In general, players might do several steps simultaneously, make mistakes in framing, and repeat previous steps. Moreover, levels might come bundled with multiple scroll libraries for the user to apply and choose from. All in all, much in the spirit of a working mathematician, the tasks of exploration, scroll application, and success are blurred in practice. See Sect. 5 for a realization of a game that allows to do all of these.

3.2 Acquiring Facts and Using Scrolls

Facts are a central part of the Frame IT Method. In our running example, we have so far only seen facts being acquired by marking/measuring things in the 3D world and by scroll application. Below, we give an extended, though non-exhaustive, compilation of ways to acquire facts.

- **Exploration of the 3D World:** Players can explore the 3D world by means of **gadgets**, which are a mechanism in the game UI to mark or measure things of interest in the game world. Our implementation includes gadgets to mark points, lines, angles, and distances among others. Upon usage, all these gadgets generate facts.
- **Scroll Application:** Successful scroll application leads to one or more facts being output.
- **Discovery, Awards, and Trade:** Serious games could be designed such that a player can stumble upon and discover facts within the world, e.g. by "talking" to non-player characters. Moreover, in more elaborate story designs, levels may come with a prize fact to earn upon success, which is then required for subsequent levels. Finally, assuming some kind of multiplayer mode, we might also allow players to share and trade facts.

Common to all ways of obtaining facts is that upon acquisition they are synchronized with the MKM system. Namely, it is supposed to serve as a single source of truth for all knowledge items. We will discuss the implementation of an appropriate framework next.

4   The **UFrameIT** Framework (Implementation)

We have implemented the FrameIT Method as a prototypical serious game framework we call UFrameIT. Concretely, we extend the existing MMT system with an interface for incremental fact synchronization and implement a general infrastructure for fact management, gadgets, scrolls, and framing in the C#-based API of the Unity game engine.

We have also instantiated the UFrameIT framework with a simple proof-of-concept game FrameWorld-1, which we describe in the next section. We separate the two concerns – even though they were developed together – to give an intuition of the relative efforts.

Figure 8 shows the main parts of the UFrameIT framework: the environment, the first-person player, the problem definition, as well as facts and scrolls at work in FrameWorld-1. It also shows the **Framing UI**, which allows **framing** and tool selection. We describe this in detail below. Lastly, in the middle we can see the laser angle finder **gadget** at work after it has been selected from the gadget bar at the bottom of the screen.

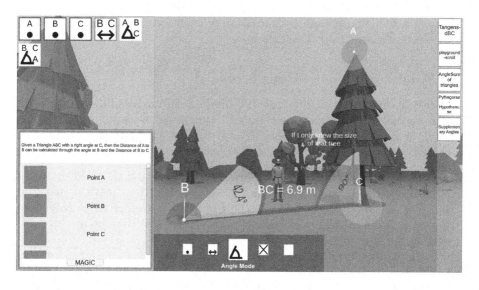

Fig. 8. Measuring facts about the world

4.1   Extending **Unity** with Facts, Scrolls, Gadgets, and Framing.

To incorporate the FrameIT Method we mainly need two things: gadgets and an interactive user interface.

Gadgets and Facts. On a technical level, gadgets consist of the following parts:

- To identify tools within the game, they need **graphical representations**. Currently, we only use a planar icon for the UI, but in the future, we plan to have 3D objects to show the gadgets in the virtual world.
- The activation of a gadget triggers **gadget events** that initialize or update its internal state. These events are used for communication between the player and the gadget.
- Gadgets give feedback to the player via **gadget visual effects**, e.g. for showing assisting previews during fact creation.
- Finally, gadgets trigger **fact events** to initiate the creation of the appropriate facts.

Facts are managed by MMT but, just as gadgets, they have graphical components: a Unity GameObject for interaction in the virtual world and an icon for interaction in the UI.

In order to develop a new gadget, there are three main modules which have to be extended: FactManager, FactSpawner and VisualEffectsManager. These modules cope with the different gadget parts described above. The FactManager is aware of the currently active gadget and handles the gadget-specific inputs made by the player. If necessary, it delegates work to the other modules. For instance, when a gadget was used successfully, it updates the global fact list (by addition or removal) and triggers the FactSpawner to arrange for the facts' in-game visualization. Moreover, for visualizing assisting previews in the course of using a gadget, the FactManager delegates and transmits the necessary data to the VisualEffectsManager. All of the modules assume that suitable fact types and gadgets producing instances of them have previously been established. Additionally, every fact type needs to be given a formalized counterpart on the MMT side. Hence, if a new gadget exceeds the current range of functionality, these parts may also need adaptation.

Framing UI. On the lower edge of the screen, players can find the **Gadget Toolbar**, which allows access and activation of the respective gadgets. To interact with the measured facts, the user can activate an overlay that freezes the underlying game and gives access to framing (cf. Fig. 8). **Facts** are depicted as small tiles and are collected in the fact inventory on the top left. Complementarily, available **scrolls** are shown on the right edge, of which the currently active scroll is shown beneath the fact inventory. Players can then fill the scrolls with facts via drag & drop. When the player clicks the "Magic" button, UFrameIT constructs and transfers the application view to MMT, which computes the pushout and, after successful verification, hands back the resulting facts.

4.2 Communication

To allow MMT to process information and give feedback according to the FrameIT Method, we use a very fine-grained communication approach. The backend server provides a RESTful-interface with endpoints to add facts (one endpoint per fact type), generate views, request pushout computations, and to list available scrolls. The corresponding payloads are transmitted in the JSON data format. There are three different types of events that trigger communication with the server:

- **Game World Triggers:** These automatically send requests during interaction with the game world but are not used for our simple example.
- **Fact List Modification:** We report all changes to the fact list to the server. Most prominently, these changes are triggered by gadgets. Each gadget-generated fact entails sending an HTTP request including the fact details to the server. On the MMT side, the putative fact is first checked for validity, then, upon success, stored as corresponding declaration(s) in the situation theory, and lastly, its generated declaration identifier is sent back to Unity.
- **Attempt of Scroll Application:** When the player tries to apply a scroll, a test for applicability is started: The mappings of the filled scroll are sent to the server and packaged into a putative view by MMT. The latter is then run through the type checker, whose outcome is reported back to the game engine. Upon success, the game engine requests the pushout computation wrt. the Problem/Solution theory pair representing the current scroll and updates the UI with the results.

5   FrameWorld-1: A Simple Serious Game in UFrameIT

FrameWorld-1 is a simple game instantiating the UFrameIT framework into a proof-of-concept game that is inspired by our running example and the playflow from Sect. 3.1. As most of the infrastructure comes from UFrameIT, the only "game contents" we had to develop for FrameWorld-1 were the game world, the problem-specific gadgets, a formalization of the background theory of 3D geometry and trigonometry, and appropriate scrolls.

5.1   A Simple Virtual World

To build a game, we require a world for the player to explore. With Unity, we simply added an object serving as ground together with the default first-person camera asset for navigation. To simplify the process of applying basic geometry, we kept the ground of the world completely flat for our first game. To bring the scene to life, we populated the scene with assets that are freely available at the Unity asset store.

Gadgets and Facts in FrameWorld-1. Gadgets are the core way of interacting with the world; for FrameWorld-1 we created three gadgets. The **pointer gadget** marks a point in the game world and produces a new fact that declares a labeled point. Upon gadget activation, objects in the environment that shouldn't be markable, e.g. the sky or existing points, are set to be ignored. Moreover, **snap zones** are activated. Placing a point within these zones positions it exactly at the center of the zone, which is necessary to accurately mark the root and the top of the tree. The user can then relate two or three different points by measuring the distance between them with a **measuring tape gadget** or the angle between them with the **laser angle finder**. An angle is defined by the selection of three existing point objects. Every single selection triggers an event that updates the internal state of the gadget. After the second point is selected, we preview the angle by following the mouse pointer until the third point has been fixed (cf. Fig. 9). Distance measuring is implemented analogously, in this case, with a preview line following the cursor. Importantly, we let the line only follow the cursor up to the height of the player and prevent connection with points which are higher than that. Even though these three gadgets were developed for FrameWorld-1, it is clear that they are generally useful for problems based on 3D geometry and can thus be shared with subsequent games.

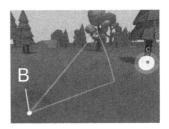

Fig. 9. Measuring angles

Fig. 10. Success

Playing the Game. The player automatically obtains a set of scrolls by starting FrameWorld-1. They learn about the puzzle they need to solve by talking to the non-player character and by subsequent exploration of the world by the means of the Frame IT Method. Delivering the height of the tree to the character talked to completes the game and triggers some visual feedback indicating success – the fireworks in Fig. 10.

5.2   Domain Knowledge and Scrolls

For FrameWorld-1, we have extended the MitM Ontology [MitM] by seven theories for 3D geometry and trigonometry, which can be found in [UFM]. We decided on 3D instead of planar geometry as the virtual world is 3D and a mapping to its 2D variant would engender an additional transformation step that we would have to communicate to the player. Additionally, this allows us to implement more advanced 3D geometry scrolls in the future.

For the scroll in the running example, we use the Problem/Solution theory pair shown in Fig. 11. The problem theory defines the required abstract situation of the scroll: a right-angled triangle, an angle, and the adjacent's length must all be known. In this context, the solution theory describes the scroll's output: the length of the opposite calculated via the tangent function. In the implementation we recognize and identify this pair by means of the meta annotations present in the problem theory.

```
theory problem : ?geometry =
  meta scrollName "OppositeLen" ▌
  meta scrollDescription "Given a triangle ABC right-angled at C, the
    distance AB can be computed from the angle at B and the distance BC" ▌
  meta solutionTheory ?tan_solution ▌

  A: Vec3 ▌ B: Vec3 ▌ C: Vec3 ▌ // triangle's endpoints ▌
  distBC_val: ℝ ▌
  distBC: DistFact B C distBC_val ▌
  angleABC_val: ℝ ▌
  angleABC: AngleFact A B C angleABC_val ▌
  angleBCA: AngleFact B C A 90.0 ▌ // required 90.0° angle at BCA ▌
▌
theory solution : ?geometry =
  include ?problem ▌
  distCA_val: ℝ ▌ = (tan angleABC_val) · distBC_val ▌
  tangentScroll: V → V → V → DistFact A C distCA_val ▌
  distCA: DistFact A C distCA_val ▌ = tangentScroll A B C ▌
▌
```

Fig. 11. MMT Problem/Solution theory pair (modified for readability)

Formalization in Detail. Recall that scrolls may represent theorems and in those cases they should only be applicable on situations fulfilling the theorem's preconditions. Fortunately, we can leverage MMT as an MKM system to enforce such conditions. For example, our background theory provides us a separate *distance type* for *every* real value of distance and two points. Using such a distance type for distBC in the problem theory allows us to enforce that only correct distance facts get mapped to it. For instance, a putative view mapping a distance fact for $|\overline{AC}|$ or even $|\overline{CB}|$ to distBC would lead to a typing error. We follow a similar approach for angle facts (cf. angleABC and angleBCA). Note that for angleBCA we fix the only correct angle of 90.0° directly in the type. In contrast, for the previous distance fact distBC and for angleABC, we used extra (unconstrained) declarations that make the actual value being mapped as the distance and the angle freely selectable. After all, these values are universally quantified over in the theorem statement.

Taking a step back from these practical experiences, we return to a conceptual level in the next section and evaluate the FrameIT Method.

6   Conceptual Evaluation

In the introduction, we have already given an account on how our approach fits on the spectrum of knowledge management in serious games. Now we evaluate it relative to two aspects in which we deviate from the other approaches.

First, we employ a **dedicated mechanism** for knowledge management instead of handling knowledge within source code. This is similar to GeoGebra, and in contrast to PhET Interactive Simulations which implements this concern in its JavaScript source code. The key benefits of doing so are:

- **Development Workflow Separation:** Traditionally, the game developer has to model complex problems within the game world, relying on frequent communication with experts to ensure that all aspects are implemented correctly. By encapsulating the knowledge integration, we can reduce the probability of mistakes during the knowledge transfer between domain experts and developers.
- **Reusing Knowledge:** As the (mathematical) background knowledge is independent from the game implementation itself, it does not rely on any specific programming language or game engine. This means that the knowledge formalization process only needs to happen once and different games can make use of it. Indeed OMDoc/MMT has been designed to support knowledge re-use in practice.
- **Reusing Game Design:** This is dual to the point above. Given a sufficiently declarative implementation API of the game engine side, the Frame IT Method allows the game to be updated by simply adapting the theory graph.

Further advantages stem from using a very **modular and expressive system** like an MKM system. Again, GeoGebra which uses a computer algebra system heads into a similar direction as we do. On the other hand, approaches reimplementing such business logic in source code, such as PhET simulations, are arguably more flexible, but not necessarily modularly so. The following features can profitably be imported from an MKM system:

- **Dependency Handling**: The MKM system can be used to track formalized dependencies of game world objects that have been given a suitable counterpart on that side. Thus, after knowledge integration, developers can often avoid to reimplement these kinds of relation handling.
- **Feedback**: The MKM system can detect at which point a player's solution fails and to some extent also why. This allows to give feedback helping players to spot and rectify problems while solving puzzles.
- **Multiple Solutions**: With careful implementation of puzzle objectives in the MKM system, the game can be made agnostic to solution paths. Thus, if there are multiple ways to complete the game, the user is free to do so by default.
- **Compound Problems/Solutions**: By treating facts and puzzle objectives in a uniform way, we can naturally construct compound problems asking for facts to be obtained by subproblems. We have presented a simple example, but it is not difficult to think of more advanced examples that require multiple scroll applications.

Nonetheless, employing a separate MKM system also introduces potential issues. In more complex games the sheer number of communication requests might impact game performance. Additionally, explicit modeling of background knowledge entails accounting for edge cases, which can be worked around in traditional (code-the-behavior) approaches.

7   Conclusion

We have presented a novel application of MKM technology: knowledge management in serious games, which we call the Frame IT Method. This principle alleviates the creation of games which, for instance, teach the application of simple mathematical models in geometry by instantiating them in virtual worlds. To realize the Frame IT Method, we have created an interface between the MMT system and Unity. This prototype implementation shows that combining a game engine with an MKM system is not only possible but indeed useful: The explicit representation of the underlying domain knowledge and the game world's situation in the MKM system allow for checking the applicability of the model on the MKM side. Consequently, our approach creates separated workflows and encourages reuse of content.

We have instantiated the UFrame IT framework to obtain FrameWorld-1, a simple serious game which challenges players to solve basic geometric problems using "scrolls" derived from 3D geometry and trigonometry. In accordance with our goals, our framework allowed to formalize knowledge in MMT largely independently from the remaining game development. Dually, we were also able to implement the game itself generically by building user-interface "gadgets", without necessitating domain expertise in geometry.

References

[Det+11] Sebastian, D., et al.: From game design elements to gamefulness: defining "Gamification". In: Proceedings of the 15th International Academic MindTrek Conference. MindTrek 2011, pp. 9–15. ACM, New York (2011). https://doi.org/10.1145/2181037.2181040

[GG] International GeoGebra Institute. Graphing Calculator - GeoGebra, 27 May 2020. https://www.geogebra.org

[MitM] MitM/core, 18 Jan 2020. https://gl.mathhub.info/MitM/core

[MML07] Mossakowski, T., Maeder, C., Lüttich, K.: The heterogeneous tool set, HETS. In: Grumberg, O., Huth, M. (eds.) TACAS 2007. LNCS, vol. 4424, pp. 519–522. Springer, Heidelberg (2007). https://doi.org/10.1007/978-3-540-71209-1_40

[MR19] Müller, D., Rabe, F.: Rapid prototyping formal systems in MMT: 5 case studies. In: LFMTP 2019. Electronic Proceedings in Theoretical Computer Science (EPTCS) (2019). https://kwarc.info/people/frabe/Research/MR_prototyping_19.pdf

[PhET] University of Colorado. PhET Interactive Simulations, 27 May 2020. https://phet.colorado.edu

[Rab13] Rabe, F.: The MMT API: a generic MKM system. In: Carette, J., et al. (eds.) Intelligent Computer Mathematics. Lecture Notes in Computer Science, vol. 7961, pp. 339-343. Springer, Heidelberg(2013). https://doi.org/10.1007/978-3-642-39320-4

[RK13] Rabe, F., Kohlhase, M.: A scalable module system. In: Information & Computation 0.230, pp. 1–54 (2013). https://kwarc.info/frabe/Research/mmt.pdf

[RKM16] Rochau, D., Kohlhase, M., Müller, D.: FrameIT reloaded: serious math games from modular math ontologies. In: Kohlhase, M., et al. (ed.) Intelligent Computer Mathematics - Work in Progress Papers (2016). http://ceur-ws.org/Vol-1785/W50.pdf

[SPEC] Kestrel Institute. The Specware System, 27 May 2020. https://www.kestrel.edu/home/projects/specware/index.html

[UFM] Formalizations for UFrameIT FrameWorld, 19 March 2020. https://gl.mathhub.info/FrameIT/FrameWorld

[Uni] Unity Technologies. Unity Realtime Development Platform. Version 2019.3.6, 19 March 2020. https://unity.com/

[Zyd05] Zyda, M.: From visual simulation to virtual reality to games. Computer **38**(9), 25–32 (2005). https://doi.org/10.1109/MC.2005.297

Formalizing Graph Trail Properties in Isabelle/HOL

Laura Kovács, Hanna Lachnitt[(✉)], and Stefan Szeider

TU Wien, Vienna, Austria
{laura.kovacs,hanna.lachnitt,stefan.szeider}@tuwien.ac.at

Abstract. We describe a dataset expressing and proving properties of graph trails, using Isabelle/HOL. We formalize the reasoning about strictly increasing and decreasing trails, using weights over edges, and prove lower bounds over the length of trails in weighted graphs. We do so by extending the graph theory library of Isabelle/HOL with an algorithm computing the length of a longest strictly decreasing graph trail starting from a vertex for a given weight distribution, and prove that any decreasing trail is also an increasing one.

Keywords: Weighted graph · Increasing/decreasing trails · Isabelle/HOL · Verified theory formalization

1 Introduction

The problem of finding a longest trail with strictly increasing or strictly decreasing weights in an edge-weighted graph is an interesting graph theoretic problem [3,7,8,14], with potential applications to scheduling and cost distribution in traffic planning and routing [5]. In this paper, we formalize and automate the reasoning about strictly increasing and strictly decreasing trail properties by developing an extendable flexible library in the proof assistant Isabelle/HOL [11].

As a motivating example consider the following (undirected) graph K_4, where each edge is annotated with a different integer-valued weight ranging from $1, \ldots, 6$:

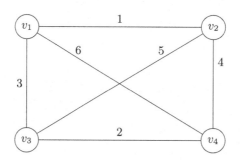

Fig. 1. Example graph K_4

C. Benzmüller and B. Miller (Eds.): CICM 2020, LNAI 12236, pp. 190–205, 2020.
https://doi.org/10.1007/978-3-030-53518-6_12

When considering K_4, the question we address in this paper is whether K_4 has a strictly decreasing trail of length $k \geq 1$. A trail is a sequence of distinct edges $(e_1, \ldots, e_k)$, $e_i \in E$ such that there exists a corresponding sequence of vertices $(v_0, \ldots, v_k)$ where $e_i = v_{i-1}v_i$. A strictly-ordered trail is a trail where the edge weights of $(e_1, \ldots, e_k)$ are either strictly increasing or strictly decreasing. Our work provides a formally verified algorithm computing such strictly-ordered trails. Note that there is a decreasing trail in K_4 starting at vertex v_3, with trail length 3; namely $(v_3v_2; v_2v_4; v_4v_3)$ is such a trail, with each edge in the trail having a higher weight than its consecutive edge in the trail. Similarly, K_4 has decreasing trails of length 3 starting from v_1, v_2, and v_4 respectively. A natural question to ask, which we address in this paper, is whether it is possible to construct a graph such that the constructed graph has 4 vertices and 5 edges, and no vertex is the starting node of a trail of length 3? We answer this question negatively, in an even more general setting, not restricted to 4 vertices and 5 edges. Similarly to the theoretical results of [8], we show that, given a graph G with n vertices and q edges, there is always a strictly decreasing trail of length at least $2 \cdot \lfloor \frac{q}{n} \rfloor$. While such a graph theoretical result has already been announced [8], in this paper we formalize the results in Isabelle/HOL and construct a Isabelle/HOL-verified algorithm computing strictly decreasing trails of length k, whenever such trails exist.

Let us note that proving that a graph G with n vertices and q edges has/does not have decreasing trails is possible for small n, using automated reasoning engines such as Vampire [9] and Z3 [6]. One can restrict the weights to the integers $1, \ldots, q$ and since $q \leq \binom{n}{2}$ there is a finite number of possibilities for each n. Nevertheless, the limit of such an undertaking is reached soon. On our machine[1] even for $n = 7$, both Vampire and Z3 fail proving the existence of strictly decreasing trails, using a 1 hour time limit. This is due to the fact that every combination of edge weights and starting nodes is tested to be a solution. Thus, the provers are not able to contribute to the process of finding an effective proof of the statement. Even for relatively small numbers n, our experiments show that state-of-the-art automated provers are not able to prove whether weighted graphs have a strictly decreasing trail of a certain length.

We also note that this limitation goes beyond automated provers. In the Isabelle proof assistant, proving that a complete graph with 3 vertices, i.e. K_3, will always contain a strictly decreasing trail of length 3 is quite exhaustive, as it requires reasoning about $3! = 6$ possibilities for a distribution of a weight function w and then manually constructing concrete trails:

$$w(v_1, v_2) = 2 \wedge w(v_2, v_3) = 1 \wedge w(v_3, v_1) = 3$$
$$\longrightarrow incTrail \ K_3 \ w[(v_3, v_2), (v_2, v_1), (v_1, v_3)]$$

Based on such limitations of automative and interactive provers, in this paper we aim at formalizing and proving existence of trails of length n, where $n \geq 1$ is a symbolic constant. As such, proving for example that graphs have trails of length 4, for a concrete n, become instances of our approach. To this end, we build upon

---

[1] Standard laptop with 1.7 GHz Dual-Core Intel Core i5 and 8 GB 1600 MHz memory.

existing works in this area. In particular, the first to raise the question of the minimum length of strictly increasing trails of arbitrary graphs were Chvátal and Komlós [4]. Subsequently, Graham and Kletman [8] proved that the lower bound of the length of increasing trails is given by $2 \cdot \lfloor \frac{q}{n} \rfloor$, as also mentioned above. In our work, we formalize and verify such results in Isabelle/HOL. Yet, our work is not a straightforward adaptation and formalization of Graham and Kletman's proof [8]. Rather, we focus on decreasing trails instead of increasing trails and give an algorithm computing longest decreasing trails of a given graph (Algorithm 1). By formalizing Algorithm 1 in Isabelle/HOL, we also formally verify the correctness of the trails computed by our approach. Moreover, we prove that any strictly decreasing trail is also an strictly increasing one, allowing this way to use our formalization in Isabelle/HOL also to formalize results of Graham and Kletman [8].

Contributions. This paper brings the following contributions.

(1) We formalize strictly increasing trails and provide basic lemmas about their properties. We improve results of [8] by giving a precise bound on the increase of trail length.
(2) We formalize strictly decreasing trails, in addition to the increasing trail setting of [8]. We prove the duality between strictly increasing and strictly decreasing trails, that is, any such decreasing trail is an increasing one, and vice versa. Thanks to these extensions, unlike [8], we give a constructive proof of the existence of strictly ordered trails (Lemma 1).
(3) We design an algorithm computing longest ordered trails (Algorithm 1), and formally verify its correctness in Isabelle/HOL. We extract our algorithm to Haskell program code using Isabelle's program extraction tool. Thus, we obtain a fully verified algorithm to compute the length of strictly-ordered trails in any given graph and weight distribution.
(4) We verify the lower bound on the minimum length of strictly decreasing trails of arbitrary graphs, and of complete graphs in particular.
(5) We build upon the Graph-Theory library by Noschinski [12], that is part of the Archive of Formal Proofs (AFP) and already includes many results on walks and general properties of graphs. We introduce the digital dataset v formalizing properties of graph trails. Our dataset consists of ∼2000 lines of Isabelle code and it took about one month for one person to finish. As far as we know this is the first formalization of ordered trails in a proof assistant.

This paper was generated from Isabelle/HOL source code using Isabelle's document preparation tool and is therefore fully verified. The source code is available online at https://github.com/Lachnitt/Ordered_Trail. The rest of the paper is organized as follows. Section 2 recalls basic terminology and properties from graph theory. We prove lower bounds on strictly increasing/decreasing trails in Sect. 3. We describe our Isabelle/HOL formalization in Isabelle/HOL in Sect. 4. We discuss further directions in Sect. 5 and conclude our paper with Sect. 6.

2   Preliminaries

We briefly recapitulate the basic notions of graph theory. A *graph* $G = (V, E)$ consists of a set V of *vertices* and a set $E \subseteq V \times V$ of *edges*. A graph is undirected if $(v_1, v_2) \in E$ implies that also $(v_2, v_1) \in E$. A graph is *complete* if every pair of vertices is connected by an edge. A graph is *loopfree* or *simple* if there are no edges $(x, x) \in E$ and *finite* if the number of vertices $|V|$ is finite. Finally, we call a graph $G' = (V', E')$ a *subgraph* of $G = (V, E)$ if $V' \subseteq V$ and $E' \subseteq E$.

If a graph is equipped with a weight function $w : E \to \mathbb{R}$ that maps edges to real numbers, it is called an *edge-weighted graph*. In the following, whenever a graph is mentioned it is implicitly assumed that this graph comes equipped with a weight function. A vertex labelling is a function $L : V \to \mathbb{N}$.

A *trail of length k* in a graph $G = (V, E)$ is a sequence $(e_1, \dots, e_k)$, $e_i \in E$, of distinct edges such that there exists a corresponding sequence of vertices $(v_0, \dots, v_k)$ where $e_i = v_{i-1} v_i$. A *strictly decreasing trail* in an edge-weighted graph $G = (V, E)$ with weight function w is a trail such that $w(e_i) > w(e_{i+1})$. Likewise, a *strictly increasing trail* is a trail such that $w(e_i) < w(e_{i+1})$. A trail is *strictly-ordered* if it is strictly increasing or strictly decreasing.

We will denote the length of a longest strictly increasing trail with $P_i(w, G)$. Likewise we will denote the length of a longest strictly decreasing trail with $P_d(w, G)$. In any undirected graph, it holds that $P_i(w, G) = P_d(w, G)$, a result that we will formally verify in Sect. 4.2.

Let $f_i(n) = \min_n P_i(w, K_n)$ denote the minimum length of an strictly increasing trail that must exist in the complete graph with n vertices. Likewise, $f_d(n) = \min_n P_d(w, K_n)$ in the case that we consider strictly decreasing trails.

3   Lower Bounds on Increasing and Decreasing Trails in Weighted Graphs

The proof introduced in the following is based on similar ideas as in [8]. However, we diverge from [8] in several aspects. Firstly, we consider strictly decreasing instead of strictly increasing trails, reducing the complexity of the automated proof (see Sect. 4). Moreover, we add tighter bounds than necessary to give a fully constructive proof in terms of an algorithm for computing the length of these trails (see Sect. 4.3). We discuss this further at the end of the section.

We start by introducing the notion of a weighted subgraph and then we built on that by specifying a family of labelling functions:

Definition 1 (Weighted Subgraph). *Let $G = (V, E)$ be a graph with weight function $w : E \to \{1, \dots, q\}$ where $|E| = q$. For each $i \in \{0, \dots, q\}$ define a weighted subgraph $G^i = (V, E^i)$ such that $e \in E^i$ iff $w(e) \in \{1, \dots, i\}$. That is, G^i contains only edges labelled with weights $\leq i$.*

Definition 2 (Labelling Function). *For each $G^i = (V, E^i)$, $n = |V|$ we define $L^i : V\{1, \dots, \frac{n(n-1)}{2}\}$ a labelling function such that $L^i(v)$ is the length of a longest strictly decreasing trail starting at vertex v using only edges in E^i.*

In Fig. 2 the example graph from Fig. 1 is revisited to illustrate these definitions. We need to prove the following property.

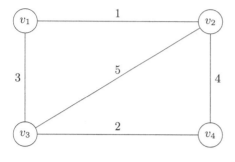

Decreasing trails from v_3 are:
$$v_3 - v_4,$$
$$v_3 - v_1 - v_2,$$
$$v_3 - v_2 - v_1,$$
$$v_3 - v_2 - v_4 - v3$$
Therefore, $L^5(v_3) = 3$.

Decreasing trails from v_1 are:
$$v_1 - v_2$$
$$v_1 - v_3 - v_4$$
Therefore, $L^5(v_1) = 2$.

Fig. 2. Graph G^5 with labelling function L^5

Lemma 1. *If $i < q$, then $\sum_{v \in V} L^{i+1}(v) \geq \sum_{v \in V} L^i(v) + 2$.*

Proof. Let e be the edge labelled with $i + 1$ and denote its endpoints with u_1 and u_2. It holds that $E^i \cup \{e\} = E^{i+1}$, therefore the graph G^{i+1} is G^i with the additional edge e. As $w(e') < w(e)$, for all $e' \in E^i$ we have $L^{i+1}(v) = L^i(v)$ for all $v \in V$ with $u_1 \neq v, u_2 \neq v$. It also holds that $L^{i+1}(u_1) = \max(L^i(u_2)+1, L^i(u_1))$ because either that longest trail from u_1 can be prolonged with edge e ($i + 1$ will be greater than the weight of the first edge in this trail by construction of L^{i+1}) or there is already a longer trail starting from u_1 not using e. We derive $L^{i+1}(u_2) = \max(L^i(u_1) + 1, L^i(u_2))$ based on a similar reasoning. See Fig. 3 for an illustration.

Note that $L^{i+1}(v) = L^i(v)$ for $v \in V \setminus \{u_1, u_2\}$, because no edge incident to these vertices was added and a trail starting from them cannot be prolonged since the new edge has bigger weight than any edge in such a trail.

If $L(u_1) = L(u_2)$, then $L^{i+1}(u_1) = L^i(u_1) + 1$ and $L^{i+1}(u_2) = L^i(u_2) + 1$ and thus the sum increases exactly by 2. If $L(u_1) > L(u_2)$ then $L^{i+1}(u_2) = L^i(u_1) + 1 \geq L^i(u_2) + 2$, otherwise $L^{i+1}(u_1) = L^i(u_2) + 1 \geq L^i(u_1) + 2$. Thus,

$$\sum_{v \in V} L^{i+1}(v) = \sum_{v \in (V - \{u_1, u_2\})} L^{i+1}(v) + L^{i+1}(u_1) + L^{i+1}(u_2)$$

$$\geq \sum_{v \in (V - \{u_1, u_2\})} L^{i+1}(v) + L^i(u_1) + L^i(u_2) + 2$$

$$= \sum_{v \in V} L^i(v) + 2.$$

$\square$

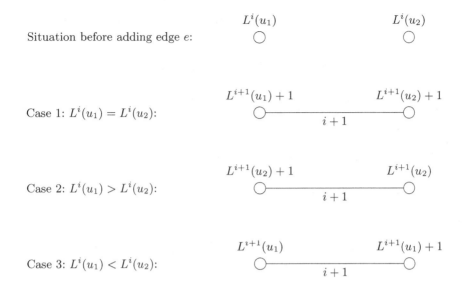

Fig. 3. Case distinction when adding edge e in Lemma 1

Note that the proof of Lemma 1 is constructive, yielding the Algorithm 1 for computing longest strictly decreasing trails. Function $findEndpoints$ searches for an edge in a graph G by its weight i and returns both endpoints. Function $findMax$ returns the maximum value of the array L.

Algorithm 1: Find Longest Strictly Decreasing Trail

> **for** $v \in V$ **do**
> $\quad\mid\ L(v) := 0$
> **end**
> **for** $i = 1; i < |E|; i + +$ **do**
> $\quad\mid\ (u, v) = findEndpoints(G, i);$
> $\quad\mid\ temp = L(u);$
> $\quad\mid\ L(u) = \max(L(v) + 1, L(u))\ ;$
> $\quad\mid\ L(v) = \max(temp + 1, L(v))\ ;$
> **end**
> return findMax(L);

Lemma 2. $\sum_{v \in V} L^q(v) \geq 2q.$

Proof. We proceed by induction, using the property $\sum_{v \in V} L^{i+1}(v) \geq \sum_{v \in V} L^i(v) + 2$ from Lemma 1. For the induction base note that $\sum_{v \in V} L^0(v) = 0$ because G^0 does not contain any edges and thus no vertex has a strictly decreasing trail of length greater than 0. $\qquad\square$

We next prove the lower bound on the length of longest strictly decreasing trails.

Theorem 1. *Let $G = (V, E)$ be an undirected edge-weighted graph such that $|V| = n$ and $|E| = q$. Let $w : E \to \{1, \ldots, q\}$ be a weight function assuming different weights are mapped to to different edges. Then, $P_d(w, G) \geq 2 \cdot \lfloor \frac{q}{n} \rfloor$ i.e., there exists a strictly decreasing trail of length $2 \cdot \lfloor \frac{q}{n} \rfloor$.*

Proof. Assume that no vertex is a starting point of a trail of length at least $2 \cdot \lfloor \frac{q}{n} \rfloor$, that is $L^q(v) < 2 \cdot \lfloor \frac{q}{n} \rfloor$, for all $v \in V$. Then, $\sum_{v \in V} L^q(v) < 2 \cdot \lfloor \frac{q}{n} \rfloor n \leq 2 \cdot q$. But this is a contradiction to Lemma 2 that postulates that the sum of the length of all longest strictly decreasing trails $\sum_{v \in V} L^q(v)$ is greater than $2 \cdot q$. Hence, there has to be at least one vertex with a strictly decreasing trail that is longer than $2 \cdot \lfloor \frac{q}{n} \rfloor$ in G^q. This trail contains a subtrail of length $2 \cdot \lfloor \frac{q}{n} \rfloor$. Since $E^q = E$ it follows that $G^q = G$, which concludes the proof.   □

Based on Theorem 1, we get the following results.

Corollary 1. *It holds that $P_i(w, G) \geq 2 \cdot \lfloor \frac{q}{n} \rfloor$ since when reversing a strictly decreasing trail one obtains a strictly increasing one. In this case, define $L^i(v)$ as the length of a longest strictly increasing trail ending at v in G^i.*   □

Corollary 2. *Let G be as in Theorem 1 and additionally assume that G is complete. Then, there exists a trail of length at least $n - 1$, i.e., $f_i(n) = f_d(n) \geq n - 1$.*   □

In [8] the authors present a non-constructive proof. As in Lemma 1 they argue that the sum of the lengths of all increasing trails is at least 2. Thus, they overestimate the increase. We however, use the exact increase therefore making the proof constructive and obtaining Algorithm 1.

4   Formalization of Trail Properties in Isabelle/HOL

4.1   Graph Theory in the Archive of Formal Proofs

To increase the reusability of our library we build upon the *Graph-Theory* library by Noschinski [12]. Graphs are represented as records consisting of vertices and edges that can be accessed using the selectors *pverts* and *parcs*. We recall the definition of the type *pair-pre-digraph*:

record 'a pair-pre-digraph = pverts :: 'a set parcs :: 'a rel

Now restrictions upon the two sets and new features can be introduced using locales. Locales are Isabelle's way to deal with parameterized theories [1]. Consider for example *pair-wf-digraph*. The endpoints of an edge can be accessed using the functions *fst* and *snd*. Therefore, conditions *arc-fst-in-verts* and *arc-snd-in-verts* assert that both endpoints of an edge are vertices. Using so-called sublocales a variety of other graphs are defined.

locale pair-wf-digraph = *pair-pre-digraph* +
assumes arc-fst-in-verts : $\bigwedge e.\ e\ \in\ parcs\ G\ \Longrightarrow\ fst\ e\ \in\ pverts\ G$
assumes arc-snd-in-verts : $\bigwedge e.\ e\ \in\ parcs\ G\ \Longrightarrow\ snd\ e\ \in\ pverts\ G$

An object of type $'b\ awalk$ is defined in *Graph-Theory.Arc-Walk* as a list of edges. Additionally, the definition *awalk* imposes that both endpoints of a walk are vertices of the graph, all elements of the walk are edges and two subsequent edges share a common vertex.

type-synonym $'b\ awalk$ = $'b\ list$

definition awalk :: $'a\ \Rightarrow\ 'b\ awalk\ \Rightarrow\ 'a\ \Rightarrow\ bool$
$awalk\ u\ p\ v\ \equiv\ u\ \in\ verts\ G\ \wedge\ set\ p\ \subseteq\ arcs\ G\ \wedge\ cas\ u\ p\ v$

We also reuse the type synonym *weight-fun* introduced in *Weighted-Graph*.

type-synonym $'b\ weight\text{-}fun$ = $'b\ \Rightarrow\ real$

Finally, there is an useful definition capturing the notion of a complete graph, namely *complete-digraph*.

4.2   Increasing and Decreasing Trails in Weighted Graphs

In our work we extend the graph theory framework from Sect. 4.1 with new features enabling reasoning about ordered trails. To this end, a trail is defined as a list of edges. We will only consider strictly increasing trails on graphs without parallel edges. For this we require the graph to be of type *pair-pre-digraph*, as introduced in Sect. 4.1.

Two different definitions are given in our formalization. Function *incTrail* can be used without specifying the first and last vertex of the trail whereas *incTrail2* uses more of *Graph-Theory's* predefined features. Moreover, making use of monotonicity *incTrail* only requires to check if one edge's weight is smaller than its successors' while *incTrail2* checks if the weight is smaller than the one of all subsequent edges in the sequence, i.e. if the list is sorted. The *equivalence between the two notions* is shown in the following.

fun *incTrail* :: $'a\ pair\text{-}pre\text{-}digraph\ \Rightarrow\ ('a\ \times\ 'a)\ weight\text{-}fun\ \Rightarrow\ ('a\ \times\ 'a)\ list\ \Rightarrow\ bool$
where
$incTrail\ g\ w\ []\ =\ True\ |$
$incTrail\ g\ w\ [e_1]\ =\ (e_1\ \in\ parcs\ g)\ |$
$incTrail\ g\ w\ (e_1 \# e_2 \# es)\ =\ (if\ w\ e_1\ <\ w\ e_2\ \wedge\ e_1\ \in\ parcs\ g\ \wedge\ snd\ e_1\ =\ fst\ e_2$
$\qquad\qquad\qquad\qquad\qquad then\ incTrail\ g\ w\ (e_2 \# es)\ else\ False)$

definition (**in** *pair-pre-digraph*) *incTrail2* **where**
$incTrail2\ w\ es\ u\ v\ \equiv\ sorted\text{-}wrt\ (\lambda e_1\ e_2.\ w\ e_1\ <\ w\ e_2)\ es\ \wedge\ (es\ =\ []\ \vee\ awalk\ u\ es\ v)$

fun *decTrail* :: $'a\ pair\text{-}pre\text{-}digraph\ \Rightarrow\ ('a\ \times\ 'a)\ weight\text{-}fun\ \Rightarrow\ ('a\ \times\ 'a)\ list\ \Rightarrow\ bool$
where
$decTrail\ g\ w\ []\ =\ True\ |$

$decTrail\ g\ w\ [e_1]\ =\ (e_1\ \in\ parcs\ g)\ |$
$decTrail\ g\ w\ (e_1\#e_2\#es)\ =\ (if\ w\ e_1\ >\ w\ e_2\ \wedge\ e_1\ \in\ parcs\ g\ \wedge\ snd\ e_1\ =\ fst\ e_2$
$$then\ decTrail\ g\ w\ (e_2\#es)\ else\ False)$$

definition (in *pair-pre-digraph*) *decTrail2* **where**
$decTrail2\ w\ es\ u\ v\ \equiv\ sorted\text{-}wrt\,(\lambda\,e_1\,e_2.\,w\,e_1\ >\ w\,e_2)\,es\ \wedge\ (es\ =\ []\ \vee\ awalk\ u\ es\ v)$

Defining trails as lists in Isabelle has many advantages including using predefined list operators, e.g., drop. Thus, we can show one result that will be constantly needed in the following, that is, that *any subtrail of an ordered trail is an ordered trail itself.*

lemma *incTrail-subtrail:*
  assumes *incTrail g w es*
  shows *incTrail g w (drop k es)*

lemma *decTrail-subtrail:*
  assumes *decTrail g w es*
  shows *decTrail g w (drop k es)*

In Isabelle we then show the equivalence between the two definitions *decTrail* and *decTrail2* of strictly decreasing trails. Similarly, we also show the equivalence between the definition *incTrail* and *incTrail2* of strictly increasing trails.

lemma (in *pair-wf-digraph*) *decTrail-is-dec-walk:*
  shows $decTrail\ G\ w\ es\ \longleftrightarrow\ decTrail2\ w\ es\ (fst\ (hd\ es))\ (snd\ (last\ es))$

lemma (in *pair-wf-digraph*) *incTrail-is-inc-walk:*
  shows $incTrail\ G\ w\ es\ \longleftrightarrow\ incTrail2\ w\ es\ (fst\ (hd\ es))\ (snd\ (last\ es))$

Any strictly decreasing trail $(e_1,\dots,e_n)$ can also be seen as a strictly increasing trail $(e_n,...,e_1)$ if the graph considered is undirected. To this end, we make use of the locale *pair-sym-digraph* that captures the idea of symmetric arcs. However, it is also necessary to assume that the weight function assigns the same weight to edge (v_i,v_j) as to (v_j,v_i). This assumption is therefore added to *decTrail-eq-rev-incTrail* and *incTrail-eq-rev-decTrail*.

lemma (in *pair-sym-digraph*) *decTrail-eq-rev-incTrail:*
  assumes $\forall\ v_1\ v_2.\ w\ (v_1,v_2)\ =\ w(v_2,v_1)$
  shows $decTrail\ G\ w\ es\ \longleftrightarrow\ incTrail\ G\ w\ (rev\ (map\ (\lambda(v_1,v_2).\ (v_2,v_1))\ es))$

lemma (in *pair-sym-digraph*) *incTrail-eq-rev-decTrail:*
  assumes $\forall\ v_1\ v_2.\ w\ (v_1,v_2)\ =\ w(v_2,v_1)$
  shows $incTrail\ G\ w\ es\ \longleftrightarrow\ decTrail\ G\ w\ (rev\ (map\ (\lambda(v_1,v_2).\ (v_2,v_1))\ es))$

4.3 Weighted Graphs

We add the locale *weighted-pair-graph* on top of the locale *pair-graph* introduced in *Graph-Theory*. A *pair-graph* is a finite, loop free and symmetric graph. We do not restrict the types of vertices and edges but impose the condition that they have to be a linear order.

Furthermore, all weights have to be integers between 0 and $\lfloor \frac{q}{2} \rfloor$ where 0 is used as a special value to indicate that there is no edge at that position. Since the range of the weight function is in the reals, the set of natural numbers $\{1,..,card\ (parcs\ G)\ div\ 2\}$ has to be casted into a set of reals. This is realized by taking the image of the function *real* that casts a natural number to a real.

locale *weighted-pair-graph* $=$ *pair-graph* $(G:: ('a::linorder)\ pair\text{-}pre\text{-}digraph)$ **for** $G +$
fixes $w :: ('a \times 'a)\ weight\text{-}fun$
assumes $dom : e \in parcs\ G \longrightarrow w\ e \in real\ `\ \{1..card\ (parcs\ G)\ div\ 2\}$
  and $vert\text{-}ge : card\ (pverts\ G) \geq 1$

We introduce some useful abbreviations, according to the ones in Sect. 2

abbreviation (in *weighted-pair-graph*$)$ $q \equiv card\ (parcs\ G)$
abbreviation (in *weighted-pair-graph*$)$ $n \equiv card\ (pverts\ G)$
abbreviation (in *weighted-pair-graph*$)$ $W \equiv \{1..q\ div\ 2\}$

Note an important difference between Sect. 3 and our formalization. Although a *weighted-pair-graph* is symmetric, the edge set contains both "directions" of an edge, i.e., (v_1, v_2) and (v_2, v_1) are both in *parcs* G. Thus, the maximum number of edges (in the case that the graph is complete) is $n \cdot (n - 1)$ and not $\frac{n \cdot (n-1)}{2}$. Another consequence is that the number q of edges is always even.

lemma (in *weighted-pair-graph*$)$ *max-arcs*:
  shows $card\ (parcs\ G) \leq n * (n - 1)$

lemma (in *weighted-pair-graph*$)$ *even-arcs*:
  shows *even* q

The below sublocale *distinct-weighted-pair-graph* refines *weighted-pair-graph*. The condition *zero* fixes the meaning of 0. The weight function is defined on the set of all vertices but since self loops are not allowed; we use 0 as a special value to indicate the unavailability of the edge. The second condition *distinct* enforces that no two edges can have the same weight. There are some exceptions however captured in the statement $(v_1 = u_2 \wedge v_2 = u_1) \vee (v_1 = u_1 \wedge v_2 = u_2)$. Firstly, (v_1, v_2) should have the same weight as (v_2, v_1). Secondly, $w(v_1, v_2)$ has the same value as $w(v_1, v_2)$. Note that both edges being self loops resulting in them both having weight 0 is prohibited by condition *zero*. Our decision to separate these two conditions from the ones in *weighted-pair-graph* instead of making one locale of its own is two-fold: On the one hand, there are scenarios where distinctiveness is not wished for. On the other hand, 0 might not be available as a special value.

locale *distinct-weighted-pair-graph* $=$ *weighted-pair-graph* $+$
  assumes $zero : \forall v_1\ v_2.\ (v_1, v_2) \notin parcs\ G \longleftrightarrow w\ (v_1, v_2) = 0$
    and $distinct : \forall (v_1, v_2) \in parcs\ G.\ \forall (u_1, u_2) \in parcs\ G.$
    $((v_1 = u_2 \wedge v_2 = u_1) \vee (v_1 = u_1 \wedge v_2 = u_2)) \longleftrightarrow w\ (v_1, v_2) = w\ (u_1, u_2)$

One important step in our formalization is to show that the weight function is surjective. However, having two elements of the domain (edges) being mapped to the same element of the codomain (weight) makes the proof complicated. We therefore first prove that the weight function is surjective on a restricted set of edges. Here we use the fact that there is a linear order on vertices by only considering edges were the first endpoint is bigger than the second.

Then, the surjectivity of w is relatively simple to show. Note that we could also have assumed surjectivity in *distinct-weighted-pair-graph* and shown that distinctiveness follows from it. However, distinctiveness is the more natural assumption that is more likely to appear in any application of ordered trails.

lemma (**in** *distinct-weighted-pair-graph*) *restricted-weight-fun-surjective*:
  $\forall k \in W. \exists (v_1, v_2) \in \{(p1, p2). (p1, p2) \in parcs\ G \wedge p2 < p1\}.\ w\ (v_1, v_2) = k$

lemma (**in** *distinct-weighted-pair-graph*) *weight-fun-surjective*:
  shows $\forall k \in W. \exists (v_1, v_2) \in parcs\ G.\ w\ (v_1, v_2) = k$

4.4   Computing a Longest Ordered Trail

We next formally verify Algorithm 1 and compute longest ordered trails. To this end, we introduce the function *findEdge* to find an edge in a list of edges by its weight.

fun *findEdge* :: $('a \times {}'a)$ *weight-fun* $\Rightarrow$ $('a \times {}'a)$ *list* $\Rightarrow$ *real* $\Rightarrow$ $('a \times {}'a)$ **where**
findEdge $f\ []\ k = undefined\ |$
findEdge $f\ (e\#es)\ k = (if\ f\ e = k\ then\ e\ else\ findEdge\ f\ es\ k)$

Function *findEdge* will correctly return the edge whose weight is k. We do not care in which order the endpoints are found, i.e. whether (v_1, v_2) or (v_2, v_1) is returned.

lemma (**in** *distinct-weighted-pair-graph*) *findEdge-success*:
  assumes $k \in W$ **and** $w\ (v_1, v_2) = k$ **and** $(parcs\ G) \neq \{\}$
  shows $(findEdge\ w\ (set\text{-}to\text{-}list\ (parcs\ G))\ k) = (v_1, v_2)$
    $\vee\ (findEdge\ w\ (set\text{-}to\text{-}list\ (parcs\ G))\ k) = (v_2, v_1)$

We translate the notion of a labelling function $L^i(v)$ (see Definition 2) into Isabelle. Function *getL G w*, in short for get label, returns the length of the longest strictly decreasing path starting at vertex v. In contrast to Definition 2 subgraphs are treated here implicitly. Intuitively, this can be seen as adding edges to an empty graph in order of their weight.

fun *getL* :: $('a::linorder)$ *pair-pre-digraph* $\Rightarrow$ $('a \times {}'a)$ *weight-fun*
    $\Rightarrow$ *nat* $\Rightarrow {}'a \Rightarrow$ *nat* **where**
getL g w 0 v = $0\ |$
getL g w (Suc i) v = $(let\ (v_1, v_2) = (findEdge\ w\ (set\text{-}to\text{-}list\ (arcs\ g))\ (Suc\ i))\ in$
    $(if\ v = v_1\ then\ max\ ((getL\ g\ w\ i\ v_2) + 1)\ (getL\ g\ w\ i\ v)\ else$
    $(if\ v = v_2\ then\ max\ ((getL\ g\ w\ i\ v_1) + 1)\ (getL\ g\ w\ i\ v)\ else\ getL\ g\ w\ i\ v)))$

To add all edges to the graph, set $i = |E|$. Recall that *card (parcs g)* $= 2*|E|$, as every edge appears twice. Then, iterate over all vertices and give back the maximum length which is found by using *getL G w*. Since *getL G w* can also be used to get a longest strictly increasing trail ending at vertex v the algorithm is not restricted to strictly decreasing trails.

definition *getLongestTrail* ::
$('a::linorder)$ *pair-pre-digraph* $\Rightarrow$ $('a \times 'a)$ *weight-fun* $\Rightarrow$ *nat* **where**
getLongestTrail g w $=$
Max (set [(getL g w (card (parcs g) div 2) v) . v $< -$ *sorted-list-of-set (pverts g)])*

Exporting the algorithm into Haskell code results in a fully verified program to find a longest strictly decreasing or strictly increasing trail.

export-code getLongestTrail **in** *Haskell* **module-name** *LongestTrail*

Using an induction proof and extensive case distinction, the correctness of Algorithm 1 is then shown in our formalization, by proving the following theorem:

theorem (in *distinct-weighted-pair-graph*) *correctness*:
  assumes $\exists v \in (pverts\ G).\ getL\ G\ w\ (q\ div\ 2)\ v\ =\ k$
  shows $\exists xs.\ decTrail\ G\ w\ xs \wedge length\ xs\ =\ k$

4.5   Minimum Length of Ordered Trails

The algorithm introduced in Sect. 4.4 is already useful on its own. Additionally, it can be used to verify the lower bound on the minimum length of a strictly decreasing trail $P_d(w, G) \geq 2 \cdot \lfloor \frac{q}{n} \rfloor$.

To this end, Lemma 1 from Sect. 3 is translated into Isabelle as the lemma *minimal-increase-one-step*. The proof is similar to its counterpart, also using a case distinction. Lemma 2 is subsequently proved, here named *minimal-increase-total*.

lemma (in *distinct-weighted-pair-graph*) *minimal-increase-one-step*:
  assumes $k + 1 \in W$
  shows

$$\left(\sum v \in pverts\ G.\ getL\ G\ w\ (k+1)\ v\right) \geq \left(\sum v \in pverts\ G.\ getL\ G\ w\ k\ v\right) + 2$$

lemma (in *distinct-weighted-pair-graph*) *minimal-increase-total*:
  shows $\left(\sum v \in pverts\ G.\ getL\ G\ w\ (q\ div\ 2)\ v\right) \geq q$

From *minimal-increase-total* we have that the sum of all labels after q div 2 steps is greater than q. Now assume that all labels are smaller than q div n. Because we have n vertices, this leads to a contradiction, which proves *algo-result-min*.

lemma (in *distinct-weighted-pair-graph*) *algo-result-min*:
shows ($\exists\, v \in pverts\; G.\; getL\; G\; w\; (q\; div\; 2)\; v \geq q\; div\; n$)

Finally, using lemma *algo-result-min* together with the *correctness* theorem of Sect. 4.4, we prove the lower bound of $2 \cdot \lfloor \frac{q}{n} \rfloor$ over the length of a longest strictly decreasing trail. This general approach could also be used to extend our formalization and prove existence of other trails. For example, assume that some restrictions on the graph give raise to the existence of a trail of length $m \geq 2 \cdot \lfloor \frac{q}{n} \rfloor$. Then, it is only necessary to show that our algorithm can find this trail.

theorem (in *distinct-weighted-pair-graph*) *dec-trail-exists*:
shows $\exists\, es.\; decTrail\; G\; w\; es \wedge length\; es = q\; div\; n$

theorem (in *distinct-weighted-pair-graph*) *inc-trail-exists*:
shows $\exists\, es.\; incTrail\; G\; w\; es \wedge length\; es = q\; div\; n$

Corollary 1 is translated into *dec-trail-exists-complete*. The proof first argues that the number of edges is $n \cdot (n-1)$ by restricting its domain as done already in Sect. 4.3.

lemma (in *distinct-weighted-pair-graph*) *dec-trail-exists-complete*:
assumes *complete-digraph n G*
shows $\exists\, es.\; decTrail\; G\; w\; es \wedge length\; es = n - 1$

4.6   Example Graph K_4

We return to the example graph from Fig. 1 and show that our results from Sects. 4.2–4.5 can be used to prove existence of trails of length k, in particular $k = 3$ in K_4. Defining the graph and the weight function separately, we use natural numbers as vertices.

abbreviation *ExampleGraph*:: *nat pair-pre-digraph* **where**
ExampleGraph $\equiv$ (|
    pverts = $\{1, 2, 3, (4::nat)\}$,
    parcs = $\{(v_1, v_2).\; v_1 \in \{1, 2, 3, (4::nat)\} \wedge v_2 \in \{1, 2, 3, (4::nat)\} \wedge v_1 \neq v_2\}$
|)

abbreviation *ExampleGraphWeightFunction* :: (*nat* × *nat*) *weight-fun* **where**
ExampleGraphWeightFunction $\equiv$ ($\lambda(v_1, v_2)$.
(*if* ($v_1 = 1 \wedge v_2 = 2$) $\vee$ ($v_1 = 2 \wedge v_2 = 1$) *then 1 else*
(*if* ($v_1 = 1 \wedge v_2 = 3$) $\vee$ ($v_1 = 3 \wedge v_2 = 1$) *then 3 else*
(*if* ($v_1 = 1 \wedge v_2 = 4$) $\vee$ ($v_1 = 4 \wedge v_2 = 1$) *then 6 else*
(*if* ($v_1 = 2 \wedge v_2 = 3$) $\vee$ ($v_1 = 3 \wedge v_2 = 2$) *then 5 else*
(*if* ($v_1 = 2 \wedge v_2 = 4$) $\vee$ ($v_1 = 4 \wedge v_2 = 2$) *then 4 else*
(*if* ($v_1 = 3 \wedge v_2 = 4$) $\vee$ ($v_1 = 4 \wedge v_2 = 3$) *then 2 else 0*)))))))

We show that the graph K_4 of Fig. 1 satisfies the conditions that were imposed in *distinct-weighted-pair-graph* and its parent locale, including for example no self loops and distinctiveness. Of course there is still some effort required for this. However, it is necessary to manually construct trails or list all possible weight distributions. Additionally, instead of $q!$ statements there are at most $\frac{3q}{2}$ statements needed.

interpretation *example*:
   distinct-weighted-pair-graph ExampleGraph ExampleGraphWeightFunction

Now it is an easy task to prove that there is a trail of length 3. We only add the fact that *ExampleGraph* is a *distinct-weighted-pair-graph* and lemma *dec-trail-exists*.

lemma *ExampleGraph-decTrail*:
   $\exists$ *xs. decTrail ExampleGraph ExampleGraphWeightFunction xs* $\wedge$
   length xs = 3

5   Discussion and Related Work

Our theory *Ordered-Trail* builds on top of the *Graph-Theory* library presented in [12]. However, this library does not formalize strictly ordered trails, nor the special weighted graphs we introduced in the locale *distinct-weighted-pair-graph*. Furthermore, our formalization extends [12] with definitions on strictly decreasing and increasing trails and provides many basic lemmas on them. Some of the main challenges in this context were the reasoning on the surjectivity of the weight function as well the correctness proof of the algorithm.

Our formalization can be easily extended and could therefore serve as a basis for further work in this field. The definitions *incTrail* and *decTrail* and the respective properties that are proven in Sect. 4.2 are the key to many other variants of trail properties.

Graham et al. [8] also showed upper bounds for trails in complete graphs by decomposing them into either into cycles or 1-factors. We are currently working on formalizing and certifying the result that

$$f_d(n) = f_i(n) = \begin{cases} n & \text{if } n \in \{3,5\}, \\ n-1 & \text{otherwise,} \end{cases}$$

that is, for complete graphs with $n = 3$ or $n = 5$ vertices there always has to be a trail of length at least n whereas for any other number n of vertices there only has to be a trail of length $n - 1$. Therefore, the lower bound that we showed in this paper is equal to the exact length with exception of two special cases. We believe that formalizing this result would be a valuable extension to the theory *Ordered-Trail*.

Another direction for further investigation are monotone paths. Graham et al. [8] show that in a complete graph with n vertices there has to be an increasing path of length at least $\frac{1}{2}(\sqrt{4n-3} - 1)$ and at most $\frac{3n}{4}$. The upper bound was afterwards improved by Calderbank, Chung and Sturtevant [3], Milans [10] and Bucić et al. [2].

Recently, other classes of graphs have been considered, e.g., trees and planar graphs [13], on random edge-ordering [14] or on hypercubes [7].

6 Conclusion

In this work we formalized strictly increasing and strictly decreasing trails in the proof assistant Isabelle/HOL. Furthermore, we showed correctness of an algorithm to find such trails. We provided a verified algorithm and program to compute monotone trails. We used this algorithm to prove the result that every graph with n vertices and q edges has a strictly decreasing trail of length at least $2 \cdot \lfloor \frac{q}{n} \rfloor$. For further work we plan to show that this is a tight bound for every n except for $n = 3$ and 5.

Our results are built on the already existing Isabelle *Graph-theory* from the Archive of Formal Proofs. Thus, our results can be used by any theory using graphs that are specified as in this library. Therefore, our theory is highly reusable and might be the basis for further work in this field.

Acknowledgements. We thank Prof. Byron Cook (AWS) for interesting discussions on reasoning challenges with ordered trails. This work was funded by the ERC Starting Grant 2014 SYMCAR 639270, the ERC Proof of Concept Grant 2018 SYMELS 842066, the Wallenberg Academy Fellowship 2014 TheProSE, the Austrian FWF research project W1255-N23 and P32441, the Vienna Science and Technology Fund ICT19-065 and the Austrian-Hungarian collaborative project 101öu8.

References

1. Ballarin, C.: Tutorial to locales and locale interpretation. In: Contribuciones científicas en honor de Mirian Andrés Gómez, pp. 123–140. Universidad de La Rioja (2010)
2. Bucic, M., Kwan, M., Pokrovskiy, A., Sudakov, B., Tran, T., Wagner, A.Z.: Nearly-linear monotone paths in edge-ordered graphs. arXiv preprint arXiv:1809.01468 (2018)
3. Calderbank, A.R., Chung, F.R., Sturtevant, D.G.: Increasing sequences with nonzero block sums and increasing paths in edge-ordered graphs. Discret. Math. **50**, 15–28 (1984)
4. Chavtal, V., Komlos, J.: Some combinatorial theorems on monocity. In: Notices of the American Mathematical Society, vol. 17, p. 943. American Mathematical Society, 201 Charles St, Providence, RI 02940-2213 (1970)
5. Cook, B., Kovács, L., Lachnitt, H.: Personal Communications on Automated Reasoning at AWS (2019)
6. De Moura, L., Bjørner, N.: Z3: an efficient SMT solver. In: Ramakrishnan, C.R., Rehof, J. (eds.) TACAS 2008. LNCS, vol. 4963, pp. 337–340. Springer, Heidelberg (2008). https://doi.org/10.1007/978-3-540-78800-3_24
7. De Silva, J., Molla, T., Pfender, F., Retter, T., Tait, M.: Increasing paths in edge-ordered graphs: the hypercube and random graphs. arXiv preprint arXiv:1502.03146 (2015)
8. Graham, R., Kleitman, D.: Increasing paths in edge ordered graphs. Periodica Math. Hung. **3**(1–2), 141–148 (1973)
9. Kovács, L., Voronkov, A.: First-order theorem proving and Vampire. In: Proceedings of CAV, pp. 1–35 (2013)
10. Milans, K.G.: Monotone paths in dense edge-ordered graphs (2015)

11. Nipkow, T., Wenzel, M., Paulson, L.C. (eds.): Isabelle/HOL - A Proof Assistant for Higher-Order Logic. LNCS, vol. 2283. Springer, Heidelberg (2002). https://doi.org/10.1007/3-540-45949-9
12. Noschinski, L.: Graph theory. Archive of Formal Proofs, April 2013. http://isa-afp.org/entries/Graph_Theory.html. Formal proof development
13. Roditty, Y., Shoham, B., Yuster, R.: Monotone paths in edge-ordered sparse graphs. Discret. Math. **226**(1–3), 411–417 (2001)
14. Yuster, R.: Large monotone paths in graphs with bounded degree. Graphs Comb. **17**(3), 579–587 (2001). https://doi.org/10.1007/s003730170031

Representing Structural Language Features in Formal Meta-languages

Dennis Müller[1,2]([✉]) [ID], Florian Rabe[1] [ID], Colin Rothgang[3],
and Michael Kohlhase[1] [ID]

[1] Computer Science, University Erlangen-Nuremberg, Erlangen, Germany
d.mueller@kwarc.info
[2] Computational Logic, University of Innsbruck, Innsbruck, Austria
[3] Mathematics, TU Berlin, Berlin, Germany

Abstract. Structural language features are those that introduce new kinds of declarations as opposed to those that only add expressions. They pose a significant challenge when representing languages in meta-languages such as standard formats like OMDOC or logical frameworks like LF. It is desirable to use shallow representations where a structural language feature is represented by the analogous feature of the meta-language, but the richness of structural language features in practical languages makes this difficult. Therefore, the current state of the art is to encode unrepresentable structural language features in terms of more elementary ones, but that makes the representations difficult to reuse and verify. This challenge is exacerbated by the fact that many languages allow users to add new structural language features that are elaborated into a small trusted kernel, which allows for a large and growing set of features.

In this paper we extend the MMT representation framework with a generic concept of structural features. This allows defining exactly the language features needed for elegant shallow embeddings of object languages. The key achievement here is to make this concept expressive enough to cover complex practical features while retaining the simplicity of existing meta-languages. We exemplify our framework with representations of various important structural features including datatype definitions and theory instantiations.

1 Introduction and Related Work

Motivation. Language design is generally subject to the expressivity-simplicity trade-off. In particular, designing a representation language for mathematics involves adequately capturing the ways how mathematical knowledge is expressed in practice. On the other hand, the language must be as simple as

---

The authors were supported by DFG grant RA-1872/3-1, KO 2428/13-1 OAF and EU grant Horizon 2020 ERI 676541 OpenDreamKit.

D. Müller—The author was supported by a postdoc fellowship of the German Academic Exchange Service (DAAD).

C. Benzmüller and B. Miller (Eds.): CICM 2020, LNAI 12236, pp. 206–221, 2020.
https://doi.org/10.1007/978-3-030-53518-6_13

possible to allow establishing meta-theoretical properties and obtaining (and maintaining!) scalable implementations. This problem is exacerbated by the fact that the language features needed in the long run are often not apparent at the beginning of a project. Moreover, depending on the availability of resources and the interests of the user community, languages and systems may be used in applications not foreseen by the developers.

Because retroactive changes become increasingly costly once meta-theory or implementation have been developed, adding new language features is often not feasible. In a curse-of-success effect, language developers may find themselves overwhelmed by feature requests from users, which they cannot add easily or at all without breaking developments by other users. Therefore, it becomes important to design languages with extensibility in mind. This is particularly difficult for *structural* features, and especially challenging for meta-languages such as standardized representation formats like OMDoc [Koh06] or logical frameworks like LF [HHP93]: These languages partially derive their value from being simple and elegant and cannot afford constantly adding features. On the other hand, they cannot afford fixing the set of structural features either: That would require encoding all other features via complex, often non-compositional translations, which are difficult to verify and preclude interoperability.

A particularly successful model used in many proof assistants has been a two-component design: firstly, a small, fixed, and carefully-designed kernel is used as the ultimate arbiter of correctness; secondly, a higher-level and more flexible component reads user input and translates it into the kernel syntax, a process we call **elaboration**. For example, major proof assistants like Coq [Coq15] and Isabelle [Pau94] have over time arrived at this model, and attention is increasingly shifting towards the elaboration component. Pure LCF systems like HOL Light [Har96] can be seen as an extreme case with the host programming language as the (Turing-complete) higher-level language.

Elaboration is typically implemented *programmatically*, i.e., via arbitrary code in the tool's underlying programming language. In the simplest case, a new kind of declaration could be introduced as a type $N <: D$ where N holds the declarations and D is an abstract interface for arbitrary declarations, together with a function $N \to \text{List}(D)$ that elaborates an instance of N into other declarations. If the logic is sufficiently strong, tools may use reflection to define programmatic elaboration inside the logic as done for Idris in [CB16] and Lean in [EUR+17]. Concrete examples of high-level language features with elaboration-based semantics include

- HOL-style subtype definitions [Gor88], elaborated into an axiomatic specification of a new type,
- Mizar's many different definition principles, elaborated into axiomatic specifications of new function symbols,
- Isabelle's so-called derived specification elements including inductive, record, and quotient types, elaborated subtype definitions of some appropriately large type, see e.g., [BHL+14],

- PVS's inductive types, elaborated into an axiomatic specification of the induction properties,
- Coq's record types, elaborated into inductive types with a single constructor,
- Coq's sections, elaborated into kernel declarations that abstract over all variables declared in the section.

As the examples already indicate, elaboration is recursive, e.g., the elaboration of an Isabelle inductive type definition may lead to a subtype definition, which is then elaborated further. It may also be nested, e.g., the elaboration of a nested Coq section first generates declarations in its parent section, which is then elaborated later.

But the elaboration-based approach has two major difficulties. Firstly, elaboration necessarily destroys the high-level structure. If only the kernel representation is effectively available to other applications (as we found is often the case, see [KR20]), it becomes harder to transfer and reuse developments. Secondly, programmatic elaboration offers a high degree of flexibility but also makes it harder to analyze or implement high-level declarations generically.

In a response to these issues, we introduced declaration patterns in [HKR12] and [Hor14]. They allowed describing elaboration *declaratively* inside the logic rather than programmatically. Declaration patterns were successful in many cases including typical logical declarations [HR15], Mizar's definition principles [IKRU13], and HOL type definitions [KR14]. But, being fully declarative, they expectedly could not cover many practically important examples. For example, to elaborate an inductive data type definition, one has to generate an inequality axiom for every pair of constructors—something that quickly becomes awkward to describe without a general purpose programming language.

Contribution. We expand on the declarative approach of [HKR12,Hor14] by extending the MMT framework with a generic extension mechanism based on programmatic elaboration. Critically, despite being very general, the declarations introduced by structural features share the same simple syntactic shape, which allows for simple specifications and uniform implementations.

Because MMT allows implementing logical frameworks such as LF, this immediately yields corresponding extensions of these. Our design was strongly motivated by and evaluated in our work on exporting proof assistant libraries [KR20], where we had to model many high-level language features of proof assistants. For example, we have already used our design to represent PVS includes [KMOR17] or Coq-style sections [MRSC19] (see Subsect. 4.2).

Overview. This paper is organized as follows. In Sect. 2, we recap the parts of OMDOC/MMT, which we use as the underlying core language. Section 3 introduces the infrastructure for structural language extensions. We look at concrete instances and develop a varied array of MMT structural features in Sect. 4 and Sect. 5. Finally, Sect. 6 concludes the paper and discusses future work.

2   Preliminaries

OMDoc is a rich representation language for mathematical knowledge with a large set of primitives motivated by expressivity and user familiarity. The MMT [RK13] language is a complete redesign of the formal core of OMDoc focusing on foundation-independence, scalability, modularity and minimality.

In Fig. 1, we show a fragment of the MMT grammar that we need in the remainder of this paper. Meta-symbols of the BNF format are given in color.

The central notion in MMT is that of a **diagram** consisting of a list of modules. For our purposes, **theories** are the only modules we need. MMT theories are named sets of statements and are used to represent formal constructs such as logical frameworks, logics, and theories. At the **declaration** level MMT has **includes** and **constants**. Constants are meant to represent a variety of OMDoc declarations and are simply named symbols with an optional type and definition. The types and definitions are MMT **expressions**, which are based on OpenMath. Expressions are ref-

Module Level		
Diagram	γ	::= Mod*
Module	Mod ::= Thy	
Theory	Thy	::= $T = \{\text{Dec}^*\}$
Statement Level		
Declaration Dec	::= $c[: E][:= E]$	
	$\mid$ Thy $\mid$ include l	
Object Level		
Expression E	::= $x \mid c \mid x : E$	
	$\mid$ $c(E^*)$	

x, c, T represent variable, constant, and theory names (strings) respectively

Fig. 1. MMT grammar

erences to bound variables x and constants c, bound variable declarations $x : E$, and complex expressions $c(E^*)$ (which include variable binding by using $x : E$ as a child).

The semantics of MMT provides an inference systems that includes in particular two judgments for typing and equality of expressions. Via Curry-Howard, the former includes provability, e.g., a theorem F is represented as a constant with type F, whose definiens is the proof. We have to omit the details here for brevity. We only emphasize that MMT is foundation-independent: The syntax does not assume any special constants (e.g., λ), and the semantics does not assume any special typing rules (e.g., functional extensionality). Instead, any such foundation-specific aspects are supplied by special MMT theories called **foundations**. For example, the foundation for the logical framework LF [HHP93] declares constants for type, λ, Π, and @ (for application) as well as the necessary typing rules. Thus, the MMT module system governs, e.g., which typing rules are available in which theory. The details can be found in [Rab17].

3   Structural Features

Before we come to a formal definition, let us consider **record types** as an example for a structural feature.

A record type R is a collection of typed (in our case, optionally additionally defined) fields $x : T$. A record **term** r is a collection of assignments $x := d$ for each field, such that if R contains $x : T$, then d has type T. In **dependent** record types, T may additionally refer to previous fields.

For any such record term $r : R$, we then have a projection operator "." such that $r.x$ has type T and (if r is not primitive) $r.x = d$. As such, a record type $R = [\![x_1 : T_1 \ldots x_n : T_n]\!]$ can be implemented as a high-level structure that elaborates into

- A single constructor $\mathrm{Con}_R : T_1 \to \ldots \to T_n \to R$,
- for each field $x : T$ in R, a projection function $\cdot.x$ of type $R \to T$, and
- Axioms asserting injectivity and surjectivity of the constructor, as well as appropriate equalities implying that constructor and projection functions commute appropriately.

We will return to this example in more detail in Subsect. 4.1.

There is a notable correspondance between record type declarations and **theories**, in that both consist (primarily) of declarations of the form $x : T$. It thus seems attractive to reuse the grammar of theories to allow for declaring record types as a high-level feature, motivating the following:

Definition 1. We extend the MMT grammar by a new production rule:

$$\mathrm{Dec} ::= d : \mathfrak{f}(E^*) = \{\mathrm{Dec}^*\}$$

We call this a **derived declaration** of the structural feature $\mathfrak{f}$. d is the name of the derived declaration, the E are its **parameters** and the Decs its **internal declarations**.

Definition 2. A **structural feature** is a triple $(\mathfrak{f}, v, \epsilon)$, where:

1. $\mathfrak{f}$ is the **name** of the feature,
2. v is a **validity predicate** on derived declarations

$$D := d : \mathfrak{f}(F_1 \ldots F_n) = \{S_1 \ldots S_m\}$$

   If $v(D)$ holds, we call D a (well-formed) **derived declaration** of $\mathfrak{f}$.
3. ϵ is called an **elaboration function**, mapping a derived declaration D of $\mathfrak{f}$ to its **elaboration**: a set of declarations, which we also call the **external declarations** of D.

Once a derived declaration is declared, we will (almost) never care about its internal declarations anymore. The corresponding structural feature checks whether a derived declaration D conforms to some specific pattern, checking its components and internal declarations separately (possibly generating errors), and **elaborates** D into a set of **external declarations** based on its constituents. Since checking often requires elaboration (and vice versa), the MMT implementation unifies ϵ and v into a single method. The external declarations specify the intended semantics of the derived declaration.

The structural feature itself is written in Scala using the MMT-API, which provides dedicated abstractions, and acts as a **rule** similarly to the typing rules mentioned in Sect. 2. Just like typing rules, structural features (or rather, their derived declarations) can thus be made available in precisely those theories where they are deemed valid.

For the rest of this paper, we will assume various extensions of LF as our foundations. If our external declarations contain **axioms**, we assume some fixed logic declared in the foundation, providing a type prop, an operator $\vdash$ of type prop $\to$ type, a typed equality operator $\doteq\, : \prod_{A:\text{type}} A \to A \to$ prop and the usual logical connectives.

However, it should be noted that the structural features presented herein can be easily adapted to any logic sufficiently strong to allow for defining (equivalents to) their external declarations.

4 Examples

We will now show the practical utility of these relatively abstract definitions in some paradigmatic cases at the declaration and module levels.

4.1 Datatypes

Inductive Types. Structural features can provide a convenient syntax for declaring inductive types. Consider for example a (parametric) type of **lists** $\text{List}(A)$ of type A, which can be defined as the inductive type generated by the two constructors $\text{nil} : \text{List}(A)$ and $\text{cons} : A \to \text{List}(A) \to \text{List}(A)$. We devise two structural features with names induct and indef, allowing us to declare inductive types and inductive definitions respectively, as in Fig. 2[1]. Naturally, parametric inductive types require a logic with (at least) shallow polymorphism.

induct Lists (A:type) | =	indef Conc (Lists, B : type, ls : List B) | =
List : type	conc : List B → List B | # 3 ++ 2
nil : List	Nil = ls
cons : A → List → List | # 1 :: 2	Cons = [b:B,l: List B] b :: (conc l)

Fig. 2. Lists as an inductive type and concatenation as an inductive definition

If the underlying logic $\mathcal{L}$ provides primitive typing features that subsume inductive types, such as W-Types, induct and indef can elaborate into their (usually syntactically cumbersome) $\mathcal{L}$-correspondents. A structural feature elaborating into W-types is described in [Mül19].

---

[1] These listings show our actual formalizations in concrete syntax and use a few semantically inessential features that go beyond the syntax introduced in Fig. 1. Most notably, # introduces a notation and | separates declaration components.

In the absence of such a typing feature, we can instead elaborate into the corresponding constructors and axioms (expressed in some logic declared in our foundation) asserting their collective injectivity and surjectivity, in the manner which we will describe shortly. Importantly, we can use the same validity predicate and feature name for both variants, preserving the syntax of the structural features across logics. This ensures that whenever $\mathcal{L}'$ extends $\mathcal{L}$ by an inductive typing feature, any $\mathcal{L}$-theory using induct and indef remains a valid $\mathcal{L}'$-theory, but the elaboration in the stronger logic will consist of **defined** constants.

Elaborating. induct A derived declaration

$$D_{ind} : \text{induct}\,(t_1 : T_1 \ldots t_n : T_n) \;=\; \{S_1 \ldots S_m\}$$

is elaborated as follows:

1. Any type-level declaration S_i : type is elaborated into

$$D_{ind}/S_i \;:\; \prod_{t_1 : T_1, \ldots, t_n : T_n} \text{type}.$$

   This allows for mutually inductive and parametric types.

   Let $I_1 \ldots I_k$ be the type-level declarations of D_{ind}. The remaining declarations need to either *i)* have type I_i, or *ii)* have type $T_1' \rightarrow \ldots \rightarrow T_k' \rightarrow I_i$ for some types $T_1' \ldots T_k'$, and are thus assumed to be constructors.
2. For each remaining $S_i : T \rightarrow I_i{}^2$, we extend the elaboration by the constructor

$$D_{ind}/S_i \;:\; \prod_{t_1 : T_1, \ldots, t_n : T_n} T \rightarrow I_i$$

3. (**No-confusion**). For each constructor S_i, we add
   - an axiom that S_i is injective in each argument, and
   - an axiom, that $S_j(a) \neq S_i(b)$ for any other constructor $S_i \neq S_j$ and sequences or arguments (a) (b) of adequate arity and types.
4. (**No-junk**). Several axioms that guarantee that the inductively defined types in the elaboration are **initial models** of their respective model category. This is the trickiest part of the construction and treated in detail in [Rot20].

Elaborating. indef Having an inductive type T_I elaborated from D_{ind}, we can design indef to allow for conveniently specifying inductive definitions and consequently (using *judgments-as-types*) proofs by induction.[3]

A derived declaration $D_{def} : \text{indef}\,(D_{ind}, t_1 : T_1 \ldots t_n : T_n) \;=\; \{S_1 \ldots S_m\}$ has to satisfy the following properties (which collectively constitute the validity predicate) in order to be considered well-formed:

---

[2] For notational simplicity, we only consider the case of unary constructors; the generalization to n-ary constructors is clear.

[3] For simplicity, we restrict ourselves to the case where D_{ind} elaborates into a single inductive type (ignoring mutual induction).

1. The first declaration S_1 has to have function type $T_I \to A$ for some type A.
2. For every constructor $\mathtt{con} : T_1' \to \ldots \to T_k' \to T_I$, there has to be an S_i with the same name, being a defined constant

$$\mathtt{con} \: : \: T_1' \to \ldots \to T_k' \to A \: := \: \lambda a_1 : T_1', \ldots, a_k : T_k'. \, t$$

The elaboration then consists of the following external declarations:

1. A constant $D_{def}/S_1 \: : \: \prod_{t_1:T_1,\ldots,t_n:T_n} T_I \to A$,
2. For every constructor $\mathtt{con} : T_1' \to \ldots \to T_k' \to T_I$ and corresponding internal declaration $\mathtt{con} \: : \: T_1' \to \ldots \to T_k' \to A \: := \: \lambda a_1 : T_1', \ldots, a_k : T_k'. \, t$, an axiom

$$D_{def}/\mathtt{con} \: : \: \prod_{t_1:T_1,\ldots,t_n:T_n} \prod_{a_1:T_1',\ldots,a_k:T_k'} \vdash D_{def}/S_1(t_1,\ldots,t_n,\mathtt{con}(a_1,\ldots,a_k)) \doteq t$$

Records. In [MRK18, Mül19], we describe an operator $\mathtt{Mod}$, which takes as argument a (reference to a) theory $\mathcal{T}$ and returns a (dependent) record type with manifest fields whose fields correspond to the declarations in $\mathcal{T}$ – effectively yielding a type of models of $\mathcal{T}$. This assumes a background logic $\mathcal{L}$ with record types as a typing feature.

For the common case that we want to have the $\mathtt{Mod}$-type be *i)* a named record type and *ii)* only need $\mathcal{T}$ in order to define $\mathtt{Mod}\,\mathcal{T}$, we can introduce a structural feature $\mathtt{rectp}$ with the same functionality as $\mathtt{Mod}$. In this case, the validity predicate accepts any theory and the elaboration simply consists of a named record with the inner declarations as fields. If a derived declaration of $\mathtt{rectp}$ has additional parameters $t_i : T_i$, these are λ-bound to the corresponding external declaration; i.e. a derived declaration

$$D_{rectp} : \mathtt{rectp}\,(R, \, t_1 : T_1, \ldots t_n : T_n) \: = \: \{s_1 \: : \: T_1'[\: := \: d_1] \ldots s_m \: : \: T_m'[\: := \: d_m]\}$$

elaborates to

$$R \: : \: \prod_{t_1:T_1,\ldots,t_n:T_n} \mathtt{type} \: := \: \lambda t_1 : T_1, \ldots, t_n : T_n. \, [\![\: s_1 \: : \: T_1'[\: := \: d_1] \ldots s_m \: : \: T_m'[\: := \: d_m] \:]\!].$$

Analogously, we can introduce a structural feature $\mathtt{rectm}$ with derived declarations $D_{rectm} : \mathtt{rectm}\,(r, \, D_{rectp}\,F_1 \ldots F_n) \: = \: \{S_1 \ldots S_m\}$, where each S_i is a defined constant whose name corresponds to an (undefined) field of R. Additional parameters $t_i : T_i$ are again λ-bound; i.e. a derived declaration

$$D_{rectm} : \mathtt{rectm}\,(D_{rectp}, \, t_1 : T_1 \ldots t_n : T_n \, R) \: = \: \{s_1 \: := \: d_1 \ldots s_m \: := \: d_m\}$$

elaborates to the named record term

$$r \: : \: \prod_{t_1:T_1,\ldots,t_n:T_n} R \: := \: \lambda t_1 : T_1, \ldots, t_n : T_n. \, \langle\, s_1 \: := \: d_1 \ldots s_m \: := \: d_m \,\rangle.$$

One big advantage of this approach in MMT surface syntax is that each field in a `rectm`-declaration can be checked separately against the corresponding field in the record type, whereas the elaborated expression $\langle\, s_1 := d_1 \ldots s_m := d_m \,\rangle$ is treated as a single term and checked as a whole. While this does not make a difference semantically, it allows for much better localization of errors and more helpful error messages.

In a logic $\mathcal{L}$ without a notion of record types, the structural feature `rectp` can instead elaborate a derived declaration in the manner described in Sect. 3.

4.2 Module System

MMT Structures. are an MMT primitive kind of theory morphisms, that essentially behave like named includes with modification: A structure $S : \mathcal{T}_1 \to \mathcal{T}_2$ makes all declarations in $\mathcal{T}_1$ accessible in $\mathcal{T}_2$, but allows for

- supplying additional names (**aliases**) to constants via @-annotations,
- changing notations of constants and
- supplying definientia for previously undefined constants.

In particular, unlike includes, multiple structures with the same domain are not idempotent. A typical example for structures is given in Fig. 3: A theory of rings is constructed using two structures for addition (from `AbelianGroup`) and multiplication (from `Monoid`) whose universes are defined to be the same type R and whose operations and units are renamed and provided with adequate notations. The axioms in the domain theories are thus automatically imported into `Ring`.

As mentioned, structures are MMT primitives. However, they can be easily defined using structural features: A derived declaration $S :$ `structure`$(\mathcal{T}_1)$ $=$ $\{S_1 \ldots S_m\}$ satisfies the validity predicate iff:

1. $\mathcal{T}_1$ is a valid theory,
2. any constant S_i shares a name with a constant in $\mathcal{T}_1$ and
3. for any defined constant $S_i = (c := d)$ with $c : T$ in $\mathcal{T}_1$, we demand that d type checks against T', where T' is T with constant references from $\mathcal{T}_1$ appropriately substituted by their S-counterparts.

The elaboration then consists simply of the appropriately modified copies of the declarations in $\mathcal{T}_1$ with their names prefixed by $S/$.

Coq-Style Sections. In [MRSC19], we present an import of the Coq Library into the MMT system. In order to preserve the original syntax of the library as closely as possible, this necessitated mirroring Coq's module system (Sections, Modules, Module Types) within MMT, which was done using structural features. Exemplary, we will look at Coq Sections.

A Coq Section is a named theory, in which it is allowed to introduce **variables** via declarations. After a section ends, its contents are accessible with all variables becoming Π-bound to all subsequent declarations.

```
theory Monoid =
        U : type
        op :  U → U → U |# 1 ∘2
        unit : U | # e
        axiom1 : ⊢ ∀ [x]  x ∘ e ≐ x
        ...
```

```
theory AbelianGroup =
        include ?Monoid
        inv :  U → U |# 1 ^−1
        axiom1 : ⊢ ∀ [x]  x ∘ (x ^−1) ≐ e
        ...
```

```
theory Ring =
        R : type
        structure  addition  : ?AbelianGroup =
                U = R |
                op @ plus |  # 1 + 2
                unit @ zero |  # O
                inv @ minus |  # − 1
        structure  multiplication  : ?Monoid =
                U = R |
                op @ times |  # 1 · 2
                unit @ one |  # I

        ...
```

Fig. 3. Theories for Monoids, Abelian groups and rings using structures

```
Section Well_founded_Nat.
     Variable A : Type.
     Variable f : A −> nat.
     Definition ltof (a b:A)
        := f a < f b.
     Definition gtof (a b:A)
        := f b > f a.
End Well_founded_Nat.
```

```
Section  Well_founded_Nat =
     A : type         | role  Variable
     f  :  A → nat  | role  Variable
     ltof  :  A → A → prop |
        = [a,b]  f a < f b
     gtof  :  A → A → prop |
        = [a,b]  f a > f b
```

Figure 4 shows an example of a Coq section. A and f are declared as variables and used like constants in the remainder of the section. The defined constant $ltof$ within the section

Fig. 4. A Coq section and its MMT counterpart

hence takes two arguments a, b. After the section is closed however, $ltof$ is used as a quaternary function, with its arguments being the type A, the function f and the two arguments a, b.

The right side of Fig. 4 shows the same Section, but expressed in MMT syntax using a new structural features `Section`. Variables are marked with the `role Variable` flag. The validity predicate accepts any theory. A derived declaration $D = Sec : \mathtt{Section}\,() = \{S_1 \ldots S_n\}$ is elaborated as follows:

1. Any constant with the `role Variable` flag is not elaborated,
2. for any other constant $S_i = c : T\,[\,:= d]$, let $v_1 : T_1 \ldots v_n : T_n$ be all variables declared in D prior to S_i. Then extend the elaboration of D by

$$Sec/c : \prod_{v_1:T_1,\ldots,v_n:T_n} T\,[\,:= \lambda v_1 : T_1, \ldots, v_n : T_n.\, d]$$

PVS-Style Includes. In [KMOR17, Mül19], we present an import of the PVS Prelude and NASA Libraries into the MMT system. One of the peculiarities of the PVS language is their prevalent use of parametric theories. These are commonly used whenever results involving multiple models of the same theory are needed; e.g. a theory of groups in PVS would be parametric in the signature of groups (i.e. $\texttt{Group}(U, \circ, e, {}^{-1})$), such that whenever a result relating two groups would be needed, the containing theory would simply import two instances of the theory of groups with different parameters. Additionally, parametric theories can be included "as is", in which case the parameters can be provided individually each time a symbol from the included theory is used (e.g. $\texttt{Group?associativity}[\mathbb{Z}, +, 0, -]$). Effectively this makes each constant in the included theory take additional arguments for the theory parameters.

While MMT supports parametric theories, they are treated quite differently than in PVS. Theory parameters need to be supplied whenever a parametric theory is included, and by the definitional property of **implicit morphisms** (which includes are, see [RM18]), at most one theory morphism between two theories may be implicit. This means that a parametric theory can only be included in another theory once with one fixed set of parameters supplied.

As with Coq sections, we hence opted for using a structural feature $\texttt{ParInclude}$ whose derived declarations take a single parameter $\mathcal{T}$ for the included theory and no inner declarations. The elaboration of such a derived declaration then consists of the constants in $\mathcal{T}$ with the theory parameters of $\mathcal{T}$ being Π-bound analogously to our treatment of Variables in Coq sections above. This treatment subsumes all possible use cases of includes in PVS.

Notably, this comes at the cost of blowing up theories massively, since any use of the feature copies all declarations of the included theory in its elaboration, slowing down various MMT services noticeably. However, since the declarations can be elaborated individually, this allows for future improvements by potentially treating the elaborations lazily.

While the grammar presented in this paper requires derived declarations to be named – as the actual abstract syntax of MMT does – the actual concrete syntax allows specific features (such as $\texttt{ParInclude}$) to omit names. This way, include-like features do not have to be named by a user, and internal names are generated instead.

4.3   Declaration Patterns

Now we recover the declarative special case introduced in [HKR12, Hor14] as a special case of our structural features.

Specification. A declaration pattern is a structural features whose elaboration is so simple that it can be specified declaratively in the meta-language. We recap the definition of [HKR12].

A **declaration pattern** is a declaration of the form $\texttt{pattern}\ P(\Gamma) = \{\Delta\}$ where P is the name of the pattern, $\Gamma = x_1 : E_1, \ldots, x_m : E_m$ is a context declaring parameters that are bound in $\Delta = D_1, \ldots, D_n$, and the D_i are declarations.

The D_i can be arbitrary declarations, and we assume they can be elaborated into constant declarations $c_1 : F_1, \ldots, c_n : F_n$.

Thus, a declaration pattern is essentially the same as a theory with some parameters. It is also similar to a parametric record type—except that it does not introduce a type, i.e., $P(e_1, \ldots, e_m)$ cannot be used as a type. The latter ensures that any declaration (including type declarations) that can be used in theories can also be used in patterns.

An **instance** of the pattern P (assumed to be declared as above) is a declaration of the form `instance` $p : P(e_1, \ldots, e_m)$ where p is the name of the instance and the e_i satisfy $e_i : E_i'$ where E' arises from E by substituting each preceding x_i with e_i. The semantics of such an instance declaration is that it induces the declarations $p/c_1 : F_1', \ldots, p/c_n : F_n'$, where the p/c_i are qualified names and the F_i' arise as above. Thus, Δ can be seen as the declarative definition of the elaboration of the instance p.

Implementation. Declaration patterns introduce two new kinds of declarations (patterns and instances), and we capture them with two structural features.

Firstly, the structural feature for patterns uses the name $\mathfrak{f} =$ `pattern`. A derived declaration $P : $ `pattern` $(A_1, \ldots, A_m)$ $=$ $\{\Delta\}$ is valid iff each A_i is of the form $x_i : E_i$ and concatenating those yields a valid context, and if the declarations in Δ are valid relative to that context. It elaborates to nothing.

Secondly, the structural feature for instances uses the name $\mathfrak{f} =$ `instance`. A derived declaration $p : $ `instance` (A) $=$ $\{\}$ is valid iff A is of the form $P(e_1, \ldots, e_m)$ for a pattern P that was declared in the current scope and the e_i satisfy the respective type constraints. Defining the elaboration of such a derived declaration is straightforward and proceeds exactly as specified above.

We do not touch on the issues of concrete syntax in this paper, it is straightforward to see that only simple notational rules are needed to make these derived declarations mimic the concrete syntax of [HKR12] entirely. This is already supported by our implementation.

Notably, the resulting implementation of declaration patterns is significantly simpler and easier to read, understand, and verify than the existing prototype implementation that had been built as a part of [Hor14]. This is because all the bureaucracy of elaboration is now covered uniformly by the framework so that the code can focus on the semantically relevant details. But more importantly, the prototype implementation was developed as an extension of MMT in a PhD thesis and was never well-integrated with the rest of the code. Such a deep integration would have gone beyond the resources and purpose of that PhD thesis. Because structural features are now deeply integrated with MMT out of the box, our new implementation is not only simpler but also better than the old prototype.

5   Module-Level Features

Definition. To simplify the presentation, we have so far only considered structural features that extend the syntax *inside* theories. But it is natural to also consider extending the module-level syntax. We specify and implement this in essentially the same way. The key step is to allow derived declarations as modules, i.e., we add a production to the MMT grammar and speak of **derived modules**:

$$\text{Mod} ::= m : \mathfrak{f}(E^*) = \{\text{Dec}^*\}$$

Module-level structural features are defined and used in the same way as above except for two subtleties. Firstly, the elaboration of a derived module may only produce other modules. This makes sense as toplevel declaration must elaborate to other toplevel declarations.

Secondly, it is difficult how to specify where a module-level structural feature may be used. For derived declaration, which occur inside a theory, this is easy: the declaration may be used if the respective structural feature rule is visible to the containing theory. But derived modules, which may occur on toplevel, do not have a containing theory. It is not desirable to introduce a global scope that would define which module-level features are in scope as that would preclude restricting a module-level feature to specific object-languages. We are still experimenting with different designs for this issue. For now we use the containing file as the scope.

Diagram Definitions. In [SR19], we added diagram expressions and diagram definitions in MMT. The former are expressions that use special constants to capture the syntax of MMT diagrams (i.e., the non-terminal γ). The latter are modules of the form **diagram** $d = E$. Their semantics is that *i)* E is evaluated into a diagram expression, say declaring theories $T_i = \{\Delta_i\}$ and *ii)* new modules $d/T_i = \{\Delta_i\}$ are created.

It is straightforward to realize this as a module-level structural feature. In fact, the implementation of structural features reported in this paper predates the work in [SR19], which already used them to implement diagram definitions.

Theory Morphisms and Logical Relations. In Sect. 2, we mentioned that MMT supports other modules than theories. Two such features have been realized so far.

Firstly, **views** are modules of the form $v : S \to T = \{\text{Dec}^*\}$. These have been a primitive feature of MMT from the beginning. We can easily realize the **syntax** of views as derived modules. This is tempting because it would allow significantly simplifying the language. However, a currently unsolved problem is that the **semantics** cannot be reduced to elaboration: A view cannot in general be elaborated into anything simpler.

Secondly, [RS13] introduced logical relations as a module-level declaration. Rabe never implemented them in MMT because they, like views, are syntactically a special case of derived modules so that it made sense to defer their implementation until a general solution for derived modules is available. We intend to revisit them in future work.

6   Conclusion

We have presented a meta-language-based infrastructure of structural features in the MMT system and some paradigmatic examples that show its power. Structural features allow flexibly extending formal mathematical languages with new kinds of declarations without having to enlarge the trusted core of the system. In a meta-logical system, structural features are especially interesting because we need them to represent object languages and because the module system itself can restrict their availability to particular object logics.

The work presented here was to a large extent motivated by and developed for building exports of theorem prover libraries. In these, structural features allowed defining derived language features of theorem prover languages so that exports could stay shallow, i.e., structure-preserving, while also capturing the deep elaboration into kernel features that is needed for verification. Without the infrastructure presented in this paper, only deep implementations would have been possible and we would have been restricted to much less structured— and thus less searchable and reusable—exports. Moreover, it will prove critical for interoperability and library translations between theorem provers: even if target and source system have the exact same structural feature, a translation is practically very difficult if the intermediate representation is based on only the elaborated declarations.

In future work, we plan to represent more advanced features of theorem prover languages, starting with Isabelle and Coq. An open theoretical question is how to translate derived declarations along views in such a way that translation commutes with elaboration—this does not hold for every structural feature, and establishing sufficient criteria would be very valuable for modular reasoning in large libraries. Finally, we will improve MMT's abilities to represent the concrete syntax of derived declarations in order to mimic even more closely arbitrary object language syntax; this will allow for prototyping domain-specific languages in a way that entirely hides the logical framework from the user.

References

[BHL+14] Blanchette, J.C., Hölzl, J., Lochbihler, A., Panny, L., Popescu, A., Traytel, D.: Truly modular (co)datatypes for Isabelle/HOL. In: Klein, G., Gamboa, R. (eds.) ITP 2014. LNCS, vol. 8558, pp. 93–110. Springer, Cham (2014). https://doi.org/10.1007/978-3-319-08970-6_7

[CB16] Christiansen, D., Brady, E.: Elaborator reflection: extending idris in idris. In: Garrigue, J., Keller, G., Sumii, E. (eds.) International Conference on Functional Programming, pp. 284–297. ACM (2016)

[Coq15] Coq Development Team: The Coq Proof Assistant: Reference Manual. Technical report, INRIA (2015)

[EUR+17] Ebner, G., Ullrich, S., Roesch, J., Avigad, J., de Moura, L.: A metaprogramming framework for formal verification. In: Proceedings of the ACM on Programming Languages, vol. 1, no. ICFP, pp. 34:1–34:29 (2017)

[Gor88] Gordon,M.: HOL: a proof generating system for higher-order logic. In: Birtwistle, G., Subrahmanyam, P. (eds.) VLSI Specification, Verification and Synthesis, pp. 73–128. Kluwer-Academic Publishers (1988)

[Har96] Harrison, J.: HOL light: a tutorial introduction. In: Srivas, M., Camilleri, A. (eds.) FMCAD 1996. LNCS, vol. 1166, pp. 265–269. Springer, Heidelberg (1996). https://doi.org/10.1007/BFb0031814

[HHP93] Harper, R., Honsell, F., Plotkin, G.: A framework for defining logics. J. Assoc. Comput. Mach. **40**(1), 143–184 (1993)

[HKR12] Horozal, F., Kohlhase, M., Rabe, F.: Extending MKM formats at the statement level. In: Jeuring, J., et al. (eds.) CICM 2012. LNCS (LNAI), vol. 7362, pp. 65–80. Springer, Heidelberg (2012). https://doi.org/10.1007/978-3-642-31374-5_5

[Hor14] Horozal, F.: A framework for defining declarative languages. Ph.D. thesis, Jacobs University Bremen (2014)

[HR15] Horozal, F., Rabe, F.: Formal logic definitions for interchange languages. In: Kerber, M., Carette, J., Kaliszyk, C., Rabe, F., Sorge, V. (eds.) CICM 2015. LNCS (LNAI), vol. 9150, pp. 171–186. Springer, Cham (2015). https://doi.org/10.1007/978-3-319-20615-8_11

[IKRU13] Iancu, M., Kohlhase, M., Rabe, F., Urban, J.: The Mizar mathematical library in OMDoc: translation and applications. J. Autom. Reason. **50**(2), 191–202 (2013)

[KMOR17] Kohlhase, M., Müller, D., Owre, S., Rabe, F.: Making PVS accessible to generic services by interpretation in a universal format. In: Ayala-Rincón, M., Muñoz, C.A. (eds.) ITP 2017. LNCS, vol. 10499, pp. 319–335. Springer, Cham (2017). https://doi.org/10.1007/978-3-319-66107-0_21

[Koh06] Kohlhase, M.: OMDoc: An Open Markup Format for Mathematical Documents (Version.12). Lecture Notes in Artificial Intelligence, vol. 4180. Springer, Heidelberg (2006). https://doi.org/10.1007/11826095

[KR14] Kaliszyk, C., Rabe, F.: Towards knowledge management for HOL light. In: Watt, S.M., Davenport, J.H., Sexton, A.P., Sojka, P., Urban, J. (eds.) CICM 2014. LNCS (LNAI), vol. 8543, pp. 357–372. Springer, Cham (2014). https://doi.org/10.1007/978-3-319-08434-3_26

[KR20] Kohlhase, M., Rabe, F.: Experiences from exporting major proof assistant libraries (2020, submitted). https://kwarc.info/people/frabe/Research/KR_oafexp_20.pdf

[MRK18] Müller, D., Rabe, F., Kohlhase, M.: Theories as types. In: Galmiche, D., Schulz, S., Sebastiani, R. (eds.) IJCAR 2018. LNCS (LNAI), vol. 10900, pp. 575–590. Springer, Cham (2018). https://doi.org/10.1007/978-3-319-94205-6_38

[MRSC19] Müller, D., Rabe, F., Sacerdoti Coen, C.: The Coq library as a theory graph. In: Kaliszyk, C., Brady, E., Kohlhase, A., Sacerdoti Coen, C. (eds.) CICM 2019. LNCS (LNAI), vol. 11617, pp. 171–186. Springer, Cham (2019). https://doi.org/10.1007/978-3-030-23250-4_12

[Mül19] Müller, D.: Mathematical knowledge management across formal libraries. Ph.D. thesis, Informatics, FAU Erlangen-Nürnberg, October 2019. https://kwarc.info/people/dmueller/pubs/thesis.pdf

[Pau94] Paulson, L.: Isabelle: A Generic Theorem Prover. Lecture Notes in Computer Science, vol. 828. Springer, Heidelberg (1994). https://doi.org/10.1007/BFb0030541

[Rab17] Rabe, F.: How to identify, translate, and combine logics? J. Log. Comput. **27**(6), 1753–1798 (2017)

[RK13] Rabe, F., Kohlhase, M.: A scalable module system. Inf. Comput. (230), 1–54 (2013). http://kwarc.info/frabe/Research/mmt.pdf

[RM18] Rabe, F., Müller, D.: Structuring theories with implicit morphisms (2018). http://wadt18.cs.rhul.ac.uk/submissions/WADT18A43.pdf

[Rot20] Rothgang, C.: Theories as inductive types, 05 2020. B.Sc. Thesis, expected May 2020

[RS13] Rabe, F., Sojakova, K.: Logical relations for a logical framework. ACM Trans. Comput. Log. (2013). http://kwarc.info/frabe/Research/RS_logrels_12.pdf

[SR19] Rabe, F., Sharoda, Y.: Diagram combinators in MMT. In: Kaliszyk, C., Brady, E., Kohlhase, A., Sacerdoti Coen, C. (eds.) CICM 2019. LNCS (LNAI), vol. 11617, pp. 211–226. Springer, Cham (2019). https://doi.org/10.1007/978-3-030-23250-4_15

Formally Verifying Proofs for Algebraic Identities of Matrices

Leonard Schmitz[✉] and Viktor Levandovskyy[✉]

Lehrstuhl D für Mathematik, RWTH Aachen University, Aachen, Germany
leonard.schmitz@rwth-aachen.de, viktor.levandovskyy@math.rwth-aachen.de

Abstract. We consider proof certificates for identities of rectangular matrices. To automate their construction, we introduce an algebraic framework and supply explicit algorithms relying on non-commutative Gröbner bases. We address not only verification, but also exploration and reasoning towards establishing new identities and even proving mathematical properties. Especially Gröbner-driven elimination theory navigates us to insightful conclusions. We present several applications, that is efficiently formalized proofs for important identities of matrices: cancellation properties of triple products with Moore–Penrose pseudoinverses, a generalized Sherman–Morrison–Woodbury formula and an automated derivation of feedback loops in the famous Youla controller parametrization from control theory.

For actual computations we employ the open source computer algebra system SINGULAR which is used as a backend by systems like SAGE and OSCAR. The non-commutative extension LETTERPLACE provides users with all the required functionality. SINGULAR has numerous conversion tools and supports various standards. Therefore, it can facilitate the integration with existing theorem provers.

Keywords: Matrix identities · Gröbner bases · Word problems · Proof certificates · Elimination theory · Proof assistant

1 Introduction

Matrices are fundamental objects in science and technology. We use symbolic computation techniques to formally prove conditional equalities between matrices. In algebras over fields, a classical approach is to reduce questions about algebraic identities to ideal membership problems, e.g. [6]. Identities of matrices, however, have a slightly different algebraic structure since rectangular matrices can only be added and multiplied with other matrices of an appropriate format. To the best of our knowledge, a systematic treatment of identities with methods of associative ring theory was initiated by [7,10,18]. Very recently in [2,8,16] a new approach extends the setting to linear operators. We show that solving

Supported by DFG TRR 195 "Symbolic Tools in Mathematics and their applications".

C. Benzmüller and B. Miller (Eds.): CICM 2020, LNAI 12236, pp. 222–236, 2020.
https://doi.org/10.1007/978-3-030-53518-6_14

ideal membership problems with methods from associative ring theory is feasible. For this, we formulate a new algebraic framework with elementary proofs to handle rectangular matrices of various sizes. Furthermore, we illustrate how elimination orderings can be used for establishing new identities. We propose easy-to-handle black box tools which do not require a full understanding of the underlying algebraic framework. These tools are then applied to prove a number of relevant matrix identities. The verifications are traditional pen-and-paper proofs that use the presented automation approach as the central proof step. We employ the non-commutative extension LETTERPLACE of the open source computer algebra system SINGULAR.

2 General Design

Every matrix with entries in some fixed field $\mathcal{K}$ has a size, that is two natural numbers encoding the number of rows and columns of this matrix. Equality of matrices and the arithmetic operations addition, subtraction and multiplication are all partial due to those sizes. Instead of starting with a tedious description of a syntax for valid matrix expressions, we shorten this process and encode matrices as polynomials with non-commuting variables. Every reasonable semantics of matrix expressions should respect the algebraic structure of polynomials. For matrices $M_1, \ldots, M_n$ and M we consider the problem

$$M_1 = 0 \wedge \cdots \wedge M_n = 0 \implies M = 0$$

which can be reduced to well-known questions about ideals in non-commutative algebras. Before introducing a formal setting, we begin the discussion with an illustrative model problem.

Lemma 1. *For arbitrary matrices $A \in \mathcal{K}^{n \times n}$, $U \in \mathcal{K}^{n \times \ell}$ and $V \in \mathcal{K}^{\ell \times n}$, $AUV = A^3$ implies $VA(UV)^2 = VA^2UVA$.*

To address this sort of problem, we interpret matrices as symbols in the free associative algebra $\mathcal{K}\langle X \rangle$ and use the tools from non-commutative Gröbner basis theory, e.g. [1,12,14]. The process begins with the choice of assumptions, encoded as a set $\mathcal{F}$ of non-commutative polynomials in which all elements of $\mathcal{F}$ *vanish as matrices*. The following black box tool provides for a suitable choice of $\mathcal{F}$ a proof for q being equal to a as a matrix.

Proof Machine for Algebraic Identities of Matrices

Assumptions $\mathcal{F} \subseteq \mathcal{K}\langle X \rangle$ (every $f \in \mathcal{F}$ must vanish as a matrix)

$\hookrightarrow$ Gröbner basis $\mathcal{G}$ (with non-commutative Buchberger's algorithm)

Question $q \in \mathcal{K}\langle X \rangle$

$\hookrightarrow$ **Answer** $a = \mathrm{NF}(q, \mathcal{G})$ (with non-commutative division algorithm)

$$\boxed{\implies q \text{ is equal to } a \text{ as a matrix}}$$

Let us discuss each step in detail. To prove that two matrices are equal, we encode them as non-commutative polynomials $q_1, q_2 \in \mathcal{K}\langle X \rangle$ and choose a set of assumptions $\mathcal{F} \subseteq \mathcal{K}\langle X \rangle$. We use the proof machine and show that q_1 and q_2 have the same normal form modulo two-sided ideal $\langle \mathcal{F} \rangle$. One way of doing this is to compute a Gröbner basis $\mathcal{G}$ of $\langle \mathcal{F} \rangle$ and to apply the division algorithm with divisors $\mathcal{G}$, input $q_1 - q_2$ and output zero. With this we obtain a *proof certificate*

$$q_1 - q_2 = \sum_{f \in \mathcal{F}} \sum_{t=1}^{k(f)} \ell_{ft} \cdot f \cdot r_{ft}$$

expressing the statement $q_1 - q_2$ in a direct dependence on $\mathcal{F}$ and where verification is the matter of elementary arithmetics. *Evaluating* the right hand side of the above expression implies that $q_1 - q_2$ vanishes as a matrix. Moreover, the right hand side provides a symbolic proof of the statement. We pick up the model problem from the beginning of this section and apply the proof machine from above.

Proof (of Lemma 1). In the notation of the proof machine let $X = \{A, U, V\}$ denote a set of symbols and $f := AUV - A^3 \in \mathcal{K}\langle X \rangle$ a polynomial such that every element in $\mathcal{F} = \{f\}$ vanishes as a matrix. We run Buchberger's algorithm on $\mathcal{F}$ with respect to the degree lexicographic ordering and linear preorder $U > V > A$. It turns out that $\mathcal{G} = \mathcal{F}$ is a Gröbner basis of the two-sided ideal $\langle \mathcal{F} \rangle$. With the division algorithm, we successively subtract multiples of f until we reach zero. In the end, we find an expression via f as follows:

$$q := VA(UV)^2 - VA^2UVA = V \cdot f \cdot UV - VA \cdot f \cdot A + VA^2 \cdot f.$$

Evaluating the right hand side of the above expression implies that q vanishes as a matrix. □

Remark 1. Generally in the free associative algebra, the ideal membership problem is semi-decidable, e.g. [13,15], meaning that there is a suitable procedure which terminates if and only if the ideal membership takes place, or runs forever otherwise.

3 Technical Details

We introduce an algebraic framework and show that solving ideal membership problems with methods originating from associative ring theory is feasible. In particular, this involves case studies and an evaluation to handle rectangular matrices of various sizes.

3.1 Encoding Matrices via Free Algebras

Given a finite set of matrices with entries in a field $\mathcal{K}$, we consider its elements as a set of symbols X. We equip this set with functions row, col : $X \to \mathbb{N}$.

Every $M \in X$ stands for a matrix and the values $\text{row}(M)$ and $\text{col}(M)$ correspond to the number of rows and columns of this matrix. Let $\mathcal{K}\langle X \rangle$ denote the free associative algebra over the free monoid $\langle X \rangle$ with string concatenation as its operation and empty word (identified with $1 \in \mathcal{K}$) as its neutral element. As a preimage of matrix products with i rows and j columns, for fixed natural numbers i and j we define a subset of $\langle X \rangle$ by

$$\mathcal{U}_{i,j} := \left\{ \prod_{k=1}^{\ell} M_k \; \middle| \; \begin{array}{l} M_k \in X, \; \ell \geq 1 \\ \text{row}(M_1) = i, \; \text{col}(M_\ell) = j \\ \text{col}(M_k) = \text{row}(M_{k+1}) \end{array} \right\}.$$

Let $\text{Span}_{\mathcal{K}}(\mathcal{U}_{i,j})$ denote a $\mathcal{K}$-vector subspace of $\mathcal{K}\langle X \rangle$ which is spanned by the elements of $\mathcal{U}_{i,j}$ from above. For arbitrary matrices we define the set of *valid relations* $\mathcal{U}_X$ by the set-theoretic union of subspaces

$$\mathcal{U}_X := \bigcup_{i,j \in \mathbb{N}} \text{Span}_{\mathcal{K}}(\mathcal{U}_{i,j}) \subseteq \mathcal{K}\langle X \rangle.$$

We recognize that $\text{Span}_{\mathcal{K}}(\mathcal{U}_{i,i})$ is a $\mathcal{K}$-subalgebra of $\mathcal{K}\langle X \rangle$ and furthermore, that $\text{Span}_{\mathcal{K}}(\mathcal{U}_{i,j})$ is a $(\text{Span}_{\mathcal{K}}(\mathcal{U}_{i,i}), \text{Span}_{\mathcal{K}}(\mathcal{U}_{j,j}))$-bimodule. However, the whole set $\mathcal{U}_X$ cannot be equipped with a common algebraic structure. We define an *evaluation* which is a family of homomorphisms of vector spaces

$$\psi_{i,j} : \text{Span}_{\mathcal{K}}(\mathcal{U}_{i,j}) \longrightarrow \mathcal{K}^{i \times j},$$

uniquely determined by $\mathcal{K}$-basis $\mathcal{U}_{i,j}$ being mapped to corresponding products of matrices. The latter is well-defined due to the construction of $\mathcal{U}_{i,j}$. For $u \in \mathcal{U}_{i,k}$ and $v \in \mathcal{U}_{k,j}$ one verifies that $\psi_{i,j}(u \cdot v) = \psi_{i,k}(u) \cdot \psi_{k,j}(v)$. Consequently, if a product of polynomials is itself contained in $\mathcal{U}_X$, the evaluation respects multiplication in $\mathcal{K}\langle X \rangle$ on the one side, and matrices of arbitrary sizes on the other. We say that polynomials $q, a \in \text{Span}_{\mathcal{K}}(\mathcal{U}_{i,j})$ are *equal as matrices* if $\psi_{i,j}(q) = \psi_{i,j}(a)$ and that q *vanishes as matrix* if $\psi_{i,j}(q)$ is the $i \times j$ zero matrix.

3.2 Gröbner Bases in Free Relations of Matrices

Let us recapitulate fundamental concepts of non-commutative Gröbner basis theory. We call a total well-ordering on $\langle X \rangle$ a *monomial ordering* if it is compatible with multiplication, i.e., for all $w, w', u, v \in \langle X \rangle$ with $w < w'$ we have $uwv < uw'v$. For nonzero $f \in \mathcal{K}\langle X \rangle$ and fixed monomial ordering let $\text{lm}(f)$ and $\text{lc}(f)$ denote the *leading monomial* and *leading coefficient* of f. Lemma 2 ensures that the set of valid relations $\mathcal{U}_X$ is invariant under the important concepts *division* and *overlapping*.

Lemma 2. *Let $f \in \text{Span}_{\mathcal{K}}(\mathcal{U}_{i,j})$ and $g \in \text{Span}_{\mathcal{K}}(\mathcal{U}_{k,\ell})$ denote two arbitrary but nonzero polynomials from the set of valid relations $\mathcal{U}_X$.*

(i) If leading monomial $\mathrm{lm}(f)$ *divides* $\mathrm{lm}(g)$, *that is*

$$\exists\, u,\, v \in \langle X \rangle:\ u \cdot \mathrm{lm}(f) \cdot v = \mathrm{lm}(g),$$

then the remainder $g - \frac{\mathrm{lc}(g)}{\mathrm{lc}(f)} u \cdot f \cdot v \in \mathrm{Span}_{\mathcal{K}}(\mathcal{U}_{k,\,\ell})$ *is valid.*

(ii) If $\mathrm{lm}(f)$ *and* $\mathrm{lm}(g)$ *overlap, that is*

$$\exists\, v,\, w,\, o \in \langle X \rangle: \mathrm{lm}(f) = vo,\ \mathrm{lm}(g) = ow,\ o \neq 1,\ \mathrm{lm}(f) \nmid w\ \text{and}\ \mathrm{lm}(g) \nmid v,$$

then the overlap relation $\frac{1}{\mathrm{lc}(f)} f \cdot w - \frac{1}{\mathrm{lc}(g)} v \cdot g \in \mathrm{Span}_{\mathcal{K}}(\mathcal{U}_{i,\,\ell})$ *is valid.*

For two polynomials f and g as above, there can be several (but finitely many) overlaps between $\mathrm{lm}(f)$ and $\mathrm{lm}(g)$. Let $\mathcal{O}(f,\,g)$ denote the set of all overlap relations of f and g. Given an input $r_0 \in \mathcal{K}\langle X \rangle$ and a *set of divisors* $\mathcal{F} \subseteq \mathcal{K}\langle X \rangle$ the *division algorithm* is performed as follows:

1. Set $i = 0$
2. If $r_i = 0$ or $\mathrm{lm}(f)$ does not divide $\mathrm{lm}(r_i)$ for all nonzero $f \in \mathcal{F}$, return r_i
3. Find $u,\, v \in \langle X \rangle$ and $f \in \mathcal{F}$ such that $u \cdot \mathrm{lm}(f) \cdot v = \mathrm{lm}(r_i)$, define

$$r_{i+1} := r_i - \frac{\mathrm{lc}(r_i)}{\mathrm{lc}(f)} u \cdot f \cdot v,\ i \mapsto i+1\ \text{and go to step 2}.$$

Since $<$ is a well-ordering and $r_0 = 0$, $r_{i+1} = 0$ or $\mathrm{lm}(r_{i+1}) < \mathrm{lm}(r_i)$ for all i, the above procedure terminates at some r_n which is called a *normal form of* r_0 *modulo* $\mathcal{F}$. A set $\mathcal{G} \subseteq \mathcal{K}\langle X \rangle$ is a *Gröbner basis* of the two-sided ideal $\langle \mathcal{G} \rangle$ with respect to a monomial ordering, if for every $f \in \langle \mathcal{G} \rangle \setminus \{0\}$ there exists $g \in \mathcal{G}$ such that $\mathrm{lm}(g)$ divides $\mathrm{lm}(f)$. *Buchberger's criterion* asserts that $\mathcal{G}$ is a Gröbner basis if and only if for every pair $(f,\, g) \in \mathcal{G} \times \mathcal{G}$ the elements in $\mathcal{O}(f,\, g)$ have normal form zero modulo $\mathcal{G}$. *Buchberger's algorithm* is the essential tool of computing for input $\mathcal{F} \subseteq \mathcal{K}\langle X \rangle$ a Gröbner bases $\mathcal{G}$ of two-sided ideal $\langle \mathcal{F} \rangle$. It has the following steps:

1. Set $\mathcal{G}_0 := \mathcal{F}$ and $i = 0$
2. Construct $\mathcal{P}_i := \bigcup_{f,\,g \in \mathcal{G}_i} \mathcal{O}(f,\, g)$ of all overlap relations in $\mathcal{G}_i$
3. Set $\mathcal{G}_{i+1} := \mathcal{G}_i \cup \{r \mid r$ is a nonzero normal form of $p \in \mathcal{P}_i$ modulo $\mathcal{G}_i\}$
4. If $\mathcal{G}_{i+1} \neq \mathcal{G}_i$ then $i \mapsto i+1$ and go to step 2
5. Return $\mathcal{G} := \bigcup_{j \geq 0} \mathcal{G}_j$.

Note that the algorithm involves two operations, namely division and overlapping from above. In the following, we make use of this observation and show that a and q are equal as matrices if $\mathcal{F}$ contains as matrix vanishing polynomials exclusively.

Theorem 1. *Let* $\mathcal{F}$ *be a finite subset of* $\mathcal{U}_X$ *and* $\mathcal{G}$ *be a Gröbner basis of two-sided ideal* $\langle \mathcal{F} \rangle$ *as an output of Buchberger's algorithm. If the division algorithm with input* $q \in \mathrm{Span}_{\mathcal{K}}(\mathcal{U}_{i,\,j})$ *and* $\mathcal{G}$ *as a set of divisors returns* $a \in \mathcal{K}\langle X \rangle$, *it follows that for every polynomial* $f \in \mathcal{F}$ *there exists a natural number* $k(f) \in \mathbb{N}$ *and polynomials* $\ell_{ft},\, r_{ft} \in \mathcal{K}\langle X \rangle$ *such that*

$$q = a + \sum_{f \in \mathcal{F}} \sum_{t=1}^{k(f)} \ell_{ft} \cdot f \cdot r_{ft} \in \mathrm{Span}_{\mathcal{K}}(\mathcal{U}_{i,\,j}).$$

Proof. With iterated application of Lemma 2, for every $g_u \in \mathcal{G}$ and $f \in \mathcal{F}$ there exist $k(f, u), i(u), j(u) \in \mathbb{N}$ and $\ell_{ftu}, r_{ftu} \in \mathcal{K}\langle X \rangle$ such that

$$g_u = \sum_{f \in \mathcal{F}} \sum_{t=1}^{k(f,u)} \ell_{ftu} \cdot f \cdot r_{ftu} \in \mathrm{Span}_{\mathcal{K}}(\mathcal{U}_{i(u), j(u)})$$

is valid. The division algorithm finds $n \in \mathbb{N}$, $g_u \in \mathcal{G}$ and $b_u, c_u \in \mathcal{K}\langle X \rangle$ such that

$$q = a + \sum_{u=1}^{n} b_u \cdot g_u \cdot c_u = a + \sum_{f \in \mathcal{F}} \sum_{u=1}^{n} \sum_{t=1}^{k(f,u)} b_u \cdot \ell_{ftu} \cdot f \cdot r_{ftu} \cdot c_u \in \mathrm{Span}_{\mathcal{K}}(\mathcal{U}_{i,j})$$

where the second equality results from substituting g_u into the representation from above. This implies that $a \in \mathrm{Span}_{\mathcal{K}}(\mathcal{U}_{i,j})$ is valid. $\qquad\square$

3.3   Black Box Tool for Gröbner-Driven Elimination

A monomial ordering is called an *elimination ordering* for a subset $X_e \subseteq X$ if for every nonzero $f \in \mathcal{K}\langle X \rangle$ with $\mathrm{lm}(f) \in \mathcal{K}\langle X \setminus X_e \rangle$ it follows that $f \in \mathcal{K}\langle X \setminus X_e \rangle$. We call $X_e \subseteq X$ the set of *eliminated matrices*. One of the most important abilities of Gröbner bases is reflected in the *Elimination Lemma*: if $\mathcal{G}$ is a Gröbner basis of an ideal $\mathcal{I} \in \mathcal{K}\langle X \rangle$ with respect to an elimination ordering for X_e then $\mathcal{G} \cap \mathcal{K}\langle X \setminus X_e \rangle$ is a Gröbner basis of $\mathcal{I} \cap \mathcal{K}\langle X \setminus X_e \rangle$. The following is our principal tool for exploration and reasoning towards establishing new identities. It finds a representation of input q in terms of output a containing no symbols X_r which are *removable with respect to* $\mathcal{F}$. The notions of *eliminated matrices* and *removable matrices* are introduced since we cannot expect to eliminate every symbol in an arbitrary polynomial q without specification on $\mathcal{F}$.

Elimination Machine for Removable Matrices

Eliminated matrices $X_e \subseteq X$ (monomial ordering which eliminates X_e)
Assumptions $\mathcal{F} \subseteq \mathcal{U}_X$

$\hookrightarrow$ Gröbner basis $\mathcal{G}$

$\hookrightarrow$ **Removable matrices** $X_r := \{M \in X_e \mid \mathrm{NF}\,(M, \mathcal{G}) \in \mathcal{K}\langle X \setminus X_e \rangle\}$

Question $q \in \mathcal{U}_X$
$\hookrightarrow$ **Answer** $a = \mathrm{NF}\,(q, \mathcal{G})$

$$\implies \quad a \in \mathcal{K}\langle X \setminus X_r \rangle$$

Let us discuss each step in detail. For a given two-sided ideal $\langle \mathcal{F} \rangle$ we compute a Gröbner basis $\mathcal{G}$ with respect to a monomial ordering which eliminates X_e. We compute the subset $X_r \subset X_e$ containing all symbols in X_e whose normal form contains no symbols in X_e. Together with the proof machine, this leads to polynomial q and a being equal as matrices. That is, the matrix considered by q has a representation in terms of matrices encoded by $X \setminus X_r$ exclusively. For every symbol $M \in X_r$ and monomial $\ell \cdot M \cdot r \in \langle X \rangle$ in q there exists a specific chain of reductions such that $\ell \cdot M \cdot r$ is reduced to $\ell \cdot \mathrm{NF}(M, \mathcal{G}) \cdot r \in \mathcal{K}\langle X \rangle$ before further reductions result in the normal form, hence $a \in \mathcal{K}\langle X \setminus X_r \rangle$. We will work with elimination orderings in the proof of Lemma 3 and Theorem 5 where more details are provided.

Remark 2. Unlike the situation described in Remark 1, we are not aware of an algorithm performing elimination. It is generally impossible to disprove that an element is contained in X_r since normal forms are not computable in all cases. The major reason is that a Gröbner basis with respect to an elimination ordering is rather infinite and not positively graded. Nevertheless, we have observed in practice that with some luck in the choice of ordering one gets finite Gröbner bases and thus solves the elimination problem completely. In other cases, where only truncated Gröbner bases are available, one obtains only a subset of the removable matrices.

3.4   Example with SINGULAR:LETTERPLACE

We employ the open source computer algebra system SINGULAR [4], more precisely its non-commutative extension LETTERPLACE [11]. SINGULAR is used as a backend by systems like SAGE [17] and OSCAR [9], supports various standards and has numerous tools for prospective integration with other systems.

The proof of Lemma 3 consists of two phases and illustrates automated exploration with elimination orderings and a straightforward verification by an ideal membership problem. Putting this together, we show invertibility of a matrix by first searching for its inverse and by verifying the defining axiomatics afterwards.

Lemma 3. *Let $A \in \mathcal{K}^{m \times \ell}$ and $B \in \mathcal{K}^{\ell \times m}$ be rectangular matrices with entries in a field $\mathcal{K}$ of characteristic zero.*

(i) *If $AB + I_m \in \mathrm{GL}_m(\mathcal{K})$ and $BA + I_\ell \in \mathrm{GL}_\ell(\mathcal{K})$ then there exists a representation of $(AB + I_m)^{-1}$ in terms of A, B, I_m, I_ℓ and $(BA + I_\ell)^{-1}$. Via symmetry the same holds for $(BA + I_\ell)^{-1}$ by exchanging A and B.*

(ii) *The existence of one inverse implies the other, that is*

$$AB + I_m \in \mathrm{GL}_m(\mathcal{K}) \Longleftrightarrow BA + I_\ell \in \mathrm{GL}_\ell(\mathcal{K}).$$

Proof. For (i) we have to construct the required representation. In the notation of the elimination machine let

$$X = \{(AB + I_m)^{-1}, \ (BA + I_\ell)^{-1}, \ A, \ B, \ I_\ell, \ I_m\}$$

denote a set of symbols with subset of eliminated matrices $X_e = \{(AB + I_m)^{-1}\}$. To encode the invertibility of $BA + I_\ell$ and to describe the identity matrices I_m

and I_ℓ we define

$$\mathcal{F}_1 = \{I_m I_m - I_m,\ I_\ell I_\ell - I_\ell,\ AI_\ell - A,\ I_m A - A,\ BI_m - B,\ I_\ell B - B,$$
$$(BA + I_\ell)^{-1}(BA + I_\ell) - I_\ell,\ (BA + I_\ell)(BA + I_\ell)^{-1} - I_\ell,$$
$$(BA + I_\ell)^{-1}I_\ell - (BA + I_\ell)^{-1},\ I_\ell(BA + I_\ell)^{-1} - (BA + I_\ell)^{-1}\}.$$

For encoding the invertibility of $AB + I_m$ we use $\mathcal{F}_2$ defined by

$$\mathcal{F}_1 \cup \{(AB + I_m)^{-1}(AB + I_m) - I_m,\ (AB + I_m)(AB + I_m)^{-1} - I_m,$$
$$(AB + I_m)^{-1}I_m - (AB + I_m)^{-1},\ I_m(AB + I_m)^{-1} - (AB + I_m)^{-1}\}.$$

Executing the computation with the code below we obtain a Gröbner basis $\mathcal{G}_2$ of two-sided ideal $\langle \mathcal{F}_2 \rangle$ with respect to an ordering which eliminates X_e. The corresponding normal form of $(AB + I_m)^{-1}$ is given by

$$a = \mathrm{NF}((AB + I_m)^{-1}, \mathcal{G}_2) = -A(BA + I_\ell)^{-1}B + I_m.$$

This provides the required representation with Theorem 1.

(ii) We show that $BA + I_\ell \in \mathrm{GL}_\ell(\mathcal{K})$ implies $AB + I_m \in \mathrm{GL}_m(\mathcal{K})$. The other implication is analogous. In $\mathcal{F}_1$ we have postulated the invertibility of $BA + I_\ell$, so the same applies to a Gröbner basis $\mathcal{G}_1$. The expression for a obtained in (i) is the same as the inverse of $AB + I_m$ modulo $\mathcal{G}_2$. Hence, it suffices to show that a is a left and a right inverse of $AB + I_m$ modulo $\mathcal{G}_1$, that is

$$\mathrm{NF}\left(a\,(AB + I_m) - I_m,\ \mathcal{G}_1\right) = 0 = \mathrm{NF}\left((AB + I_m)\,a - I_m,\ \mathcal{G}_1\right).$$

$\square$

The following source code for SINGULAR realizes all computations and gives explanations for each command being used.

```
LIB "freegb.lib";
ring r = 0,(ABpIi,BApIi,A,B,Il,Im),lp;  // field of char 0,
//names of variables (like ABpIi) and monomial ordering (lp)
ring R = freeAlgebra(r,11);     // free algebra up to length 11
option(redSB); option(redTail); // min reduced GBs option
poly ABpI = A*B + Im;   poly BApI = B*A + Il;
ideal F1 = Im*Im - Im, Il*Il - Il, A*Il - A, Im*A - A,
B*Im - B, Il*B - B, BApI*BApIi - Il, BApIi*BApI - Il,
BApIi*Il - BApIi, Il*BApIi - BApIi;
ideal F2 = F1, ABpI*ABpIi - Im, ABpIi*ABpI - Im,
ABpIi*Im - ABpIi, Im*ABpIi - ABpIi;
ideal G1 = twostd(F1);  ideal G2 = twostd(F2); // truncated GBs
poly a = NF(ABpIi, G2);    // division by G2 with remainder a
a;                         // synonymous to print(a);
> -A*BApIi*B+Im     // output of the previous command
```

```
NF(a*(A*B+Im)-Im, G1);
> 0
NF((A*B+Im)*a-Im, G1);
> 0
```

Remark 3. Both Gröbner bases $\mathcal{G}_1$ and $\mathcal{G}_2$ in the proof are finite. Notably, we can prove that the restriction to the field of characteristic zero is not essential for this theorem. Also, for each of the three constructive statements in the Lemma we can provide a symbolic proof in terms of the original assumptions $\mathcal{F}_i$ by hiding the Gröbner component $\mathcal{G}_i$. For instance, let $\mathcal{G}_2[11]$ denote the eleventh element of $\mathcal{G}_2$ considered in the code. In (i) the reduction of $(AB + I_m)^{-1}$ with divisors $\mathcal{G}_2$ requires subtraction by the element

$$\mathcal{G}_2[11] = (AB + I_m)^{-1} + A(BA + I_\ell)^{-1}B - I_m.$$

The latter is expressed via $\mathcal{F}_2$ as

$$\begin{aligned}
\mathcal{G}_2[11] &= A(BA + I_\ell)^{-1} \cdot \mathcal{F}_2[5] \cdot (AB + I_m)^{-1} - A(BA + I_\ell)^{-1} \cdot \mathcal{F}_2[5] - \mathcal{F}_2[14] \\
&\quad - A(BA + I_\ell)^{-1} \cdot \mathcal{F}_2[6] \cdot (AB + I_m)^{-1} + A \cdot \mathcal{F}_2[6] \cdot (AB + I_m)^{-1} \\
&\quad + A \cdot \mathcal{F}_2[8] \cdot B(AB + I_m)^{-1} - A(BA + I_\ell)^{-1}B \cdot \mathcal{F}_2[11] + \mathcal{F}_2[11].
\end{aligned}$$

In (ii) polynomial $b := a(AB + I_m) - I_m$ is reduced to zero modulo $\mathcal{G}_1$ as follows:

$$b = -A \cdot \mathcal{G}_1[10] \cdot B - A(BA + I_\ell)^{-1} \cdot \mathcal{G}_1[3] - \mathcal{G}_1[6] \cdot B + \mathcal{G}_1[5] \cdot B + \mathcal{G}_1[1].$$

By expressing the elements $\mathcal{G}_1[i]$ via $\mathcal{F}_1$ as above, we can algorithmically construct a lengthy expression for b which involves only $\mathcal{F}_1$. Both constructions belong to the *lifting* mechanism.

4   Applications

We present several illustrations of concrete mathematical investigations where the tools from above have been applied successfully. These reach from various practically relevant identities concerning Moore–Penrose pseudoinverses to an automated derivation of feedback loops in the Youla controller parametrization.

4.1   The Moore–Penrose Pseudoinverse

Various generalizations of matrix inverses play an important role in science. Especially the Moore–Penrose pseudoinverse has been in the center of investigation over the last decades, e.g. [3,5]. Indeed, there are countless applications in linear least squares approximation and minimal Euclidean norm solutions. As an immediate consequence of Gauss elimination, one obtains *generalized inverses* as a first step towards Moore–Penrose pseudoinverses.

Lemma 4. *For a matrix $A \in \mathcal{K}^{m \times \ell}$ over a field $\mathcal{K}$ there exists $B \in \mathcal{K}^{\ell \times m}$ with $ABA = A$ and $BAB = B$. Every such B is called a* generalized inverse *of A.*

Proof. Let us consider the non-trivial case $\text{rank}_\mathcal{K}(A) = r < \min\{m, \ell\}$ such that there are matrices

$$\begin{bmatrix} C \\ D \end{bmatrix}, \; [F\ G] = \begin{bmatrix} C \\ D \end{bmatrix}^{-1} \in \mathcal{K}^{m \times m} \quad \text{and} \quad [P\ Q], \; \begin{bmatrix} R \\ T \end{bmatrix} = [P\ Q]^{-1} \in \mathcal{K}^{\ell \times \ell}$$

which transform A to block matrix

$$\begin{bmatrix} C \\ D \end{bmatrix} A \, [P\ Q] = \begin{bmatrix} CAP & CAQ \\ DAP & DAQ \end{bmatrix} = \begin{bmatrix} I_r & 0 \\ 0 & 0 \end{bmatrix} \in \mathcal{K}^{m \times \ell}.$$

Every polynomial in

$$
\begin{aligned}
\mathcal{F} = \{ & I_m I_m - I_m, \; FC + GD - I_m, \; I_m G - G, \; GI_{m-r} - G, \; I_m F - F, \\
& FI_r - F, \; I_m A - A, \; AI_\ell - A, \; I_{m-r}D - D, \; DI_m - D, \; TQ - I_{\ell-r}, \\
& DG - I_{m-r}, \; DF, \; DAP, \; DAQ, \; I_r C - C, \; CI_m - C, \; CG, \; I_r I_r - I_r, \\
& CF - I_r, \; RP - I_r, \; CAP - I_r, \; I_r R - R, \; RI_\ell - R, \; CAQ, \; RQ, \\
& I_\ell P - P, \; PI_r - P, \; I_\ell I_\ell - I_\ell, \; PR + QT - I_\ell, \; I_\ell Q - Q, \; QI_{\ell-r} - Q, \\
& TP, \; I_{\ell-r}T - T, \; TI_\ell - T, \; I_{\ell-r}I_{\ell-r} - I_{\ell-r}, \; I_{m-r}I_{m-r} - I_{m-r} \}
\end{aligned}
$$

vanishes as a matrix. A Gröbner basis of the two-sided ideal $\langle \mathcal{F} \rangle$ with respect to the degree reverse lexicographic ordering is finite and given by

$$\mathcal{F} \cup \{AP - F, \; FR - A, \; AQ, \; DA, \; CA - R\}.$$

For instance, this provides a factorization $A = FR$ of A into matrices of full rank. With $b := PCAPC$ the division algorithm reduces both $AbA - A$ and $bAb - b$ to zero. Therefore $PCAPC$ is a generalized inverse of A. $\qquad \square$

For the remaining of this subsection we restrict ourselves to the field $\mathbb{C}$ of complex numbers. All of the following statements also hold under less restrictive assumptions on the field, but this is a topic of a forthcoming article.

Definition 1. *For a matrix $A \in \mathbb{C}^{m \times \ell}$ let $A^* = \overline{A}^T \in \mathbb{C}^{\ell \times m}$ denote its* adjoint *matrix. Every matrix $A^+ \in \mathbb{C}^{\ell \times m}$ which satisfies*

$$AA^+A = A, \; A^+AA^+ = A^+, \; (A^+)^*A^* = AA^+ \quad \text{and} \quad A^*(A^+)^* = A^+A$$

is called a Moore–Penrose pseudoinverse *of A.*

Theorem 2. *Let $A \in \mathbb{C}^{m \times \ell}$. If a Moore–Penrose pseudoinverse $A^+ \in \mathbb{C}^{\ell \times m}$ exists, then it is unique.*

Proof. We prove uniqueness by showing that any two Moore–Penrose pseudoinverses are already equal to each other, that is for Moore–Penrose pseudoinverses B_1, $B_2 \in \mathbb{C}^{\ell \times m}$ we use the set of symbols

$$X = \{A, \ B_1, \ B_2, \ A^*, \ B_1^*, \ B_2^*\}$$

such that every relation in

$$\mathcal{F}_i = \{AB_iA - A, \ B_iAB_i - B_i, \ AB_i - B_i^*A^*, \ B_iA - A^*B_i^*\}$$

with $i \in \{1, 2\}$ vanishes as a matrix by the axiomatics. We compute a Gröbner basis of $\langle \mathcal{F}_1 \cup \mathcal{F}_2 \rangle$ with respect to the degree reverse lexicographic ordering and obtain the following finite set:

$$\begin{aligned}
\mathcal{G} = \{&B_2 - B_1, \ A^*B_2^* - A^*B_1^*, \ AB_1B_1^*B_1 - B_1^*B_1, \ B_1B_2^* - B_1B_1^*, \\
&B_1^*A^* - AB_1, \ B_2^*A^* - AB_1, \ B_2^*B_1 - B_1^*B_1, \ AA^*B_1^* - A, \\
&A^*B_1^*B_1 - B_1, \ AA^*AB_1 - AA^*, \ B_1A - A^*B_1^*, \ A^*AB_1B_1^* - A^*B_1^*\}.
\end{aligned}$$

Since every polynomial in $\mathcal{F}_i$ vanishes as a matrix it follows that $B_2 - B_1 \in \mathcal{G}$ vanishes. This implies the uniqueness of Moore–Penrose pseudoinverses. □

Cancellation properties of triple products with Moore–Penrose pseudoinverses have been investigated in [3]. Illustrating the abilities of our methods, we address the first of many equivalences established in the paper. Note that the original proof requires a tedious verification. In order to accomplish it, a special language is developed. On the contrary, our approach delivers an efficiently formalized proof without using any additional theory.

Theorem 3. *For all $B \in \mathbb{C}^{m \times \ell}$, $Y \in \mathbb{C}^{\ell \times k}$ and $C \in \mathbb{C}^{k \times o}$ the following properties hold:*

$$C(BYC)^+B = Y^+ \iff (BY)^+B = Y^+ \ \text{ and } \ C(YC)^+ = Y^+.$$

Proof. For encoding the underlying axiomatics we use symbols X given by

$$\{B, Y, C, B^*, Y^*, C^*, (BY)^*, (YC)^*, (BYC)^*, B^+, Y^+, C^+,$$
$$(BY)^+, (YC)^+, (BYC)^+, B^{+*}, Y^{+*}, C^{+*}, (BY)^{+*}, (YC)^{+*}, (BYC)^{+*}\}$$

and for every $x \in \{B, C, Y, BY, YC, BYC\}$ we define

$$\begin{aligned}
\mathcal{F}_x = \{&xx^+x - x, \ x^+xx^+ - x^+, \ x^*x^{+*}x^* - x^*, \\
&x^{+*}x^*x^{+*} - x^{+*}, \ xx^+ - x^{+*}x^*, \ x^+x - x^*x^{+*}\}.
\end{aligned}$$

Together with relations reflecting the multiplication of adjoints we set

$$\mathcal{F} = \bigcup_x \mathcal{F}_x \ \cup \ \{(BY)^* - Y^*B^*, \ (BYC)^* - C^*Y^*B^*, \ (YC)^* - C^*Y^*\}$$

and $\mathcal{F}' = \mathcal{F} \cup \{C(BYC)^+B - Y^+\}$. We fix the degree lexicographic ordering such that the first implication is proved by

$$\mathrm{NF}((BY)^+B - Y^+, \langle \mathcal{F}' \rangle) = 0 = \mathrm{NF}(C(YC)^+ - Y^+, \langle \mathcal{F}' \rangle)$$

whereas the latter implication follows from

$$\mathrm{NF}(\, C(BYC)^+B - Y^+, \, \left\langle \mathcal{F} \cup \left\{ (BY)^+B - Y^+, \, C(YC)^+ - Y^+ \right\} \right\rangle \,) = 0.$$

$\square$

The Sherman–Morrison–Woodbury formula provides a cheap way to compute the inverse of a matrix numerically. It has found application in Broyden's method. Recently, this formula has been generalized by [5] with all inverse matrices replaced by Moore-Penrose pseudoinverses. A computer-supported proof follows in a straightforward fashion and without additional insight.

Theorem 4. *Let $A \in \mathbb{C}^{m \times \ell}$, $U \in \mathbb{C}^{m \times k}$, $C \in \mathbb{C}^{k \times o}$ and $V \in \mathbb{C}^{o \times \ell}$ be matrices such that $V = VA^+A$, $U = US^+S$, $V = C^+CV$, $U = UCC^+$, $V = SS^+V$ and $U = AA^+U$. This implies the Sherman–Morrison–Woodbury formula*

$$(A + UCV)^+ = A^+ - A^+U(C^+ + VA^+U)^+VA^+$$

for Moore–Penrose pseudoinverses.

4.2   Youla Controller Parametrization

The Youla controller parametrization, e.g. [19, 20], is a famous result from control theory. For a field $\mathbb{K}$ and a given matrix $P := C(s \cdot I_n - A)^{-1}B + D \in \mathcal{R}_0^{p \times m}$ with entries in a subring $\mathcal{R}_0$ of the field of rational functions $\mathcal{K} = \mathbb{K}(s)$ one is interested in finding such a matrix $K \in \mathcal{K}^{m \times p}$, that the block matrix

$$W = \begin{bmatrix} I_m & -K \\ -P & I_p \end{bmatrix} \in \mathcal{K}^{(m+p) \times (m+p)}$$

becomes invertible. Additionally, one is looking for such K, that the entries from the inverse of W lie in a subring $\mathcal{R}$ of $\mathcal{R}_0$. Traditionally in control theory, $\mathcal{R}_0$ contains all *proper fractions* and $\mathcal{R}$ is the ring of all $\varphi \in \mathcal{R}_0$ which induce complex functions with all their poles having negative real part, i.e. satisfying

$$a \geq 0 \implies \lim_{t \to a+bi} \varphi(t) \in \mathbb{C}.$$

However, the statement can be formulated and proved independently of traditional choices in the following purely algebraic setting.

Theorem 5. *For an arbitrary field $\mathbb{K}$ let $\mathcal{R}$ and $\mathcal{R}_0$ denote rings such that $\mathbb{K} \subseteq \mathcal{R} \subseteq \mathcal{R}_0 \subseteq \mathcal{K} := \mathbb{K}(s)$. Furthermore, let*

$$A \in \mathbb{K}^{n \times n}, B \in \mathbb{K}^{n \times m}, C \in \mathbb{K}^{p \times n},$$
$$F \in \mathbb{K}^{m \times n}, L \in \mathbb{K}^{n \times p} \ and \ D \in \mathbb{K}^{p \times m}$$

denote matrices with

$$P := C(s \cdot I_n - A)^{-1} B + D \in \mathcal{R}_0^{p \times m}$$

and

$$(s \cdot I_n - A - BF)^{-1}, \ (s \cdot I_n - A - LC)^{-1} \in \mathcal{R}^{n \times n}.$$

Let M, U_0, V_0 and N be blocks in the expression

$$\begin{bmatrix} M & U_0 \\ N & V_0 \end{bmatrix} := \begin{bmatrix} F \\ C + DF \end{bmatrix} (s \cdot I_n - A - BF)^{-1} \begin{bmatrix} B & -L \end{bmatrix} + \begin{bmatrix} I_m & 0 \\ D & I_p \end{bmatrix}.$$

(i) One has $V_0 \in \mathrm{GL}_p(\mathcal{K})$ and

$$\tilde{V}_0 := -F(s \cdot I_n - A - LC)^{-1}(B + LD) + I_m \in \mathrm{GL}_m(\mathcal{K}).$$

(ii) Let $Q_y \in \mathcal{K}^{m \times p}$ such that $V_0 + NQ_y \in \mathrm{GL}_p(\mathcal{K})$. The choice

$$K := (U_0 + MQ_y)(V_0 + NQ_y)^{-1} \in \mathcal{K}^{m \times p}$$

implies that

$$\begin{bmatrix} I_m & -K \\ -P & I_p \end{bmatrix} \in \mathrm{GL}_{m+p}(\mathcal{K})$$

with its inverse given by

$$H = \begin{bmatrix} H_{11} & H_{12} \\ H_{21} & H_{22} \end{bmatrix} \in \mathcal{K}^{(m+p) \times (m+p)},$$

and where the H_{ij} have explicit representations in terms of A, B, C, F, L, D, Q_y, I_m, I_p, I_n, $(s \cdot I_n - A - BF)^{-1}$ and $(s \cdot I_n - A - LC)^{-1}$.
(iii) If the entries of Q_y are in $\mathcal{R}$, then the same holds for the entries of H.

Proof. (i) We show the invertibility of V_0 and $\tilde{V}_0$. Since $\mathcal{K} = \mathbb{K}(s)$, the matrix

$$s \cdot I_n - A - BF - LC - LDF \in \mathcal{K}^{n \times n}$$

is invertible over the field $\mathcal{K}$. Adding this fact to the other assumptions which describe invertibility, the elimination machine finds representations

$$V_0^{-1} = (C + DF)(s \cdot I_n - A - BF - LC - LDF)^{-1} L + I_p$$

and $\tilde{V}_0^{-1} = -U_0 V_0^{-1} N + M$.

(ii) By choosing the elimination ordering to be `lp` (see SINGULAR [4] user's manual for its description) the elimination machine produces the representation

$$\begin{aligned}
H_{11} = {} & F(s \cdot I_n - A - BF)^{-1} BQ_y C(s \cdot I_n - A - LC)^{-1} B \\
& + F(s \cdot I_n - A - BF)^{-1} BQ_y C(s \cdot I_n - A - LC)^{-1} LD \\
& + Q_y C(s \cdot I_n - A - LC)^{-1} B + F(s \cdot I_n - A - BF)^{-1} BQ_y D \\
& + Q_y C(s \cdot I_n - A - LC)^{-1} LD + Q_y D \\
& - F(s \cdot I_n - A - BF)^{-1} LC(s \cdot I_n - A - LC)^{-1} B \\
& - F(s \cdot I_n - A - BF)^{-1} LC(s \cdot I_n - A - LC)^{-1} LD \\
& - F(s \cdot I_n - A - BF)^{-1} LD + I_m.
\end{aligned}$$

The representations for H_{12}, H_{21} and H_{22} follow in an analogous way, look similar and are therefore omitted.

(iii) Follows from the explicit presentations of H_{ij} in (ii) since all involved matrices have entries in $\mathcal{R}$.

$\square$

Remark 4. Note that the additional assumption in the proof of (i) does not follow from the setup in an obvious way, and has to be inserted manually. On the other hand, this assumption is not required in the proof of (ii) and (iii).

5 Conclusion

We have supplied not only theoretic results but concrete tools for formal verification of algebraic identities. These tools provide an error-free and fast base for mathematicians, engineers and all others who need computer-supported investigation with matrices in their daily work. A collection of known identities can be put in form of an online database, similar to the well-known DLMF, OEIS and DDMF. Our computational tools can be integrated into other projects, like theorem provers.

Acknowledgements. We are grateful to Eva Zerz (Aachen) and Bernd Sturmfels (Leipzig) for fruitful discussions. We also thank Mariia Anapolska and Sven Gross for carefully reading preliminary versions of this article. The authors have been supported by Project II.6 of SFB-TRR 195 "Symbolic Tools in Mathematics and their Applications" of the German Research Foundation (DFG).

References

1. Bergman, G.: The diamond lemma for ring theory. Adv. Math. **29**, 178–218 (1978)
2. Chenavier, C., Hofstadler, C., Raab, C.G., Regensburger, G.: Compatible rewriting of noncommutative polynomials for proving operator identities. https://arxiv.org/abs/2002.03626 (2020)
3. Damm, T., Wimmer, H.K.: A cancellation property of the Moore-Penrose inverse of triple products. J. Aust. Math. Soc. **86**(1), 33–44 (2009)
4. Decker, W., Greuel, G.M., Pfister, G., Schönemann, H.: SINGULAR 4-1-3 – A computer algebra system for polynomial computations (2020). http://www.singular.uni-kl.de
5. Deng, C.Y.: A generalization of the Sherman-Morrison-Woodbury formula. Appl. Math. Lett. **24**(9), 1561–1564 (2011)
6. Grégoire, B., Pottier, L., Théry, L.: Proof certificates for algebra and their application to automatic geometry theorem proving. In: Sturm, T., Zengler, C. (eds.) ADG 2008. LNCS (LNAI), vol. 6301, pp. 42–59. Springer, Heidelberg (2011). https://doi.org/10.1007/978-3-642-21046-4_3
7. Helton, J., Kronewitter, F.: Computer algebra in the control of singularly perturbed dynamical systems (1999). http://math.ucsd.edu/~ncalg/DELL/SingPert/singpertcdc99.pdf

8. Hofstadler, C., Raab, C.G., Regensburger, G.: Certifying operator identities via noncommutative Gröbner bases. ACM Commun. Comput. Algebra **53**, 49–52 (2019)

9. Joswig, M., Fieker, C., Horn, M., et al.: The OSCAR project (2020). https://oscar.computeralgebra.de

10. Kronewitter, F.D.: Using noncommutative Gröbner bases in solving partially prescribed matrix inverse completion problems. Linear Algebra Appl. **338**(1–3), 171–199 (2001)

11. Levandovskyy, V., Abou Zeid, K., Schönemann, H.: SINGULAR: LETTERPLACE – A singular 4-1-3 subsystem for non-commutative finitely presented algebras (2020). http://www.singular.uni-kl.de

12. Mora, T.: Groebner bases in non-commutative algebras. In: Gianni, P. (ed.) ISSAC 1988. LNCS, vol. 358, pp. 150–161. Springer, Heidelberg (1989). https://doi.org/10.1007/3-540-51084-2_14

13. Mora, T.: An introduction to commutative and non-commutative Gröbner bases. Theor. Comput. Sci. **134**, 131–173 (1994)

14. Mora, T.: Solving Polynomial Equation Systems IV: vol. 4. Buchberger Theory and Beyond. Cambridge University Press, Cambridge (2016)

15. Pritchard, F.L.: The ideal membership problem in non-commutative polynomial rings. J. Symb. Comput. **22**(1), 27–48 (1996)

16. Raab, C.G., Regensburger, G., Poor, J.H.: Formal proofs of operator identities by a single formal computation. https://arxiv.org/abs/1910.06165 (2019)

17. Stein, W., et al.: Sage Mathematics Software. The Sage Development Team (2020)

18. Wavrik, J.J.: Rewrite rules and simplification of matrix expressions. Comput. Sci. J. Moldova **4**(3), 360–398 (1996)

19. Youla, D.C., Jabr, H.A., Bongiorno, J.J.: Modern Wiener-Hopf design of optimal controllers. II: the multivariable case. IEEE Trans. Autom. Control **21** 319–338 (1976)

20. Zhou, K., Doyle, J.C., Glover, K.: Robust and Optimal Control. Prentice Hall, Upper Saddle River (1996)

AutoMSC: Automatic Assignment of Mathematics Subject Classification Labels

Moritz Schubotz[1,2(✉)], Philipp Scharpf[3], Olaf Teschke[1], Andreas Kühnemund[1],
Corinna Breitinger[2,3], and Bela Gipp[2,3]

[1] FIZ-Karlsruhe, Berlin, Germany
{moritz.schubotz,olaf.teschke,andreas.kuhnemund}@fiz-karlsruhe.de
[2] Bergische Universität Wuppertal, Wuppertal, Germany
{schubotz,breitinger,gipp}@uni-wuppertal.de
[3] University of Konstanz, Konstanz, Germany
{philipp.scharpf,corinna.breitinger,bela.gipp}@uni-konstanz.de

Abstract. Authors of research papers in the fields of mathematics, and other math-heavy disciplines commonly employ the Mathematics Subject Classification (MSC) scheme to search for relevant literature. The MSC is a hierarchical alphanumerical classification scheme that allows librarians to specify one or multiple codes for publications. Digital Libraries in Mathematics, as well as reviewing services, such as zbMATH and Mathematical Reviews (MR) rely on these MSC labels in their workflows to organize the abstracting and reviewing process. Especially, the coarse-grained classification determines the subject editor who is responsible for the actual reviewing process.

In this paper, we investigate the feasibility of automatically assigning a coarse-grained primary classification using the MSC scheme, by regarding the problem as a multi class classification machine learning task. We find that the our method achieves an F_1-score of over 77%, which is remarkably close to the agreement of zbMATH and MR (F_1-score of 81%). Moreover, we find that the method's confidence score allows for reducing the effort by 86% compared to the manual coarse-grained classification effort while maintaining a precision of 81% for automatically classified articles.

Keywords: Document classification · Applications of machine learning · Mathematical Subject Classification · Digital mathematical libraries · Mathematical information retrieval

1 Introduction

zbMATH[1] has classified more than 135k articles in 2019 using the Mathematics Subject Classification (MSC) scheme [6]. With more than 6,600 MSC codes, this classification task requires significant in-depth knowledge of various sub-fields of

---

[1] https://zbmath.org/.

© Springer Nature Switzerland AG 2020
C. Benzmüller and B. Miller (Eds.): CICM 2020, LNAI 12236, pp. 237–250, 2020.
https://doi.org/10.1007/978-3-030-53518-6_15

mathematics to determine the fitting MSC codes for each article. In summary, the classification procedure of zbMATH and MR is two-fold. First, all articles are pre-classified into one of 63 primary subjects spanning from general topics in mathematics (00), to integral equations (45), to mathematics education (97). In a second step, subject editors assign fine-grained MSC codes in their area of expertise, i.a. with the aim to match potential reviewers.

The automated assignments of MSC labels has been analyzed by Rehurek and Sojka [9] in 2008 on the DML-CZ [13] and NUMDAM [3] full-text corpus. They report a micro-averaged F_1 score of 81% for their public corpus. In 2013 Barthel, Tönnies, and Balke performed automated subject classification for parts of the zbMATH corpus [2]. They criticized the micro averaged F_1 measure, especially, if the average is applied only to the best performing classes. However, they report a micro-averaged F_1 score of 67.1% for the zbMATH corpus. They suggested training classifiers for a precision of 95% and assigning MSC class labels in a semi-automated recommendation setup. Moreover, they suggested to measure the human baseline (inter-annotator agreement) for the classification tasks. Moreover, they found that the combination of mathematical expressions and textual features improves the F_1 score for certain MSC classes substantially. In 2014, Schöneberg and Sperber [11] implement a method that combined formulae and text using an adapted Part of Speech Tagging approach. Their paper reported a sufficient precision of >.75, however, it did not state the recall. The proposed method was implemented and is currently being used especially to pre-classify general journals [7] with additional information, like references. For a majority of journals, coarse- and fine-grained codes can be found by statistically analyzing the MSC codes from referenced documents matched within the zbMATH corpus. The editor of zbMATH hypothesizes that the reference method outperforms the algorithm developed by Schöneberg and Sperber. To confirm or reject this hypothesis was one motivation for this project.

The positive effect of mathematical features is confirmed by Suzuki and Fujii [15], who measured the classification performance based on an arXiv and mathoverflow dataset. In contrast, Scharpf et al. [10] could not measure a significant improvement of classification accuracy for the arxiv dataset when incorporating mathematical identifiers. In their experiments Scharpf et al. evaluated numerous machine learning methods, which extended [4,14] in terms of accuracy and run-time performance, and found that complex compute-intensive neural networks do not significantly improve the classification performance.

In this paper, we focus on the coarse-grained classification of the *primary MSC subject number* (pMSCn) and explore how current machine learning approaches can be employed to automate this process. In particular, we compare the current state of the art technology [10] with a part of speech (POS) preprocessing based system customized for the application in zbMATH from 2014 [11].

We define the following research questions:

1. Which evaluation metrics are most useful to assess the classifications?
2. Do mathematical formulae as part of the text improve the classifications?
3. Does POS preprocessing [11] improve the accuracy of classifications?
4. Which features are most important for accurate classification?
5. How well do automated methods perform in comparison to a human baseline?

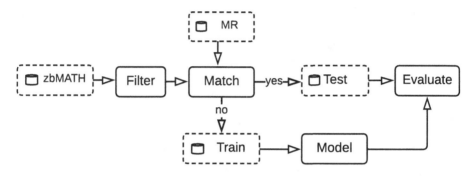

Fig. 1. Workflow overview.

2 Method

To investigate the given set of problems, we first created test and training datasets. We then investigated the different pMSCn encodings, trained our models and evaluated the results, cf Fig. 1.

2.1 Generation of a Test and Training Dataset

Filter Current High Quality Articles: The zbMATH database has assigned MSC codes to more than 3.6 M articles. However, the way in which mathematical articles are written has changed over the last century, and the classification of historic articles is not something we aim to investigate in this article. The first MSC was created in 1990, and has since been updated every ten years (2000, 2010, and 2020) [5]. With each update, automated rewrite rules are applied to map the codes from the old MSC to the next MSC version, which is connected with a loss of accuracy of the class labels. To obtain a coherent and high quality dataset for training and testing, we focused on the more recent articles from 2000 to 2019, which were classified using the MCS version 2010, and we only considered selected journals[2]. Additionally, we restricted our selection to English articles and limited ourselves to abstracts rather than reviews of articles. To be able to compare methods that are based on references and methods using text and title, we only selected articles with at least one reference that could be matched to another article. In addition, we excluded articles that were not yet published and processed. The list of articles is available from our website: https://automsceval.formulasearchengine.com.

Splitting to Test and Training Set: After applying the filter criteria as mentioned above, we split the resulting list of 442,382 articles into test and training sets. For the test set, we aimed to measure the bias of our zbMATH classification labels. Therefore, we used the articles for which we knew the classification labels by the MR service as the training set from a previous research project [1]. The resulting test set consisted of $n = 32,230$ articles, and the training set contained 410,152 articles. To ensure that this selection did not introduce additional bias, we also computed the standard ten-fold cross validation, cf. Sect. 3.

Definition of Article Data Format: To allow for reproducibility, we created a dedicated dataset from our article selection, which we aim to share with other researchers. However, currently, legal restrictions apply and the dataset can not yet be provided for anonymous download at this date. However, we can grant access for research purposes as done in the past [2]. Each of the 442,382 articles in the dataset contained the following fields:

de. An eight-digit ID of the document[3].
labels. The actual MSC codes (see Footnote 3).
title. The English title of the document, with LaTeX macros for mathematical language [12].
text. The text of the abstract with LaTeX macros.
mscs. A comma separated list of MSC codes generated from the references.

These 5 fields were provided as CSV files to the algorithms. The `mscs` field was generated as follows: For each reference in the document, we looked up the MSC codes of the reference. For example, if a certain document contained the references A, B, C that are also in the documents in zbMATH and the MSC codes of A, B, C are a_1 and a_2, b_1, and $c_1 - c_3$, respectively, then the field `mscs` will read $a_1 a_2, b_1, c_1 c_2 c_3$.

After training, we required each of our tested algorithms to return the following fields in CSV format for the test sets:

de (integer). Eight-digit ID of the document.
method (char(5)). Five-letter ID of the run.
pos (integer). Position in the result list.

---

[2] The list of selected journals is available from https://zbmath.org/?q=dt%3Aj+st %3Aj+py%3A2000-2019.
[3] The fields `de` and `labels` must not be used as input to the classification algorithm.

coarse (integer). Coarse-grained MSC subject number.
fine (char(5), optional). Fine-grained MSC code.
score (numeric, optional). Self-confidence of the algorithm about the result.

We ensured that the fields de, method and pos form a primary key, i.e., no two entries in the result can have the same combination of values. Note that for the current multi-class classification problem, pos is always 1, since only the primary MSC subject number is considered.

2.2   Definition of Evaluation Metrics

While the assignment of all MSC codes to each article is a multi-label classification task, the assignment of the primary MSC subject, which we investigate in this paper, is only a multi-class classification problem. With $k = 63$ classes, the probability of randomly choosing the correct class of size c_i is rather low $P_i = \frac{c_i}{n}$. Moreover, the dataset is not balanced. In particular, the entropy $H = -\sum_{i=1}^{k} P_i \log P_i$, can be used to measure the imbalance $\widehat{H} = \frac{H}{\log k}$ by normalizing it to the maximum entropy $\log k$.

To take into account the imbalance of the dataset, we used weighted versions of precision p, recall r, and the F_1 measure f. In particular, the precision $p = \frac{\sum_{i=1}^{k} c_i p_i}{n}$ with the class precision p_i. r and F_1 are defined analogously.

In the test set, no entries for the pMSCn 97 (Mathematics education) were included, thus

$$\widehat{H} = \frac{H}{\log k} = \frac{3.44}{\log 62} = .83$$

Moreover, we eliminate the effect of classes with only few samples by disregarding all classes with less than 200 entries. While pMSCn with few samples have little effect on the average metrics, the individual values are distracting in plots and data tables. Choosing 200 as the minimum evaluation class size reduces the number of effective classes to $k = 37$, which only has a minor effect on the normalized entropy as it is raised to $\widehat{H} = .85$. The chosen value of 200 can be interactively adjusted in the dynamic result figures we made available online[4]. Additionally, the individual values for P_i that were used to calculate H are given in the column p in the table on that page. As one can experience in the online version of the figures, the impact on the choice of the minimum class size is insignificant.

2.3   Selection of Methods to Evaluate

In this paper, we compare 12 different methods for (automatically) determining the primary MSC subject in the test dataset:

zb1 Reference MSC subject numbers from zbMATH.

---

[4] https://autoMSCeval.formulasearchengine.com.

mr1 Reference MSC subject numbers from MR.

titer According to recent research performed on the arXiv dataset [10], we chose a machine learning method with a good trade-off between speed and performance. We combined the `title`, abstract `text`, and reference `mscs` of the articles via string concatenation. We encoded these string sources using the *TfidfVectorizer* of the Scikit-learn[5] python package. We did not alter the *utf-8* encoding, and did not perform accent striping, or other character normalization methods, with the exception of lower-casing. Furthermore, we used the *word* analyzer without a custom stop word list, selecting tokens of two or more alphanumeric characters, processing unigrams, and ignoring punctuation. The resulting vectors consisted of float64 entries with *l2* norm unit output rows. This data was passed to Our encoder. The encoder was trained on the training set to subsequently transform or vectorize the sources from the test set. We chose a lightweight *LogisticRegression* classifier from the python package Scikit-learn. We employed the *l2* penalty norm with a 10^{-4} tolerance stopping criterion and a 1.0 regularization. Furthermore, we allowed intercept constant addition and scaling, but no class weight or custom random state seed. We fitted the classifier using the *lbfgs* (Limited-memory BFGS) solver for 100 convergence iterations. These choices were made based on a previous study in which we clustered arXiv articles.

refs Same as `titer`, but using only the `mscs` as input[6].

titls Same as `titer`, but using only the `title` as input (see Footnote 6).

texts Same as `titer`, but using only the `text` as input (see Footnote 6).

tite Same as `titer`, but without using the `mscs` as input (see Footnote 6).

tiref : Same as `titer`, but without using the abstract `text` as input (see Footnote 6).

teref : Same as `titer`, but without using the `title` as input (see Footnote 6).

ref1 We used a simple SQL script to suggest the most frequent primary MSC subject based on the `mscs` input. This method is currently used in production to estimate the primary MSC subject.

uT1 We adjusted the JAVA program posLingue [11] to read from the new training and test sets. However, we did not perform a new training and instead reused the model that was trained in 2014. However, for this run, we removed all mathematical formulae from the `title` and the abstract `text` to generate a baseline.

uM1 The same as uT1 but in this instance, we included the formulae. We slightly adjusted the formula detection mechanism, since the way in which formulae are written in zbMATH had changed [12]. This method is currently used in production for articles that do not have references with resolvable `mscs`.

3 Evaluation and Discussion

After executing each of the methods described in the previous section, we calculated the precision p, recall r, and F_1 score f for each method, cf. Table 1.

---

[5] https://swmath.org/software/8058 [8].

[6] Each of these sources was encoded and classified separately.

Overall, we find that results are similar whether we used zbMATH or MR as a baseline in our evaluation. Therefore, we will use zbMATH as the reference for the remainder of the paper. All data, including the test results using MR as the baseline is available from: https://automsceval.formulasearchengine.com.

Table 1. Precision p, recall r and F_1-measure f with regard to the baseline zb1 (left) and mr1 (right).

	p	r	f		p	r	f
zb1	1	1	1	zb1	0.817	0.807	0.81
mr1	0.814	0.814	0.812	mr1	1	1	1
titer	0.772	0.778	0.773	titer	0.776	0.775	0.772
refs	0.748	0.753	0.746	refs	0.743	0.743	0.737
titls	0.637	0.627	0.623	titls	0.644	0.632	0.627
texts	0.699	0.709	0.699	texts	0.704	0.709	0.699
refl	0.693	0.648	0.652	refl	0.693	0.646	0.652
uT1	0.656	0.642	0.645	uT1	0.653	0.636	0.639
uM1	0.655	0.639	0.644	uM1	0.652	0.632	0.636
tiref	0.76	0.764	0.76	tiref	0.762	0.761	0.758
teref	0.769	0.774	0.77	teref	0.771	0.77	0.767
tite	0.713	0.722	0.713	tite	0.72	0.724	0.715

Effect of Mathematical Expressions and Part-of-Speech Tags: By filtering out all mathematical expressions in the current production method uT1 in contrast to uM1 we could receive information on the impact of mathematical expressions on classification quality. We found that the overall F_1 score without mathematical expressions $f_{uT1} = 64.5\%$ is slightly higher than the score with mathematical expressions $f_{uM1} = 64.4\%$. Here, the main effect is an increase in recall from 63.9% to 64.2%. Additionally, a class-wise investigation showed that for most classes, uT1 outperformed uM1, cf. Fig. 2. Exceptions are pMSCn 46 (Functional analysis) and 17 (Nonassociative rings and algebras) where the inclusion of math tags raised the F_1-score slightly.

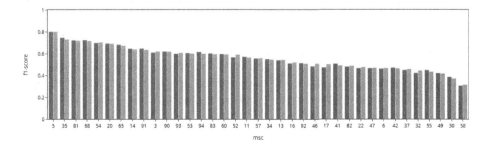

Fig. 2. Mathematical symbols in title and abstract text do not improve the classification quality. Method uT1 = left bar; method uM1 = right bar

We evaluated the effect of *part of speech tagging* (POS), by comparing `tite` with `uM1`. $f_{\text{tite}} = .713$ clearly outperformed $f_{uM1} = .64$. This held true for all MSC subjects, cf. Fig. 3. We modified posLingo to output the POS tagged text and used this text as input and retrained scikit learn classifier `tite2`. However, this method did not lead to better results than `tite`.

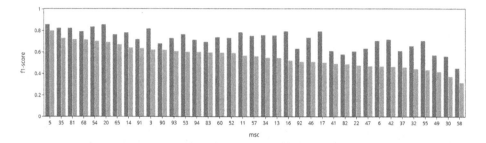

Fig. 3. Part-of-speech tagging for mathematics does not improve the classification quality. Method `uM1` = left bar, method `tite` = right bar.

Effect of Features and Human Baseline: The newly developed method combined method [10] works best in a combined approach that uses `title`, abstract `text`, and references `titer` $f_{\text{titer}} = 77.3\%$. This method performs significantly better than methods that omit either one of these features. The best performing single feature method was `refs` $f_{\text{refs}} = 74.6\%$) followed by `text` $f_{\text{text}} = 69.9\%$ and `titls` $f_{\text{titls}} = 62.3\%$. Thus, automatically generating the MSC subject while including the references appears to be a very valuable strategy. This becomes evident also when comparing the scores of approaches that only considered two features. For the approaches that excluded `title` (i.e. `teref` $f_{\text{text}} = 77\%$) or abstract `text` (i.e. `tiref` $f_{\text{text}} = 76\%$), the performance remained notably higher than when the approach excluded the reference `mscs` (`tite` $f_{\text{text}} = 71.3\%$) However, it is also worth pointing out that the naive reference-based method, `ref1` $f_{\text{text}} = 65.2\%$, which is currently being used in production still performs more poorly than just using `tite` despite this approach ignoring references. In conclusion, we can say that training a machine learning algorithm that weights all information from the fine grained MSC codes is clearly better than the majority vote of the references, cf. Fig. 4.

Even the best performing machine learning algorithm, `titer` with $f_{\text{titer}} = 77.3\%$, is worth than using the classification by human experts from MR, the other mathematics publication reviewing service, resulted in a baseline of `mr1` $f_{mr1} = 81.2\%$. However, there is no foundation that could allow us to determine which of the primary MSC subjects, either from MR or zbMATH, are truly correct. Assigning a two-digit label to mathematical research papers – which often cover overlapping themes and topics within mathematics – remains a challenge even to humans, who struggle to conclusively label publications as belonging

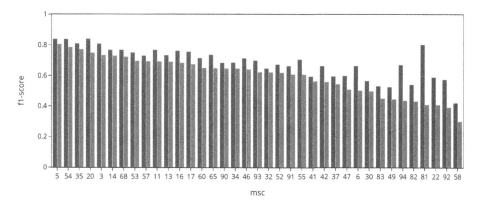

Fig. 4. Machine learning method (`refs`, left) clearly outperforms current production (`ref1`, right) method using references as only source for classification.

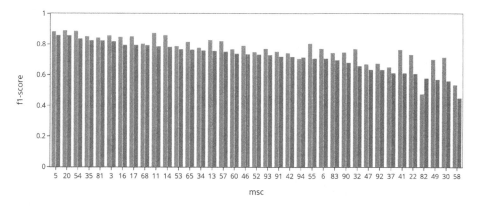

Fig. 5. For many pMSCn the best automatic method (`titer`, right) gets close to the performance of the human baseline (`mr1` left)

to only a single class. While for some classes, expert agreement is very high, e.g. for class 20 agreement is 89.1%, for other classes, such as 82, agreement is only at 47.6% regarding the F_1 score, cf., Fig. 5. These discrepancies reflect the intrinsic problem that mathematics cannot be fully reflected by a hierarchical system. The differences in classifications made among the two reviewing services are likely also a reflection of emphasizing different facets of evolving research, which often derive from differences in the reviewing culture.

We also investigated the bias introduced by the non-random selection of the training set. Performing ten fold cross validation on the entire dataset yielded an accuracy of $f_{titer,10} = .776$ with a standard deviation $\sigma_{titer,10} = .002$. Thus, test set selection does not introduce a significant bias.

After having discussed the strengths and weaknesses of the individual methods tested, we now discuss how the currently best-performing method, `titer`, can be improved. One standard tool to analyze misclassifications is a confusion

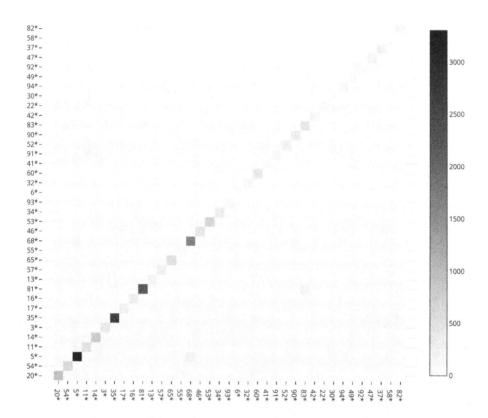

Fig. 6. Confusion matrix `titer`

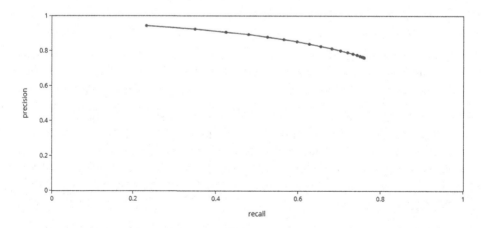

Fig. 7. Precision recall curve `titer`.

matrix, cf., Fig. 6. In this matrix, off-diagonal elements of the matrix indicate that two sets of classes are often mixed by the classification algorithm. The x axis shows the true labels, while the y axis shows the predicted labels. The most frequent error of *titer* was that 68 (Computer science) was classified as 5 (Combinatorics). Moreover, 81 (Quantum theory) and 83 (Relativity and gravitational theory) were often mixed up.

However, in general the number of misclassifications were small and there was no immediate action that one could take to avoid special cases of misclassification that do not involve a human expert.

Since `titer` outperforms both the text-based and reference based methods currently used in zbMATH, we decided to develop a restful API that wraps our trained model into a service. We use pythons fastAPI under unicorn to handle higher loads. Our system is available as a docker container and can thus be scaled on demand. To simplify development and testing, we provide a static HTML page as a micro UI, which we call *AutoMSC*. This UI displays not only lists/suggests the most likely primary MSC subjects but also the less likely MSC subjects. We expect that our UI can support human experts, especially whenever the most likely MSC subject seems unsuitable. The result is displayed as a pie-chart, cf., Fig. 8 from https://automscbackend.formulasearchengine.com. To use the system in practice, an interface to the citation matching component of zbMATH would be desired to paste the actual references rather than the MSC subjects extracted from the references. Moreover, looking at the precision-recall curve (Fig. 7) for `titer`, suggests that one can also select a threshold for falling back to manual classification. For instance, if one requires a precision that is as high as the precision of the other human classifications by MR, one would need to only consider suggestions with a score >0.5. This would automatically classify 86.2% of the 135k articles being annually classified by subject experts at zbMATH/MR and thus significantly reduce the number of articles that humans must manually examine without a loss of classification quality. This is something we might develop in the future.

4   Conclusion and Future Work

Returning to our research questions, we summarize our findings as follows: First, we asked which metrics are best suited to assess classification quality. We demonstrated that the classification quality for the primary MSC subject can be evaluated with classical information retrieval methods such as precision, recall and F_1-score. We share the observation Barthel, Tönnies, and Balke [2] that the averages do not reflect the performance of outliers, cf. Fig. 1, 2, 3 and 4. However, for our methods the difference between the best and worst performing class was significantly smaller than reported by [2].

Second, we wanted to find out whether taking into account the mathematical formulae contained in publications could improve the accuracy of classifications. In accordance with [10], we did not find evidence that mathematical expressions improved pMSCn classification. However, we did not evaluate advanced encodings of mathematical formulae. This is will be a subject of future work, cf. Fig. 1.

Third we evaluated the effect of POS-preprocessing [11] and found that modern machine learning methods do not benefit from the POS tagging based model developed by [11], cf. Fig. 2.

Fourth we evaluated which features are most important for an accurate classification. We conclude that references have the highest prediction power, followed by the abstract text and title.

Finally, we evaluated the performance of automatic methods in comparison to a human baseline. We found that our best performing method has an F_1 score of 77.2%. The manual classification is significantly better for most classes, cf. Fig. 4. However, the self-reported `score` can be used to reduce the manual classification effort by 86.2%, without a loss in classification quality.

In the future, we plan to extend our automated methods to predict full MSC codes. Moreover, we would like to be able to assign pMSCn to document sections, since we realize that some research just does not fit into one of the classes. We also plan to extend the application domain to other mathematical research artifacts, such as blog posts, software, or dataset descriptions. As a next step, we plan to generate pMSCn from authors using the same methods we applied for references. We speculate that authors will have a high impact on the classification, since authors often publish in the same field. For this purpose, we are leveraging our prior research on affiliation disambiguation, which could be used as fallback method for junior authors, who have not yet established a track record. Another extension is a better combination of the different features. Especially when performing research on the full MSC code-generation, we will need to use a different encoding for the MSC from references and authors. However, this new encoding requires more main memory for the training of the model and cannot be done on a standard laptop. Thereafter, we will re-investigate the impact of mathematical formulae since the inherently combined representation of text and formulae was not successful.

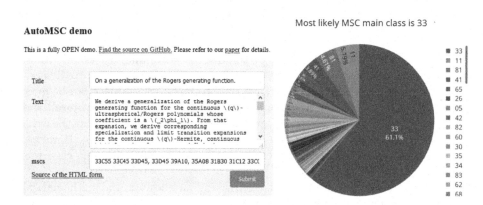

Fig. 8. Classification frontend

Our work represents a further step in the automation of Mathematics Subject Classification and can thus support reviewing services, such as *zbMATH* or *Mathematical Reviews*. For accessible exploration, we have made the best-performing approaches available in our *AutoMSC* implementation and have shared our code on our website. We envision that other application domains requiring an accurate labeling of publications into their respective Mathematics Subject Classification, for example, research paper recommendation systems, or reviewer recommendation systems, will also be able to benefit from this work. AutoMSC delivers comparable results to human experts in the first stage of MSC labeling, all without requiring manual labor or trained experts. In the future, zbMATH will use our new method for all journals that used to employ the method by Schöneberg and Sperber [11] introduced in 2014.

Acknowledgments. This work was supported by the German Research Foundation (DFG grant GI 1259-1). The authors would like to express their gratitude to Felix Hamborg, and Terry Ruas for their advice in the most recent machine learning technology.

References

1. Bannister, A., et al.: Editorial: on the road to MSC 2020. EMS Newslett. **2018**–**6**(108), 3–4 (2018). https://doi.org/10.4171/news/108/1
2. Barthel, S., Tönnies, S., Balke, W.-T.: Large-scale experiments for mathematical document classification. In: Urs, S.R., Na, J.-C., Buchanan, G. (eds.) ICADL 2013. LNCS, vol. 8279, pp. 83–92. Springer, Cham (2013). https://doi.org/10.1007/978-3-319-03599-4_10
3. Bouche, T., Labbe, O.: The new numdam platform. In: Geuvers, H., England, M., Hasan, O., Rabe, F., Teschke, O. (eds.) CICM 2017. LNCS (LNAI), vol. 10383, pp. 70–82. Springer, Cham (2017). https://doi.org/10.1007/978-3-319-62075-6_6
4. Evans, I.: Semi-supervised topic models applied to mathematical document classification. Ph.D. thesis, University of Bath, Somerset, UK (2017)
5. Ion, P., Sperber, W.: MSC 2010 in SKOS – the transition of the MSC to the semantic web. Eur. Math. Soc. Newsl. **84**(2012), 55–57 (2010)
6. Kühnemund, A.: The role of applications within the reviewing service zbMATH. PAMM **16**(1), 961–962 (2016). https://doi.org/10.1002/pamm.201610459
7. Mihaljević-Brandt, H., Teschke, O.: "Journal profiles and beyond: what makes a mathematics journal "general"?" English. Eur. Math. Soc. Newsl. **91**, 55–56 (2014)
8. Pedregosa, F., et al.: "Scikit-learn: machine learning in Python". English. J. Mach. Learn. Res. **12**, 2825–2830 (2011)
9. Řehůřek, R., Sojka, P.: Automated classification and categorization of mathematical knowledge. In: Autexier, S., Campbell, J., Rubio, J., Sorge, V., Suzuki, M., Wiedijk, F. (eds.) CICM 2008. LNCS (LNAI), vol. 5144, pp. 543–557. Springer, Heidelberg (2008). https://doi.org/10.1007/978-3-540-85110-3_44
10. Scharpf, P., et al.: Classification and clustering of arXiv documents, sections, and abstracts comparing encodings of natural and mathematical language. In: Proceedings of ACM/IEEE JCDL (2020)

11. Schöneberg, U., Sperber, W.: POS tagging and its applications for mathematics -Text Analysis in Mathematics. In: Watt, S.M., Davenport, J.H., Sexton, A.P., Sojka, P., Urban, J. (eds.) CICM 2014. LNCS (LNAI), vol. 8543, pp. 213–223. Springer, Cham (2014). https://doi.org/10.1007/978-3-319-08434-3_16
12. Schubotz, M., Teschke, O.: "Four decades of TeX at zbMATH". English. Eur. Math. Soc. Newslett. **112**, 50–52 (2019)
13. Sojka, P., Rehurek, R.: Classification of multilingual mathematical papers in DML-CZ. In: Proceedings of the 1st Workshop on Recent Advances in Slavonic Natural Languages Processing, RASLAN 2007, pp. 89–96. Masaryk University (2007)
14. Sojka, P., et al.: Quo vadis, math information retrieval. In: Horák, A., Rychlý, P., Rambousek, A., Tribun, E.U. (eds.) The 13th Workshop on Recent Advances in Slavonic Natural Languages Processing, RASLAN 2019, Karlova Studanka, Czech Republic, 6–8 December 2019, pp. 117–128 (2019)
15. Suzuki, T., Fujii, A.: Mathematical document categorization with structure of mathematical expressions. In: 2017 ACM/IEEE Joint Conference on Digital Libraries, JCDL 2017, Toronto, ON, Canada, 19-23 June 2017, pp. 119–128. IEEE Computer Society (2017). https://doi.org/10.1109/JCDL.2017.7991566

Maintaining a Library of Formal Mathematics

Floris van Doorn[1] , Gabriel Ebner[2] , and Robert Y. Lewis[2(✉)]

[1] University of Pittsburgh, Pittsburgh, PA 15260, USA
fpvdoorn@gmail.com
[2] Vrije Universiteit Amsterdam, 1081 HV Amsterdam, The Netherlands
gebner@gebner.org, r.y.lewis@vu.nl

Abstract. The Lean mathematical library mathlib is developed by a community of users with very different backgrounds and levels of experience. To lower the barrier of entry for contributors and to lessen the burden of reviewing contributions, we have developed a number of tools for the library which check proof developments for subtle mistakes in the code and generate documentation suited for our varied audience.

Keywords: Formal mathematics · Library development · Linting

1 Introduction

As a tool for managing mathematical knowledge, a proof assistant offers many assurances. Once a result has been formalized, readers can confidently believe that the relevant definitions are fully specified, the theorem is stated correctly, and there are no logical gaps in the proof. A body of mathematical knowledge, represented by formal definitions and proofs in a single theorem proving environment, can be trusted to be coherent.

Logical coherence, however, is only one of many properties that one could wish of a mathematical corpus. The ideal corpus can be modified, extended, and queried by users who do not have expert knowledge of the entire corpus or the underlying system. Proof assistant libraries do not always fare so well in this respect. Most of the large mathematical libraries in existence are maintained by expert users with a significant time cost. While external contributions are easily checked for logical consistency, it typically takes manual review to check that contributions cohere with the system in other ways—e.g., that lemmas are correctly marked for use with a simplification tactic. It can be difficult or impossible for outsiders to understand the library well enough to contribute themselves.

The first author is supported by the Sloan Foundation (grant G-2018-10067). The second and third authors receive support from the European Research Council (ERC) under the European Union's Horizon 2020 research and innovation program (grant agreement No. 713999, Matryoshka) and from the Dutch Research Council (NWO) under the Vidi program (project No. 016.Vidi.189.037, Lean Forward).

© Springer Nature Switzerland AG 2020
C. Benzmüller and B. Miller (Eds.): CICM 2020, LNAI 12236, pp. 251–267, 2020.
https://doi.org/10.1007/978-3-030-53518-6_16

The mathlib library [15] is a corpus of formal mathematics, programming, and tactics in the Lean proof assistant [16] that is managed and cultivated by a community of users. The community encourages contributions from novice users, and the rapid growth of the library has threatened to overwhelm its appointed maintainers. The maintenance difficulty is compounded by the library's extensive use of type classes and context-dependent tactics. Misuse of these features is not always easy to spot, but can lead to headaches in later developments.

To ease the burdens on new users and maintainers alike, we have incorporated into mathlib tools for checking meta-logical properties of declarations and collecting, generating, and displaying documentation in an accessible way. The use of these tools has already had a large impact on the community. We aim here to explain the goals and design principles of these tools. While some details are specific to Lean and mathlib, we believe that these considerations apply broadly to libraries of formal mathematical knowledge.

2   Lean and mathlib

Lean offers a powerful metaprogramming framework that allows Lean programs to access the system's syntax and core components [8]. All of the linting tools described in Sect. 3 are implemented in Lean, without the need for external plugins or dependencies. They are distributed as part of the mathlib library.

Lean metaprograms are frequently used to implement *tactics*, which transform the proof state of a declaration in progress. They can also implement top-level *commands*, which interact with an environment outside the context of a proof. Examples include #find, which searches for declarations matching a pattern, and mk_simp_attribute, which defines a new collection of simplification lemmas. *Transient* commands like #find, which do not modify the environment, customarily start with #. Tactics and commands interact with the Lean environment and proof state through the tactic monad, which handles side effects and failure conditions in a purely functional way. Finally, Lean supports tagging declarations with *attributes* as a way to store metadata. Within the tactic monad, metaprograms can access the list of declarations tagged with a certain attribute.

The mathlib project is run by a community of users and encourages contributions from people with various backgrounds. The community includes many domain experts, people with expert knowledge of the mathematics being formalized but who are less familiar with the intricacies of the proof assistant. Linting and documentation are useful for every user of every programming language, but are especially helpful for such domain experts, since they often work on deep and intricate implementations without a broad view of the library.

An example of this is seen in mathlib's *structure hierarchy* [15, Sect. 4]. The library extensively uses type classes to allow definitions and proofs to be stated at the appropriate level of generality without duplication. Type classes are a powerful tool, but seemingly innocent anti-patterns in their use can lead to unstable and unusable developments. Even experienced users find it difficult to avoid these patterns, and they easily slip through manual code review.

The mathlib library and community are growing at a fast pace. As of May 15, 2020, the library contains over 170,000 lines of non-whitespace, non-comment code, representing a 25% increase over five months, and 42,000 declarations, excluding internal and automatically generated ones, a 23% increase. Contributions have been made by 85 people, a 16% increase over the same time period. 264 commits were made to the mathlib git repository in April 2020; while a small number were automatically generated, each commit typically corresponds to a single approved pull request. We display more statistics about the project's growth on the community website.[1] The library covers a wide range of subject matter, enough to serve as a base for numerous projects that have formalized complex and recent mathematical topics [5, 7, 11].

3   Semantic Linting

Static program analysis, the act of analyzing computer code without running the code, is widely used in many programming languages. An example of this is *linting*, where source code is analyzed to flag faulty or suspicious code. Linters warn the user about various issues, such as syntax errors, the use of undeclared variables, calls to deprecated functions, spacing and formatting conventions, and dangerous language features.

In typed languages like Lean, some of these errors are caught by the elaborator or type checker. The system will raise an error if a proof or program has a different type than the declared type or if a variable is used that has not been introduced. However, other problems can still be present in developments that have been accepted by Lean. It is also possible that there are problems with the metadata of a declaration, such as its attributes or documentation. These mistakes are often not obvious at the time of writing a declaration, but will manifest at a later time. For example, an instance might be declared that will never fire, or is likely to cause the type class inference procedure to loop.

We have implemented a package of semantic linters in mathlib to flag these kinds of mistakes. These linters are *semantic* in the sense that they take as input a fully elaborated declaration and its metadata. This is in contrast to a *syntactic* linter, which takes as input the source code as plain text. The use of semantic linters allows us to automatically check for many commonly made mistakes, using the abstract syntax tree (the elaborated term in Lean's type theory) for the type or value of a declaration. Syntactic linters would allow for testing of e.g. the formatting of the source code, but would not help with many of the tests we want to perform.

The linters can be used to check one particular file or all files in mathlib. Running the command `#lint` at any point in a file prints all the linter errors up to that line. The command `#lint_mathlib` tests all imported declarations in mathlib. Occasionally a declaration may be permitted to fail a lint test, for example, if it takes an unused argument to satisfy a more general interface. Such lemmas are tagged with the attribute `@[nolint]`, which takes a list of tests that

---

```
/-- Reports definitions and constants that are missing doc strings -/
meta def doc_blame_report_defn : declaration → tactic (option string)
| (declaration.defn n _ _ _ _ _) := doc_string n >> return none <|>
    return "def missing doc string"
| (declaration.cnst n _ _ _) := doc_string n >> return none <|> return
    "constant missing doc string"
| _ := return none

/-- A linter for checking definition doc strings -/
@[linter, priority 1450] meta def linter.doc_blame : linter :=
{ test := λ d, mcond (bnot <$> has_attribute' `instance d.to_name)
    (doc_blame_report_defn d) (return none),
  no_errors_found := "No definitions are missing documentation.",
  errors_found := "DEFINITIONS ARE MISSING DOCUMENTATION STRINGS" }
```

Fig. 1. A linter that tests whether a declaration has a documentation string.

the declaration is allowed to fail. The continuous integration (CI) workflow of mathlib automatically runs the linters on all of mathlib for every pull request made to the library.

For some of the mistakes detected by our linters, it is reasonable to ask whether they should even be allowed by the system in the first place. The core Lean tool aims to be small, permissive, and customizable; enforcing our linter rules at the system level would cut against this philosophy. Projects other than mathlib may choose to follow different conventions, or may be small enough to ignore problems that hinder scalability. Stricter rules, of course, can create obstacles to finishing a project. By incorporating our checks into our library instead of the core Lean system, we make them available to all projects that depend on mathlib without forcing users to comply with them.

3.1 Linter Interface

A linter is a wrapper around a metaprogram with type `declaration → tactic (option string)`. Given an input declaration d, the test function returns `none` if d passes the test and `some error_msg` if it fails. These test functions work within the `tactic` monad in order to access the elaborator and environment, although some are purely functional and none modify the environment. The type `linter` bundles such a test function with formatting strings.

The package of linters is easily extended: a user simply defines and tags a declaration of type `linter`. In Fig. 1 one sees the full definition of the `doc_blame` linter, described in Sect. 3.2.

We have focused on implementing these linters with actionable warning messages. Since the errors they detect are often subtle and can seem mysterious to novice users, we try to report as clearly as possible what should change in a declaration in order to fix the warning.

3.2   Simple Linters

A first selection of mathlib linters checks for simple mistakes commonly made when declaring definition and theorems.

Duplicated Namespaces. Declaration names in Lean are hierarchical, and it is typical to build an interface for a declaration in its corresponding namespace. For example, functions about the type list have names such as list.reverse and list.sort. Lean's namespace sectioning command inserts these prefixes automatically. However, users often write a lemma with a full name and then copy it inside the namespace. This creates identifiers like list.list.reverse; it can be difficult to notice the duplication without careful review. The dup_namespace linter flags declarations whose names contain repeated components.

Definitions vs. Theorems. Lean has separate declaration kinds for definitions and theorems. The subtle differences relate to byte code generation and parallel elaboration. It is nearly always the case that a declaration should be declared as a theorem if and only if its type is a proposition. Because there are rare exceptions to this, the system does not enforce it. The def_lemma linter checks for this correspondence, so that the user must explicitly approve any exceptions.

Illegal Constants. The Lean core library defines a > b to be b < a, and similarly for a ≥ b. These statements are convertible, but some automation, including the simplifier, operates only with respect to syntactic equality. For this reason, it is convenient to pick a normal form for equivalent expressions. In mathlib, we prefer theorems to be stated in terms of < instead of >. The ge_or_gt linter checks that the disfavored constants do not appear in the types of declarations.

Unused Arguments. A very common beginner mistake is to declare unnecessary arguments to a definition or theorem. Lean's useful mechanisms for auto-inserting parameters in namespaces and sections can unfortunately contribute to this. The unused_arguments linter checks that each argument to a declaration appears in either a subsequent argument or the declaration type or body.

Missing Documentation. The mathlib documentation guidelines require every definition to have a doc string (Sect. 4). Since doc strings are accessible by metaprograms, we are able to enforce this property with a linter, called doc_blame (Fig. 1). Missing doc strings are the most common linter error caught in CI.

3.3   Type Class Linters

Lean and mathlib make extensive use of *type classes* [21] for polymorphic declarations. Of the 42,000 declarations in mathlib, 465 are type classes and 4600 are type class instances. In particular, type classes are used to manage the hierarchy of mathematical structures. Their use allows definitions and theorems to be stated at high levels of generality and then applied in specific cases without extra effort. Arguments to a declaration are marked as *instance implicit* by surrounding them with square brackets. When this declaration is applied, Lean runs a depth-first backward search through its database of instances to satisfy the argument. Type classes are a powerful tool, but users often find the underlying algorithms opaque, and their misuse can lead to performance issues [20]. A collection of linters aims to warn users about this misuse.

Guiding Type Class Resolution. Instances can be assigned a positive integer *priority*. During type class resolution the instances with a higher priority are tried first. Priorities are optional, and in mathlib most instances are given the default priority. Assigning priorities optimally is difficult. On the one hand, we want to try instances that are used more frequently first, since they are most likely to be applicable. On the other hand, we want to try instances that fail more quickly first, so that the depth-first search does not waste time on unnecessary searches.

While we cannot automatically determine the optimal priority of instances, there is one class of instances we want to apply last, namely the *forgetful instances*. A forgetful instance is an instance that applies to every goal, like the instance comm_group α → group α, which forgets that a commutative group is commutative. Read backward as in the type class inference search, this instance says that to inhabit group α it suffices to inhabit comm_group α.

Forgetful instances contrast with *structural instances* such as comm_group α → comm_group β → comm_group ($\alpha \times \beta$). We want to apply structural instances before forgetful instances, because if the conclusion of a structural instance unifies with the goal, it is almost always the desired instance. This is not the case for forgetful instances, which are always applicable, even if the extra structure or properties are not available for the type in question. In this case, the type class inference algorithm will do an exhaustive search of the new instance problem, which can take a long time to fail. The instance_priority linter enforces that all forgetful instances have priority below the default.

Another potential problem with type class inference is the introduction of metavariables in the instance search. Consider the following definition of an *R*-module type class.

```
class module (R : Type u) (M : Type v) :=
(to_ring : ring R)
(to_add_comm_group : add_comm_group M)
(to_has_scalar : has_scalar R M)
/- some propositional fields omitted -/
```

If we make the projection module.to_ring an instance, we have an instance of the form module R M → ring R. This means that during type class inference, whenever we search for the instance ring α, we will apply module.to_ring and then search for the instance module α ?m, where ?m is a metavariable. This type class problem is likely to loop, since most module instances will apply in the case that the second argument is a variable.

To avoid this, in mathlib the type of module actually takes as arguments the ring structure on R and the group structure on M. The declaration of module looks more like this:

```
class module (R : Type u) (M : Type v) [ring R] [add_comm_group M] :=
(to_has_scalar : has_scalar R M)
/- some propositional fields omitted -/
```

Using this definition, there is no instance from modules to rings. Instead, the ring structure of R is carried as an argument to the module structure on M. The dangerous_instance raises a warning whenever an instance causes a new type class problem that has a metavariable argument.

Misused Instances and Arguments. Misunderstanding the details of type class inference can cause users to write instances that can never be applied. As an example, consider the theorem which says that given a continuous ring homomorphism f between uniform spaces, the lift of f to the completion of its domain is also a ring homomorphism. The predicate is_ring_hom f is a type class in mathlib, and this theorem was originally written as a type class instance:

```
is_ring_hom f → continuous f → is_ring_hom (completion.map f)
```

However, continuous f is not a type class, and this argument does not appear in the codomain is_ring_hom (completion.map f). There is no way for the type class resolution mechanism to infer this argument and thus this instance will never be applied. The impossible_instance linter checks declarations for this pattern, warning if a non-type class argument does not appear elsewhere in the type of the declaration.

A dual mistake to the one above is to mark an argument as instance implicit even though its type is not a type class. Since there will be no type class instances of this type, such an argument will never be inferable. The incorrect_type_class_argument linter checks for this. While the linter is very simple, it checks for a mistake that is difficult to catch in manual review, since it requires complete knowledge of the mathlib instance database.

Missing and Incorrect Instances. Most theorems in mathlib are type-polymorphic, but many hold only on *inhabited* types. (Readers used to HOL-based systems should note that Lean's type theory permits empty types, e.g. an inductive type with no constructors.) Inhabitedness is given by a type class argument, so in order to apply these theorems, the library must contain many instances of the inhabited type class. The has_inhabited_instance linter checks, for each concrete Type-valued declaration, that conditions are given to derive that the type is inhabited.

The inhabited type class is itself Type-valued. One can computably obtain a witness t : T from an instance of inhabited T; it is possible to have multiple distinct (nonconvertible) instances of inhabited T. Sometimes the former property is not necessary, and sometimes the latter property can create problems. For instance, instances deriving inhabited T from has_zero T and has_one T would

```
@[simp] lemma zero_add (x : N) : 0 + x = x := /- ... -/

example (x : N) : 0 + (0 + x) = x := by simp
```

Fig. 2. Example usage of the simplifier.

lead to non-commuting diamonds in the type class hierarchy. To avoid this, math-lib defines a weaker type class, `nonempty`, which is `Prop`-valued. Lean propositions are *proof-irrelevant*, meaning that any two terms of the same `Prop`-valued type are indistinguishable. Thus `nonempty` does not lead to non-commuting diamonds, and is safe to use in situations where `inhabited` instances would cause trouble.

The `inhabited_nonempty` linter checks for declarations with `inhabited` arguments that can be weakened to `nonempty`. Suppose that a `Prop`-valued declaration takes an argument `h : inhabited T`. Since Lean uses dependent types, `h` may appear elsewhere in the type of the declaration. If it doesn't, it can be weakened to `nonempty T`, since the elimination principles are equivalent for `Prop`-valued targets. Weakening this argument makes the declaration more widely applicable.

3.4 Linters for Simplification Lemmas

Lean contains a `simp` tactic for (conditional) term rewriting. Similar tactics, such as Isabelle's `simp` [17], are found in other proof assistants. Users can tag theorems using the `@[simp]` attribute. The theorems tagged with this attribute are collectively called the *simp set*. The `simp` tactic uses lemmas from the simp set, optionally with extra user-provided lemmas, to rewrite until it can no longer progress. We say that such a fully simplified expression is in *simp-normal form* with respect to the given simp set.

The simplifier is used widely: `mathlib` contains over 7000 simp lemmas, and the string `by simp` occurs almost 5000 times, counting only a small fraction of its invocations. However, care needs to be taken when formulating simp lemmas. For example, if both `a = b` and `b = a` are added as simp lemmas, then the simplifier will loop. Other mistakes are more subtle. We have integrated several linters that aid in declaring effective simp lemmas.

Redundant Simplification Lemmas. We call a simp lemma redundant if the simplifier will never use it for rewriting. This redundancy property depends on the whole simp set: a simp lemma is not redundant by itself, but due to other simp lemmas that break or subsume it. One way a simp lemma can be redundant is if its left-hand side is not in simp-normal form.

Simplification proceeds from the inside out, starting with the arguments of a function before simplifying the enclosing term. Given a term `f (0 + a)`, Lean will first simplify `a`, then it will simplify `0 + a` to `a` using the simp lemma `zero_add` (Fig. 2), and then finally simplify `f a`.

A lemma stating `f (0 + x) = g x` will never be used by the simplifier: the left-hand side `f (0 + x)` contains the subterm `0 + x` which is not in simp-normal form. Whenever the simplifier tries to use this lemma to rewrite a term, the arguments to `+` have already been simplified, so this subterm can never match.

It is often not immediately clear whether a term is in simp-normal form. The first version of the `simp_nf` linter only checked that the arguments of the left-hand side of a simp lemma are in simp-normal form. This first version identified more than one hundred lemmas across `mathlib` violating this condition. In some cases, the lemma satisfied this condition in the file where it was declared, but later files contained simp lemmas that simplified the left-hand side.

Simp lemmas can also be redundant if one simp lemma generalizes another simp lemma. The simplifier always picks the *last* simp lemma that matches the current term. (It is possible to override this order using the `@[priority]` attribute.) If a simp lemma is followed by a more general version, then the first lemma will never be used, such as `length_singleton` in the following example. It is easy to miss this issue at first glance since `[x]` and `x::xs` look very different, but `[x]` is actually parsed as `x:: []`.

```
@[simp] lemma length_singleton : length [x] = 1 := rfl
@[simp] lemma length_cons : length (x::xs) = length xs + 1 := rfl
```

Both of these issues are checked by the `simp_nf` linter. It runs the simplifier on the left-hand side of the simp lemma, and examines the proof term returned by the simplifier. If the proof of the simplification of the left-hand side uses the simp lemma itself, then the simp lemma is not redundant. In addition, we also assume that the simp lemma is not redundant if the left-hand side does not simplify at all, as is the case for conditional simp lemmas. Otherwise the linter outputs a warning including the list of the simp lemmas that were used.

Commutativity Lemmas. Beyond conditional term rewriting, Lean's simplifier also has limited support for ordered rewriting with commutativity lemmas such as `x + y = y + x`. Naively applying such lemmas clearly leads to non-termination, so the simplifier only uses these lemmas if the result is smaller as measured by a total order on Lean terms. Rewriting with commutativity lemmas results in nice normal forms for expressions without nested applications of the commutative operation. For example, it reliably solves the goal `f (m + n) = f (n + m)`. However, in the presence of nested applications, the results are unpredictable:

```
example (a b : ℤ) : (a + b) + -a = b := by simp /- works -/
example (a b : ℤ) : a + (b + -a) = b := by simp /- fails -/
```

The `simp_comm` linter checks that the simp set contains no commutativity lemmas.

Variables as Head Symbols. Due to the implementation of Lean's simplifier, there are some restrictions on simp lemmas. One restriction is that the head symbol of the left hand side of a simp lemma must not be a variable. For example, in the hypothetical (conditional) lemma

∀ f, is_homomorphism f → f (x + y) = f x + f y

the left-hand side has head symbol f, which is a bound variable, and therefore the simplifier will not rewrite with this lemma. The simp_var_head linter ensures that no such lemmas are accidentally added to the simp set.

4 Documentation

Programming language documentation serves very different purposes for different audiences, and proof assistant library documentation is no different. When creating documentation for Lean and mathlib, we must address users who

- are new to Lean and unfamiliar with its syntax and paradigms;
- would like an overview of the contents of the library;
- would like to understand the design choices made in an existing theory;
- would like a quick reference to the interface for an existing theory;
- need to update existing theories to adjust to refactorings or updates;
- would like to learn to design and implement tactics or metaprograms; and
- would like a quick reference to the metaprogramming interface.

Many of these goals are best served with user manuals or tutorials [2]. Such documents are invaluable, but there is a high cost to maintaining and updating them. They are most appropriate for material that does not often change, such as the core system syntax and logical foundations. From the perspective of library maintenance, we are particularly interested in *internal documentation*, that is, documentation which is directly written in the mathlib source files. Since the library evolves very quickly, it is essential to automatically generate as much of the reference material as possible. Furthermore, human-written text should be close to what it describes, to make it harder for the description and implementation to diverge.

We focus here on a few forms of this internal documentation. *Module documentation*, written at the top of a mathlib source file, is intended to describe the theory developed in that file, justify its design decisions, and explain how to use it in further developments. (A Lean source file is also called a *module.*) *Declaration doc strings* are written immediately before definitions and theorems. They describe the behavior or content of their subject declarations. In supported editors, these doc strings are automatically displayed when the cursor hovers over a reference to the declaration. *Decentralized documentation* is not localized to a particular line or file of the library, although it may originate in a certain place; it is expected to be collected and displayed post hoc. An example of this is tactic documentation: mathlib defines hundreds of interactive tactics in dozens of files, but users expect to browse them all on a single manual page.

Some features of proof assistants (and of Lean and mathlib in particular) encourage a different style of documentation from traditional programming languages. Since Lean propositions are proof-irrelevant, only the statement of a theorem, not its proof term, can affect future declarations. Thus theorems are self-documenting in a certain sense: the statement of a theorem gives a complete account of its content, in contrast to a definition of type $\mathbb{N} \to \mathbb{N}$, for example. We require doc strings on all mathlib definitions but allow them to be omitted from theorems. While it is often helpful to have the theorem restated or explained in natural language, the manual burden of writing and maintaining these strings for the large amount of simple lemmas in mathlib outweighs the gain of the natural language restatement. Nonetheless, doc strings are strongly encouraged on important theorems and results with nonstandard statements or names.

4.1   Generation Pipeline

In the style of many popular programming languages, we generate and publish HTML documentation covering the contents of mathlib. The generation is part of mathlib's continuous integration setup.

Perhaps unusually for this kind of tool, our generator does not examine the mathlib source files. Instead, it builds a Lean environment that imports the entire library and traverses it using a metaprogram. The metaprogramming interface allows access to the file name, line number, and doc string for any particular declaration, along with module doc strings. By processing a complete environment we can display terms using notation declared later in the library, and include automatically generated declarations that do not appear in the source. We can also associate global information with declarations: for example, we can display a list of instances for each type class.

The generation metaprogram produces a JSON file that contains all information needed to print the module, declaration, and decentralized documentation. A separate script processes this database into a searchable HTML website.[2]

4.2   Declaration Display

The majority of the documentation is oriented around modules. For each Lean source file in mathlib, we create a single HTML page displaying the module documentation and information for each declaration in that file. Declarations appear in the same order as in the source, with an alphabetical index in a side panel. For each declaration, we print various pieces of information (Fig. 3).

The declaration name is printed including its full namespace prefix. Lean declarations have four possible kinds: theorem, definition, axiom, and constant. We print the declaration kind and use it to color the border of the entry for a visual cue. The type of the declaration is printed with implicit arguments hidden by default. This gives an easy reference as to how the declaration can be applied. Each type can be expanded to display all arguments. When a declaration has a doc string, it is displayed beneath the type.

Lean represents the type former and constructors of an inductive type as separate constants. We display them together, mirroring the Lean syntax for an

---

[2] https://leanprover-community.github.io/mathlib_docs/.

```
@[class]                                              ⏻ view source
structure normed_space (α : Type u_5) (β : Type u_6) {…} :
    Type (max u_5 u_6)
(to_module : module α β)
(norm_smul : ∀ (a : α) (b : β), ‖a • b‖ = ‖a‖ * ‖b‖)
```

A normed space over a normed field is a vector space endowed with a norm
which satisfies the equality ‖c • x‖ = ‖c‖ ‖x‖.

▼ Instances

- complex.normed_space.restrict_scalars_real
- normed_field.to_normed_space
- prod.normed_space
- pi.normed_space

Fig. 3. The generated documentation entry for the `normed_space` type class. The
implicit arguments can be expanded by clicking on {...}.

inductive definition. Similarly, we print the constructor and fields of a structure
mirroring the input syntax.

We do not display all of the attributes applied to a declaration, but show those
in a predefined list, including `simp` and `class`. For declarations tagged as type
classes, we display a collapsible list of instances of this class that appear elsewhere
in the library. For definitions, we display a collapsible list of the equational
lemmas that describe their associated reduction rules. We also link to the exact
location where the declaration is defined in the source code.

We believe that this display achieves many of our design goals. The module
documentation provides an overview of a particular theory for newcomers and
general implementation details for experts. The declaration display serves as
an API reference, displaying information concisely with more details readily
available. The same framework works to document both the formalization and
the metaprogramming components of `mathlib`.

4.3   Tactic Database

Lean proofs are often developed using tactics. Custom tactics can be written
in the language of Lean as metaprograms, and `mathlib` includes many such tactics [15, Sect. 6]. It is essential for us to provide an index of the available tools
explaining when and how to use them. Tactic explanations are an example of
decentralized documentation. Their implementations appear in many different
files, interspersed with many other declarations, but users must see a single unified list. These same concerns apply to the commands defined in `mathlib`, as well
as to attributes and hole commands, which we do not discuss in this paper.

It is inconvenient to maintain a database of tactics separate from the library.
Since `mathlib` changes rapidly, such a database would likely diverge from the

```
structure tactic_doc_entry :=
(entry_name                : string)
(category                  : doc_category)
(decl_names                : list name)
(tags                      : list string := [])
(description               : string      := "")
(inherit_description_from  : option name := none)

add_tactic_doc
{ entry_name := "linarith",
  category   := doc_cagetory.tactic,
  tags       := ["arithmetic", "decision procedure"],
  decl_names := [`tactic.interactive.linarith] }
```

Fig. 4. The information stored in a tactic documentation entry, and the standard way to register an entry. The text associated with this entry will be the declaration doc string of `tactic.interactive.linarith`.

library before long. In addition, the doc strings for tactics—which appear as tooltips in supported editors—often contain the same text as a tactic database entry. To avoid these issues, we provide a command `add_tactic_doc` that registers a new tactic documentation entry. Another command retrieves all tactic doc entries that exist in the current environment.

A tactic doc entry (Fig. 4) contains six fields. The command `add_tactic_doc` takes this information as input. To avoid duplicating information, the `description` field is optional, as this string has often already been written as a declaration doc string. When `description` is empty, the command will source it from the declaration named in `inherit_description_from` (if provided) or the declaration named in `decl_names` (if this list has exactly one element). The HTML generation tool links each description to its associated declarations.

The `entry_name` field titles the entry. This is typically the name of the tactic or command, and is used as the header of the doc entry. The `category` field is either `tactic`, `command`, `hole_command`, or `attribute`. These categories are displayed on separate pages. The `decl_names` field lists the declarations associated with this doc entry. Many entries document only a single tactic, in which case this list will contain one entry, the implementation of this tactic.

The `tags` field contains an optional list of tags. They can be used to filter entries in the generated display. The command can be called at any point in any Lean file, but is typically used immediately after a new tactic is defined, to keep the documentation close to the implementation in the source code. The HTML display allows the user to filter declarations by tags—e.g. to view only tactics related to arithmetic.

4.4 Library Notes

The interface surrounding a definition is often developed in the same file as that definition. We typically explain the design decisions of a given module in the

```
-- declare a library note about instance priority
/-- Certain instances always apply during type class resolution... -/
library_note "lower instance priority"

-- reference a library note in a declaration doc string
/-- see Note [lower instance priority] -/
@[priority 100]
instance t2_space.t1_space [t2_space α] : t1_space α := ...

-- print all existing library notes
run_cmd get_library_notes >>= trace
```

Fig. 5. Library notes can be declared, referenced, and collected anywhere in mathlib.

file-level documentation. However, some design features have a more distributed flavor. An example is the priority of type class instances (Sect. 3.3). There are guidelines for choosing a priority for a new instance, and an explanation why these guidelines make sense, but this explanation is not associated with any particular module: it justifies design decisions made across dozens of files.

We use a mechanism that we call *library notes* (Fig. 5), inspired by a technique used in the Glasgow Haskell Compiler [14] project to document these distributed design decisions. A library note is similar to a module doc string, but it is identified by a name rather than a file and line. As with tactic doc entries, we provide commands in mathlib to declare new library notes and retrieve all existing notes.

The documentation processing tool generates an HTML page that displays every library note in mathlib. When these notes are referenced in other documentation entries with the syntax Note [note name], they are linked to the entry on the notes page. Library notes are also often referenced in standard comments that are not displayed in documentation. These references are useful for library developers to justify design decisions in places that do not face the public.

5 Conclusion

Although there are a growing number of large libraries of formal proofs, both mathematical and otherwise, little has been written about best practices for maintaining and documenting these libraries. Ringer et al. [18] note the gap between proof engineering and software engineering in this respect. Andronick [1] describes the large-scale deployment of the seL4 verified microkernel, focusing on the social factors that have led to its success; Bourke et al. [4] describe technical aspects of maintaining this project. Other discussions of large libraries [3,10] touch on similar topics. Wenzel [22] explains the infrastructure underlying the Isabelle Archive of Formal Proofs (AFP), including progress toward building the AFP with semantic document markup.

Sakaguchi [19] describes a tool for checking and validating the hierarchy of mathematical structures in the Coq Mathematical Components library [13], a task in the same spirit as our type class linters. Cohen et al. [6] implement a related tool which greatly simplifies changing this hierarchy.

It is hard to quantify the effect that our linters and documentation have had on the mathlib community. Fixing issues identified by the `instance_priority` and `dangerous_instance` linters led to performance boosts in the library. Removing unusable instances and simplification lemmas has also improved performance and decluttered trace output. More noticeable is the effect on the workload of maintainers, who can now spend more review time on the deeper parts of library submissions. Similarly, inexperienced contributors worry less about introducing subtle mistakes into the library. Users at all levels report frequent use of the HTML documentation, especially to find information that is not easily available in an interactive Lean session, such as the list of instances of a given type class.

So far we have only implemented the very basic sanity checks on simp lemmas described in Sect. 3.4. There are also other properties of term rewriting systems that we want for the simp set, such as confluence and termination. Kaliszyk and Sternagel [12] have used completion of term rewriting systems to automatically derive a simp set for the HOL Light standard library. We plan to implement a more manual approach, where a linter detects the lack of local confluence and prints a list of equations for the non-joinable critical pairs. It is then up to the user to decide how to name, orient, and generalize these new equations.

The current linter framework considers each declaration locally, but we anticipate the need for global tests. The `simp_nf` linter already goes beyond strictly local checking: it considers the entire simp set. Another global linter could check the termination of the simp set. This is a much harder challenge, since checking termination is undecidable in general. We plan to investigate the integration of external termination checkers such as AProVE [9].

While many of the features we present are specific to Lean, we believe that the general considerations apply more broadly: automated validation and documentation seem essential for a sustainable and scalable library of formal proofs. Especially in regard to documentation, there is a definite path for coordination between libraries and systems, possibly aided by tools from the mathematical knowledge management community.

Acknowledgments. We thank Jeremy Avigad and Jasmin Blanchette for comments on a draft of this paper, and Bryan Gin-ge Chen for many contributions to the mathlib documentation effort.

References

1. Andronick, J.: Successes in deployed verified software (and insights on key social factors). In: ter Beek, M.H., McIver, A., Oliveira, J.N. (eds.) FM 2019. LNCS, vol. 11800, pp. 11–17. Springer, Cham (2019). https://doi.org/10.1007/978-3-030-30942-8_2

2. Avigad, J., de Moura, L., Kong, S.: Theorem Proving in Lean. Carnegie Mellon University (2014)
3. Bancerek, G., et al.: The role of the Mizar Mathematical Library for interactive proof development in Mizar. J. Autom. Reasoning 61(1–4), 9–32 (2018). https://doi.org/10.1007/s10817-017-9440-6
4. Bourke, T., Daum, M., Klein, G., Kolanski, R.: Challenges and experiences in managing large-scale proofs. In: Jeuring, J., et al. (eds.) CICM 2012. LNCS (LNAI), vol. 7362, pp. 32–48. Springer, Heidelberg (2012). https://doi.org/10.1007/978-3-642-31374-5_3
5. Buzzard, K., Commelin, J., Massot, P.: Formalising perfectoid spaces. In: Proceedings of the 9th ACM SIGPLAN International Conference on Certified Programs and Proofs, CPP 2020, pp. 299–312. Association for Computing Machinery, New York (2020). https://doi.org/10.1145/3372885.3373830
6. Cohen, C., Sakaguchi, K., Tassi, E.: Hierarchy Builder: algebraic hierarchies made easy in Coq with Elpi, February 2020. https://hal.inria.fr/hal-02478907
7. Dahmen, S.R., Hölzl, J., Lewis, R.Y.: Formalizing the solution to the cap set problem. In: Harrison, J., O'Leary, J., Tolmach, A. (eds.) 10th International Conference on Interactive Theorem Proving (ITP 2019). Leibniz International Proceedings in Informatics (LIPIcs), vol. 141, pp. 15:1–15:19. Schloss Dagstuhl-Leibniz-Zentrum fuer Informatik, Dagstuhl, Germany (2019). https://doi.org/10.4230/LIPIcs.ITP.2019.15
8. Ebner, G., Ullrich, S., Roesch, J., Avigad, J., de Moura, L.: A metaprogramming framework for formal verification. PACMPL 1(ICFP), 34:1–34:29 (2017). https://doi.org/10.1145/3110278
9. Giesl, J., et al.: Analyzing program termination and complexity automatically with AProVE. J. Autom. Reasoning 58(1), 3–31 (2017). https://doi.org/10.1007/s10817-016-9388-y
10. Gonthier, G., et al.: A machine-checked proof of the odd order theorem. In: ITP 2013, pp. 163–179 (2013). https://doi.org/10.1007/978-3-642-39634-2_14
11. Han, J.M., van Doorn, F.: A formal proof of the independence of the continuum hypothesis. In: Proceedings of the 9th ACM SIGPLAN International Conference on Certified Programs and Proofs, CPP 2020, pp. 353–366. Association for Computing Machinery, New York (2020). https://doi.org/10.1145/3372885.3373826
12. Kaliszyk, C., Sternagel, T.: Initial experiments on deriving a complete HOL simplification set. In: Blanchette, J.C., Urban, J. (eds.) PxTP 2013. EPiC Series in Computing, vol. 14, pp. 77–86. EasyChair (2013)
13. Mahboubi, A., Tassi, E.: Mathematical Components (2017)
14. Marlow, S., Peyton-Jones, S.: The Glasgow Haskell Compiler. In: Brown, A., Wilson, G. (eds.) The Architecture of Open Source Applications, Volume II (2012)
15. The mathlib Community: The Lean mathematical library. In: CPP, pp. 367–381. ACM, New York(2020). https://doi.org/10.1145/3372885.3373824
16. de Moura, L., Kong, S., Avigad, J., van Doorn, F., von Raumer, J.: The Lean theorem prover (system description). In: Felty, A.P., Middeldorp, A. (eds.) CADE 2015. LNCS (LNAI), vol. 9195, pp. 378–388. Springer, Cham (2015). https://doi.org/10.1007/978-3-319-21401-6_26
17. Nipkow, T., Wenzel, M., Paulson, L.C. (eds.): Isabelle/HOL - A Proof Assistant for Higher-Order Logic. LNCS, vol. 2283. Springer, Heidelberg (2002). https://doi.org/10.1007/3-540-45949-9
18. Ringer, T., Palmskog, K., Sergey, I., Gligoric, M., Tatlock, Z.: QED at large: a survey of engineering of formally verified software. Found. Trends® Program. Lang. 5(2–3), 102–281 (2019). https://doi.org/10.1561/2500000045

19. Sakaguchi, K.: Validating mathematical structures. arXiv (2020). https://arxiv.org/abs/2002.00620
20. Selsam, D., Ullrich, S., de Moura, L.: Tabled typeclass resolution (2020). https://arxiv.org/abs/2001.04301
21. Wadler, P., Blott, S.: How to make ad-hoc polymorphism less ad-hoc. In: Proceedings of POPL 1989, pp. 60–76 (1989). https://doi.org/10.1145/75277.75283
22. Wenzel, M.: Isabelle technology for the Archive of Formal Proofs with application to MMT (2019). https://arxiv.org/abs/1905.07244

System Descriptions and Datasets

The Tactician

A Seamless, Interactive Tactic Learner and Prover for Coq

Lasse Blaauwbroek[1,2(✉)], Josef Urban[1], and Herman Geuvers[2]

[1] Czech Technical University, Prague, Czech Republic
lasse@blaauwbroek.eu,josef.urban@gmail.com
[2] Radboud University, Nijmegen, The Netherlands
herman@cs.ru.nl

Abstract. We present Tactician, a tactic learner and prover for the Coq Proof Assistant. Tactician helps users make tactical proof decisions while they retain control over the general proof strategy. To this end, Tactician learns from previously written tactic scripts and gives users either suggestions about the next tactic to be executed or altogether takes over the burden of proof synthesis. Tactician's goal is to provide users with a seamless, interactive, and intuitive experience together with robust and adaptive proof automation.

1 Introduction

The Coq Proof Assistant [3] is an Interactive Theorem Prover in which one proves lemmas using tactic scripts. Individual tactics in these scripts represent actions that transform the proof state of the lemma currently being proved. A wide range of tactics exist, with a wide range of sophistication, from simple inference steps to entire decision procedures and heuristic search procedures.

When proving a lemma, the user's challenge is to observe the current proof state and select the appropriate tactic and its arguments to be used. Often the user makes this decision based on experience with previous proofs. If the current proof state is similar to a previously encountered situation, then one can expect that an effective tactic in that situation might also be effective now. Hence, the user is continuously matching patterns of proof states in their mind and selects the correct tactic based on these matches.

That is not the only task the user performs, however. When working on a mathematical development, the user generally has two roles: (1) As a *strategist*, the user comes up with appropriate lemmas and sometimes decides on the main structure of complicated proofs. (2) As a *tactician*, the user performs the long and somewhat mindless process of mental pattern matching on proof states, applying corresponding tactics until the lemma is proved. Many of the steps in the tactician's role will be considered as "obvious" by a mathematician. Our

This work was supported by the European Regional Development Fund under the project AI&Reasoning (reg. no. CZ.02.1.01/0.0/0.0/15_003/0000466) and by the *AI4REASON* ERC Consolidator grant nr. 649043.

C. Benzmüller and B. Miller (Eds.): CICM 2020, LNAI 12236, pp. 271–277, 2020.
https://doi.org/10.1007/978-3-030-53518-6_17

system is meant to replicate the pattern matching process performed in this role, alleviating the user from this burden. Hence, we have aptly named it Tactician.

To perform its job, Tactician can learn from existing proofs, by looking at how tactics modify the proof state. Then, when proving a new lemma, the user can ask the system to recommend previously used tactics based on the current proof state and even to complete the whole proof using a search procedure based on these tactic recommendations.

In our previous publication, we describe technical details on the machine learning techniques employed by Tactician and measure its current automation against Coq's standard library [1]. This paper instead gives a quick introduction to Tactician from the user perspective. Details on installation and usage of Tactician can be found on the project's website http://coq-tactician.github.io. There, we also explain how Tactician can be used on large projects with complex dependencies.

2   Design Principles

For our system, we start with the principal goal of learning from previous proofs to aid the user with proving new lemmas. In Coq, there are essentially two notions of proof: (1) proof terms expressed in the Gallina language (Coq's version of CIC [9]); (2) tactic proof scripts written by the user that can then generate a Gallina term. Although it is possible to employ machine learning on both notions, we choose to learn from tactic scripts for two reasons. (1) Tactic scripts are more high-level and forgiving, which is more suitable for machine learning. (2) Working on the tactic level allows the user to introduce domain-specific information to aid the system by writing new tactics. One can teach Tactician about such tactics merely by using them in hand-written proofs a couple of times, after which the system will automatically start to use them.

Apart from the principal goal described above, Tactician's most important objective is to be usable and remain usable by actual Coq users. To achieve this usability, Tactician needs to be pleasant to all parties involved, which we express in four basic "friendliness" tenets: *user-friendly*, *installation-friendly*, *integration-friendly*, and *maintenance-friendly*. More concretely, it should be usable in any editor, with minimal configuration and no time spent training a ML model. Instead, the system should learn on the fly. Tactician should be tightly integrated with Coq, implemented as a plugin in OCaml without requiring external toolkits. To ensure ease of installation and to prevent it from becoming abandonware, it should be entered into the Coq Package Index [2].

The tight integration with Coq make Tactician function both in Coq's interactive mode and compilation mode. In the next two sections, we describe how the system is integrated with these modes.

3   Interactive Mode of Operation

We illustrate the interactive mode of operation of Tactician using the schematic in Fig. 1. When the user starts a new Coq development file—say X.v—the first

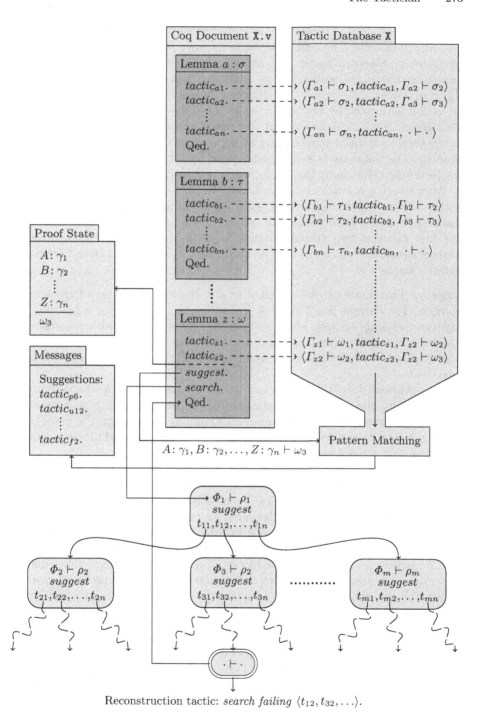

Fig. 1. A schematic overview of Tactician in its interactive mode of operation.

thing Tactician does is create an (in-memory) empty tactic database X corresponding to this file. The user then starts to prove lemmas as usual. Behind the scenes, every executed tactic, e.g. $tactic_{a1}$, is saved into the database accompanied by the proof states before and after tactic execution, in this case, $\langle \Gamma_{a1} \vdash \sigma_1, tactic_{a1}, \Gamma_{a2} \vdash \sigma_2 \rangle$. The difference between these two states represents the action performed by the tactic, while the state before the tactic represents the context in which it was useful. By recording many such triples for a tactic, we create a dataset representing an approximation of that tactic's semantic meaning. The database is kept synchronized with the user's movement within the document throughout the entire interactive session.

After proving a few lemmas by hand, the user can start to reap the fruits of the database. For this, the tactics suggest and search are available. We illustrate their use in the schematic when "Lemma z : ω" is being proven. The user first executes two normal tactics. After that, Coq's proof state window displays a state for which the user is unsure what tactic to use. Here Tactician's tactics come in.

suggest. This tactic can be executed to ask Tactician for a list of recommendations. The current proof state $A : \gamma_1, B : \gamma_2, \ldots, Z : \gamma_n \vdash \omega_3$ is fed into the pattern matching engine, which will perform a comparison with the states in the tactic database. From this, an ordered list of recommendations is generated and displayed in Coq's messages window, where the user can select a tactic to execute.

search. Alternatively, the system can be asked to search for a complete proof. We start with the current proof state, which we rename to $\Phi_1 \vdash \rho_1$ for clarity. Then a search tree is formed by repeatedly running suggest on the proof state and executing the suggested tactics. This tree can be traversed in various ways, finishing only when a complete proof has been found.

If a proof is found, two things happen. (1) The Gallina proof term that is found is immediately submitted to Coq's proof engine, after which the proof can be closed with Qed. (2) Tactician generates a reconstruction tactic search failing $\langle t_{12}, t_{32}, \ldots \rangle$ which is displayed to the user (see the bottom of the figure). The purpose of this tactic is to provide a modification resilient proof cache that also functions when Tactician is not installed. Normally, the lemma can be reproved using the list of tactics $\langle t_{12}, t_{32}, \ldots \rangle$. "Failing" that (due to definitional changes), a new search is initiated to recover the proof. To use the cache, the user should copy it and replace the original search invocation with it in the source file.

4   Compilation Mode of Operation

This mode is visualized in Fig. 2. After the file X.v has been finished, one might want to depend on it in other files. This requires the file to be compiled into a binary X.vo file. The compilation is performed using the command coqc X.v. Tactician is integrated into this process. During compilation, the tactic database is rebuilt in the same way as in interactive mode and then included in the .vo file.

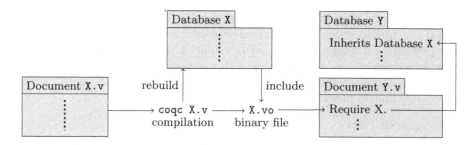

Fig. 2. A schematic overview of Tactician in its compilation mode of operation.

When development X.v is then **Required** by another development file Y.v, the tactic database of X.v is automatically inherited.

5   A Concrete Example

We now give a simple example use-case based on lists. Starting with an empty file, Tactician is immediately ready for action. We proceed as usual by giving a standard inductive definition of lists of numbers with their corresponding notation and a function for concatenation.

```
Inductive list :=              Fixpoint concat ls₁ ls₂ :=
| nil  : list                  match ls₁ with
| cons : nat -> list -> list.  | []     => ls₂
Notation "[]"    := nil.       | x::ls₁' => x::(ls₁' ++ ls₂)
Notation "x::ls" := (cons x ls).   end where "ls₁++ls₂":=(concat ls₁ ls₂).
```

We wish to prove some standard properties of concatenation. The first is a lemma stating that the empty list [] is the right identity of concatenation (the left identity is trivial).

```
Lemma concat_nil_r ls : ls ++ [] = ls.
```

With Tactician installed, we immediately have access to the new tactics **suggest** and **search**. Neither tactic will produce a result when used now since the system has not had a chance to learn from proofs yet. Therefore, we will have to prove this lemma by hand.

```
Proof. induction ls.
- simpl. reflexivity.
- simpl. f_equal. apply IHls.
Qed.
```

The system has immediately learned from this proof (it was even learning during the proof) and is now ready to help us with a proof of the associativity of concatenation.

```
Lemma concat_assoc ls₁ ls₂ ls₃ : (ls₁ ++ ls₂) ++ ls₃ = ls₁ ++ (ls₂ ++ ls₃).
```

Now, if we execute `suggest`, it outputs the ordered list `induction ls`$_1$, `simpl`, `f_equal`,... Indeed, using `induction` as our next tactic is not unreasonable. We can repeatedly ask `suggest` for a recommendation after every tactic we input, which sometimes gives us good tactics and sometimes bad tactics. However, we can also eliminate the middle-man and execute the `search` tactic, which immediately finds a proof.

```
Proof. search. Qed.
```

To cache the proof that is found for the future, we can copy-paste the reconstruction tactic that Tactician prints into the source file. This example shows how the system can quickly learn from very little data and with minimal effort from the user. Of course, this also scales to much bigger developments.

6   Related Work

Tactician takes its main inspiration from the TacticToe [5] system for HOL4. Our work is similar to TacticToe in principle, but diverges significantly in the implementation details due to the large differences between HOL4 and Coq, both their logical system and practical implementation, see [1].

The most significant distinguishing factor of Tactician to other systems for Coq is its user-friendliness. There are many other interesting ML systems for Coq, such as ML4PG [8], SEPIA [6], GamePad [7], CoqGym [11], and Prover-Bot9001 [10]. However, all of these systems are either difficult to install, can only be used with one editor, need a long time to train their models or do not have an end-user interface at all. Many such systems are geared towards the AI community rather than towards the Theorem Proving community. CoqHammer [4] is the only other system we know of for Coq that has tight integration with Coq and is directly usable for end-users. For more detailed related work, see [1].

References

1. Blaauwbroek, L., Urban, J., Geuvers, H.: Tactic learning and proving for the Coq proof assistant. In: LPAR23. EPiC Series in Computing, vol. 73, pp. 138–150. EasyChair (2020)
2. Coq Development Team: Coq package index. https://coq.inria.fr/opam/www
3. Coq Development Team: The Coq proof assistant, version 8.11.0, October 2019
4. Czajka, L., Kaliszyk, C.: Hammer for Coq: automation for dependent type theory. J. Aut. Reasoning **61**(1–4), 423–453 (2018)
5. Gauthier, T., Kaliszyk, C., Urban, J.: TacticToe: Learning to reason with HOL4 tactics. In: LPAR. EPiC Series in Computing, vol. 46, pp. 125–143. EasyChair (2017)
6. Gransden, T., Walkinshaw, N., Raman, R.: SEPIA: search for proofs using inferred automata. In: Felty, A.P., Middeldorp, A. (eds.) CADE 2015. LNCS (LNAI), vol. 9195, pp. 246–255. Springer, Cham (2015). https://doi.org/10.1007/978-3-319-21401-6_16

7. Huang, D., Dhariwal, P., Song, D., Sutskever, I.: Gamepad: a learning environment for theorem proving. In: ICLR (Poster). OpenReview.net (2019)

8. Komendantskaya, E., Heras, J., Grov, G.: Machine learning in proof general: interfacing interfaces. UITP. EPTCS **118**, 15–41 (2012)

9. Paulin-Mohring, C.: Inductive definitions in the system Coq rules and properties. In: Bezem, M., Groote, J.F. (eds.) TLCA 1993. LNCS, vol. 664, pp. 328–345. Springer, Heidelberg (1993). https://doi.org/10.1007/BFb0037116

10. Sanchez-Stern, A., Alhessi, Y., Saul, L.K., Lerner, S.: Generating correctness proofs with neural networks. In: arXiv/CoRR. abs/1907.07794 (2019)

11. Yang, K., Deng, J.: Learning to prove theorems via interacting with proof assistants. In: ICML, Proceedings of Machine Learning Research, vol. 97, pp. 6984–6994 (2019)

Tree Neural Networks in HOL4

Thibault Gauthier[✉]

Czech Technical University in Prague, Prague, Czech Republic
email@thibaultgauthier.fr

Abstract. We present an implementation of tree neural networks within the proof assistant HOL4. Their architecture makes them naturally suited for approximating functions whose domain is a set of formulas. We measure the performance of our implementation and compare it with other machine learning predictors on the tasks of evaluating arithmetical expressions and estimating the truth of propositional formulas.

1 Introduction

Applying machine learning to improve proof automation has been an essential topic in the theorem proving community and contributed to the rise of powerful automation such as hammers [2]. In these systems, the current machine learning predictors learn the premise selection task with relative success. However, these predictors typically rely on a set of syntactic features, and thus, they can hardly discover semantic patterns. To solve this issue, we propose in this work to rely on deep learning models to automatically infer appropriate features that better approximates object semantics. The success of this approach depends heavily on how the design of the neural network architecture encodes and processes the input objects. For example, the space invariance of convolutional neural networks makes them successful at interpreting images. Moreover, recurrent networks can process arbitrarily long sequences of tokens, which is necessary for learning text-based tasks. In the case of formulas, tree neural networks(TNNs) [8] capture the compositional nature of the underlying functions as their structure dynamically imitates the tree structure of the formula considered.

That is why we implement TNNs in HOL4 [9] and evaluate their pattern recognition abilities on two tasks related to theorem proving. The first task is to estimate the value of an expression. It is an example of evaluating a formula in a Tarski-style model, which can be in general useful for conjecturing and approximate reasoning. The second task is to estimate the truth of a formula. Acquiring this ability is important for discarding false conjectures and flawed derivations. These two tasks are only a sample of the many theorem proving tasks that could be learned. We believe that deep learning models such as TNNs could be useful to guide automated theorem provers. In practice, the existence

This work has been supported by the European Research Council (ERC) grant AI4REASON no. 649043 under the EU-H2020 programme. We would like to thank Josef Urban for his contributions to the final version of this paper.

ⓒ Springer Nature Switzerland AG 2020
C. Benzmüller and B. Miller (Eds.): CICM 2020, LNAI 12236, pp. 278–283, 2020.
https://doi.org/10.1007/978-3-030-53518-6_18

of an implementation of a deep learning predictor in HOL4 is a valuable tool for improving proof automation methods in this proof assistant. Experiments on the implemented TNNs presented in this paper can be replicated by following the instructions in the file[1] from the HOL4 repository[2] after switching to this commit[3].

2   Tree Neural Networks

Let $\mathbb{O}$ be a set of operators (functions and constants) and $\mathbb{T}_{\mathbb{O}}$ be all terms built from operators in $\mathbb{O}$. A TNN is to approximate a function from $\mathbb{T}_{\mathbb{O}}$ to $\mathbb{R}^n$. A TNN consists of a head network N_{head} and a mapping that associates to each operator $f \in \mathbb{O}$ a neural network N_f. If the operator f has arity a, it is to learn a function from $\mathbb{R}^{a \times d}$ to $\mathbb{R}^d$. And the head network N_{head} is to approximate a function from $\mathbb{R}^d$ to $\mathbb{R}^n$. The natural number d is called the *dimension* of the embedding space. For a TNN, an embedding function $E : \mathbb{T}_{\mathbb{O}} \mapsto \mathbb{R}^d$ can be recursively defined by:

$$E(f(t_1, \ldots, t_a)) =_{def} N_f(E(t_1), \ldots, E(t_a))$$

The head network "decodes" the embedding of the term considered in $\mathbb{R}^d$ into an element of the output space $\mathbb{R}^n$. Figure 1 shows how the computation follows the tree structure of the input term.

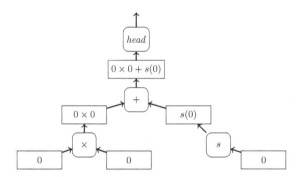

Fig. 1. Computation flow of a tree neural network on the arithmetical expression $0 \times 0 + s(0)$. The operator s stands for the successor function. Rectangles represent embeddings (in $\mathbb{R}^d$) and rounded squares represent neural networks.

In both experiments, the TNNs have neural network operators (including the head network) with one hidden layer and with a embedding dimension $d = 12$. we follow a training schedule over 200 epochs using a fixed learning rate of 0.02 and we double the batch size after every 50 epochs from 8 to 64.

---

[1] https://github.com/HOL/examples/AI_TNN/README.md.
[2] https://github.com/HOL-Theorem-Prover/HOL.
[3] c679f0c69b397bede9fefef82197f33ec495dd8a.

3   Arithmetical Expression Evaluation

The aim of this task is to compute the value x of a given arithmetical expression. Since the output of the TNN is a fixed vector in $\mathbb{R}^n$, we restrict the objective to predicting the four binary digits of x modulo 16. We say that a prediction is accurate if the four predicted real numbers rounded to the nearest integer corresponds to the four binary digits.

The bottom-up architecture of the TNN is ideally suited for this task as it is a natural way to evaluate an expression. And since the knowledge of the structure of the formula is hard-coded in the tree structure, we expect the TNN to generalize well. The experiments rely on a training set of 11990 arithmetical expressions and a testing set of 10180 arithmetical expressions. These expressions are constructed using the four operators $0, s, +$ and $\times$. The deepest subterms of the expressions are made of unary numbers between 0 and 10 (e.g. $s^8(0) + s(s^3(0) \times s^2(0)))$. For further inspection, the datasets are available in this repository[4].

Table 1. Percentage of accurate predictions on different test sets

Predictors	Train	Test
NearestNeighbor [5]	100.0	11.7
LibLinear [7]	84.4	18.3
XGBoost [3]	99.5	16.8
NMT [1]	100.0	77.2
TreeHOL4	97.7	90.1

In Table 1, we compare the accuracy of our TNN predictor (TreeHOL4) with feature-based predictors. These predictors are quite successful in the premise selection task in ITP Hammers [2]. We experiment with these predictors using a standard set of syntactical features, which consists of all the subterms of the arithmetical expressions. This requires almost no engineering. The accuracy of these predictors on the test set is only slightly better than random (6.25%). The obvious reason is that it is challenging to compute the value of an expression by merely comparing its subterms with features of terms in the training set. This highlights the need for some feature engineering using these predictors. As a final comparison, we test the deep learning recurrent neural model NMT with parameters taken from those shown as best in the informal-to-formal task [10]. This is a sequence-to-sequence model with attention, typically used for machine translation. We use prefix notation for representing the terms as sequences for NMT and used one class per output modulo 16 instead of the 4-bit encoding as NMT performed better with those. Despite the perfect training accuracy, the testing accuracy of NMT is below the TNN.

---

[4] https://github.com/barakeel/arithmetic_datasets.

4   Propositional Truth Estimation

The aim of this task is to teach a TNN to estimate if a propositional formula is true or not. For this propositional task, we re-use the benchmark created by the authors of [6] which can be downloaded from this repository[5]. There, each problem is of the form $A \Vdash ?B$. To re-use the implication operator, we instead solve the equivalent task of determining if $A \Rightarrow B$ is universally true or not.

Moreover, the propositional formulas contain boolean variables and a direct representation in our TNN would create one neural network operator for each named variables (up to 25 in the dataset). Our solution is to encode all variables using two operators x and $prime$. First, we index the variables according to their order of appearance in the formula. Second, each variable x_i is replaced by the term $prime^i(x)$. Thus, the input formulas are now represented by terms built from the set of operators $\{x, prime, \Rightarrow, \neg, \vee, \wedge\}$.

Table 2 compares the results of our TNNs (TreeHOL4) on the truth estimation task with the best neural network architectures for this task. The first three architectures are the best extracted from the table of results in [6]. The first one is a tree neural network similar to ours, which also indexes the variables. A significant difference is that we use the $prime$ operator to encode variables while they instead rely on data augmentation by permuting the indices of variables. The second one replaces feedforward networks by LSTMs. The third architecture bases its decision on simultaneously using multiple embeddings for boolean variables. That is why this architecture is named PossibleWorld. In contrast, the TopDown architecture [4] inverts the structure of the TNNs, and combines the embedding of boolean variables (that are now outputs) using recurrent networks. The results on the test set demonstrate that our implementation of TNN is at least as good as the one in [6] as it beats it on every test set. Overall, the more carefully designed architectures for this task (PossibleWorld and Top-Down) outperform it. One thing to note is that these architectures typically rely on a much larger embedding dimension (up to $d = 1024$ for the TopDown architecture). Our TNN implementation rivals with the best architectures on the exam dataset, which consists of 100 examples extracted from textbooks.

Table 2. Percentage of accurate predictions

Architecture	easy	hard	big	mass	exam
Tree	72.2	69.7	67.9	56.6	85.0
TreeLSTM	77.8	74.2	74.2	59.3	75.0
PossibleWorld	98.6	96.7	93.9	73.4	96.0
TopDown	95.9	83.2	81.6	83.6	96.0
TreeHOL4	86.5	77.8	79.2	61.2	98.0

---

[5] https://github.com/deepmind/logical-entailment-dataset.

5   Usage

Our deep learning modules allow HOL4 users to train a TNN on a chosen supervised learning task with little development overhead. The function `train_tnn` from the module `mlTreeNeuralNetwork` is available for such purpose. Its three arguments are a schedule, an initial TNN, and a couple consisting of training examples and testing examples.

Examples. Given the objective functions $o_1, \ldots, o_n$, an example for a term t is:

$$[(h_1(t), l_1), \ (h_2(t), l_2), \ldots, (h_n(t), \ l_n)]$$

where l_i is the list of real numbers between 0 and 1 returned by $o_i(t)$ and h_i is the head operator with objective o_i. The term t is expected to be lambda-free with each operator appearing with a unique arity. Each task in our experiments is defined by a single objective on a set of training examples.

Initial TNN. To create an initial TNN, the user first needs to gather all operators appearing in the examples. Then, given an embedding dimension d, for each operator f with arity a the list of dimensions of N_f is to be defined as:

$$[a \times d, u_1, \ldots, u_k, d]$$

The natural numbers $u_1, \ldots, u_k$ are sizes of the intermediate layers that can be freely chosen by the user. In the case of a head operator h_i, the input dimension is to be d and the output dimension is to be the length of the list l_i. From the operators (including heads) and the associated dimensions, the user can randomly initialize the weights of the TNN by calling `random_tnn`.

Schedule. The schedule argument is a list of records containing hyperparameters for the training such as the number of threads, the number of epochs, the learning rate and the size of the batches. Here is a typical training schedule:

```
[{batch_size = 16, learning_rate = 0.02, ncore = 4, nepoch = 50,  ... },
 {batch_size = 32, learning_rate = 0.02, ncore = 4, nepoch = 100, ... }]
```

In this schedule, training is performed with a batch size of 16 for 50 epochs which is then increased to 32 for the next 100 epochs.

6   Conclusion

In this paper, we presented an implementation of tree neural networks(TNNs) in HOL4 that can be used to learn a function on HOL4 formulas from examples. Compared to the other machine learning predictors, it excels on the arithmetical evaluation task as the TNN architecture reflects perfectly the implied bottom-up computation. It also exhibits excellent performance on propositional formulas. It yields a better accuracy than an existing implementation of TNNs but comes short of more involved architectures tailored for this particular task. As a way forward, we would like to see if the observed TNNs pattern recognition abilities (understanding) transfer to other tasks such as premise selection or high-order unification, which could have a more direct benefit for proof automation.

References

1. Vaswani, A., et al.: Attention is all you need. In: Guyon, I., et al. (eds.) Advances in Neural Information Processing Systems 30: Annual Conference on Neural Information Processing Systems 2017, 4–9 December 2017, Long Beach, CA, USA, pp. 5998–6008 (2017). http://papers.nips.cc/paper/7181-attention-is-all-you-need
2. Blanchette, J.C., Kaliszyk, C., Paulson, L.C., Urban, J.: Hammering towards QED. J. Formalized Reasoning **9**(1), 101–148 (2016). https://doi.org/10.6092/issn.1972-5787/4593
3. Chen, T., Guestrin, C.: XGBoost: a scalable tree boosting system. In: Proceedings of the 22nd ACM SIGKDD International Conference on Knowledge Discovery and Data Mining, 13–17 August 2016, San Francisco, CA, USA, pp. 785–794 (2016). https://doi.org/10.1145/2939672.2939785
4. Chvalovský, K.: Top-down neural model for formulae. In: 7th International Conference on Learning Representations, ICLR 2019, 6–9 May 2019, New Orleans, LA, USA (2019). https://openreview.net/forum?id=Byg5QhR5FQ
5. Cover, T.M., Hart, P.E.: Nearest neighbor pattern classification. IEEE Trans. Inf. Theory **13**(1), 21–27 (1967). https://doi.org/10.1109/TIT.1967.1053964
6. Evans, R., Saxton, D., Amos, D., Kohli, P., Grefenstette, E.: Can neural networks understand logical entailment? In: 6th International Conference on Learning Representations, ICLR 2018, Vancouver, BC, Canada, 30 April–3 May 2018, Conference Track Proceedings (2018). https://openreview.net/forum?id=SkZxCk-0Z
7. Fan, R., Chang, K., Hsieh, C., Wang, X., Lin, C.: LIBLINEAR: a library for large linear classification. J. Mach. Learn. Res. **9**, 1871–1874 (2008). https://dl.acm.org/citation.cfm?id=1442794
8. Kiperwasser, E., Goldberg, Y.: Easy-first dependency parsing with hierarchical tree LSTMs. TACL **4**, 445–461 (2016)
9. Slind, K., Norrish, M.: A brief overview of HOL4. In: Mohamed, O.A., Muñoz, C., Tahar, S. (eds.) TPHOLs 2008. LNCS, vol. 5170, pp. 28–32. Springer, Heidelberg (2008). https://doi.org/10.1007/978-3-540-71067-7_6
10. Wang, Q., Kaliszyk, C., Urban, J.: First experiments with neural translation of informal to formal mathematics. In: Rabe, F., Farmer, W.M., Passmore, G.O., Youssef, A. (eds.) CICM 2018. LNCS (LNAI), vol. 11006, pp. 255–270. Springer, Cham (2018). https://doi.org/10.1007/978-3-319-96812-4_22

Interpreting Mathematical Texts in Naproche-SAD

Adrian De Lon, Peter Koepke$^{(\boxtimes)}$, and Anton Lorenzen

Rheinische Friedrich-Wilhelms-Universität Bonn, Bonn, Germany
koepke@math.uni-bonn.de

Abstract. Naproche-SAD is a *natural proof assistant* based on the controlled natural input language ForTheL. Integrating ForTheL into LaTeX allows to leverage type setting commands for the disambiguation and structuring of mathematical texts, with high-quality mathematical typesetting coming for free. A new generic parsing mechanism allows the translation of texts into other formal languages besides the original first-order internal format of Naproche-SAD. We can generate correct Lean code from ForTheL statements which may be useful for writing readable fabstracts.

1 Natural Proof Assistants

Leading proof assistants have enabled spectacular successes like fully formal and certified proofs of the four-color theorem or of the Kepler conjecture. On the other hand proof assistants have so far not been widely adopted in mathematical practice since their input languages look like conventional programming languages, use unfamiliar foundations and require a lot of detail that seem to be mathematically irrelevant (see also [15]).

To facilitate the use of formal methods in the mathematical community at large proof assistants should employ:

1. input languages which are close to the mathematical vernacular, including symbolic expressions;
2. familiar text structurings that support, e.g., the axiomatic definition-theorem-proof approach;
3. underlying logics that correspond to strong foundations in set theory or type theory;
4. automatic handling of tedious formalization details that are usually left implicit;
5. strong automatic proof checking to approximate proof granularities found in the mathematical literature.

In principle, these points were already addressed in the early years of interactive theorem proving, e.g., in the Mizar project [7], see also [4]. Other proof assistants have implemented Mizar-like proof languages with declarative proof

© Springer Nature Switzerland AG 2020
C. Benzmüller and B. Miller (Eds.): CICM 2020, LNAI 12236, pp. 284–289, 2020.
https://doi.org/10.1007/978-3-030-53518-6_19

structures [14]. Note, however, that the Mizar language is a restricted formal language that is *not* part of commonly used mathematical English.

To reach an even higher degree of naturality, a small number of experimental proof assistants accept proofs in controlled natural languages (CNL) which are fully formal subsets of common natural English (with symbolic mathematical terms). Moreover, input texts may be structured just like proof texts in the published mathematical literature. This development should eventually lead to systems that one may term *natural proof assistants*. In this paper we highlight some aspects of points 1–3 in view of recent improvements [12] to the previous Naproche-SAD release [3]. More technical details are contained in an informal system description that we are also submitting to this conference.

2   Naproche-SAD and ForTheL

The Evidence Algorithm project (EA) which was started by V. Glushkov was inspired by the idea of a system to assist actual mathematical work [13]. It was centered around the development of a controlled natural language for mathematics called ForTheL (Formula Theory Language). The project culminated in the implementation of the proof assistant SAD (System for Automated Deduction) in the PhD work of Andrei Paskevich [11].

Independently, the Naproche (Natural Proof Checking) initiative [10] developed a controlled natural language on top of classical first-order logic, with an emphasis on techniques from formal linguistics. The PhD thesis of Marcos Cramer demonstrated that formal grammars and discourse representation theory could deal adequately and efficiently with mathematical proof texts [1].

A few years ago Naproche has adopted and extended the ideas and algorithms of SAD (see [2], [5]) because of SAD's superior logical setup and performance. Naproche-SAD accepts and proof-checks texts like

Definition 1. *A natural number p is prime iff $p \neq 0, 1$ and for every k such that $k \mid p$, we have $k = p$ or $k = 1$.*

Theorem 1 (Euclid's lemma). *If p is prime and $p \mid m \cdot n$ then $p \mid m$ or $p \mid n$.*

By stripping away pretty-printing commands in the LATEX source of this text fragment one obtains a valid text in the ForTheL proof language for Naproche-SAD. This can be done by a simple filter or by hand. The stripped text proof-checks in Naproche-SAD within the context of a larger file that formalizes a sufficient amount of arithmetic and contains a standard proof of the theorem. Such formalizations are representative of a growing library of proof-checked ForTheL texts from various fields of mathematics [9].

ForTheL, the proof language of Naproche-SAD, is a controlled natural language (CNL). Its design goes back to the 1980s and was based on extensive studies of published mathematical texts. It was found that a large part of mathematical language can be simply built up from fixed patterns which consist of (multiple) words and symbols. Formal production rules of the ForTheL grammar are based on patterns without further analysis of its constituent tokens. On the other hand ForTheL gives a lot of freedom for the creation of patterns, allowing rather arbitrary ASCII sequences as tokens.

For the above sample text, the pattern "natural number $(-)$" with a slot $(-)$ for some other term can be introduced by a language extension of the form

```
Signature. A natural number is a notion.
```

Internally this generates a unary predicate `aNaturalNumber()` which can be addressed by phrases like "x is a natural number" or "for all natural numbers". Note that after "natural number" is parsed there is no attempt to break this down into "natural" and "number". This corresponds to the mathematical practice of taking "natural number" as an "atomic" notion whose meaning cannot be derived from meanings of "natural" and "number".

3   ForTheL and LaTeX

Mathematical typography and typesetting is a prominent part of mathematical culture. An iconic formula like $e^{i\pi} = -1$ uses non-Latin letters (π) and a two-dimensional arrangement of letters to denote certain constants and operations. Typography and typesetting carry semantic information that is utilizable in mathematical text processing.

These days mathematicians routinely do their own typesetting using LaTeX or related software. LaTeX has become the universal format for editing and exchanging mathematics. It provides fonts and symbols to distinguish many mathematical objects and notions. Environments like `\begin{theorem}` ... `\end{theorem}` mark statements to be proved and define scopes for assumptions and variable declarations. The original ForTheL language has only primitive theorem and proof environments. Special symbols have to be simulated by "ASCII-art".

Therefore we are integrating ForTheL into LaTeX, extending features of the original Naproche input language. This work uses some previous experiences with the Naproche input language. A grammatically correct ForTheL text is supposed to be a valid LaTeX file in the context of appropriate document classes and packages. Further benefits will be achieved by semantically enriched versions of LaTeX.

The previous version of Naproche-SAD [3] used a parser which employed an internal parser combinator library. We are replacing the ASCII syntax with a LaTeX-based syntax. The old parser had some logical transformations interwoven with the parsing process, assuming that the target would only be first-order logic. We have now separated the parser module from further logical processing. This required a change of internal representations. Whereas the old parser produced blocks of tagged first-order formulas, we replaced this with a higher-level abstract syntax tree, which is not committed to any particular foundational framework and is also amenable to type-theoretic semantics.

Text Mode and Math Mode. A characteristic feature of ordinary mathematical language is the intuitive distinction between ordinary text and specific mathematical terms and phrases. In LaTeX, this is reflected by commands for switching between text mode and math mode. This distinction is often crucial for disambiguations like between the article "a" and the mathematical variable "a", recognizable by different typesettings. In the old parser, patterns definitions such as "the closure of X as a metric space" resulted either in the unintended pattern "the closure of $(-)$ as $(-)$ metric space" or gave a nondescript parser error.

Another example is that the phrase "vector space" may be parsed as the structure vector space or as a vector named space, provided that both vectors and vector spaces have been defined previously. This led to surprising errors, requiring awkward rephrasings to fix. With the new syntax, variables only occur within math environments which removes many ambiguities.

Ease of Learning and Compatibility. A significant advantage of the new syntax is that most mathematicians are already comfortable with using LaTeX, which eases the learning curve for the CNL. We can also re-use some of the existing tooling around LaTeX: editors, syntax-highlighters, bibliography managers, metadata extractors, etc.

Generating Documents. We provide a custom LaTeX package that makes a CNL text a valid LaTeX document. This way we get prettyprinted documents for free! Furthermore we allow patterns to contain LaTeX commands. The above sample text is prettyprinted from the following *ForTheL* source:

```
\begin{definition}
  A natural number $p$ is prime iff $p \neq 0, 1$
  and for every $k$ such that $k \divides p$,
  we have $k = p$ or $k = 1$.
\end{definition}
\begin{theorem}[Euclid's lemma]
  If $p$ is prime and $p \divides m\mul n$
  then $p \divides m$ or $p \divides n$.
\end{theorem}
```

Expression Parsing. The old syntax made no distinction between symbolic expressions and word patterns, both were parsed as patterns. This approach was flexible, allowing free mixing of words and symbols in patterns. The downside was that parsing of symbolic expressions was complicated and had no mechanism for operator precedences. With the new distinction between math and text content, it seems natural to investigate alternative approaches. We are currently experimenting with more traditional precedence-based expression parsers.

Expression parsing is complicated by allowing relator chaining, as in "$a < b < c = d$". Some operators (e.g. logical connectives) should have lower precedence than relators, and some should have higher precedence (e.g. arithmetic operations). We address this by maintaining two operator tables, along with the list of relators, and parsing expressions in three steps.

Introduction of Grammatical Number. Naproche-SAD used to have no concept of grammatical number, treating singular and plural forms completely synonymously. This can lead to ambiguities. For example, treating "is"/"are" synonymously in "the maximum of x and y is/are smaller than z" creates an ambiguity; with the first interpretation being "(the maximum of x and y) is smaller than z" and the second interpretation being "(the maximum of x) and y are smaller than z", where the maximum is understood as an operation on a list or set. This ambiguity can be resolved with grammatical number.

4   ForTheL and Types

ForTheL is a language with soft types which are called *notions*. One can introduce notions like *integer* and modify them with adjectives like *positive*. In the current Naproche-SAD system dependent notions in n parameters are translated into $(n+1)$-ary relation symbols and processed in classical first-order logic.

Since many established interactive theorem provers are based on type theories, it appears natural to translate ForTheL into (dependent) type theory. Parsing of ForTheL texts should yield an internal representation that can be translated alternatively into FOL or type theory.

Translating to Lean. Lean [8] is a proof assistant with a growing library of mathematical texts [6] from a wide variety of undergraduate courses up to some formalizations of research mathematics. We have implemented a translation from the new syntax to Lean definitions. We include some predefined commands mapping to basic definitions from Leans stdlib and mathlib, such as `\naturals`, `\rationals`, `\divides`, etc.

The above sample text renders as the correct and idiomatic Lean fragment:

```
def prime (p : ℕ) : Prop :=
  p ≠ 0 ∧ p ≠ 1 ∧ (∀ k, has_dvd.dvd k p -> k = p ∨ k = 1)
theorem euclids_lemma {p} {n} {m} : prime p ∧ has_dvd.dvd p (m * n)
  -> has_dvd.dvd p m ∨ has_dvd.dvd p n := omitted
```

The Transformation. We translate pattern definitions to definitions of propositions, and theorems to Lean-theorems. Premises become arguments and the statement the result type of the theorem. Patterns inside the premises and statement will not be unrolled, but rather refer to the Lean definitions defined previously (like `prime` above). We use the optional argument of the amsthm environments (in this case Euclid's lemma) to pick an appropriate Lean name, with a fallback to `thm0`, `thm1`, etc.

5   Future Work

The naturalness of an interactive system is the result of a large number of small natural features. We shall continue to enhance Naproche-SAD in this direction.

One important example is the handling of common type coercions: Given a rational number q and a natural number n, the expression $q = n$ type-checks in Lean thanks to implicit coercions, while $n = q$ does not, as Lean cannot "undo" the specialization of $=$ to the natural numbers. Having coercions depend on the order of arguments is undesirable for natural language texts. While it is of course possible for users to supply coercions manually, we plan on addressing this issue by adding a system that manages subtyping relations. We are also evaluating the possibility of translating ForTheL proofs to Lean tactics.

References

1. Cramer, M.: Proof-checking mathematical texts in controlled natural language. Ph.D. thesis, University of Bonn (2013)
2. Frerix, S., Koepke, P.: Automatic proof-checking of ordinary mathematical texts. In: CICM Informal Proceedings (2018). http://ceur-ws.org/Vol-2307/paper13.pdf
3. Frerix, S., Wenzel, M., Koepke, P.: Isabelle/Naproche (2019). https://sketis.net/2019/isabelle-naproche-for-automatic-proof-checking-of-ordinary-mathematical-texts
4. Harrison, J., Urban, J., Wiedijk, F.: Interactive theorem proving. In: Gabbay, D.M., Siekmann, J., Woods, J. (eds.) Computational Logic of the Handbook of the History of Logic, vol. 9, pp. 266–290. Elsevier, Amsterdam (2014)
5. Koepke, P.: Textbook Mathematics in the Naproche-SAD System. In: CICM Informal Proceedings (2019). http://cl-informatik.uibk.ac.at/cek/cicm-wip-tentative/FMM4.pdf
6. Lean community: The Lean mathematical library. https://github.com/leanprover-community/mathlib
7. Mizar. http://mizar.org/
8. de Moura, L., Kong, S., Avigad, J., van Doorn, F., von Raumer, J.: The Lean theorem prover. In: Automated Deduction - CADE-25 (2015)
9. Naproche community: A ForTheL Library. https://github.com/naproche-community/FLib
10. Naproche. https://korpora-exp.zim.uni-duisburg-essen.de/naproche/
11. Paskevich, A.: Méthodes de formalisation des connaissances et des raisonnements mathématiques: aspects appliqués et théoriques. Ph.D. thesis, Université Paris 12 (2007)
12. Prototype CNL. https://github.com/adelon/nave
13. Glushkov, V.M.: Some problems in the theories of automata and artificial intelligence. Cybern. Syst. Anal. **6**, 17–27 (1970). https://doi.org/10.1007/BF01070496
14. Wenzel, M.: Isabelle/Isar - a versatile environment for human-readable formal proof documents. Ph.D. thesis, TU Munich (2002)
15. Wiedijk, F.: The QED manifesto revisited. In: From Insight to Proof, Festschrift in Honour of Andrzej Trybulec, pp. 121–133 (2007)

TGView3D: A System for 3-Dimensional Visualization of Theory Graphs

Richard Marcus(✉) , Michael Kohlhase , and Florian Rabe

Computer Science, FAU Erlangen-Nürnberg, Erlangen, Germany
richard.marcus@fau.de

Abstract. We describe the TGView3D system, an interactive graph viewer optimized for exploring mathematical knowledge as 3D graphs. To exploit all three spatial dimensions, it extends the commonly-used force-directed layout algorithms with hierarchical components that are more suitable for the typical structure of mathematical knowledge. TGView3D can also communicate with OMDoc-based knowledge management tools in order to offer semantic, mathematics-specific interaction with the graphs.

1 Introduction

Digital libraries of both informal and formal mathematics have reached enormous sizes. For instance, at least half a dozen theorem prover libraries exceed 10^5 statements. Thus, it is getting more and more difficult to organize this knowledge in a way that humans can understand and access it. While library sources, generated presentations, and IDEs such as PIDE [Wen19] give good access to local knowledge structures, global properties of the induced knowledge spaces are very difficult to assess.

Theory graphs provide a good representation for these global properties: the nodes are **theories** and their edges **theory morphisms** that define interrelations between theories. Concretely, we use OMDoc/MMT [Koh06, RK13], which distinguishes multiple kinds of morphisms for theory graphs: Most importantly, **inclusions** represent the inheritance relation, and **views** represent translations and interpretations.

However, standard graph visualization techniques are not ideal for theory graphs. Inclusions are highly prevalent and induce a directed acyclic subgraph, which captures the primary structure of the graph, in particular the inheritance hierarchy; therefore, they must be prioritized in the layout. Views may introduce cycles or connect very distant theories; therefore, they must be layouted with care to avoid intersecting edges, which can lead to a messy layout, especially in

The authors were supported by DFG grant RA-1872/3-1, KO 2428/13-1 OAF and EU grant Horizon 2020 ERI 676541 OpenDreamKit. They are also grateful for hardware support from and very helpful discussions about layout algorithms with Roberto Grosso and Marc Stamminger as well as Jonas Müller.

C. Benzmüller and B. Miller (Eds.): CICM 2020, LNAI 12236, pp. 290–296, 2020.
https://doi.org/10.1007/978-3-030-53518-6_20

the 2-dimensional case. For example, we have never been satisfied with the visualization and user interaction features that state-of-the-art tools could provide for our own graph of logic formalizations (LATIN; see [Cod+11]), containing (only) a few hundred nodes and many includes representing the modular design of logics and views representing logic translations. We will use this LATIN theory graph as a running example.

Superseding our previous two-dimensional theory graph viewer [RKM17], TGView3D is a three-dimensional theory graph visualization tool that adapts traditional force-directed layout algorithms to make use of hierarchies and clusters in theory graphs, using an approach similar to [DKM06] except extended to three dimensions.

TGView3D is based on the **Unity** game engine [UGE]. While there are dedicated tools for interactive 3D graph visualization such as **Gephi** [BHJ09] or web applications and frameworks (e.g., based on WebGL), we opted for Unity as it allows fast implementation of typical 3D interactions and flexible platform support as well as efficient rendering of large graphs. Unity also allows building two versions of TGView3D: a WebGL version that we can embed into browser-based interfaces for casual users, and executables for VR hardware that offer better performance for power users.

While Unity is proprietary, all of our code is licensed under GPLv3 and is available at https://github.com/UniFormal/TGView3D. The web application runs at https://tgview3d.mathhub.info and a demo video for the VR executable is available at https://youtube.com/watch?v=Mx7HSWD5dwg.

2   Layouting and Interaction

3D Layouting. To compute the layout for large graphs, force-directed graph drawing is the typical choice. It introduces forces so that nodes repel each other in general but that connected ones attract each other, aiming at a layout of connected groups of nodes and short edges. However, this approach does not offer special treatment for directed edges, and in theory graphs the directed acyclic inheritance hierarchy is a central cognitive aspect. To better visualize this, layered graph drawing can be used instead. This 2D approach first places the nodes on a minimal number of layers with all edges pointing in the same direction and then minimizes edge crossings by reordering the nodes within their layers. While successful for the inclusion hierarchy, the restriction to layers makes it difficult to incorporate arbitrary additional edges. The latter is needed all the time for theory graphs, where edges relating distant nodes are among the most interesting. A key benefit of the 3D approach is that we can utilize the third spatial dimensions to devise layout algorithms that cater to the structure of mathematical knowledge. Concretely, we can map the hierarchy to the graph vertically and still get the advantages of force-directed layout algorithms.

However, static layers in the style of layered graph drawing (cf. Fig. 1) are still problematic in this combination: it prevents nodes from forming groups vertically, which can lead to inefficient use of space, e.g. all nodes could end

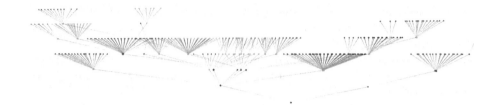

Fig. 1. LATIN graph with static layers

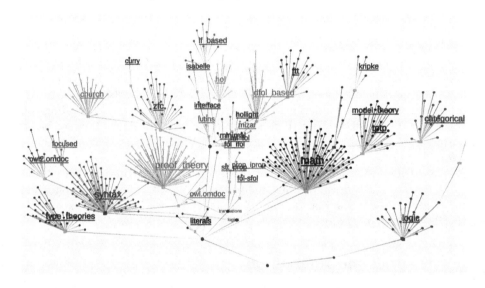

Fig. 2. LATIN graph with hierarchic forces

up on a single layer. Therefore, we use a less restrictive **relative hierarchy** instead, i.e., we aim at a consistent edge direction going from bottom to top. We accomplish this by adding a force that pushes nodes connected by inclusions either downwards or upwards without statically fixing a set of layers. In many cases, this hierarchic force already influences the layout sufficiently to yield good visualizations. But we also added a way to force every node that includes N to appear above N: we first position the nodes in any way that conforms to the hierarchy (e.g., placing them all on the same layer) and then restrict the force-directed node movement so that nodes may only "overtake" each other in the correct direction. This achieves our goals to preserve the relative hierarchy while allowing the force-directed algorithm to work relatively freely (cf. Fig. 2).

Now, the layout algorithm can organize the theory graph efficiently: hierarchic relations create a vertical ordering, and minimizing the length of other edges creates node groups. Adding the view edges to the layout in Fig. 2 would then reorganize the positions of node clusters but keep the relative hierarchy intact.

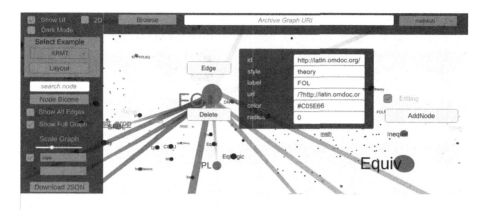

Fig. 3. TGView3D user interface: theory FOL within LATIN

Interaction. Figure 3 gives an example of the TGView3D user interface. It shows the node for the FOL theory in the LATIN graphs with its attributes. Nodes and edges may be typed, and colors are used to differentiate the types visually. Users explore the theory graph by moving through the 3-dimensional visualization and using interaction features that can be accessed within the UI. Additionally, we provide graph editing features for advanced users like developers or library maintainers, e.g., adding and removing nodes and edges.

Compared to 2D, the nodes have more space to form recognizable clusters, but a problem of the 3D-visualization is the visual overlap induced by the placement of nodes along the third dimensions. To cope with this, TGView3D provides the option to hide parts in the distance, thus presenting the user a vertical slice of the graph. Even so, showing all types of edges at once can still result in cluttered layouts, but, since users often want to focus on certain aspects of the theory graph, the main interaction concepts in TGView3D revolve around giving users control over the layout composition. Accordingly, TGView3D allows the user to hide currently not required edge types and, optionally, recalculate the layout based on this selection. The latter, in particular, can be used to analyze how the types of theory morphisms affect the graph layout and thus to get insights about different dependencies in the theory graph.

Another core feature is following the inheritance hierarchy of inclusions. In practice, this means that we need to support the transition between inspecting the graph globally and exploring local structures. Both are important for mathematical knowledge: looking at the whole graph at once reveals groups of theories and dependencies between these groups, whereas the relation between individual nodes give insights about the respective theories and theory morphisms. Given the limitations of space, separating groups visually by packing nodes closely together will eventually result in too much local overlap, while a more even spread makes it harder to recognize clusters. Therefore, TGView3D gives the user direct control over the node spacing in addition to the possibility of moving through the graph. To allow crawling through the graph and focusing on the local neighborhood of nodes, we give users the option to hide all edges except those of selected nodes. Last, to bridge the gap between local and global exploration, TGView3D can also compute **node bicones**, which show the transitive inclusions of a node, i.e., the two trees of nodes that can be reached by following the inclusion relation forwards and backwards. This gives the user information about the role of an individual node in relation to the full graph.

Hierarchical Clustering. In MMT theory graphs, all nodes and edges are labeled in two orthogonal ways: with their logical URI, which follows the namespace structure chosen by the user, and their physical source URL, which follows the project and folder structure of the source files. TGView3D uses this information to define clusters, which are visualized by using the same color for the respective nodes and adding a cluster label. Beyond that, TGView3D permits collapsing these clusters into a single bigger node to reduce graph complexity and enable step-wise graph exploration. In that case, all edges of the original nodes are propagated to the cluster node. This also allows for nested clusters, which is important to efficiently reduce the graph to a size where humans can recognize clear structures and computers can handle the computational load better. With this method, we can compress the graph shown in Fig. 2 drastically (cf. Fig. 4) and still show all edge types at the same time.

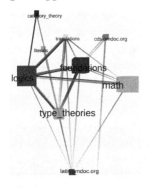

Fig. 4. LATIN graph: hierarchic clustering

Indeed, mathematical libraries often yield large theory graphs with a single connected component, and theory graphs visualizations should not always be self-contained. As an complementary approach to clustering, TGView3D can also be opened with a subgraph built for a particular theory, containing some neighborhood of that theory. The key difference is that instead of collapsing nodes into clusters, the user preselects a certain cluster to reduce the size of the loaded graph. In that case, TGView3D reveals the origin of external nodes and gives users the option to load the respective subgraphs to add them to the current one, thus gradually increasing the size of the visible subgraph.

Integration with Other Systems. While TGView3D is a standalone system, one of its key motivations is to serve as a component of our larger MathHub system (hosted at https://MathHub.info), a web portal for formal mathematical libraries in OMDoc/MMT format. In particular, the access of subgraphs via namespaces is enabled by the MMT system. For integration with other systems in general, the TGView3D web application is

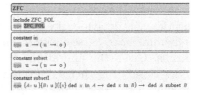

Fig. 5. Source view in MathHub

called by URL parameters that govern which graph to load. It can call other systems by opening URLs attached to the nodes and edges, e.g., in response to user interaction. Thus, every library, namespace, and theory viewed in Math-Hub allows opening a corresponding subgraph in TGView3D in a new page. Vice versa, the MMT URI of every node or edge in TGView3D can be used to view the sources of the respective object in MathHub (cf. Fig. 5). It is also straight-forward to add the functionality of opening nodes and edges in a locally running version of MMT's source editor instead.

3 Conclusion and Future Work

TGView3D is an interactive 3D graph viewer that can handle hierarchical relations and clusters efficiently. While it can handle arbitrary graphs, it is designed to particularly support theory graphs as they occur in mathematical libraries. Therefore, it allows for hierarchical clustering and filtering methods and our layout algorithm makes use of the third spatial dimension to visualize hierarchies and optimize the node organization in a force-directed manner.

In addition to continuous improvements to the graph viewer itself, future work will be to create an ecosystem that simplifies the process of importing different kinds of graphs into TGView3D. Extending this, we want to allow more customizability and offer preconfigured builds that are tailored towards domain-specific use cases.

References

[BHJ09] Bastian, M., Heymann, S., Jacomy, M.: Gephi: an open source software for exploring and manipulating networks. In: Third International AAAI Conference on Weblogs and Social Media (2009)

[Cod+11] Codescu, M., Horozal, F., Kohlhase, M., Mossakowski, T., Rabe, F.: Project abstract: logic atlas and integrator (LATIN). In: Davenport, J.H., Farmer, W.M., Urban, J., Rabe, F. (eds.) CICM 2011. LNCS, vol. 6824, pp. 289–291. Springer, Heidelberg (2011). https://doi.org/10.1007/978-3-642-22673-1_24. https://kwarc.info/people/frabe/Research/CHKMR_latinabs_11.pdf

[DKM06] Dwyer, T., Koren, Y., Marriott, K.: Drawing directed graphs using quadratic programming. IEEE Trans. Visual Comput. Graph. **12**(4), 536–548 (2006)

[Koh06] Kohlhase, M.: OMDoc - An Open Markup Format for Mathematical Documents [Version 12]. LNAI, vol. 4180. Springer, Heidelberg (2006). https://doi.org/10.1007/11826095. http://omdoc.org/pubs/omdoc1.2.pdf

[RK13] Rabe, F., Kohlhase, M.: A scalable module system. Inf. Comput. **230**, 1–54 (2013). http://kwarc.info/frabe/Research/mmt.pdf

[RKM17] Rupprecht, M., Kohlhase, M., Müller, D.: A flexible, interactive theory-graph viewer. In: Kohlhase, A., Pollanen, M. (eds.) MathUI 2017: The 12th Workshop on Mathematical User Interfaces (2017). http://kwarc.info/kohlhase/papers/mathui17-tgview.pdf

[UGE]   Unity Game Engine. https://unity3d.com. Accessed 03 July 2019

[Wen19] Wenzel, M.: Interaction with formal mathematical documents in Isabelle/PIDE. In: Kaliszyk, C., Brady, E., Kohlhase, A., Sacerdoti Coen, C. (eds.) CICM 2019. LNCS, vol. 11617. Springer, Cham (2019). https://doi.org/10.1007/978-3-030-23250-4_1

Simple Dataset for Proof Method Recommendation in Isabelle/HOL

Yutaka Nagashima[1,2](✉) (iD)

[1] Czech Technical University in Prague, Prague, Czech Republic
Yutaka.Nagashima@cvut.cz
[2] University of Innsbruck, Innsbruck, Austria

Abstract. Recently, a growing number of researchers have applied machine learning to assist users of interactive theorem provers. However, the expressive nature of underlying logics and esoteric structures of proof documents impede machine learning practitioners, who often do not have much expertise in formal logic, let alone Isabelle/HOL, from achieving a large scale success in this field. In this data description, we present a simple dataset that contains data on over 400k proof method applications along with over 100 extracted features for each in a format that can be processed easily without any knowledge about formal logic. Our simple data format allows machine learning practitioners to try machine learning tools to predict proof methods in Isabelle/HOL without requiring domain expertise in logic.

1 Introduction

As our society relies heavily on software systems, it has become essential to ensure that our software systems are trustworthy. Interactive theorem provers (ITPs), such as Isabelle/HOL [20], allow users to specify desirable functionalities of a system and prove that the corresponding implementation is correct in terms of the specification.

A crucial step in developing proof documents in ITPs is to choose the right tool for a proof goal at hand. Isabelle/HOL, for example, comes with more than 100 proof methods. Proof methods are sub-tools inside Isabelle/HOL. Some of these are general purpose methods, such as `auto` and `simp`. Others are special purpose methods, such as `intro_classes` and `intro_locales`. The Isabelle community provides various documentations [20] and on-line supports to help new Isabelle users learn when to use which proof methods.

Previously, we developed `PaMpeR` [17], a proof method recommendation tool for Isabelle/HOL. Given a proof goal specified in a proof context, `PaMpeR` recommends a list of proof methods likely to be suitable for the goal. `PaMpeR` learns

This work was supported by the European Regional Development Fund under the project AI & Reasoning (reg. no.CZ.02.1.01/0.0/0.0/15_003/0000466) and by NII under NII-Internship Program 2019-2nd call.

© Springer Nature Switzerland AG 2020
C. Benzmüller and B. Miller (Eds.): CICM 2020, LNAI 12236, pp. 297–302, 2020.
https://doi.org/10.1007/978-3-030-53518-6_21

which proof method to recommend to what kind of proof goal from proof documents in Isabelle's standard library and the Archive of Formal Proofs [10].

The key component of PaMpeR is its elaborate feature extractor. Instead of applying machine learning algorithms to Isabelle's proof documents directly, PaMpeR first applies 113 assertions to the pair of a proof goal and its underlying context. Each assertion checks a certain property about the pair and returns a boolean value. Some assertions check if a proof goal involves certain constants or types defined in the standard library. Others check the meta-data of constants and types appearing in a goal. For example, one assertion checks if the goal has a term of a type defined with the codatatype keyword.

When developing PaMpeR, we applied these 113 assertions to the proof method invocations appearing in the proof documents and constructed a dataset consisting of 425,334 unique data points.

Note that this number is strictly smaller than all the available proof method invocations in Isabelle2020 and the Archive of Formal Proofs in May 2020, from which we can find more than 900k proof method invocations. One obvious reason for this gap is the ever growing size of the available proof documents. The other reason is that we are intentionally ignoring compound proof methods while producing data points. We decided to ignore them because they may pollute the database by introducing proof method invocations that are eventually back-tracked by Isabelle. Such backtracking compound methods may reduce the size of proof documents at the cost of introducing backtracked proof steps, which are not necessary to complete proofs. Since we are trying to recommend proof methods appropriate to complete a proof search, we should not include data points produced by such backtracked steps.

We trained PaMpeR by constructing regression trees [3] from this dataset. Even though our tree construction is based on a fixed height and we did not take advantage of modern development of machine learning research, our cross evaluation showed PaMpeR can correctly predict experts' choice of proof methods for many cases. However, decision tree construction based on a fixed height is an old technique that tends to cause overfitting and underfitting. We expect that one can achieve better performance by applying other algorithms to this dataset.

In the following we present the simple dataset we used to train PaMpeR. Our aim is to provide a dataset that is publicly available at Zenodo [15] and easily usable for machine learning practitioners without backgrounds in theorem proving, so that they can exploit the latest development of machine learning research without being hampered by technicalities of theorem proving.

2   The PaMpeR Dataset

Each data point in the dataset consists of the following three entries:

- the location of a proof method invocation,
- the name of the proof method used there,
- an array of 0s and 1s expressing the proof goal and its context.

The following is an example data point:

```
Functors.thy119 simp 1,0,0,0,0,0,0,0,0,0,0,0,0,0,1,...
```

This data point describes that in the theory file named `Functors.thy`, a proof author applied the `simp` method in line 119 to a proof goal represented by the sequence of 1s and 0s where 1 indicates the corresponding assertion returns true while 0 indicates the otherwise.

This dataset has important characteristics worth mentioning. Firstly, this dataset is heavily imbalanced in terms of occurrences of proof methods. Some general purpose methods, such as `auto` and `simp`, appear far more often than other lesser known methods: each of `auto` and `simp` accounts more than 25% of all proof method invocations in the dataset, whereas no proof methods account for more than 1% of invocations except for the 15 most popular methods.

Secondly, this dataset only serves to learn what proof methods to apply, but it does not describe how to apply a proof method. None of our 113 assertions examines arguments passed to proof methods. For some proof methods, notably the `induct` method, the choice of arguments is the hardest problem to tackle, whereas some methods rarely take arguments at all. We hope that users can learn what arguments to pass to proof methods from the use case of these methods in existing proof documents once they learn which methods to apply to their goal.

Thirdly, it is certainly possible that `PaMpeR`'s feature extractor misses out certain information essential to accurately recommend some methods. This dataset was not built to preserve the information in the original proof documents: we built the dataset, so that we can effectively apply machine learning algorithms to produce recommendations.

Finally, this dataset shows only one way to prove a given goal, ignoring alternative possible approaches to prove the same goal. Consider the following goal: `"True ∨ False"`. Both `auto` or `simp` can prove this goal equally well; however, if this goal appeared in our dataset our dataset would show only the choice of the proof author, say `auto`, ignoring alternative proofs, say `simp`.

One might guess that we could build a larger dataset that also includes alternative proofs by trying to complete a proof using various methods, thus converting this problem into a multi-label problem. That approach would suffer from two problems. Firstly, there are infinitely many ways to apply methods since we often have to apply multiple proof methods in a sequence to prove a conjecture. Secondly, some combinations of methods are not appropriate even though they can finish a proof in Isabelle. For example, the following is an alternative proof for the aforementioned proposition:

```
lemma "True ∨ False" apply(rule disjI1) apply auto done
```

This is a valid proof script, with which Isabelle can check the correctness of the conjecture; however, the application of the `rule` method is hardly appropriate since the subsequent application of the `auto` method can discharge the proof without the preceding `rule`. For these reasons we take the proof methods chosen by human proof authors as the correct choice while ignoring other possibilities.

3   Overview of 113 Assertions

The 113 assertions we used to build the dataset roughly fall into the following two categories:

1. assertions that check terms and types appearing in the first sub-goal, and
2. assertions that check how such terms and types are defined in the underlying proof context.

The first kind of assertions directly check the presence of constructs defined in the standard library. For example, the 56th assertion checks if the first sub-goal contains `Filter.eventually`, which is a constant defined in the standard library since the presence of this constant may be a good indicator to recommend the special purpose proof method called `eventually_elim`. A possible limitation of these assertions is that these assertions cannot directly check the presence of user-defined constructs because such constructs may not even exist when we develop the feature extractor.

The second kind of assertions address this issue by checking how constructs appearing in the first sub-goal are defined in the proof context. For example, the 13th assertion checks if the first sub-goal involves a constant that has one of the following related rules: the `code` rule, the `ctr` rule, and the `sel` rule.

These related rules are derived by Isabelle when human engineers define new constants using the `primcorec` keyword, which is used to define primitively corecursive functions. Since this assertion checks how constants are defined in the background context, it can tell that the proof goal at hand is a coinductive problem. Therefore, if this assertion returns `true`, maybe the special purpose method called `coinduct` would be useful, since it is developed for coinductive problems. The advantage of this assertions is that it can guess if a problem is a coinductive problem or not, even though we did not have that problem at hand when developing the assertion.

Due to the page limit, we expound the further details of the 113 assertions in our accompanying Appendix [14].

4   The Task for Machine Learning Algorithms

The task for machine learning algorithms is to predict the name of a promising proof method from the corresponding array of boolean values. Since we often have multiple equivalently suitable methods for a given proof goal, this learning task should be seen as a multi-output problem: given an array of boolean values machine learning algorithms should return multiple candidate proof methods rather than only one method. Furthermore, this problem should be treated as a regression problem rather than a classification problem, so that users can see numerical estimates about how likely each method is suitable for a given goal.

5   Conclusion and Related Work

We presented our dataset for proof method recommendation in Isabelle/HOL. Its simple data format allows machine learning practitioners to try out various algorithms to improve the performance of proof method recommendation.

Kaliszyk *et al.* presented HolStep [9], a dataset based on proofs for HOL Light [7]. They developed the dataset from a multivariate analysis library [8] and the proof of the Kepler conjecture [6]. They built HolStep for various tasks, which does not include proof method prediction. While their dataset explicitly describes the text representations of conjectures and dependencies of theorems and constants, our dataset presents only the essential information about proof documents as an array of boolean values.

Blanchette *et al.* mined the Archive of Formal Proofs [2] and investigated the nature of proof developments, such as the size and complexity of proofs [12]. Matichuk *et al.* also studied the Archive of Formal Proofs to understand leading indicators of proof size [12]. Neither of their projects aimed at suggesting how to write proof documents: to the best of our knowledge we are the first to mine a large repository of ITP proofs using hand crafted feature extractors.

Our dataset does not contain information useful to predict what arguments to pass to each method. Previously we developed, smart_induct [16], to address this problem for the induct method in Isabelle/HOL, using a domain-specific language for logical feature extraction [13].

Recently a number of researchers have developed meta-tools that exploit existing proof methods and tactics and brought stronger proof automation to ITPs [1,4,5,11,18,19]. We hope that our dataset helps them improve the performance of such meta-tools for Isabelle/HOL.

References

1. Bansal, K., Loos, S.M., Rabe, M.N., Szegedy, C., Wilcox, S.: HOList: an environment for machine learning of higher order logic theorem proving. In: Proceedings of the 36th International Conference on Machine Learning, ICML 2019, Long Beach, California, USA (2019). http://proceedings.mlr.press/v97/bansal19a.html
2. Blanchette, J.C., Haslbeck, M.W., Matichuk, D., Nipkow, T.: Mining the archive of formal proofs. In: Kerber, M., Carette, J., Kaliszyk, C., Rabe, F., Sorge, V. (eds.) CICM 2015. LNCS, vol. 9150, pp. 3–17. Springer, Heidelberg (2015). https://doi.org/10.1007/978-3-319-20615-8_1
3. Breiman, L., Friedman, J.H., Olshen, R.A., Stone, C.J.: Classification and Regression Trees. Wadsworth (1984)
4. Gauthier, T., Kaliszyk, C., Urban, J.: TacticToe: learning to reason with HOL4 tactics. In: LPAR-21, 21st International Conference on Logic for Programming, Artificial Intelligence and Reasoning, Maun, Botswana (2017). http://www.easychair.org/publications/paper/340355
5. Gransden, T., Walkinshaw, N., Raman, R.: SEPIA: search for proofs using inferred automata. In: Felty, A., Middeldorp, A. (eds.) CADE 2015. LNCS, vol. 9195, pp. 246–255. Springer, Cham (2015). https://doi.org/10.1007/978-3-319-21401-6_16

6. Hales, T.C., et al.: a formal proof of the Kepler conjecture. CoRR abs/1501.02155 (2015). http://arxiv.org/abs/1501.02155

7. Harrison, J.: HOL light: a tutorial introduction. In: Srivas, M., Camilleri, A. (eds.) FMCAD 1996. LNCS, vol. 1166, pp. 265–289. Springer, Heidelberg (1996). https://doi.org/10.1007/BFb0031814

8. Harrison, J.: The HOL light theory of euclidean space. J. Autom. Reason. **50**(2), 173–190 (2013). https://doi.org/10.1007/s10817-012-9250-9

9. Kaliszyk, C., Chollet, F., Szegedy, C.: HolStep: A machine learning dataset for higher-order logic theorem proving. In: 5th International Conference on Learning Representations, ICLR 2017, Toulon, France, Conference Track Proceedings (2017)

10. Klein, G., Nipkow, T., Paulson, L., Thiemann, R.: The archive of formal proofs (2004). https://www.isa-afp.org/

11. Komendantskaya, E., Heras, J.: Proof mining with dependent types. In: Geuvers, H., England, M., Hasan, O., Rabe, F., Teschke, O. (eds.) CICM 2017. LNCS, vol. 10383, pp. 303–318. Springer, Cham (2017). https://doi.org/10.1007/978-3-319-62075-6_21

12. Matichuk, D., Murray, T.C., Andronick, J., Jeffery, D.R., Klein, G., Staples, M.: Empirical study towards a leading indicator for cost of formal software verification. In: 37th IEEE/ACM International Conference on Software Engineering, ICSE 2015, Florence, Italy, vol. 1 (2015). https://doi.org/10.1109/ICSE.2015.85

13. Nagashima, Y.: LiFtEr: language to encode induction heuristics for Isabelle/HOL. In: Lin, A. (ed.) APLAS 2019. LNCS, vol. 11893, pp. 266–287. Springer, Cham (2019). https://doi.org/10.1007/978-3-030-34175-6_14

14. Nagashima, Y.: Appendix to "simple dataset for proof method recommendation in Isabelle/HOL (dataset description)", May 2020. https://doi.org/10.5281/zenodo.3839417

15. Nagashima, Y.: Simple dataset for proof method recommendation in Isabelle/HOL, May 2020. https://doi.org/10.5281/zenodo.3819026

16. Nagashima, Y.: Smart induction for Isabelle/HOL (tool paper). CoRR abs/2001.10834 (2020). https://arxiv.org/abs/2001.10834

17. Nagashima, Y., He, Y.: PaMpeR: proof method recommendation system for Isabelle/HOL. In: Proceedings of the 33rd ACM/IEEE International Conference on Automated Software Engineering, ASE 2018, Montpellier, France, 3–7 September 2018, pp. 362–372 (2018). https://doi.org/10.1145/3238147.3238210

18. Nagashima, Y., Kumar, R.: A proof strategy language and proof script generation for Isabelle/HOL. In: de Moura, L. (ed.) CADE 2017. LNCS, vol. 10395, pp. 528–545. Springer, Cham (2017). https://doi.org/10.1007/978-3-319-63046-5_32

19. Nagashima, Y., Parsert, J.: Goal-oriented conjecturing for Isabelle/HOL. In: Rabe, F., Farmer, W., Passmore, G., Youssef, A. (eds.) CICM 2018. LNCS, vol. 11006, pp. 225–231. Springer, Cham (2018). https://doi.org/10.1007/978-3-319-96812-4_19

20. Nipkow, T., Paulson, L.C., Wenzel, M.: Isabelle/HOL - A Proof Assistant for Higher-Order Logic. Lecture Notes in Computer Science, vol. 2283. Springer, Heidelberg (2002). https://doi.org/10.1007/3-540-45949-9

Dataset Description: Formalization of Elementary Number Theory in Mizar

Adam Naumowicz$^{(\boxtimes)}$ (iD)

Institute of Informatics, University of Bialystok,
Ciolkowskiego 1M, 15-245 Bialystok, Poland
adamn@mizar.org

Abstract. In this paper we present a dataset based on the Mizar formalization of selected problems related to elementary number theory. The dataset comprises proofs of problems on several levels of difficulty. They are available in the form of full proofs, proof sketches, as well as bare statements equipped with suitable environments importing necessary notions from the Mizar Mathematical Library. The elementary character of the underlying theory makes the data particularly suitable as a starting point for developing courses in interactive theorem proving based mathematics education and recreational mathematics activities.

Keywords: Mizar formalization · Number theory · Mathematics education · Recreational mathematics

1 Introduction

The centrally maintained library of formalizations developed using Mizar [3], the Mizar Mathematical Library (MML [2]), contains over $60,000$ theorems and $12,000$ definitions. The data is organized into more than $1,300$ files representing *articles* on various topics. As such, the huge and somewhat eclectic library does not appear to be the best resource for introducing the Mizar way of formalizing mathematics to new users or facilitating introductory Mizar-based courses for math students. For this reason we have started developing a set of easy to comprehend Mizar data files which can provide a better starting point for educational activities. The set is based on examples from elementary number theory which has an initially relatively steep learning curve, few prerequisites and provides a great selection of self-contained proofs. Number theory proofs very often carry an extra recreational component – statements can amuse the audience by simplicity and elegance of their form, references to specific occasions, years or dates and so on. Such tasks are in line with the educational entertainment approach to learning which helps perceive the formalization as a challenging but rewarding activity. We believe that thanks to mastering the elementary techniques and familiarizing with the theory's basic methods one can be prepared to approach the study and/or formalization of further, more advanced problems.

The Mizar processing has been performed using the infrastructure of the University of Bialystok High Performance Computing Center.

C. Benzmüller and B. Miller (Eds.): CICM 2020, LNAI 12236, pp. 303–308, 2020.
https://doi.org/10.1007/978-3-030-53518-6_22

2   Underlying Informal Data

Our dataset is intended to gradually formalize the content of the book *"250 Problems in Elementary Number Theory"* [14] by Waclaw Sierpinski. Sierpinski had numerous contributions to many fields of mathematics, but number theory was his first main area of interest. The above-mentioned book was published by Elsevier and Polish National Publishers in the series *Modern Analytic and Computational Methods in Science and Mathematics* exactly half a century ago - in 1970. Thus, our paper is a humble tribute to Sierpinski, whose prolific and diverse research resulted in over 700 papers and 50 books. The content of the book covers the following chapters: I. Divisibility of Numbers, II. Relatively Prime Numbers, III. Arithmetic Progressions, IV. Prime and Composite Numbers, V. Diophantine Equations, VI. Miscellanea.

Our initial dataset uses data corresponding to ten first problems from the first chapter. Unlike other sources used in many Mizar formalization projects (handbooks [4], whole theories [5], particular theorems [9], research papers [10], etc.) this material comprises self-contained and relatively short proofs, so the work on the formalization can easily be split, given necessary formal environment and necessary hints. They can form a number of similar yet slightly different tasks which can be solved/formalized independently by individuals or in groups.

3   Dataset Characteristics

Similarly to the informal original, the dataset comprises Mizar proofs of problems on several levels of difficulty. They are available in the form of full proofs, proof sketches, as well as bare statements equipped with suitable environments [12] importing necessary notions from the MML. Some ideas were drawn from F. Wiedijk's notion of formal proof sketches [18] and J. Alama's mizar-items [1] (developed as a means to do reverse mathematics over MML). The generation of respective files was achieved by means of standard Mizar tools for extracting article abstracts [6], and optimizing formalization environments [11]. Building a suitable formalization environment of notions to be imported from the MML is sometimes a non-trivial task itself, since many number theory facts are scattered around the current library and take care of their various dependencies – apart from proper number theory files, users also need to look for relevant information in formalizations concerning cryptography (e.g. article PEPIN) or set theory (article ABIAN), etc. Although the material contained in the problems is elementary, the collected proofs allow learning also more advanced Mizar proof methods, like schemes or using Mizar flexary logical connectives [8] (see references in Table 1).

3.1   Dataset Organization

The dataset is available for download as a compressed `number.zip` archive[1]. All the files are compatible with the current official Mizar ver. 8.1.09 bundled with

---

[1] http://mizar.uwb.edu.pl/~softadm/number/.

MML ver. 5.57.1355 (04 June 2019)[2]. The underlying Mizar article is now also available in the MML as article NUMBER01 [13].

The data is located in directories: nump001 – nump010 corresponding to ten initial problems from Sierpinski's book. Each directory contains subdirectories with:

- a bare statement (`statement/nump0XYt.miz`)
- a proof sketch (`sketch/nump0XYs.miz`)
- a full proof (`proof/nump0XYp.miz`)

and an extra file `references` (extracted theorems and schemes) to consult before attempting the proof. Each `*.miz` file contains its environment. In case of bare statements, environment not only lacks theorems and schemes, but also other notions imported in proofs (to allow creating alternative proofs, which are shorter, more elegant, etc.). The sketches are proof skeletons which, apart from the problem statement, contain a working proof structure which can be filled in as is, or modified by hand within the restriction of a given environment. Having the proof environment right is sometimes not trivial [12], and so the proof sketch form allows the less experienced users to start developing the proofs immediately and getting to know the Mizar's notion of obviousness by observing which inferences are accepted. Proof sketches have all references removed (including references to local labels, but the labels are left in the source). Moreover, **then** linking is preserved to keep the proof flow resembling the informal original.

In some cases, following Sierpinski's proofs directly requires introducing a few lemmas (not readily available in the current MML) in order not to complicate the proof itself. Some users may find it useful to try the `::$V-` and `::$V+` pragmas to skip proof checking over certain parts of the file.

The proof sketches could also be fed into ATP-based MizAR [7,17] automation within the Emacs mode [16] to automate proof search. Moreover, the files can be HTML-ized [15] once they get processed by the Mizar verifier.

3.2   Some Technical Issues

Beginner Mizar users working with this dataset should be aware of some technical issues.

E.g., a simple glitch can be seen in the statement of the very first problem: Sierpinski refers to *positive integers*, whereas a preferred Mizar way is to use *natural numbers* with their built-in automation. The literal encoding of statements with *positive integers* is of course possible, but requires a technical and superfluous (as far as the integrity of the MML is concerned) registration (see e.g. the `nump001t` file).

We also face numerous differences in the writing style if we intend to mimic natural language reasoning. E.g., in Mizar we use a lot of **then** linking to previous statements instead of using handy congruence chains ubiquitous in informal

---

[2] http://mizar.uwb.edu.pl/system/index.html#download.

divisibility proofs. It would be useful to have the Mizar language understand some sort of iterative congruence similar to the iterative equality feature.

Less trivially, at first it might not be that easy to see a clear connection between the elegant informal statement of problem:

9. Prove that for every positive integer n the number $3(1^5 + 2^5 + \ldots + n^5)$ **is divisible by** $1^3 + 2^3 + \ldots + n^3$.

and its corresponding (somewhat ugly and technical looking) rendering in Mizar:

```
for s1,s2 being XFinSequence of NAT, n being Nat st
(len s1=n+1 & for i being Nat st i in dom s1 holds s1.i=i|^5) &
(len s2=n+1 & for i being Nat st i in dom s2 holds s2.i=i|^3)
holds Sum s2 divides 3*Sum s1;
```

which employs 0-based finite sequences to represent the ellipses available in traditional mathematics. However, one may note here that this Mizar encoding is slightly more general than the original statement, because it also covers the trivial case of $n = 0$ (so n does not have to be strictly positive) since 0^3 divides 0^5 according to the definition of the reflexive 'divides' predicate.

Table 1 shows more information about the data corresponding to particular problems, the estimation of their size and the number of references extracted to form the sketches. One can also see e.g. which problem can be used to illustrate the use of natural induction, or which proof is based on Fermat's little theorem. Moreover, some proofs make use of either 0- or 1-based finite sequences to encode informal ellipses – because of already available MML theories one or the other approach can be preferable.

Table 1. Characteristics of dataset problems.

Problem #	Size (in lines)	References extracted	Lemmas required	Schemes used	Other comments
1	39	6	–	–	–
2	105	10	2	–	–
3	80	17	–	Infinite sequence existence	–
4	58	14	–	–	–
5	77	30	–	–	Fermat's little theorem
6	54	19	–	–	Fermat's little theorem (due to Kraichik)
7	93	27	–	–	Fermat's little theorem
8	163	31	2	Induction	0-based finite sequences
9	69	12	–	Infinite sequence existence	0-based finite sequences
10	159	32	2	–	1-based finite sequences

4   Conclusion and Future Work

The described dataset was created to serve the following main purposes: facilitating theorem proving education (including self-education), promoting proof methodology based on gap filing proof development/refinement, providing simple data for proof exchange and comparison of different formalization environments and frameworks, and being a starting point for further, more advanced number theory developments.

In its current form the data can already be used as a basis for an elementary theorem proving course for students with only rudimentary number theory background. Naturally, there are several ways we can make this data grow and become more generally useful: either continue completing the proofs from the divisibility of numbers chapter, start the formalization work (in parallel) on other chapters, or just formulate a number of next theorems in each chapter to boost development by others/students.

Furthermore, as it usually happens when starting the formalization of a less-developed branch of mathematics, especially if there is a possibility to compare the data developed in various systems, the work may help identify weaker points of a given proof system and streamline further research to devise better solutions or improve the current implementations.

References

1. Alama, J.: mizar-items: exploring fine-grained dependencies in the Mizar mathematical library. In: Davenport, J.H., Farmer, W.M., Urban, J., Rabe, F. (eds.) CICM 2011. LNCS, vol. 6824, pp. 276–277. Springer, Heidelberg (2011). https://doi.org/10.1007/978-3-642-22673-1_19
2. Bancerek, G., et al.: The role of the Mizar mathematical library for interactive proof development in Mizar. J. Autom. Reason. **61**(1–4), 9–32 (2018)
3. Bancerek, G., et al.: Mizar: state-of-the-art and beyond. In: Kerber, M., Carette, J., Kaliszyk, C., Rabe, F., Sorge, V. (eds.) CICM 2015. LNCS (LNAI), vol. 9150, pp. 261–279. Springer, Cham (2015). https://doi.org/10.1007/978-3-319-20615-8_17
4. Bancerek, G., Rudnicki, P.: A compendium of continuous lattices in MIZAR. J. Autom. Reasoning **29**(3–4), 189–224 (2002)
5. Grabowski, A.: Tarski's geometry modelled in Mizar computerized proof assistant. In: Ganzha, M., Maciaszek, L.A., Paprzycki, M. (eds.) Proceedings of the 2016 Federated Conference on Computer Science and Information Systems, FedCSIS 2016, Gdańsk, Poland, 11–14 September 2016. Annals of Computer Science and Information Systems, vol. 8, pp. 373–381. IEEE (2016)
6. Grabowski, A., Kornilowicz, A., Naumowicz, A.: Mizar in a nutshell. J. Formalized Reason. **3**(2), 153–245 (2010)
7. Kaliszyk, C., Urban, J.: Mizar 40 for mizar 40. J. Autom. Reason. **55**(3), 245–256 (2015)
8. Kornilowicz, A.: Flexary connectives in Mizar. Comput. Lang. Syst. Struct. **44**, 238–250 (2015)
9. Kornilowicz, A., Naumowicz, A.: Niven's theorem. Formalized Math. **24**(4), 301–308 (2016)

10. Naumowicz, A.: An example of formalizing recent mathematical results in Mizar. J. Appl. Log. **4**(4), 396–413 (2006)
11. Naumowicz, A.: Tools for MML environment analysis. In: Kerber, M., Carette, J., Kaliszyk, C., Rabe, F., Sorge, V. (eds.) CICM 2015. LNCS (LNAI), vol. 9150, pp. 348–352. Springer, Cham (2015). https://doi.org/10.1007/978-3-319-20615-8_26
12. Naumowicz, A.: Towards standardized Mizar environments. In: Świątek, J., Borzemski, L., Wilimowska, Z. (eds.) ISAT 2017. AISC, vol. 656, pp. 166–175. Springer, Cham (2018). https://doi.org/10.1007/978-3-319-67229-8_15
13. Naumowicz, A.: Elementary number theory problems. Part I. Formalized Math. **28**(1), 115–120 (2020)
14. Sierpiński, W.: 250 Problems in Elementary Number Theory. Elsevier, Amsterdam (1970)
15. Urban, J.: XML-izing Mizar: making semantic processing and presentation of MML easy. In: Kohlhase, M. (ed.) MKM 2005. LNCS (LNAI), vol. 3863, pp. 346–360. Springer, Heidelberg (2006). https://doi.org/10.1007/11618027_23
16. Urban, J.: Mizarmode - an integrated proof assistance tool for the Mizar way of formalizing mathematics. J. Appl. Log. **4**(4), 414–427 (2006)
17. Urban, J., Rudnicki, P., Sutcliffe, G.: ATP and presentation service for Mizar formalizations. J. Autom. Reason. **50**(2), 229–241 (2013)
18. Wiedijk, F.: Formal proof sketches. https://www.cs.ru.nl/~freek/pubs/sketches2.pdf

Guiding Inferences in Connection Tableau by Recurrent Neural Networks

Bartosz Piotrowski[1,2]([⊠]) and Josef Urban[1]

[1] Czech Institute of Informatics, Robotics and Cybernetics, Prague, Czech Republic
[2] Faculty of Mathematics, Informatics and Mechanics, University of Warsaw,
Warsaw, Poland
bartoszpiotrowski@post.pl

Abstract. We present a dataset and experiments on applying recurrent neural networks (RNNs) for guiding clause selection in the connection tableau proof calculus. The RNN encodes a sequence of literals from the current branch of the partial proof tree to a hidden vector state; using it, the system selects a clause for extending the proof tree. The training data and learning setup are described, and the results are discussed and compared with state of the art using gradient boosted trees. Additionally, we perform a conjecturing experiment in which the RNN does not just select an existing clause, but completely constructs the next tableau goal.

Keywords: Connection tableau · Neural networks · Internal guidance

1 Introduction

There is a class of machine learning sequence-to-sequence architectures based on recurrent neural networks (RNNs) which are successfully used in the domain of natural language processing, in particular for translation between languages [2]. Recently, such architectures proved useful also in various tasks in the domain of symbolic computation [6,10,14,16]. The models *encode* the source sequence to a *hidden vector state* and *decode* from it the target sequence.

In this work, we employ such neural methods to choose among the non-deterministic steps in connection-style theorem proving. In more detail, we want to learn the *hidden proving states* that correspond to the evolving proof trees and condition the next prover steps based on them. I.e., from a set of connection tableau proofs we create a dataset (Sect. 2) of *source-target* training examples of the form (*partial_proof_state, decision*) that we then use to train the neural models (Sect. 3). The results are reported in Sect. 4. Section 5 shows an additional experiment with predicting (conjecturing) tableau goals.

B. Piotrowski—Supported by the grant 2018/29/N/ST6/02903 of National Science Center, Poland.
J. Urban—Supported by the *AI4REASON* ERC Consolidator grant nr. 649043 and by the Czech project AI&Reasoning CZ.02.1.01/0.0/0.0/15_003/0000466 and the European Regional Development Fund.

C. Benzmüller and B. Miller (Eds.): CICM 2020, LNAI 12236, pp. 309–314, 2020.
https://doi.org/10.1007/978-3-030-53518-6_23

The connection tableau seems suitable for such methods. The connection proofs grow as branches of a tree rooted in a starting clause. The number of options (clauses) to choose from is relatively small compared to saturation-style provers, where the number of clauses grows quickly to millions during the search. The tableau branches representing the proof states can be the sequential input to the RNNs, which can then decode one or more decisions, i.e., choices of clauses.

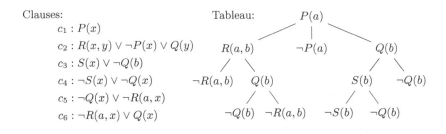

Clauses:

$c_1 : P(x)$

$c_2 : R(x, y) \vee \neg P(x) \vee Q(y)$

$c_3 : S(x) \vee \neg Q(b)$

$c_4 : \neg S(x) \vee \neg Q(x)$

$c_5 : \neg Q(x) \vee \neg R(a, x)$

$c_6 : \neg R(a, x) \vee Q(x)$

Fig. 1. Closed connection tableau for a set of clauses.

2   A Dataset for Connection-Style Internal Guidance

The experimental data originate from the Mizar Mathematical Library (MML) [7] translated [15] to the TPTP language. We have used the leanCoP connection prover [13] to produce 13822 connection proofs from the Mizar problems.

The connection tableau calculus searches for *refutational proofs*, i.e., proofs showing that a set of first-order clauses is *unsatisfiable*. Figure 1 (adapted from Letz et al. [11]) shows a set of clauses and a *closed connection tableau* constructed from them, proving their unsatisfiability. A closed tableau is a tree with nodes labeled by literals where each branch is *closed*. A *closed* branch contains a pair of *complementary literals* (identical but with opposite polarities). An *open* branch can be extended with descendant nodes by applying one of the input clauses. This *extension* step can often be performed with several different clauses – this is the main non-determinism point. Choosing the correct clause advances the proof, whereas choosing wrongly leads to redundant exploration followed by backtracking.

The training data for choosing good clauses were extracted from the proofs as follows. First, formulas in the proofs were made more uniform by substituting for each universal variable the token VAR and for each Skolem function the token SKLM. For each non-root and non-leaf node n in each proof tree, we exported two types of paths, which form two kinds of input data for the neural architecture:

(1) $P_{\text{lits}}(r \to n)$ – the literals leading from the root r to the node n,
(2) $P_{\text{cls}}(r \to n)$ – the clauses that were chosen on the way from the root r to n.

The output data are created as follows. For each node n we record the decision (i.e., the clause) that led to the proof. Let clause(n) be the clause selected at node n. For instance, if n is the node labeled by $R(a, b)$ in Fig. 1, clause(n) = c_6.

The pairs $\big(P_{\mathrm{lits}}(r \to n), \mathrm{clause}(n)\big)$ and $\big(P_{\mathrm{cls}}(r \to n), \mathrm{clause}(n)\big)$ constitute two different sets of training examples for learning clause selection. Each of these sets contains 567273 pairs. Additionally, we have constructed similar data in which the output contains not only the choice of the next clause, but a sequence of two or three such consecutive choices. All these data sets[1] were split into training, validation and testing sets – the split was induced by an initial split of the proofs in proportions 0.6, 0.1 and 0.3, respectively.

3   Neural Modelling and Evaluation Metric

As a suitable sequence-to-sequence recurrent neural model we used an implementation of a neural machine translation (NMT) architecture by Luong et al. [12], which was already successfully used for symbolic tasks in [16] and [14]. All the hyperparameters used for training were inherited from [16].

Let $subsequent\_clauses_i(P_{\mathrm{lits/cls}}(r \to n))$ be a set of i-long sequences of clauses found in the provided proofs, following a given path of literals/clauses from the root to a node n.[2] Let $clauses\_from\_model_k^i(P_{\mathrm{lits/cls}}(r \to n))$ be a set of k i-long sequences of clauses decoded from the NMT model (we decoded for $k = 1$ or $k = 10$ most probable sequences using the *beam search* technique [5]). We consider the prediction from the model for a given path of literals/clauses as successful if the sets $subsequent\_clauses_i(P_{\mathrm{lits/cls}}(r \to n))$ and $clauses\_from\_model_k^i(P_{\mathrm{lits/cls}}(r \to n))$ intersect. The metric of predictive accuracy of the model is the proportion of successful predictions on the test set.

4   Results

The average results for the above metric are shown in Table 1. We can see that predicting the next clause is much more precise than predicting multiple clauses. The accuracy of predicting the next clause(s) from a sequence of clauses is lower than predicting the next clause(s) from a sequence of literals, which means the literals give more precise information for making the correct decision.

We have also investigated how the performance of NMT depends on the length of the input sequences. The results for the

Table 1. Predictive accuracy of the NMT system trained on two types of source paths (literals or clauses), decoding 1–3 consecutive clauses. 1 or 10 best outputs were decoded and assessed.

	Paths of literals		Paths of clauses	
# clauses to decode	1 best output	10 best outputs	1 best output	10 best outputs
1	0.64	0.72	0.17	0.36
2	0.11	0.19	0.03	0.07
3	0.05	0.07	0.01	0.02

---

[1]   The tableau proofs and the sequential training data extracted from it are available at https://github.com/BartoszPiotrowski/guiding-connection-tableau-by-RNNs.

[2]   E.g., for the proof from Fig. 1, we have $(c_4) \in subsequent\_clauses_1(P_{\mathrm{lits}}(P(a) \to S(b)))$, $(c_6, c_5) \in subsequent\_clauses_2(P_{\mathrm{lits}}(P(a) \to R(a,b)))$, $(c_6) \in subsequent\_clauses_1(P_{\mathrm{cls}}(c_1 \to c_2))$, or $(c_3, c_4) \in subsequent\_clauses_1(P_{\mathrm{cls}}(c_1 \to c_2))$.

neural model trained on the paths of literals as the input are shown in the second row of Table 2. As expected, the longer the input sequence, the better is the prediction. The neural model was capable of taking advantage of a more complex context. This differs significantly with the path-characterization methods using manual features (as in [9]) that just average (possibly with some decay factor) over the features of all literals on the path.

To compare with such methods, we trained a classifier based on gradient boosted trees for this task using the XGBoost system [1], which was used for learning feature-based guidance in [9]. To make the task comparable to the neural methods, we trained XGBoost in a multilabel setting, i.e., for each partial proof state (a path of literals) it learns to score all the available clauses, treated as labels. Due to limited resources, we restrict this comparison to the MPTP2078 subset of MML which has 1383 different labels (the clause names).

The average performance of XGBoost on predicting the next clause from the (featurized) path of literals was 0.43. This is lower than the performance of the neural model, also using literals on the path as the input (0.64). The XGBoost performance conditioned on the length of the input path is shown in the third row of Table 2. XGBoost is outperforming NMT on shorter input sequences of literals, but on longer paths, XGBoost gets significantly worse. The performance of the recurrent neural model grows with the length of the input sequence, reaching 0.85 for input length 8. This means that providing more context significantly helps the recurrent neural methods, where the hidden state much more precisely represents (encodes) the whole path. The feature-based representation used by XGBoost cannot reach such precision, which is likely the main reason for its performance flattening early and reaching at most 0.51.

Table 2. Predictive accuracy of the NMT and XGBoost systems for different lengths of input sequences consisting of literals.

Length	1	2	3	4	5	6	7	8
NMT	0.19	0.48	0.64	0.70	0.68	0.72	0.79	0.85
XGB	0.43	0.35	0.42	0.39	0.47	0.41	0.51	0.46

Table 3. Predictive accuracy of conjecturing literals by the NMT system for input sequences of different lengths.

Length	1	2	3	4	5	6	7	all
NMT	0.04	0.05	0.08	0.11	0.14	0.16	0.34	0.08

5   Conjecturing New Literals

As an additional experiment demonstrating the power of the recurrent neural methods we constructed a data set for *conjecturing* new literals on the paths in the tableau proofs. The goal here is not to select a proper literal, but to *construct* it from the available symbols (the number of them for the MML-based data set is 6442). This task is impossible to achieve with the previous methods that can only *rank* or *classify* the available options. Recurrent neural networks are, on the other hand, well-suited for such tasks – e.g., in machine translation, they can learn how to compose grammatically correct and meaningful sentences.

It turns out that this more difficult task is to some extent feasible with NMT. Table 3 shows that NMT could propose the right next literal on the path in a significant number of cases. Again, there is a positive dependence between the length of the input sequence and the predictive performance. Most of the times the correct predictions involve short literals, whereas predicting longer literals is harder. The proposed longer literals often not only do not match the right ones but have an improper structure (see Table 4 for examples of the NMT outputs).

Table 4. Literals conjectured by NMT *vs.* the correct ones. (1) is an example of a correctly predicted output; in (2) NMT was wrong but proposed a literal which is similar to the proper one; (3) shows a syntactically incorrect literal produced by NMT.

	NMT prediction	Correct output
(1)	`m1_subset_1(np__1,k4_ordinal1)`	`m1_subset_1(np__1,k4_ordinal1)`
(2)	`m1_subset_1(SKLM,k1_zfmisc_1(SKLM))`	`m1_subset_1(SKLM,SKLM)`
(3)	`k2_tarski(SKLM,SKLM)=k2_tarski(SKLM`	`k2_tarski(SKLM,SKLM)=k2_tarski(SKLM,SKLM)`

6   Conclusion and Future Work

In this work, we proposed RNN-based encoding and decoding as a suitable representation and approach for learning clause selection in connection tableau. This differs from previous approaches – both neural and non-neural – by emphasizing the importance of the evolving proof state and its accurate encoding. The approach and the constructed datasets also allow us to meaningfully try completely new tasks, such as automatically conjecturing the next literal on the path. The experimental evaluation is encouraging. In particular, it shows that the longer the context, the more precise the recurrent methods are in choosing the next steps, unlike the previous methods. The evaluation and data sets have focused (as similar research studies [4,8]) on the machine learning performance, which is known to underlie the theorem proving performance. Future work includes integrating such methods into ATP systems and ATP evaluation similar to [3,9].

References

1. Chen, T., Guestrin, C.: XGboost: a scalable tree boosting system. ACM SIGKDD **2016**, 785–794 (2016)
2. Cho, K., van Merrienboer, B., Gülçehre, Ç., Bahdanau, D., Bougares, F., Schwenk, H., Bengio, Y.: Learning phrase representations using RNN encoder-decoder for statistical machine translation. EMNLP **2014**, 1724–1734 (2014)
3. Chvalovský, K., Jakubuv, J., Suda, M., Urban, J.: ENIGMA-NG: efficient neural and gradient-boosted inference guidance for E. CADE **27**, 197–215 (2019)
4. Evans, R., Saxton, D., Amos, D., Kohli, P., Grefenstette, E.: Can neural networks understand logical entailment? In: ICLR 2018 (2018)
5. Freitag, M., Al-Onaizan, Y.: Beam search strategies for neural machine translation. In: NMT@ACL 2017, pp. 56–60 (2017)

6. Gauthier, T.: Deep reinforcement learning for synthesizing functions in higher-order logic. CoRR (2019). http://arxiv.org/abs/1910.11797
7. Grabowski, A., Kornilowicz, A., Naumowicz, A.: Mizar in a nutshell. J. Formalized Reasoning **3**(2), 153–245 (2010)
8. Kaliszyk, C., Chollet, F., Szegedy, C.: Holstep: a machine learning dataset for higher-order logic theorem proving. In: ICLR 2017 (2017)
9. Kaliszyk, C., Urban, J., Michalewski, H., Olšák, M.: Reinforcement learning of theorem proving. NeurIPS **2018**, 8836–8847 (2018)
10. Lample, G., Charton, F.: Deep learning for symbolic mathematics. CoRR (2019). http://arxiv.org/abs/1912.01412
11. Letz, R., Mayr, K., Goller, C.: Controlled integration of the cut rule into connection tableau calculi. J. Autom. Reasoning **13**, 297–337 (1994)
12. Luong, M., Brevdo, E., Zhao, R.: Neural machine translation (seq2seq) tutorial (2017). https://github.com/tensorflow/nmt
13. Otten, J., Bibel, W.: leanCoP: lean connection-based theorem proving. J. Symb. Comput. **36**(1–2), 139–161 (2003)
14. Piotrowski, B., Urban, J., Brown, C.E., Kaliszyk, C.: Can neural networks learn symbolic rewriting? CoRR (2019). https://arxiv.org/pdf/1911.04873.pdf
15. Urban, J.: MPTP 0.2: Design, implementation, and initial experiments. J. Autom. Reasoning **37**(1–2), 21–43 (2006)
16. Wang, Q., Kaliszyk, C., Urban, J.: First experiments with neural translation of informal to formal mathematics. In: Rabe, F., Farmer, W.M., Passmore, G.O., Youssef, A. (eds.) CICM 2018. LNCS (LNAI), vol. 11006, pp. 255–270. Springer, Cham (2018). https://doi.org/10.1007/978-3-319-96812-4_22

First Neural Conjecturing Datasets and Experiments

Josef Urban[(⊠)] and Jan Jakubův

Czech Institute of Informatics, Robotics and Cybernetics, Prague, Czech Republic
Josef.Urban@gmail.com

Abstract. We describe several datasets and first experiments with creating conjectures by neural methods. The datasets are based on the Mizar Mathematical Library processed in several forms and the problems extracted from it by the MPTP system and proved by the E prover using the ENIGMA guidance. The conjecturing experiments use the Transformer architecture and in particular its GPT-2 implementation.

1 Introduction and Related Work

Automated creation of suitable conjectures is one of the hard problems in automated reasoning over large mathematical corpora. This includes tasks such as (i) conjecturing suitable intermediate lemmas (cuts) when proving a harder conjecture, and (ii) unrestricted creation of interesting conjectures based on the previous theory (i.e., theory exploration). Starting with Lenat's AM [10], several systems such as the more specialized Graffitti by Fajtlowicz [4], and Colton's HR [3] have been developed, typically using heuristics for theory exploration or limited brute-force enumeration, controlled e.g. by the type system [7].

Our motivation is the work of Karpathy[1] with recurrent neural networks (RNNs). One of his experiments used the Stacks project, generating LaTeX-style pseudo-mathematics that looked quite credible to non-experts. We have repeated these experiments over the Mizar library using Karpathy's RNNs in 2016, but the results did not seem convincing. The neural methods have however improved since, coming up with stronger methods and systems such as attention, transformer and GPT-2 [12]. The experiments described here started by testing GPT-2 on the Mizar library, gradually producing several more datasets.

Related work includes research on the informal-to-formal grammar-based and neural translation [8,9,16,17]. There it was found that PCFGs and RNNs with attention work well on some informal-to-formal datasets, can learn analogies from the data, and can be used to produce multiple formal outputs of which some are new provable conjectures. In [16] we use this together with type checking to set up a data-augmentation loop between the neural learner and the type-checker. Such learning-reasoning loops are also planned for the datasets presented here. Similar experiments are done in [6] and by Chvalovský[2].

---

[1] http://karpathy.github.io/2015/05/21/rnn-effectiveness/.

[2] http://aitp-conference.org/2019/abstract/AITP_2019_paper_27.pdf, http://aitp-conference.org/2020/abstract/paper_21.pdf.

© Springer Nature Switzerland AG 2020
C. Benzmüller and B. Miller (Eds.): CICM 2020, LNAI 12236, pp. 315–323, 2020.
https://doi.org/10.1007/978-3-030-53518-6_24

Gauthier has been working on term synthesis using Monte-Carlo Tree Search and reinforcement learning with semantic feedback [1,5].

2 Datasets

The datasets for neural conjecturing are available from our web page[3]. We have so far experimented with the following data:

1. All Mizar articles (MML version 1147), stripped of comments and concatenated together[4]. This is 78M of uncompressed text.
2. Text version of the HTML export [14] of the MML articles[5]. This unpacks to 156 MB. It additionally contains disambiguation features such as full types of variables, full names of theorems and the thesis is printed after every natural deduction step. This seems useful for neural conjecturing because the context is repeated more often.
3. Tokenized TPTP proofs[6] of 28271 Mizar theorems translated by the MPTP system [15]. The proofs are produced by the E prover [13] equipped with recent ENIGMA guidance [2]. This unpacks to 658 MB.
4. A subselection of the used Mizar premises from the 28271 proofs printed in prefix notation[7]. These files always start with the conjecture, and the premises are printed in the order in which E used them in its proof. This unpacks to 53 MB.

Below we show short examples of the four kinds of data, all for the theorem ZMODUL01:103:

```
theorem
  for W being strict Submodule of V holds W /\ W = W
  proof
    let W be strict Submodule of V;
    the carrier of W = (the carrier of W) /\ (the carrier of W);
    hence thesis by Def15;
  end;

theorem :: ZMODUL01:103
for V being Z_Module
for W being strict Submodule of V holds W /\ W = W
proof
let V be Z_Module; ::_thesis: for W being strict Submodule of V holds W /\ W = W
let W be strict Submodule of V; ::_thesis: W /\ W = W
 the carrier of W = the carrier of W /\ the carrier of W ;
hence  W /\ W = W by Def15; ::_thesis: verum
end;

fof ( d15_zmodul01 , axiom , ! [ X1 ] : ( ( ( ( ( ( ( ( ( ( ~ ( v2_struct_0 ( X1 ) ) ) & ...
fof ( idempotence_k3_xboole_0 , axiom , ! [ X1 , X2 ] : k3_xboole_0 ( X1 , X1 ) = X1 ...
fof ( t103_zmodul01 , conjecture , ! [ X1 ] : ( ( ( ( ( ( ( ( ( ( ~ ( v2_struct_0 ( X1 ) ) ) ...
fof ( c_0_3 , plain , ! [ X118 , X119 , X120 , X121 ] : ( ( X121 != k7_zmodul01 ( X118 , ...
cnf ( c_0_6 , plain , ( X1 = k7_zmodul01 ( X4 , X2 , X3 ) | v2_struct_0 ( X4 ) | ...
```

```
c! b0   c=> c& c~ cv2_struct_0 b0 c& cv13_algstr_0 b0 c& cv2_rlvect_1 b0 c& cv3_rlvect_1 ...
c! b0   c=> c& c~ cv2_struct_0 b0 c& cv13_algstr_0 b0 c& cv2_rlvect_1 b0 c& cv3_rlvect_1 ...
c! b0   c! b1  c= ck3_xboole_0 b0 b0 b0
```

3 Experiments

The basic experiment for each dataset consists of training the smallest (117 M parameters) version of GPT-2 on a NVIDIA GeForce GTX 1080 GPU with 12 GB RAM, producing random unconditioned samples during the training. The produced samples and the most recent trained models are available from our web page[8]. The published models can be used for conditional and unconditional generation of Mizar-like texts, proofs and premise completion. The samples contain megabytes of examples of what can be generated and how the generated texts improve during the training. The training on the third dataset was stopped early. The large number of redundant tokens such as brackets and commas led us to produce the fourth dataset that uses the punctuation-free prefix notation and much shorter summary of the E proof (just the premises in their order). The training for datasets 1, 2 and 4 has been running for several weeks, with the performance still slowly improving. See Fig. 1 in Appendix A for a sample training and loss on dataset 2. There are many interesting conjectures generated during the unconditioned sampling. The trained models can be directly used by Mizar users for auto-completion of their texts. Some examples compared to real theorems are shown below. More semantic evaluation on the textual datasets (1 and 2) could be done in various ways. We imagine that a proper Mizar environment will have to be guessed, some assumptions may be automatically added, etc.

```
# real MML theorem
theorem :: YELLOW10:61
for S, T being non empty up-complete Poset
for X being Subset of S
for Y being Subset of T st X is property(S) & Y is property(S) holds
[:X,Y:] is property(S)

# generated similar "theorem"
theorem :: WAYBEL30:56
for R being complete Lattice
for X being Subset of [:R,R:] st X is upper & X is property(S) holds
[:X,X:] is property(S)

# real MML theorem
theorem :: SEQ_4:47
for X being non empty real-membered set
for Y being real-membered set st X c= Y & Y is bounded_below holds
lower_bound Y <= lower_bound X

# generated similar "theorem"
theorem Th33: :: SEQ_4:33
for X being real-membered set
for Y being real-membered set st Y is bounded_below & X c= Y holds
lower_bound Y <= lower_bound X

# generated "theorem" with "proof"
theorem Th23: :: STIRL2_1:23
for X, Y being finite set st not X is empty & X c= Y & card X = card Y holds X = Y
```

---

[8] http://grid01.ciirc.cvut.cz/~mptp/nn_conj20/samples/, http://grid01.ciirc.cvut.cz/~mptp/nn_conj20/models/.

```
proof
let X, Y be finite set ; ::_thesis: ( not X is empty & X c= Y & card X = card Y implies X = Y )
assume that
A1: not X is empty and A2: X c= Y and A3: card X = card Y ; ::_thesis: X = Y
 card (Y \ X) = (card Y) - (card X) by A1, A3, CARD_2:44;
then A4: card (Y \ X) = ((card Y) - 1) - (card X) by CARD_1:30;
 X = Y \ X by A2, A3, Th22;
hence  X = Y by A4, XBOOLE_0:def_10; ::_thesis: verum
end;
```

3.1 Conditioned Completion

We have also done two initial experiments with proof and formula completion. The data and results for them are available from our web page[9]. In the first experiment, we use a model trained on Dataset 4 (premises), and ask the model to auto-complete 369 theorems from the CARD series of Mizar. For each conjecture we produce 10 premise selections using beam search, and we use different temperatures and beam search parameters. An interesting phenomenon is that with low temperatures, practically all conjectured premises are known Mizar theorems. I.e., the task reduces to standard premise selection. With higher temperatures, GPT-2 starts producing premises (lemmas) that are not among the existing Mizar theorems, but are still well-typed. Even higher temperatures lead to non-well-typed or even unparsable lemmas. The next section provides a more involved ATP evaluation done on a larger dataset.

The second experiment was done over Dataset 2 and a set of 462 partial formulas from the CARD articles. The model trained on Dataset 2 is then (again using beam search) asked to auto-complete these formulas. Mizar users can also play with such autocompletion via a web server[10] using this model. For example,

```
for M, N being Cardinal holds
```

results in the following (selected) auto-completions (more are available online[11]):

```
( M = N iff M,N are_equipotent )
( M = N iff not 0 in M ) by ORDINAL3:8;
M *' N = N *' M
( M in N iff not M c= N )
the_rank_of M = the_rank_of N by Th77;
nextcard (Sum M) = M *' N
```

3.2 Initial ATP Evaluation

The first larger ATP (semantic) evaluation uses the fourth dataset following the setting introduced for such evaluations in [6]. After training GPT-2 on the 28271 ENIGMA proofs, we produce (using beam search) 12 GPT-2 premise predictions for a set of 31792 theorems of which 6639 are not among the training ones.

---

[9] http://grid01.ciirc.cvut.cz/~mptp/nn_conj20/samples/premises/,   http://grid01.ciirc.cvut.cz/~mptp/nn_conj20/samples/html2/.

[10] http://grid01.ciirc.cvut.cz:8000/.

[11] http://grid01.ciirc.cvut.cz/~mptp/nn_conj20/samples/html2/00cardmizout1_t1.

This yields 381432 predictions,[12] deduplicated to 193320 unique predictions. The predictions are converted back to TPTP from the polish notation, creating ATP problems. We distinguish between the premises that already exist as Mizar theorems and definitions, and the new formulas (conjectures) introduced by GPT-2. 108564[13] of the created problems contain no new conjectures, i.e., GPT-2 works there as a standard premise selector similar to [11].

Most (86899) of these ATP problems[14] can be quickly shown to be countersatisfiable by E prover.[15] This shows the first difference between syntactic loss as used by the ML/NLP community and semantic usefulness. GPT-2's loss is geared towards mimicking the length of the original texts with a small number of syntactic mistakes. In premise selection, the underlying task is to generate premises that have sufficient logical power. Overshooting is better than making a mistake and observing the usual length of the text. 11866 of the problems can be proved in 6 s, resulting in proofs of 8105 theorems. This is not yet an interesting number, because GPT-2 does not observe the *chronological order* of premises. E.g., 4350 of the proofs use only a single premise – typically GPT-2 suggested the proved theorem itself as a premise. Still, some predictions are chronologically correct and lead to correct new proofs. E.g. for theorem XXREAL_1:48,[16] which is not in the training set, the fifth GPT-2 sample proposed 7 premises[17] of which 5 were used in a quickly found new E proof[18] (see Appendix A for details).

Next we evaluate[19] the 44524 problems[20] that do use at least one newly proposed premise. We have not strictly enforced the chronology, but remove the theorem itself from axioms if proposed. 34675 of the problems are then found countersatisfiable by E in 1 s and for 1515 a proof is found. The conjectures may be interesting, even though hard to prove automatically: E.g. for GROUPP_1:T10[21] a valid, though not quite trivial strengthening from finite to general groups is proposed, see Appendix A for details.

In total, GPT-2 proposed in this experiment 52515 new syntactically correct formulas[22] that deduplicate to 33100. Some are clearly false, yet quite natural to ask: e.g. for dozens of theorems like SINCOS10:17[23] – "sec is increasing on $[0, \pi/2)$" – GPT-2 makes the conjecture that every differentiable function is increasing.[24] In this particular case we can likely disprove the conjecture since there are counterexamples in the MML. Similarly, in FUNCTOR1:9[25], to prove

---

[12] http://grid01.ciirc.cvut.cz/~mptp/nn_conj20/results/preds3.tar.gz.

[13] http://grid01.ciirc.cvut.cz/~mptp/nn_conj20/results/preds5.tar.gz.

[14] http://grid01.ciirc.cvut.cz/~mptp/nn_conj20/results/preds6.tar.gz.

[15] We used E with 6 s time limit and its auto-schedule mode for this initial check.

[16] http://grid01.ciirc.cvut.cz/~mptp/7.13.01_4.181.1147/html/xxreal_1.html#T48.

[17] http://grid01.ciirc.cvut.cz/~mptp/nn_conj20/results/t48_xxreal_1___5.

[18] http://grid01.ciirc.cvut.cz/~mptp/nn_conj20/results/t48_xxreal_1___5.out.

[19] http://grid01.ciirc.cvut.cz/~mptp/nn_conj20/results/preddatagpt1.out.tar.gz.

[20] http://grid01.ciirc.cvut.cz/~mptp/nn_conj20/results/preddatagpt1.tar.gz.

[21] http://grid01.ciirc.cvut.cz/~mptp/7.13.01_4.181.1147/html/groupp_1.html#T10.

[22] http://grid01.ciirc.cvut.cz/~mptp/nn_conj20/results/out4.tar.gz.

[23] http://grid01.ciirc.cvut.cz/~mptp/7.13.01_4.181.1147/html/sincos10.html#T17.

[24] http://grid01.ciirc.cvut.cz/~mptp/nn_conj20/results/t17_sincos10___1.

[25] http://grid01.ciirc.cvut.cz/~mptp/7.13.01_4.181.1147/html/functor1.html#T9.

that the composition of full functors is full, GPT-2 proposes to reduce fullness to faithfulness, likely because a previous theorem[26] says that faithfulness is preserved under composition. See Appendix A for details.

Finally we use standard premise selection (although we could recurse and use GPT-2) and E with the ENIGMA guidance to try to prove the 52515 new formulas.[27] This yields 9000–10000 proofs,[28] depending on how we run premise selection and E. While some proofs are long, it seems that we are not yet capable of proving the more interesting conjectures and we still need more ATP strengths. E.g., the longest ATP proof shows that `-infty is non empty`, where `-infty` is defined as `[0,REAL]`. A slightly more useful conjecture which is also hard to prove[29] is the strengthening of the symmetry of the `are_homeomorphic` predicate[30] from non-empty to arbitrary spaces.

Funding. Funded by the *AI4REASON* ERC Consolidator grant nr. 649043 and by the Czech project AI&Reasoning CZ.02.1.01/0.0/0.0/15_003/0000466 and the European Regional Development Fund. We thank K. Chvalovský and T. Gauthier for discussions.

A   Additional Data From the Experiments

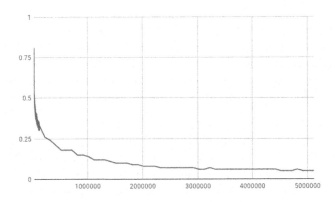

Fig. 1. Dataset 2 training and loss.

---

[26] http://grid01.ciirc.cvut.cz/~mptp/7.13.01_4.181.1147/html/functor1.html#T7.

[27] http://grid01.ciirc.cvut.cz/~mptp/nn_conj20/results/preddata128.tar.gz.

[28] http://grid01.ciirc.cvut.cz/~mptp/nn_conj20/results/preddata128.out.tar.gz.

[29] http://grid01.ciirc.cvut.cz/~mptp/nn_conj20/results/t20_borsuk_3___7__1.

[30] http://grid01.ciirc.cvut.cz/~mptp/7.13.01_4.181.1147/html/borsuk_3.html#R2.

A.1   XXREAL 1:48 and its GPT-2 predictions

theorem Th48: :: XXREAL_1:48
for p, r, s, q being ext−real number st p < r & s <= q holds
[.r,s.[c=].p,q.[

Following are the Mizar premises in the order proposed by GPT-2. The fifth and sixth were not needed for the ATP proof.

theorem Th3: :: XXREAL_1:3
for t, r, s being ext−real number holds t in [.r,s.[iff r <= t & t < s

let X be ext−real−membered set ; let Y be set ;
pred X c= Y means : Def8: :: MEMBERED: def 8
for e being ext−real number st e in X holds e in Y;

let r, s be ext−real number ;
cluster [.r,s.[→ ext−real−membered ;

theorem Th2: :: XXREAL_0:2
for a, b, c being ext−real number st a <= b & b <= c holds a <= c

let X be ext−real−membered set ; cluster → ext−real for Element of X;

theorem :: SUBSET:1
for a, b being set st a in b holds a is Element of b;

theorem Th4: :: XXREAL_1:4
for t, r, s being ext−real number holds t in].r,s.[iff r < t & t < s

A.2   GROUPP_1:10 and its generalization conjectured by GPT-2

theorem Th10: :: GROUPP_1:10
for G being finite Group for N being normal Subgroup of G st
N is Subgroup of center G & G ./. N is cyclic holds G is commutative

The generalization that avoids finiteness:

for G being Group for N being normal Subgroup of G st
N is Subgroup of center G & G ./. N is cyclic holds G is commutative

We don't have an ATP proof of the generalization yet. We thank algebraists Michael Kinyon and David Stanovský for confirming that this generalization is provable. Based on this example Stanovský commented that related Mizar theorems can be similarly generalized.

A.3   SINCOS10:17 and a false conjecture by GPT-2

theorem Th17: :: SINCOS10:17
sec | [.0 ,(PI / 2).[is increasing

GPT-2 generated the following conjecture, which is false. Along with another GPT-2 conjecture about the differentiability of sec on the interval, this results in an ATP proof of SINCOS10:17.

for X **being** set **for** f **being** Function **of** REAL, REAL **holds**
f is differentiable_on X **implies** f | X is increasing

A.4   FUNCTOR1:9 and a GPT-2 conjecture reducing it to FUNCTOR1:7

theorem Th9: :: FUNCTOR1:9
for C1 **being** non empty AltGraph **for** C2, C3 **being** non empty reflexive AltGraph
for F **being** feasible FunctorStr **over** C1,C2 **for** G **being** FunctorStr **over** C2,C3
st F is full & G is full **holds** G * F is full

for C1, C2 **being** AltGraph **for** F **being** FunctorStr **over** C1,C2 **holds**
F is full **iff** F is faithful & F is feasible

theorem Th7: :: FUNCTOR1:7
for C1 **being** non empty AltGraph **for** C2, C3 **being** non empty reflexive AltGraph
for F **being** feasible FunctorStr **over** C1,C2 **for** G **being** FunctorStr **over** C2,C3
st F is faithful & G is faithful **holds** G * F is faithful

References

1. Brown, C.E., Gauthier, T.: Self-learned formula synthesis in set theory. CoRR, abs/1912.01525 (2019)
2. Chvalovský, K., Jakubův, J., Suda, M., Urban, J.: ENIGMA-NG: efficient neural and gradient-boosted inference guidance for E. In: Fontaine, P. (ed.) CADE 2019. LNCS (LNAI), vol. 11716, pp. 197–215. Springer, Cham (2019). https://doi.org/10.1007/978-3-030-29436-6_12
3. Colton, S.: Automated Theory Formation in Pure Mathematics. Distinguished Dissertations. Springer, London (2012). https://doi.org/10.1007/978-1-4471-0147-5
4. Fajtlowicz, S.: On conjectures of Graffiti. Ann. Discrete Math. **72**(1–3), 113–118 (1988)
5. Gauthier, T.: Deep reinforcement learning in HOL4. CoRR, abs/1910.11797 (2019)
6. Gauthier, T., Kaliszyk, C., Urban, J.: Initial experiments with statistical conjecturing over large formal corpora. In: CICM 2016 WiP Proceedings, pp. 219–228 (2016)
7. Johansson, M., Rosén, D., Smallbone, N., Claessen, K.: Hipster: integrating theory exploration in a proof assistant. In: Watt, S.M., Davenport, J.H., Sexton, A.P., Sojka, P., Urban, J. (eds.) CICM 2014. LNCS (LNAI), vol. 8543, pp. 108–122. Springer, Cham (2014). https://doi.org/10.1007/978-3-319-08434-3_9
8. Kaliszyk, C., Urban, J., Vyskočil, J.: Automating formalization by statistical and semantic parsing of mathematics. In: Ayala-Rincón, M., Muñoz, C.A. (eds.) ITP 2017. LNCS, vol. 10499, pp. 12–27. Springer, Cham (2017). https://doi.org/10.1007/978-3-319-66107-0_2
9. Kaliszyk, C., Urban, J., Vyskočil, J.: Learning to parse on aligned corpora (Rough Diamond). In: Urban, C., Zhang, X. (eds.) ITP 2015. LNCS, vol. 9236, pp. 227–233. Springer, Cham (2015). https://doi.org/10.1007/978-3-319-22102-1_15
10. Lenat, D.B.: AM: an artificial intelligence approach to discovery in mathematics as heuristic search. Ph.D thesis, Stanford (1976)
11. Piotrowski, B., Urban, J.: Stateful Premise Selection by Recurrent Neural Networks (2020)
12. Radford, A., et al.: Language models are unsupervised multitask learners. OpenAI Blog **1**(8), 9 (2019)
13. Schulz, S.: System description: E 1.8. In: McMillan, K., Middeldorp, A., Voronkov, A. (eds.) LPAR 2013. LNCS, vol. 8312, pp. 735–743. Springer, Heidelberg (2013). https://doi.org/10.1007/978-3-642-45221-5_49

14. Urban, J.: XML-izing Mizar: making semantic processing and presentation of MML easy. In: Kohlhase, M. (ed.) MKM 2005. LNCS (LNAI), vol. 3863, pp. 346–360. Springer, Heidelberg (2006). https://doi.org/10.1007/11618027_23
15. Urban, J.: MPTP 0.2: design, implementation, and initial experiments. J. Autom. Reasoning **37**(1–2), 21–43 (2006)
16. Wang, Q., Brown, C.E., Kaliszyk, C., Urban, J.: Exploration of neural machine translation in autoformalization of mathematics in Mizar. In: CPP, pp. 85–98 (2020)
17. Wang, Q., Kaliszyk, C., Urban, J.: First experiments with neural translation of informal to formal mathematics. In: Rabe, F., Farmer, W.M., Passmore, G.O., Youssef, A. (eds.) CICM 2018. LNCS (LNAI), vol. 11006, pp. 255–270. Springer, Cham (2018). https://doi.org/10.1007/978-3-319-96812-4_22

A Contextual and Labeled Math-Dataset Derived from NIST's DLMF

Abdou Youssef[1,2]([✉]) and Bruce R. Miller[2]

[1] The George Washington University, Washington DC, WA, USA
ayoussef@gwu.edu
[2] NIST, Gaithersburg, USA
{youssef,bruce.miller}@nist.gov

Abstract. Machine Learning (ML) and Natural Language Processing (NLP) have started to be applied to math language processing and math knowledge discovery. To fully utilize ML in those areas, there is a pressing need for Math labeled datasets. This paper presents a new dataset that we have derived from the widely used Digital Library of Mathematical Functions (DLMF) of NIST. The dataset is structured and labeled in a specific way. For each math equation and expression in the DLMF, there is a record that provides annotational and contextual elements. An accompanying dataset is also generated from the DLMF. It consists of "Simple XML" files, each organized as **marked-up sentences** within a marked-up hierarchy of paragraphs/subsections/sections. The math in each sentence is marked up in a way that enables users to extract the actual context of math elements, at various levels of granularity, for contextualized processing. This context-rich, sentence-oriented, equation/expression-centered, symbol-labeled dataset is motivated by the fact that much of ML-based NLP algorithms are sentence oriented.

1 Introduction

Machine Learning (ML) and ML-based Natural Language Processing (NLP) have started to be applied to math language processing (MLP), math knowledge discovery (MKD), and document processing in STEM fields [1,3,5–7]. This holds great promise for advancement in those areas, but to accomplish that, we need labeled math-datasets to train and test ML models, such as classifiers, part-of-math taggers, summarizers, translators, question-answering systems, and word embedding models. Unlike in traditional ML-NLP applications, there is a dearth of labeled datasets for MLP and MKD. Ginev and Miller introduced recently a large dataset labeled at a coarse granularity [2], but no math dataset labeled at fine granularity is available at this time.

In this paper, we present a new dataset[1] that we have derived from the widely used Digital Library of Mathematical Functions (DLMF) of NIST [4]. For reasons stated in Sect. 3, the dataset consists of two twin datasets: the *per-expression dataset*, and the *Simple-XML dataset*.

---

[1] For now, the dataset is at https://github.com/abdouyoussef/math-dlmf-dataset/.

© Springer Nature Switzerland AG 2020
C. Benzmüller and B. Miller (Eds.): CICM 2020, LNAI 12236, pp. 324–330, 2020.
https://doi.org/10.1007/978-3-030-53518-6_25

Table 1. Names, values and explanations of the fields of equation records.

Field name	Field value and its explanation
Equation-number	The unique equation number of the equation in DLMF
Permalink	A unique URL of the equation
Xml-id	A unique XML ID of the equation within the DLMF
Tex	LaTeX encoding of the equation, surrounded by dollar signs
Content-tex	LaTeX encoding of the equation, but using DLMF-defined semantic Latex macros
Constraints	A number of name:value fields encoding the constraints of the equation, if any, in both LaTeX and content-tex
Symbols-defined	A number of name:value fields where the name is "symbol", and the value is in turn a number of name:value fields encoding and describing a math symbol in the equation, where the description gives the meaning of the symbol, which can be viewed as a symbol label in the ML sense
Symbols-used	Similar to the symbols-defined values above, except that each symbol has an additional idref:value field where the latter value provides the ID where the original definition of that symbol is located in the DLMF
Meaning	The meaning or role of the symbol in question[a]
Idref	A unqiue ID reference to the location where a symbol is initially defined in the DLMF
Context-references	A number of name:value fields that provide context-identifying references and titles of the textual units containing the equation, such as subsection and section titles, as detailed in Table 2

[a] The meanings of symbols are provided by the DLMF, and were determined by the DLMF authors and editors. As those labels were meant for human readers rather than for any machine learning/NLP applications, no formalized "levels" of meaning were provided. We decided to keep those meaning labels as currently provided, pending future elaborations.

The per-expression dataset is structured and labeled at fine granularity. For each math equation or expression in the DLMF, there is a record that provides a number of related elements, both contextual and annotational. The Simple-XML dataset consists of "Simple XML" files, where the contents of each Simple-XML file are organized as **marked-up sentences** within the marked-up hierarchy of paragraphs/subsections/sections inherited form the original DLMF files. Each sentence consists of its text and math XML-elements with their own unique IDs. The details of those twin datasets are in Sect. 2.

Insert 1. An equation record in the per-expression dataset

Equation:
  equation-number: 5.2.2
  permalink: http://dlmf.nist.gov/5.2.E2
  xml-id: C5.S2.E2
  tex: `$\psi\left(z\right)=\Gamma'\left(z\right)/\Gamma\left(z\right)$`
  content-tex: `$\digamma@{z}=\EulerGamma'@{z}/\EulerGamma@{z}$`
  constraints:
    tex: `$z\neq 0,-1,-2,\dots$`
  symbols-defined:
    symbol:
      tex: `$\psi\left(\NVar{z}\right)$`
      content-tex: `$\digamma@{\NVar{z}}$`
      meaning: psi (or digamma) function
  symbols-used:
    symbol:
      tex: `$\Gamma\left(\NVar{z}\right)$`
      content-tex: `$\EulerGamma@{\NVar{z}}$`
      idref: C5.S2.E1
      meaning: gamma function
    symbol:
      tex: `$z$`
      idref: C5.S1.p2.t1.r4
      meaning: complex variable
  context-references:
    sentence-xmlid: C5.S2.Px1.p1.s6
    sentence-num-in-section: 6
    sentence-num-in-chapter: 27
    sentence-num-in-corpus: 4550
    para-xmlid: C5.S2.Px1.p1
    para-num-of-sentences: 7
    paragraph-xmlid: C5.S2.Px1
    paragraph-title: Euler's Integral
    subsection-xmlid: C5.S2.SS1
    subsection-title: Gamma and Psi Functions
    section-xmlid: C5.S2
    section-title: Definitions
    chapter-xmlid: C5
    chapter-title: Gamma Function
End-equation

Insert 2. A sentence element in the Simple-XML dataset

```
<sentence sentence-num-in-para="6" sentence-num-in-section="6"
    xml:id="C5.S2.Px1.p1.s6">
  <Math equation-number="5.2.2" mode="display" xml:id="C5.S2.E2">
    \psi\left(z\right) =
      \Gamma'\left(z\right)/\Gamma\left(z\right), if \neq 0,-1,-2,\dots
  </Math>.
</sentence>
```

The full context of each equation or expression is easily and quickly derivable from the twin datasets, which enables users to identify and fully extract the sentence containing a given equation/expression, as well as neighboring sentences or full paragraphs, for contextualized processing needed in many MLP tasks.

Table 2. Names, values and explanations of the <u>context</u> fields of equation records.

Field name	Field value and its explanation
Sentence-xmlid	A unique sentence ID within the *Simple-XML* files of the DLMF
Sentence-num-in-section	The in-section number of the sentence containing the equation
Sentence-num-in-chapter	The in-chapter number of the sentence containing the equation
Sentence-num-in-corpus	The in-corpus number of the sentence containing the equation
Para-xmlid	A unique ID of the *physical* paragraph of the equation
Para-num-of-sentences	The number of sentences in the physical paragraph of the equation
Paragraph-xmlid	A unique XML ID of the *logical* paragraph of the equation
Paragraph-title	The title of the logical paragraph of the equation
Subsection-xmlid	A unique XML ID of the subsection containing the equation
Subsection-title	The title of the subsection containing the equation
Section-xmlid	A unique XML ID of the section containing the equation
Section-title	The title of the section containing the equation
Chapter-xmlid	A unique XML ID of the chapter containing the equation
Chapter-title	The title of the chapter containing the equation

2   Description of the Datasets

We produced the datasets by writing Java software to process the DLMF XML source files and to extract from them the twin datasets, including the JSON version of the per-expression dataset. This section describes the details and sizes of the datasets.

2.1   The Per-Expression Dataset

The per-expression dataset, represented in both a textual format and the JSON format, is organized by records, one per equation and one per math expression. Each equation-record starts and ends with the keywords *Equation:* and *End-equation* on separate lines, and has fields of name:value pairs. The name of each field is a meaningful string, and the value is a text string that can be a LATEX encoding, an ID, or a sequence of name:value fields. Insert 1 gives an example of such a record, and Tables 1 and 2 specify the fields. Note that expression-records are similar to equation-records except that they start and end with the keywords *Expression:* and *End-expression*, and do not have the following fields: equation-number, permalink, constraints, symbols-used, and symbols-defined.

2.2   The Simple-XML Dataset

In the Simple-XML dataset, each section of the DLMF is a lean XML file, structured as a tree of section and subsections. Each subsection consists of paragraphs, and each paragraph is a sequence of marked-up sentences that contain text and/or marked-up math elements. Each sentence element has valuable XML attributes, including the xml-id attribute of the sentence (see Insert 2 for an illustration). That way, from a given equation record in the per-expression dataset, one can retrieve the sentence-xmlid field value and use it to retrieve the actual sentence from the right file in Simple-XML dataset, and indeed retrieve the contents of even broader contexts (*e.g.*, paragraph).

2.3   Dataset Size

The whole dataset has 20,040 sentences; 25,930 math elements; and 8,494 numbered equations. The uncompressed size of the per-expression dataset in textual format is 26.5 MB, and in JSON format is 83.5 MB. The uncompressed size of the Simple-XML dataset is 15.7 MB. Thus the total size is 125.7 MB.

3   Justification of the Data Model of the Datasets

The data model of our twin datasets is justified by the following considerations:

- Much of deep learning in NLP, and by extension in MLP/MKD, works on the sentence (occasionally paragraph) level, such as in word embedding, and classification at the micro level (*e.g.*, part-of-math (POM) tagging) and macro level (*e.g.*, classifying paragraphs [2] as definitions, assertions, proofs, etc.).
- The datasets are envisioned to have multiple uses that require different kinds of features. For example, training and testing classifiers for POM tagging of symbols require not only math symbols and their tags, but also the textual context, local and distant. Similarly, harvesting definitions and distributed (i.e., non-local) constraints of equations requires textual contexts, local and distant. Thus, besides symbols and their labels, a math dataset must provide math/text context(*e.g.*, full equation and full sentence).

– As the application of ML to MLP and MKD is in a nascent stage, users do not yet fully know what features to define and use. Therefore, it is advisable at this time to provide adequate contextual information from which potentially useful features can be defined and readily extracted.
– Why split the dataset into two separate ones? The first two applications in the next section provide some justification for the separation of the two twin datasets, and illustrate the "interaction" between the two of them.

4   A Sample of Potential Uses of the Datasets

The following is but a short list of applications that can make use of the datasets:

Harvesting non-local constraints/conditions: The constraints of some equations are not directly attached to the equations, but are embedded in local (*i.e.*, nearby) text or distant text, i.e., in local or distant context. The equation information in the per-expression dataset tells us whether or not there are explicit constraints provided therein; if not provided, then the context-references portion in the per-expression dataset tells us where to locate the (layers of) textual context in the Simple-XML dataset where search can be conducted for constraints and conditions pertaining to that equation.

Harvesting non-local definitions: While the DLMF provides *in-situ* metadata (meaning, definitions, and/or references to definitions) about the symbols of a *numbered equation*, it does not do so for *expressions*. This necessitates harvesting the definitions of in-expression symbols in local/distant contexts. To find a definition of a target symbol occurring in a given expression, we can first look inside the per-expression dataset for the symbol definition in the blocks of the equations surrounding the expression. If none is found, we turn to the Simple-XML dataset to locate the textual context where search for definitions of the target symbol can be conducted. It is customary for authors to put definitions of math symbols a few sentences before or after the actual use of those symbols; therefore, searching for symbol definitions in surrounding sentences is therefore an often fruitful endeavor.

POM tagging of math symbols: The per-expression dataset with its *in-situ* definitions can serve as a training and testing dataset (in 80–20 split) for training POM tagging classifiers.

Scoping: Scoping of multi-symbol math constructs, such as functions applied at variables, functions with superscripts and/or subscripts, determinant of a matrix, the arguments of sums ($\sum$), and so on, presents challenging but promising disambiguation applications of the twin datasets.

References

1. Gao, L., et al.: Preliminary exploration of formula embedding for mathematical information retrieval: can mathematical formulae be embedded like a natural language? arXiv:1707.05154 (2017)

2. Ginev, D., Miller, B.: Scientific statement classification over arXiv:1908.10993, August 2019
3. Kstovski, K., Blei, D.M.: Equation embeddings. arXiv:1803.09123, March 2018
4. Olver, F.W.J., et al. (eds.): NIST Digital Library of Mathematical Functions. https://dlmf.nist.gov/, Release 1.0.20 of 1 September 2018
5. Youssef, A.: Part-of-math tagging and applications. In: Geuvers, H., England, M., Hasan, O., Rabe, F., Teschke, O. (eds.) CICM 2017. LNCS (LNAI), vol. 10383, pp. 356–374. Springer, Cham (2017). https://doi.org/10.1007/978-3-319-62075-6_25
6. Youssef, A., Miller, B.R.: Deep learning for math knowledge processing. In: Rabe, F., Farmer, W.M., Passmore, G.O., Youssef, A. (eds.) CICM 2018. LNCS (LNAI), vol. 11006, pp. 271–286. Springer, Cham (2018). https://doi.org/10.1007/978-3-319-96812-4_23
7. Youssef, A., Miller, B.R.: Explorations into the use of word embedding in math search and math semantics. In: Kaliszyk, C., Brady, E., Kohlhase, A., Sacerdoti Coen, C. (eds.) CICM 2019. LNCS (LNAI), vol. 11617, pp. 291–305. Springer, Cham (2019). https://doi.org/10.1007/978-3-030-23250-4_20

Abstracts of Invited Talks

Formalizing Undergraduate Mathematics

Kevin Buzzard$^{(\boxtimes)}$

Imperial College, London, UK
`k.buzzard@imperial.ac.uk`

Abstract. Most research pure mathematicians do not use computer theorem provers. One of the reasons for this: computer theorem provers cannot currently prove new theorems at research level in any of the mainstream areas of pure mathematical research, and proofs are the currency of pure mathematics. Note however that most research pure mathematicians did an undergraduate degree in mathematics, and in fact no computer theorem prover can prove—or even *state*—all the theorems in an undergraduate pure maths degree. These systems have been around for decades, and that is how far we have got – one would struggle to formalise the *questions* on most final year undergraduate pure mathematics courses, in any of the modern ITP systems.

We have to start somewhere if we want to get research mathematicians interested in these new technologies. I will talk about my vision for Lean's mathematics library `mathlib`, currently over 50 percent of the way through formalising the proofs in the pure mathematics courses in Imperial College's undergraduate mathematics degree.

© Springer Nature Switzerland AG 2020
C. Benzmüller and B. Miller (Eds.): CICM 2020, LNAI 12236, p. 333, 2020.
https://doi.org/10.1007/978-3-030-53518-6

Formally Verified Constraints Solvers: A Guided Tour

Catherine Dubois[✉]

École Nationale Supérieure d'Informatique pour l'Industrie et l'Entreprise,
Samovar Évry Courcouronnes, Paris, France
catherine.dubois@ensiie.fr

Abstract. Constraint solvers are complex tools implementing tricky algorithms and heuristics manipulating intricate data structures. It is well-known that they have bugs. Certifying the output of such tools is extremely important in particular when they are used for critical systems or in verification tools. There are mainly two ways for having confidence in the computed results: making the solver produce not only the output but also proof logs that can be easily verified by an external checker or proving the correctness of the solver itself. The former approach is widespread in the Boolean satisfiability community through formats such as DRAT [11] which can be considered as a standard. The latter approach has been followed for example for developing Compcert [8] and sel4 [6] respectively a C compiler developed and formally verified with the help of the Coq proof assistant Coq and a micro-kernel developed and formally verified with the proof assistant Isabelle/HOL.

This talk focusses on Constraint Programming (CP) solvers on finite domains (FD) [2] and explores the work developed for some years by the author and some other researchers around the Coq formalization of such CP(FD) solvers. The starting point is the development, in 2012, of a formally verified CP(FD) solver limited to binary constraints [3] implementing a classical filtering algorithm, AC3 [9] and one of its extension AC2001 [4], both looking for arc consistency. It is proved sound and complete. A variant implementing bound consistency has also been formalized and proved sound and complete. Recent work[1] concerns the Coq formalization of a pre-processor that transforms a constraint satisfaction problem containing non-binary constraints into an equivalent binary constraint satisfaction problem, allowing for resolution of more complex CP programs. Different representations of domains are investigated, simple ordered lists or lists of intervals [7]. The Coq formalization of Regin's filtering algorithm [10] for the global constraint alldifferent that enforces some variables to be assigned to distinct values is under progress. But here, contrary to the previous formalizations, a large amount of results from graph theory (maximal matching, augmenting path, etc) is needed and requires an intensive proof effort because there is no corresponding off-the-shelf Coq library.

---

[1] The work presented in [5] concerns ternary constraints but has been recently extended to n-ary constraints.

C. Benzmüller and B. Miller (Eds.): CICM 2020, LNAI 12236, pp. 334–335, 2020.
https://doi.org/10.1007/978-3-030-53518-6

Many ingredients are thus present to build a reference implementation that could be used as a second shot verifier in some critical cases or to validate existing solvers.

The talk discusses the main challenges of such a research work: efficiency, genericity, development of mathematical theorems or reuse of such theorems formalized in other proof assistants (like Berge's theorem recently formalized by Abdulaziz and al in [1] in Isabelle/HOL, required in the **alldifferent** context), etc. A last, but not least, important challenge is to convince the CP community to use such formal tools (The work presented in [5] concerns ternary constraints but has been recently extended to n-ary constraints.).

Thanks. The work presented here is joint work with A. Butant, M. Carlier, V. Clément, S. Elloumi, A. Gotlieb, A. Ledein and H. Mlodecki. I am very grateful to them.

References

1. Abdulaziz, M., Mehlhorn, K., Nipkow, T.: Trustworthy graph algorithms (invited talk). In: Rossmanith, P., Heggernes, P., Katoen, J. (eds.) 44th International Symposium on Mathematical Foundations of Computer Science, MFCS 2019, Aachen, Germany, 26–30 August 2019, volume 138 of LIPIcs, pp. 1:1–1:22. Schloss Dagstuhl - Leibniz-Zentrum für Informatik (2019)
2. Bessiere, C.: Constraint propagation. In: Handbook of Constraint Programming, chapter 3. Elsevier, Amsterdam (2006)
3. Carlier, M., Dubois, C., Gotlieb, A.: A certified constraint solver over finite domains. In: Giannakopoulou, D., Méry, D. (eds.) FM 2012. LNCS, vol. 7436, pp. 116–131. Springer, Heidelberg (2012). https://doi.org/10.1007/978-3-642-32759-9_12
4. Christian Bessiere, R.Y., Régin, J.-C., Zhang, Y.: An optimal coarse-grained arc consistency algorithm. Artif. Intell. **165**, 165–185 (2005)
5. Dubois, C.: Formally verified decomposition of non-binary constraints into equivalent binary constraints. In: Journées Francophones des Langages Applicatifs, Les Rousses, France (2019)
6. Klein, G., et al.: sel4: formal verification of an operating-system kernel. Commun. ACM **53**(6), 107–115 (2010)
7. Ledein, A., Dubois, C.: Facile en coq : vérification formelle des listes d'intervalles. In: Journées Francophones des Langages Applicatifs, Gruissan, France (2020)
8. Leroy, X.: Formal verification of a realistic compiler. Commun. ACM **52**, 107–115 (2009)
9. Mackworth, A.: Consistency in networks of relations. Art. Intel. **8**(1), 99–118 (1977)
10. Régin, J.-C.: A filtering algorithm for constraints of difference in CSPs. In: 12th National Conference on Artificial Intelligence (AAAI 1994), pp. 362–367 (1994)
11. Wetzler, N., Heule, M.J.H., Hunt, W.A.: DRAT-trim: efficient checking and trimming using expressive clausal proofs. In: Sinz, C., Egly, U. (eds.) SAT 2014. LNCS, vol. 8561, pp. 422–429. Springer, Cham (2014). https://doi.org/10.1007/978-3-319-09284-3_31

Author Index

Printed in the United States
By Bookmasters